CREATED
UNEQUAL

ALSO BY JAMES K. GALBRAITH

Balancing Acts: Technology, Finance, and the American Future

JAMES K. GALBRAITH

CREATED UNEQUAL

The Crisis in American Pay

A Century Foundation Book

The University of Chicago Press

The University of Chicago Press, Chicago 60637

University of Chicago Press edition 2000

Printed in the United States of America
05 04 03 02 01 00   6 5 4 3 2 1

Library of Congress Cataloging-in-Publication Data

Galbraith, James K.
　　Created unequal : the crisis in American pay / James K. Galbraith.
　　　　p.　　cm.
　　Originally published: New York : Free Press. 1998.
　　Includes bibliographical references and index.
　　ISBN 0-226-27879-4 (pbk. : alk. paper)
　　1. Wages—United States.　2. Income distribution—United
States.　3. Labor market—United States.　4. Social conflict—
United States.　5. United States—Economic policy—1981–1993.
6. United States—Economic policy—1993–　I. Title.

HD4975.G28　2000
331.2′973—dc21

00-044707

♾ The paper used in this publication meets the minimum requirements
of the American National Standard for Information Sciences—
Permanence of Paper for Printed Library Materials, ANSI Z39.48-1992.

FOR YING

Second, however, there has been, as we know and discussed over the years, a significant opening up of income spreads, largely as a function of technology and of education with the increased premium of college education over high school, and high school over high school dropouts becoming stronger. The whole spread goes right through the basic system. It is a development which I feel uncomfortable with. There is nothing monetary policy can do to address that, and it is outside the scope, so far as I am concerned, of the issues with which we deal.

—Alan Greenspan, Testimony to Congress, March 5, 1997

CONTENTS

PART FOUR: POLICIES

FOREWORD

The spectacular run-up of the stock market during the 1990s has become the symbol of a resurgent American economy. To hear your broker tell it, we live in the best of times. Inflation is low; employment is up; and fear of international rivals such as Germany and Japan has become only a vague memory.

At least through the end of 1997, however, national economic performance since the recession of 1990–91 had failed to match that experienced during previous recoveries. Still, because of its duration, the period of sustained, if modest, growth served as the foundation for a renewal of national confidence about the future. Moreover, the longer the economy continues steady growth, the more likely that the total addition to GDP and national wealth from this phase of the business cycle will be substantial, even by historical standards.

For many Americans, this glowing portrait of current economic conditions reflects their personal experiences. For many others, however, it is something that they hear about only on the news. So far, in one important respect, the 1990s seem unlikely to break a pattern that has now persisted for nearly a generation: high inequality in income and wealth. The basic facts about this phenomenon are well known. Since the early 1970s, income inequality has increased dramatically, while average wages for middle-income earners barely kept pace with inflation, and those at the bottom of the scale actually fell in real terms. Inequality of wealth also widened, with the gaps between haves and have-nots escalating to levels last experienced during the Great Depression.

Economists have focused considerable research on the growing inequalities of income. The long list of suspects includes "skill-biased" technological change, economic globalization, deindustrialization, new production practices, declining union membership, and "winner-take-all" markets. But because these suspected causes of inequality are perceived to be forces of the private, free-market economy, many view them as unfortunate necessities—the belief is that governmental intervention to soften their impact would be worse. Direct action to alter the underlying circumstances is said to be playing with fire. Were it not for the real misfortunes caused by income stagnation and decline, it would be amusing that in the political sphere, even the most modest proposals to relieve inequality prompt outcries against "class warfare."

In the pages that follow, economist James Galbraith raises the possibility that the government has in fact been engaging in class warfare all along, with middle- and lower-income Americans losing at every step of the way. Their fortunes have declined not because of inexorable, uncontrollable market forces, Galbraith argues, but because government policy has been managed in a way that drove inequality up. Tight money, a high dollar, and high unemployment have driven the rise of inequality—not the autonomous forces of technology and trade. The implication of Galbraith's approach is that the only way to reverse course is through direct government action. Passivity will only continue the war.

Professor Galbraith has been on target often lately, especially in his insistence that the negative consequences of reductions in unemployment were greatly exaggerated by many economists. He reviews and strengthens his arguments in this area in this work. Indeed the idea of a fixed level for the "non-accelerating inflation rate of unemployment" (NAIRU) has been shattered by that hardest critic of all: empirical evidence. Today, even Federal Reserve chairman Alan Greenspan expresses public skepticism about the existence of such a specific and predictable number. The strongest adherents of NAIRU must today acknowledge that their certainty about the dire consequences of an unemployment level below 6 (or even 7) percent was misguided. Galbraith was right about this, well ahead of his colleagues.

When it comes to inequality, Galbraith brings, most of all, a willingness to look at the evidence we have with remarkably fresh eyes. His insights and conclusions are certain to be at the center of the continuing debate about the causes of the present discontent among working Americans and the remedies for it.

The Twentieth Century Fund/Century Foundation has energetically sought to document, understand the causes of, and develop ideas for alleviating economic inequality. We have supported Edward Wolff's important report, *Top Heavy,* on the increasing inequality of wealth. We also sponsored Robert Kuttner's *Everything for Sale: The Virtues and Limits of Markets,* which devotes considerable attention to the connections between inequality and markets. Our roster of forthcoming books includes the economists Barry Bluestone and Bennett Harrison's analysis of the relationship between economic growth and inequality, economics writer Jeffrey Madrick's exploration of slow productivity improvements, Cornell political scientist Jonas Pontusson's investigation into why inequality is so much worse in the United States than in other developed countries, journalist Simon Head's reporting on the role of technology in inequality, Harvard's Theda Skocpol's proposals for federal action to alleviate inequality, and Wolff's examination of the extent to which schooling may or may not help eliminate inequality.

On behalf of the Trustees of the Twentieth Century Fund/Century Foundation, I thank Galbraith for this bold and thoughtful contribution to our understanding of one of the nation's most important public policy questions.

Richard C. Leone, President
The Twentieth Century Fund/Century Foundation
December 1997

PREFACE TO THE PAPERBACK EDITION

What caused increasing inequality in America? How can pay gaps be reduced? Is the pay distribution a matter of supply and demand, of the force of technology on the demand for skill, so that the right policies lie mainly in the area of education and training? Or should a serious egalitarian focus first on full employment, lower interest rates, stronger unions and a higher minimum wage? More generally, is there a tradeoff between inequality and unemployment, as many people suppose? Or are these two evils instead two sides of the same economic coin?

The debates have changed markedly since this book first raised these questions. The natural rate of unemployment and the notion of skill bias in technological change—two foundation stones of the orthodox academic view—have since lost their luster and many adherents. The idea that full employment works *against* inequality, that there is no tradeoff, is now widely accepted. Discussions of how to reduce inequality today are, for the most part, properly focused on sustaining full employment and on raising pay standards through such measures as the minimum wage and the Earned Income Tax Credit.

This is progress. It occurred mainly because, between 1994 and 2000, the United States experienced steadily falling unemployment and then sustained full employment, with unemployment rates near 4 percent. Minimum wages were increased, and until mid-1999 interest rates were kept stable. In this way the central proposition, the conditional forecast, of *Created Unequal* received an out-of-sample test, almost immediately after the book appeared. This is what every social scientist, of course, secretly dreads, but in my case the fates were kind. Wage inflation, though widely predicted year after year, never emerged. So much for the natural rate hypothesis. And while these years witnessed an accelerated boom in the new technologies, pay inequalities in the larger economy *declined.* This was especially true in manufacturing, where the effects of technological change ought to have been most apparent—undermining the hypothesis of skill bias in the demand for labor.

This outcome—so far—validates much more than my public policy arguments, which are after all about a particular country in a particular time, matters that are necessarily transitory to some degree. It also lends weight to the larger and deeper implications of the work. This is not political but academic, not directed at policymakers but rather at the structure and content of modern economics.

For a half century, since the passage of Keynesianism into the major textbooks of the early postwar years, the teaching and thought of modern economics has been divided between macro and micro. The former is said to be concerned with the big concepts of output, growth, employment, and inflation; the latter with the rational foundations of individual and business choice. This division served as a great practical convenience, for it allowed a small group of practically-minded and policy-oriented thinkers, mostly liberals, to coexist inside the profession with a much larger group of scholars who focused their work on micro-theory. Most of the latter were more conservative in their policy views, generally believing that competitive markets produced good results and government policies should only minimally interfere.

Serious theorists, however, have never liked the macro/micro division. It clearly implies inadequacy on both sides: macro-theory lacks micro-foundation, while micro-theory lacks application to the most important questions that policymakers must face. Since the 1970s, microeconomists have mounted a concerted effort to subsume macroeconomics and build a consistent theory of the whole economy on the foundation of rational individual choice in competitive market settings. This campaign reflected both political and academic ambition. Pure theorists saw it as a necessary step toward unifying economics under a single conceptual roof, rooted in the principles of rationality, foresight, and competition. The politically minded, for their part, saw it as a way to undermine the interventionist policy lessons inherited from Keynes.

But this project has failed. The microeconomics of general competitive equilibrium, the great project of welfare theory that seemed so promising when I entered graduate school twenty-five years ago, has petered out. In its place we find a vast and inchoate body of work, often based on game theory and leading to propositions about multiple equilibria, continuous equilibria, Nash solutions, and a myriad of other concepts. At the same time, ideas of imperfect and asymmetric information corrosively undermine the claim that a rationalist micro-theory can support any general conclusions about macro policy. And the project of explaining the business cycle from micro-foundations and rational expectations remains stuck at the starting gate after many years, forced to rely on "exogenous shocks" to explain the central problem of that theory, namely the scale and period of economic fluctuations.

The failure of micro-foundations led me to a radically contrarian view. I concluded that the project of unifying economics would have to start at the other end of the discipline and proceed from the top down. It would have to be based not on the neoclassical theory of rational choice but instead on the great work of Keynes himself, on the unification of money and production into a single and coherent economic theory. Macroeconomics, in other words, would have to provide the foundation for the study of phenomena at the sub-macro level. The structure of relative pay—from the traditional viewpoint a quintessential micro-theoretic problem—presented itself as the ideal test of the power of a macro-theoretic approach. If Keynesian principles could explain the evolution of inequality, the jurisdiction of microeconomics over the theory of value would be removed in a single stroke.

I realized, of course, that no one would take any such proposition on faith. To win adherents, I would have to show concrete progress toward the resolution of key *empirical* issues. And that would require a research strategy designed explicitly to elicit information from data sets organized at the aggregative social level. Traditional econometric techniques, built for the micro-theoretic project and adapted to sample surveys, would not work.

The research project of this book is based on two principles. First, to understand the evolution of inequalities of pay, one has to measure them as directly and as precisely as possible, with frequent and accurate observations over time. I demonstrate a way of doing this from data sets concerned with manufacturing pay and earnings. Second, to understand the main forces underlying patterns of change in a distribution, one must be able to identify the main social structures underlying those forces. This is an exercise in taxonomy—a neglected topic among economists, but a vital one in any empirical science. This book presents principles of numerical taxonomy that will, I believe, have wide application in macro-theoretic social science.

Generally speaking, the empirical work in the volume has withstood scrutiny to date, and the methods have proved themselves in other contexts as well. On one matter, though, the work originally presented in these pages now needs to be revised. In Chapter 8, I report a measure of pay inequalities in the American economy going back to 1920. Due to a gap in the earnings data for the years 1948–1957, I made the assumption that pay inequality could be guessed from the known movement of a measure of family income inequality.

FIGURE P.1

WAGE RATE INEQUALITY 1920–1998

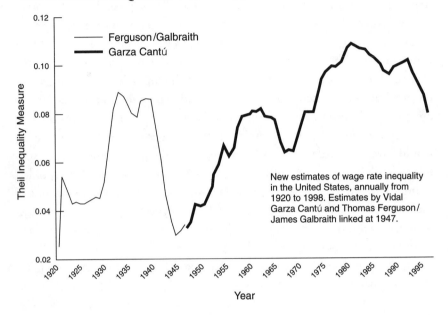

New estimates of wage rate inequality in the United States, annually from 1920 to 1998. Estimates by Vidal Garza Cantú and Thomas Ferguson/James Galbraith linked at 1947.

The resulting series showed stable behavior in the 1950s, and increasing inequality in the 1970s and 1980s, to levels still well below those of the 1930s.

We have since located the missing data, thanks to the efforts of Vidal Garza Cantú, and we now know that the linking assumption was incorrect. Direct measures of earnings inequality in manufacturing in the 1950s show surprisingly large increases, mainly during the recessions of those years, and a return by the end of the decade to levels of pay inequality that rivaled those of the Great Depression. (A number of independent checks of the data confirm the reliability of the new estimates.) Figure P.1 presents the new time-series going back to 1920, linking the new estimates to those of Thomas Ferguson and myself for the period 1920 to 1947. Data cover agriculture and manufacturing in the earlier period and manufacturing in the later one; data on services are not included.

Two important conclusions follow from the new measures. First, the relationship between pay inequality in manufacturing and unemployment is even stronger than previously thought, for this relationship holds in the 1950s (when unemployment rose sharply on several occasions) as well as in earlier and later times. The relative stability of the larger measure of *income inequality* in the 1950s (if indeed those measures, which were based on tax return information, are correct) must therefore be attributed to the emergence of large government transfer programs (Social Security) and the continuation of wartime progressivity in tax rates, rather than to the stability of the wage structure.

Second, the new measures make it clear that pay inequalities in the 1970s and 1980s rose from a higher base than previously believed and reached levels far exceeding those of the 1930s. Thus the improvement since 1994 has brought our measure of pay inequality back down, at best, to mid-Depression levels or a bit below—surely yet another reason to keep the reduction of inequality as a high priority on any economic policy agenda.

The last several years have also witnessed confusing trends in the relationship between pay and incomes. While measures of wage and pay inequality have clearly declined, measures of family *income inequality* have continued to rise. Why is this the case and what social meaning should we attach to it?

Part of the discrepancy is due to differences between the tabulation of wages and salaries, which accrue to jobs and to individuals; and the tabulation of incomes, which accrue to households and families. For instance, social trends toward more low-income single-person households, or toward more high-income two-earner households, are both likely to raise income inequality even if the distribution of pay to jobs does not change. It is even possible for income inequality to rise on this account while pay inequality is falling, which may account for some of the phenomenon we observed during the second half of the 1990s.

Changes in family structure and household demographics have varying social interpretations. Some are certainly troubling, but others, such as those reflecting the economic emancipation of women, may be desirable. Such changes must be evaluated against particular criteria of desirable family structure—a topic well beyond the reach of this study. Still, changes in family composition are not directly due to labor market incentives, and it is hard to attribute them to the effects of technological change, or of trade, for that matter.

The sharply increasing earnings by the top few percent of households (particularly those who receive the bulk of dividend and capital gains income) was a larger cause of rising income inequalities in the late 1990s. This period was a time of rapidly increasing corporate and business profits, and in a steeply rising stock market, the few who hold most of the stock will necessarily experience a disproportionate share of the gains. Since capital gains count in incomes, this will drive up inequality of household incomes, but the effect will not appear in data restricted to pay.

Is the rise of capital gains and associated earnings from profits good or bad? Many deplore the increasing inequalities of wealth that it seems to reflect. And surely, in principle, they are correct to do so: vast inequalities of wealth cannot be entirely good for a democratic country.

But a word of realistic caution is in order. Against the reality of increased and unequal financial wealth, one must also consider the nature of the system under which we live. Given a capitalist system, rising asset prices are partly a reflection of the performance of the economy as a whole at full employment. You cannot have, as a practical matter, an economic boom without a stock boom. So the question becomes: is it better to live with the distributional consequences of a profits boom, or not to have the boom in the first place? Here, for once, I side with the capitalists; surely it is better to have both than neither.

For these reasons, I maintain that the principal focus of work on economic inequality should be on inequalities of pay, and that the central issue remains reducing inequalities among the many millions for whom wages and salaries remain the major sources of income. The key objective should be to maintain decent employment and a prosperous standard of living for the 130 million working Americans and their families. It is on this population that the prosperity and future of the country depend. Let a robustly progressive tax system—including taxes on capital income—largely take care of the others.

And so, has the crisis in American pay now ended? Alas, it has not. Certainly there has been progress toward greater equality in pay structures—especially in manufacturing. So far, however, there is only slight evidence of a closing gap between manufacturing pay and pay in the much larger services sector. This is because the political forces on which wages in services depend have yet to be felt on behalf of this large but weakly organized population. There is still work to do, but whether it will be completed remains in doubt. Minimum and average wages still need to rise substantially before the pay crisis will come to an end.

Even so, it is good to know, with much more assurance than would have been possible even two years ago, which particular policy measures will work effectively to reduce inequality and what the gravest dangers to progress are. The key policy message at present is clear: *full employment works*. Full employment is a distinct, important accomplishment, and we must fight to preserve it. As we fight, we need to recognize that while the evidence favors a policy geared toward sustained full employment, nothing in the evidence guarantees such policies will in fact be pursued—either by Congress, the Administration, or the Federal Reserve.

ACKNOWLEDGMENTS

Famine is a political event. It is not caused by drought, flood, or other natural disaster alone. Whether one examines the experience of Ireland in 1846, Ukraine in 1933, Bengal in 1943, or China in 1960, everywhere and always one finds the mark of policy—specific governmental actions that deprived the poor of their livelihoods or their incomes.

We owe this teaching to Amartya Sen, and few economists dispute it. But it raises a question: Can smaller increases in economic inequality be viewed in a similar way? Are famines different, except in degree? It seems impossible for there to be a difference *except* of degree. For if natural disasters could cause an enduring increase in the inequality of incomes, they could in principle be sufficiently serious on occasion to cause famine. But they don't.

This book is a reflection on the power of economic policy, particularly its power to achieve an evil result. Usually such results are not so serious as famines. They lack the drama and also the closure that follows. They are a little bit banal. Yet, like famines, they are invariably depicted by those sympathetic to the existing structures of authority as the sad consequence of natural forces. I believe, on the contrary, that where the evil concerned is a rise in the inequality of economic incomes, one can usually find the sources in political decisions.

The search for these sources is, to some extent, inherently statistical. Since it is not possible to write a book of this kind without exposing pieces of it to critical review along the way, certain parts have already seen the light of the printed page. In particular, Chapter 10 is adapted from an essay, "Time to Ditch the NAIRU," which appeared in the winter 1997 *Journal of Economic Perspectives,* itself based on an earlier working paper supported by the Jerome Levy Economics Institute of Bard College. This has now also appeared in greatly changed form as "Dangerous Metaphor: The Fiction of the Labor

Market." I thank the editors of the *JEP* and Dimitri Papadimitriou of Levy for their help and for permission to make use of this material.

Chapter 15, which provides international comparisons of inequality, is adapted from a paper first presented to a conference in Dubrovnik, Republic of Croatia, in October 1996. That paper will appear in somewhat greater detail in a conference volume edited by Soumitra Sharma entitled *John Maynard Keynes: Keynesianism into the Twenty-first Century,* with permissions all around. My ruminations on what should be done with the Federal Reserve are familiar to readers of *Reclaiming Prosperity,* edited by Todd Schafer and Jeff Faux, though modified here.

The other chapters are original for this book, although inevitably ideas, phrases, and even short arguments assayed elsewhere, notably in the *American Prospect, Challenge,* the *Nation,* the *Texas Observer,* and *Dissent,* creep in from time to time. I thank the editors of these excellent publications for their indulgence and for the help they have given to my prose. I especially thank Bob Kuttner, a great friend and editor, who got me started on this whole project and has supported it in many ways. For help with the statistical work of Chapters 5 to 9, I am grateful to several seminar audiences, most especially at the Center for Non-linear Dynamics of the Department of Physics at the University of Texas at Austin, the Berkeley Roundtable on the International Economy and the Berkeley Labor and Economy History Seminars, and the 1996 Post-Keynesian Workshop in Knoxville, and for the excellent economists and statisticians at CERGE, the Center for Economic Research and Graduate Education, Charles University, Prague, Czech Republic, who were patient enough to work through my procedures and give them at least some conditional signs of approval. Kresimir Zigic and Myron Tegze deserve special thanks in this regard. Audiences in China, notably at the planning commissions in Chengdu and Wuhan, were intensely stimulating, but I was especially delighted by an afternoon spent at Huazhong University of Science and Technology, Wuhan, in early 1996; my thanks to Chang Pei-kang and his associates there.

I am grateful for conversations and correspondence with Eileen Appelbaum, Dean Baker, Michael Bernstein, Barry Bluestone, Carlo Brumat, Martin Carnoy, Lawrence Chimerine, Steve Cohen, Paul Davidson, John Dunlop, Robert Eisner, Benjamin Friedman, Wynne Godley, Robert Heilbroner, Doug Henwood, Abel Hibert, David Howell, Jorge Braga de Macedo, Michael Mandler, Larry Mishel, Jefferson Morley, Elke Muchlinski, Steven Nickell, Chris Niggle, Richard Parker, Kunibert Raffer, Michael Reich, Robert Reich, Henry Reuss, Derek Shearer, Hans Singer, Dan Slottje,

Robert Solow, and Roger Tollison. In the course of discussions on these issues, Thomas Ferguson has become a coauthor; I appreciate his permission to make use of a small part of our joint work on the years 1920 to 1947 here. That I have been deeply influenced over many years by Adrian Wood will be apparent below. The late Hyman Minsky devoted an unforgettable afternoon to these ideas, on a day when he didn't have many left.

Among my colleagues at the University of Texas at Austin, I have received help and encouragement from Leigh Boske, Ed George, Gordon Hanson, Michael Marder, Steve Magee, Ray Marshall, Michael Oden, Brian Roberts, Bill Spelman, Chandler Stolp, Robert Wilson and, as always, from Walt Rostow. Paulo Du Pin Calmon of the University of Brasilia, no longer my student, has been my enduring coauthor and statistical co-conspirator. I thank the dean of the LBJ School of Public Affairs during this period, Max Sherman, for supporting my research through the Policy Research Institute and in particular for academic leave to finish this work in the fall of 1997. The students in my 1995 master's seminar on inequality at the LBJ School equally have my thanks.

My most important collaborators in this phase of my work have been my Ph.D. students in public policy at the Lyndon B. Johnson School of Public Affairs. First among these is Lu Jiaqing—last name first here in correct Chinese form—a relentlessly logical thinker. The other members of this talented group are Maureen Berner, Amy Calistri, Pedro Filipe Teixeira da Conceição, Vidal Garza Cantu, and Junmo Kim, all of whom will be publishing related work within a year or two. Another gifted Ph.D. student, Yusuk Lee, compiled the bibliography from my disorderly records, and Matt Wilson provided helpful comments on infrastructure. Also at the LBJ School, my assistant, Patricia Ni Kennelly, provided help and support as I struggled with these words.

Two people provided detailed comments on the manuscript. One was William (Sandy) Darity, Jr., of the University of North Carolina, a scholar of unrivaled depth. The other was my father, John Kenneth Galbraith, who read the unreadable early versions and told me pitilessly that it had to be reorganized, and reorganized again.

This book would not have been written without the patient support of the Twentieth Century Fund. I am especially grateful to President Richard Leone of the fund for unfailing encouragement, to Greg Anrig and David Smith of the fund for critical comments on earlier drafts, to two anonymous referees—one highly encouraging and the other highly constructive—and to Beverly Goldberg who handled discussions with the publisher. At the Free Press,

Bruce Nichols provided superb editing in a very short time, and Carol de Onís supervised copyediting, which was accomplished with great skill by Beverly Miller.

Tang Ying, herself born at the end of the last great Chinese famine, brought her outsider's perspective to this work and made it possible for me to retain mine. *Xiang qin, Xiang ai* . . .

My big children, Douglas and Margaret, provided patient and understanding encouragement, more than they know, and during this project a new little one was born: Eve, created more than equal.

All remaining errors in this book are my responsibility alone.

Part One

IDEAS

1

THE CRISIS OF
WAGES AND TRANSFERS

Is this improvement in the circumstances of the lower ranks of
the people to be regarded as an advantage or an inconveniency? The answer seems at first sight abundantly plain. Ser-
vants, labourers and workmen of different kinds, make up the
far greater part of every political society. But what improves
the circumstances of the greater part can never be regarded as
an inconveniency to the whole.

—Adam Smith, *Inquiry into the Nature and Causes of the Wealth of*
Nations, 1776, Book I, Chapter VII

This is a book about pay. It is about the gap between good and
bad jobs, about what can be earned in America in decent as
compared with mediocre employment. This gap was once quite small. But
the gap has grown, and now it is wider than at any other time since the Great
Depression. It so wide that it has come, once again, to threaten the social solidarity and stability of the country. It has come, I believe, to undermine our
sense of ourselves as a nation of equals. In this way, rising inequality presents
a stark challenge to American national life.

The most visible sign of this challenge has emerged not in the marketplace
or on the factory floor, as one might possibly expect, but in politics. It sur-
faces in bitter discussions of budgets, welfare, and entitlement programs. A
high degree of inequality causes the comfortable to disavow the needy. It increases the social and the psychological distance separating the haves from

3

the have-nots, making it easier to imagine that defects of character or differences of culture, rather than an unpleasant turn in the larger schemes of economic history, are at the root of the separation. It is leading toward the transformation of the United States from a middle-class democracy into something that more closely resembles an authoritarian quasi democracy, with an overclass, an underclass, and a hidden politics driven by money.

To put the matter the other way around, economic equality blurs the distinctions between persons. It makes people feel similar to other people. In this way, equality casts a veil of ignorance over the comparative future of individual fortunes. As we know from the philosopher John Rawls,[1] this ignorance, rather than equality itself, is the key to fairness in social choice. A just society, providing for the less fortunate in an equable way, is one that people would freely choose for themselves, without knowledge of their own position within it.

Inequality lifts the veil. Inequality is information; it is knowledge. With high inequality, of income and of wealth, it becomes easy to know whether one is likely in the long run to be a net gainer, or a net loser, from public programs of family assistance, pension security, and health care. The more inequality there is in the present, the more definite is each person's sense of his or her own position, both in the present and for the future. The rich feel more secure; the poor feel less hopeful. High inequality therefore weakens the willingness to share at the same time that it concentrates resources in hands least inclined to be willing. In this way, and for this reason, inequality threatens the ability of society as a whole to provide for the weak, the ill, and the old.

The rise in inequality is the cause of our dreadful political condition. It is the cause of the bitter and unending struggle over the Transfer State, of the ugly battles over welfare, affirmative action, health care, social security, and the even uglier preoccupation in some circles with the alleged relationship of race, intelligence, and earnings. The "end of welfare as we knew it," to take a recent example, became possible only as rising inequality ensured that those who ended welfare did *not* know it, that they were detached from the life experiences of those on the receiving end.

Crisis is a misused word, particularly by alarmists who have presented us in recent years with a budget crisis, a Medicare crisis, and a social security crisis. None of those alleged crises really is. They all rest on specious claims about financial abstractions, on scare stories about impending bankruptcy—whether of the government as a whole or of particular government trust funds. They all fade when the economic news is good, only to return when hard times make the public receptive. But they serve the same underlying purpose: to legitimize the reduction of social welfare and social security programs, to withdraw resources from the social to the private realm. And they all enjoy support from the same social quarter: the financial and commercial interests of the wealthy. The real crisis is the underlying attack on the elderly, the poor, and the ill, and the tragic willingness of many working people to join it.

What brought this crisis into being? According to popular perception, rising inequality is a kind of black rain, a curse of obscure origin and no known remedy, a matter of mystery covered by words like *downsizing, deregulation,* and *globalization.* There is a view that capitalism has simply become more savage, a matter of the temper of the times and a new brutality of markets.[2] Many speak of a paradox in which the social evil of rising inequality accompanies rising average incomes and general prosperity for the country as a whole, a single dark cloud in a silver sky.

But is higher inequality, as many believe, something that "just happens"? Or does it serve a deeper purpose, one that is to be expected and accepted? Is the splitting apart of America an accident, or is it the inevitable incident of technological progress and the spread of free markets, a by-product of change and modernity? Is it the cost we must pay for the efficiencies of worldwide production and trade? Is it the price of comparatively low unemployment? Is it a side effect—disagreeable perhaps but a necessary aspect of our development toward a better future?

The idea that rising inequality serves a deeper purpose emerges from the economics profession, which has produced a kind of instant wisdom on the subject—a set of views, usually presented as orthodox, but in fact established with great haste and in considerable disorder in recent years. To a predominant faction within the economics profession, the "why" of rising inequality has been answered by a single, all-encompassing phrase: *skill-biased technological change.*

The term *technology* is very broad, and in many presentations the specific nature of "skill-biased" technological change remains vague.[3] Still, many economists today believe that a main cause of rising inequality lies in the spread of information technologies, and especially in the computer revolution. Massive investment in computers has, they argue, led to a transformation of the workplace. A rush to information technologies has driven up the relative demand for workers trained to use the new technologies. Since only so many well-trained, computer-literate workers are available at the outset of this process, market forces require that they be paid increasing amounts. And so "the rate of return" to skill increases. Inequality rises because those who are more skilled already hold positions near the top of the wage ladder, so their gains stretch the wage structure. Demand for unskilled labor falls, reducing comparative pay at the bottom of the wage scale.

This majority view on the "why" question has led to a split view on two other questions: *whether* inequality ought to be considered a social problem, and *what* should be done about it.

The strictest believers in the free market argue that rising inequality is not a problem; the market's dictate in this matter should be respected, even celebrated. The reasoning behind this position is a textbook case in the further economics of supply and demand. A shortfall of computer skills, caused by increasing demand for those skills, reflects the rising productivity of those who have mastered computers relative to those who have not. This causes the wage of the computer-skilled to rise. That rising relative wage sends a signal to the labor market, where it is received by everyone from college students to displaced middle managers in late middle age. They decode the message and head back to school. Soon computer courses will be overflowing, the labor markets will be flooded with newly numerate job applicants, and the premium associated with computer skills will disappear. The problem is self-liquidating, unless the transformations of skill-biased technological change continue in the next period, in which case the sequence of corrective responses must be repeated.

According to this line of argument, the wage gap produced by the skill differential is actually *necessary*, so long as the mismatch persists. It is the signal that tells the market to produce a greater number of workers with computer skills. To reduce the gap artificially, so to speak, by raising the wages of the unskilled, would only thwart the market. It would produce unemployment among the unskilled, since their wages would now lie above their worth—a story often told to account for the persistence of high unemployment in Europe. It would discourage retraining and perpetuate the shortage of skills. It might even have the perverse effect of slowing future technological improvements, since employers can scarcely be expected to pursue paths of innovation for which they cannot find an adequately talented workforce.

There is a respectable liberal dissent from this position, and it lies in arguing that although the price mechanism may work eventually, it doesn't work quickly enough. Thus, there is a social benefit in accelerating the creation of new skills, or in making access to retraining more equal. A forward-looking policy can anticipate future technological developments and prepare the workforce to meet the challenges to come; it can match expected shifts in demand with policy-driven shifts in supply. Hence there is a case, on the center-left of our reputable politics, for subsidies to education and for training programs. Affirmative action for women and minorities can also be justified; such measures help distribute the privileged positions in the distribution of skills to members of groups that have historically been excluded from privileged positions.

It is no accident that education and affirmative action hold their prominent positions on the beleaguered liberal agenda. Access to education is a gateway to opportunity in America, and few doubt (in public) that additional years in the classroom are socially useful. Distributing such access across ethnicities and genders is a way to achieve some diversity in the higher professions and in political and social elites. From a political standpoint, a program of support for education helps to relieve the financial anxieties of struggling middle-class families, who are known to vote. It is comparatively immune from attack by economists, for it leaves the pricing mechanisms of the labor market alone. And it is unlikely to incur criticism from the larger run of society's intellectuals either, for they stand to benefit from expanded subsidies to their own employment.

Yet the notion that equalizing *skills* will equalize *incomes* rests on a confusion—a confusion between equity in access to lottery tickets and equity in the value of the prizes. It is one thing for a program to hold out, subsidize, and support new chances for individuals to compete on the educational and career ladders. It is something different to promise that the ladder itself will become shorter and wider as a result of an increase in the numbers crowding their way up the rungs. It is something entirely different to suppose that each new entrant and reentrant in the educational sweepstakes will enjoy a chance of success equally high as those who have already entered and won. It is something entirely different, something bold and ingenious, to promise that we can return to the middle-class solidarity of three decades ago, entirely by diffusing knowledge through the population and by allowing free labor markets to work.

This is the marvelous adjustment that both sides of the debate—the education activists and the free-market purists—are implicitly promising. They are promising an adjustment of the structure of economic outcomes to the distribution of human skills. They are promising, in effect, that the inequalities occasioned by technological change will take care of themselves.[4]

One may reasonably pose the question, When?

Twenty years into the computer revolution, and nearly thirty years since the start of rising inequality, many millions have acquired the skills appropriate to the age. Word processing, accounting and calculating on spreadsheets, e-mail and the Internet, computer graphics and publication, computer-aided design: none of this is any longer esoteric. Yet the readjustment of incomes to a wider and more equal distribution of skill levels hasn't even begun to happen.[5] Indeed, so far as one can measure skills by educational attainment, the reverse has occurred and continues to occur. Educational differentials have narrowed, with policy help. Yet wage differentials widened sharply in the 1970s and 1980s; since the mid-1980s the most charitable interpretation of the data is that differentials have remained stable at historically high levels. As Martin Carnoy has eloquently pointed out, this bitter irony is especially poignant for black Americans, who have narrowed the educational gap separating them from whites, only to slip further behind in average earnings.[6]

The skills-shortage hypothesis—the idea that computers or other forms of skill-enhancing technology are mainly responsible for what has happened to the wage structure—and the idea that education can cure the problem are, I believe, fantasies. They are comforting fantasies for politicians, policymakers, and business interests, for they lay the blame for the phenomenon of rising inequality on workers themselves (if they fail to keep up with changing times, whose responsibility is that?), they ensure us that something good will come of it anyway (hey, isn't technology wonderful?), and they exonerate the state. For these same reasons, they are also dangerous fantasies, for they insulate us from a serious discussion of why inequality has risen and what might be done about it. This is true even though we do subsidize education (and should do so), affirmative action for disadvantaged groups is a good thing (or so I believe), we have heavily supported the introduction of new technologies to the schools, and computers and other inventions have generally enriched and eased our lives. Measures such as these can be good and socially useful without having application to the crisis of inequality in the wage structure.

In this book I argue that rising inequality in the wage structure is neither inevitable nor mysterious nor necessary nor the dark side of a good thing: rather, it was brought on mainly by bad economic performance. Its principal causes lie in the hard blows of recession, unemployment, and slow economic growth, combined with the effects of inflation and political resistance to raising the real value of the minimum wage. These are blows that, when once delivered, are not erased in any short period of economic recovery. They can be reversed, and in American history have been reversed, only by sustained periods of full employment alongside controlled inflation and a determined drive toward social justice. We last saw such a movement in this country in the 1960s, and before that only during World War II.

What caused bad economic performance? The answer is plainly visible to anyone with an open mind and a reasonable grasp of the evidence. Economic policy, and very specifically monetary policy, changed. Beginning in 1970,[7] the government abandoned the goal of full employment and instead turned its attention to a fight against inflation. For this purpose, only one instrument was deemed suitable: high interest rates brought into being by the Federal Reserve. There followed a repeated sequence of recessions, each justified at the time as the unfortunate consequence of external shocks and events beyond national control. The high unemployment that recessions produced generated, I shall demonstrate, the rise in inequality that destroyed the middle class. For this, the Federal Reserve, under its reputable chairmen Arthur F. Burns, Paul A. Volcker, and Alan Greenspan, stands primarily responsible.

As a matter of secondary importance, rising wage inequality is also linked to economic globalization, a touchy and contentious issue. As a share of the U.S. economy, trade has been expanding since the late 1960s, and imports of manufactures from developing countries, in particular, grew dramatically in the early 1980s. The effects on wages, now thoroughly debated in a large literature, are measurable and significant, though not so vast as economic nationalists sometimes contend.[8] It would be absurd to pretend that imports from low-wage countries have no effect on American wages; it is equally wrong to argue, as we sometimes hear from both left and right, that the Mexican and Chinese tails wag the dog of the American wage structure.

Globalization may be irreversible, but its consequences for economic and social inequality are not cast in concrete, and so it is also incorrect to argue that the new global economy necessarily dictates a politics of unrestricted laissez-faire. The cause of higher inequality as trade has expanded lies, rather, in the *way* American trade expanded, particularly under the huge overvaluation of the dollar and debt crises of the early 1980s. Because of this peculiar, harsh, unnecessary, and policy-created pattern, globalized trade has pulled our manufacturing wage structure in two directions at once: it has gradually layered the United States between the rich countries and the poor, and America has tended to become the leading industrial economy of both the First and the Third Worlds. This was unnecessary and it can be changed. We need not fear trade relations with poor countries so long as we properly fulfill our own responsibilities in the trading system.

Thus, whether one examines the international or the domestic aspects of rising inequality, the imprint of economic policy is clear. Things could have been different if economic policy had followed a different course. Things *should* have been different, because different choices were possible in the past.

Moreover, our situation can be changed now. We know it can be changed, because policies are available that have worked to reduce inequality in the past, in both the United States and other countries. Indeed, policies are working now that have slowed the increase in wage inequality. The task we face today is not so much to invent such policies but to recognize them and push them forward further and faster than we have so far dared to do.

There is an even bigger story just under the surface of this argument. It is that the ostensibly private, free-market character of the changes in the wage structure is an illusion. Relative wages are much more a matter of politics, and much less a matter of markets, than is generally believed. They are subject to the powerful effects of public policy, albeit policy governed in large measure by private interest and private pressures and frequently hidden from view. Public policies before 1970 largely supported a middle-class society, but not so later on. It follows that deep issues of macroeconomic policy, international economic order, and the role of the state have to be addressed before policies adequate to this crisis may be forthcoming. We have to acknowledge the essentially contingent, reversible, and public causes of the inequality crisis, and we must be willing to take actions that are direct, forceful, and sustained in order to bring it to an end.

From 1945 through 1970, the state maintained a wide range of protections for low-wage, less educated, more vulnerable workers, so that a broadly equal pattern of social progress was sustained despite, even in those distant years, rapid technological change. These protections were held in place by a stable macroeconomic policy that avoided sharp or prolonged disruptions to economic growth, and in particular by a monetary policy that was subordinated to these larger objectives. In those years, the government *as a whole* was committed to the pursuit of full employment, price stability, and high rates of economic growth. Following 1970, technological change continued, but the protections were withdrawn, and at the same time macroeconomic policy became much more unstable. The state shifted its support from the economy in general, the macroeconomy, to specific leading sectors of the economy— in fact, to the firms and industries most devoted to technological change. Monetary policy led the way, by declaring its independence from the larger objectives of economic policy, and its responsibility for the defeat of inflation above all other economic goals.

Wage equality and the middle-class character of American society were victims, in short, of the war on inflation. The wage structure cracked and crumbled under the assault of policies that stabilized the price level at the expense of comparatively low-income working Americans—in 1970, 1974, 1980,

1981, and most recently in 1990. These policies were led and implemented by the Federal Reserve, though with the acquiescence of the rest of the government, which chose the politically easy path of assigning responsibility for fighting inflation to the central bank. It follows that if we wish to restore patterns of wage equality befitting a society that is truly middle class, we need two things: a return to policies of sustained full employment and an entirely different approach, when necessary, to inflation. We will return to this point.

This book focuses primarily on wages as the major story of inequality in working America, the fundamental issue in the politics of inequality, and the driving story behind the larger social changes that come when inequality increases. Wages and salaries account for over half of all income flows and for most of the incomes of the 135 million Americans in the labor force, plus their dependents. It is also true, if my calculations are correct, that even if there had been no increase in the inequality of nonwage incomes in America since 1970 and no change in the relation of wages to profits, the rise in U.S. inequality would still have been among the highest in the industrial world.

My focus on wage income is also partly driven by theoretical interests, data, and a desire to add something to the literature and debate. Hourly wage rates are of interest here because they are the fundamental outcome of the work contract. Statements about the effect of technology or trade on wage structures are about hourly wage rates in theory; differences in hours worked, nonwage incomes, or family structures have nothing to do with it. Yet empirical research on inequality often has relied on broader measures of income inequality, such as normal weekly earnings or annual earnings, with the risk that fluctuating hours or spells of unemployment may obscure what is happening to wage rates.

Individual earnings—weekly, monthly, or annual—combine the effects of the hourly wage rate with fluctuations in hours worked. Even if all hourly wages were equal, and even if there were no sources of income other than personal labor, personal earnings would not be equal because different people would work differing numbers of hours through the week, the month, and the year. Some of this is by choice: certain people prefer more hours of work and the associated income; others prefer less. Some is not by choice, because in the real world unemployment falls on some people against their will.

Incomes differ from earnings because of income from capital, including dividends, interest, realized capital gains, and partnership profits. Also, many people receive modest incomes in the form of public assistance and transfers from the government, including social security and welfare. Nonwage incomes account for more than 40 percent of total income today and are clearly a major source of inequality, especially since the distribution of capital ownership is so uneven.

Finally, people form themselves into families, and family income is the ultimate determinant of the standard of living. Families with multiple earners rise toward the top of the family income distribution, while families with just one earner fall toward the bottom. As the number of single-headed households rises, so too will inequality. This pattern is compounded in the real world by the grim fact that single-headed households also comprise, to a large extent, those with the most unstable employment experiences and the lowest hourly wages.

All of these elements combine to generate the structure of incomes and of inequalities that we all live with. I argue, however, that inequality in wage rates is the foundation of the whole structure. This is partly because wages and salaries remain such a large fraction of total incomes and also because the distribution of certain other forms of income, such as private pensions, depends directly on each recipient's past history of earnings and hence on the inequality of the wage structure.

Beyond this, I believe that increases in the inequality of the wage structure have repercussions through the outer layers that lead to higher inequality at the levels of individual earnings, individual incomes, and family incomes. Higher inequality in wage rates tends to polarize the experience of unemployment: jobs paying higher wages are more stable, and those at the bottom become contingent and experience the brunt of ups and downs in labor demand. Higher inequality in family incomes produces higher transfer payments—both public, because more people fall into poverty, and private, because more people incur debts and interest burdens in the effort to maintain parities of living standards despite disparities of income. Finally, wage and income inequality bleed through to family structures. Doubling up and breaking up are both consequences in part of economic stress; hence the rise in inequality due to changes in family structure is partly an aftershock of rising wage and salary inequality and unemployment.

The politics of inequality tends to be mainly about transfer payments, for the straightforward reason that transfer payments are mediated by the state, and politics is about the state. The support of these populations who live directly or indirectly off the toil of those who are currently working is the story of our political life. Typically, when we speak of transfers, we refer to the retired elderly and the poor. I will argue, however, that the politics of transfers actually involves three distinct groups, and I would add *interest receivers* to the poor and the elderly as a population with a direct interest in state policy—namely, the interest rate. The difference between these groups is that while the poor are poor, the elderly tend to be lower middle class and the population of significant interest receivers stretches from the upper middle to the very highest reaches of the income distribution.

In the larger scheme of the economy and the government budget, transfer payments to poor people other than the elderly are minor. The now-defunct welfare program Aid to Families with Dependent Children (AFDC), housing assistance, food stamps, and state-supported general relief programs have been vital to those who rely on them. But these programs are comparatively small in budget terms, tiny in relation to the size of the economy, and with perhaps one important exception—the earned income tax credit—they have been falling since the early 1980s.

The elderly are a different case. This is a group for whom the news of the past generation has been good on the whole. To a very large degree, the elderly have escaped both poverty and the labor market over a quarter-century's time, as well as the crushing burdens of the cost of medical care. They have done so, of course, through government assistance. Social security goes back to 1935, but for the first generation of its existence, large numbers of the elderly remained poor. It was only beginning in the early 1970s that increases in retirement earnings and medical care under social security, as well as supplemental security income for the disabled and destitute, permitted many older people to quit working earlier and to live better in retirement than they otherwise would or than any previous generation of the elderly has ever done.

Some of these large improvements were accidental, or the result of political competition during the election season of 1972.[9] But the accomplishment was nevertheless very real. A whole economy now revolves around an emancipated elderly population; such a thing hardly existed thirty years ago. And among the elderly, the war against poverty has been a resounding success. According to a report from the Census Bureau, the poverty rate of elderly people fell from 35.2 percent in 1959 to 10.5 percent in 1995, a rate lower than that of the working population.[10]

What of transfers to the rich? According to one study, the average pretax income of the top 1 percent of American families more than doubled over fifteen years after 1977, reaching $676,000 per year in 1992.[11] This group of the very rich relies on wages and salaries for less than half their income. The other half flows from the distribution of wealth, a controversial and important topic that I will substantially neglect, except for a few words to situate interest in this complex pattern.[12]

At the very top of the income distribution, net capital gains are extremely important. In 1988, they accounted for 22.1 percent of the income of the top 1 percent of taxpaying families, and that group received over 68 percent of all gains. Capital gains overall totaled $153 billion; of this, nearly $105 billion went to the top percentile. Partnership net profits, another critical item, totaled $56 billion in 1988 and flowed almost exclusively to the top percentile.

Interest income overall is five times larger than capital gains and more stable, and it has grown more as a share of total income than any other category, rising particularly sharply with the rise in interest rates, from 4.6 percent of total personal income in 1977 to 8.2 percent in 1982—an increase larger than the whole defense budget and on a par with social security payments.[13] It is true that interest income is not so concentrated as capital gains and partnership incomes. Interest is earned in significant quantities by significant numbers of moderately wealthy—say, the top 10 percent rather than the very top percentile, both directly and through holdings in pension funds. As compared with capital gains, the rise in interest income represents an important source of transfers to this comparatively large group. Obviously many of them have debts themselves, so not all of interest flows are redistributive. But as one moves up the wealth ladder, net creditors come to predominate over net debtors; on balance, the payment of interest represents a net flow from middle-income debtors and from the government itself (that is, from taxpayers) to creditors among the comparatively well-to-do.[14]

The trouble comes when we add the burdens of the three nonworking populations together and present the bill to the working population. Transfers to the truly poor are minor and declining. But when we count transfer payments to the rich, in the form of interest on private and public debts, alongside transfer payments to the elderly, in the form of government programs, the increase in total transfers as a share of personal income over forty years has been dramatic. Interest payments and government programs together accounted for about 11 percent of all personal income in the 1950s. Today the share is about 30 percent, with transfers accounting for over 16 percent and interest for over 13 percent of the total.

This phenomenon we may call the rise of the Transfer State. As a result of it, we have in place in the United States today not one but two competing welfare systems. One is a private one disproportionately for the rich, based on their ownership of financial assets. The other is a public one, mainly for the retired population, with dribs and drabs for the younger poor. Both are financed mainly by working Americans, who pay taxes to the state and interest to their creditors, and then try to live on the remainder. Both are administered, in important ways, by the government, for it is the government that sets the tax rate on payrolls to fund social security, and it is the government, through the Federal Reserve system, that sets the key interest rate on loans.[15]

My argument is that rising inequality in the wage structure underlies both the evident crisis of public transfers and the not-so-evident but insidious problems of a rising burden of net interest obligations. As the wage structure became less equal, both public and private transfers rose, and the public transfer burden, which inevitably bears the brunt of public attention and efforts at legislative remedy, became the enduring crisis of our political life. Was this accidental? I think not.

Why do more equally paid societies tolerate higher public transfer burdens, and why do these systems fall into crisis when inequality rises? There are at least three reasons. The first of these concerns the nature of the transfers themselves, the second concerns the attitudes and political involvement of the rich, and the third concerns the bargain as it appears to the middle class.

First, more equal societies have less poverty. The burden of support for the nonelderly poor is therefore less, and the political controversies surrounding the notion of aid to the undeserving tend not to arise. The social problems of the poor tend to be seen much more as the social problems of the temporarily poor—a category into which many people can imagine themselves falling, for example, through loss of employment. Thus, there is greater and wider support for what is, in any event, a smaller and less onerous burden. Transfer programs themselves can then be generous enough to blur the distinction between the poor and the middle class, and the stigma of poverty falls away.

Second, more equal societies have fewer rich people. In a society of broadly based equality, the proportion of those opting out of public services, of those for whom public pension plans are financially insignificant, becomes a politically negligible fringe. But as a society polarizes, the rich develop an ethos all their own—an ethos of exaggerated individualism, of independence from the state and rejection of public institutions. The usual political response to this development—certainly the response in the United States—has been to allow the wealthy to reduce their share of payment for the burden. (In the United States, for instance, the cap on payroll earnings taxable for social security is a clear example of this; so too are tax provisions benefiting the wealthy, such as special rates for capital gains.) This then has the effect of shifting the burden of supporting transfer programs from the wealthy toward the middle class, a burden that becomes heavier as transfers increase and the weight of income shifts up the scale from the middle class toward the wealthy.

Third, more equal societies will tend to have lower *private* transfer burdens—less private capital, less debt, less conspicuous consumption and pecuniary emulation. People are willing to pay higher taxes for social insurance if they face a lower burden of private debts. Moreover, in a middle-class society, public services come to be seen as collective assets—something from which the population at large benefits directly. What might be a bad social bargain at 30 percent of income, when benefits are thought to flow mainly to the unworthy, seems like a much better deal even at 40 percent of income, when benefits flow back to the population at large (for example, in the form of Canadian medical care, French trains and mass transit, and the German system of free universities). This explains why these amenities enjoy such widespread support—as has the social security system in the United States.

One answer to the inequality crisis, indeed the principal answer offered by the small cohort of true progressives who have survived in political life, is to engage in a stalwart defense of progressive taxation and generous public assistance programs, including social security. This has been the work of angels.[16] And in the preservation of the income tax and the social security system, so far it has been not without a share of successes. Tax reform in 1986 and in 1993 demonstrated that the theme of fairness in the tax structure is a powerful political force; liberals need not flinch from progressive taxation for political reasons.

But in the long run, the battle cannot be won by reacting to ever-rising inequality with ever-increasing compensatory transfers, for as society grows increasingly unequal, the political economy of compensatory transfers becomes oppressive. Claustrophobia, a sense of lack of mobility, of flexibility, a loss of liquidity, of possibility and of freedom set in. In the squeeze between entitlements, public interest payments, and private spending, public services are degraded, downgraded, and debased; they become symbols of the shabby, amenities to avoid. The social bargain exempting the rich from their share of the burden—for instance, through caps on income subject to social security payroll taxes and reduced tax rates on capital gains—comes to grate on the middle class as much as the burden itself.

An economy of tax slaves and debt peons is, at its worst, an economy of frightened and frustrated people. The American working population is angry because it has both the rich and the elderly on its back, even as it divides into mutually hostile and distrusting camps, and because the economic bargain involved in continuing to carry both looks increasingly bad for those who can least afford it. Lacking public solutions to the problems of life on the treadmill, and lacking also the political parties, platforms, and organizations to put them into effect, it is not surprising that people become open to the appeal of every man for himself, and ultimately the power of this appeal will become irresistible.

The signs of this are unmistakable. The antistate political operatives of the wealthy seek allies by offering small tax breaks to those near the top of the wage structure, while chipping away at programs and benefits from the bottom up. There results a form of class warfare—a warfare of code words and indirection—fed by cynical ploys and schemes of diversion. In this way economic polarization and political retrogression mutually reinforce each other.

In the United States, the first target of this assault was federal assistance to the very poor, and particularly to young, single mothers. Conservatives and their academic allies fueled their assault on welfare with a powerful rhetoric of welfare reform built on displacement. The frustration generated by a high burden of transfers, of which very little goes to poor people in practice, was channeled into resentment of the supposed privileges and supposed depravities of welfare recipients.[17] The resulting anger led to the abolition of AFDC in 1996, along with deep cuts in the eligibility of even legal landed immigrants for such programs as food stamps and Supplemental Security Income.[18]

Still another manifestation of the same phenomenon is the drive to mandate balance—a deficit of zero—in the budget of the U.S. government, a proposal often accompanied by proposals to reduce taxes and make increasing taxes constitutionally difficult.[19] If the objective were budget balance per se, it would make little sense to put an extra barrier in the way of an increase in tax rates. The inconsistency of joining the two proposals reveals the true purpose, which is to increase the pressure for cuts in federal government spending. Since advocates of balancing the budget are usually strong supporters of the defense budget and since federal interest payments cannot be reduced by fiat, the effect is to focus this pressure on cuts in transfer spending.

In the initial rounds, the agenda focused on scapegoats on one side (the poor, immigrants) and on generalized assaults on public spending (the balanced budget amendment). But this moment is past. The debate now centers openly on the core program of the New Deal social architecture, which was social security, and on the core accomplishment of the Great Society, which was Medicare. Led from secure bastions on Wall Street by investment bankers,[20] a campaign against the social security system, in particular, has moved into the gap left by the successful crusade against welfare.

The arguments advanced for "reform" of the social security system are, of course, quite different in kind from those heard against welfare.[21] One does not berate the elderly for their lack of work ethic (even though the reduction of working hours by able-bodied elderly men has been far more dramatic over the past twenty years than that of young black women). Instead we hear a financial argument, to the effect that the trust funds from which social security retirement benefits are paid will be depleted over the next thirty or forty years. This projection, accompanied by dire warnings of bankruptcy and crisis, is said to justify either a large reduction in future benefits or else the transfer of trust fund revenues into mandatory private savings accounts. In either case, the effect is to privatize what was previously social, to reduce both present and future transfers, and to cut the support for the elderly poor to the benefit of the elderly rich.[22]

These arguments do not, in fact, reflect a consensus of experts or of reputable work on social security.[23] But the fact is that they are widely accepted, because they appeal to an increasing sense of self-interest on the part of influential communities. This has occurred, I believe, only because for a sufficient group *within* the broad middle, the increasing stratification of wages and salaries, combined with the increasing burden of public and private transfers, means that there is an increasingly powerful economic incentive to opt out, to take one's own pro rata share of the commonweal, and to go it alone.

The heart of the problem lies not with the structure of transfer programs but with the structure of wages and incomes that both breeds the Transfer State and makes it unsustainable. It lies in the splitting apart of the middle class that once dominated the social and psychological landscape in this country, of the great Middle America that was created by World War II and built up through the two and a half decades that followed. This great polarization leads toward the dissociation of the rich, the debt and tax peonage of the middle, and the seeming intractability of the poor, all of which combine to produce the vulnerability of our social programs. For this reason, no amount of debunking, whether of Charles Murray or Peter Peterson, is likely to defuse the march to demolition of the New Deal. Only a reestablishment of the middle-class solidarity that supported the New Deal for a generation can do that and lay the groundwork for widely shared social progress into the future.

To summarize bluntly, in rising inequality we long ago cut back on public universities, mass transit, housing, parks, and the arts. We have now decided that we cannot afford the poor. But since cutting the poor saves very little money, it follows that we cannot afford to maintain both the elderly and the wealthy at their current levels of income and consumption. Perhaps we could afford the elderly, perhaps we could afford the rich, each taken alone as matters stand. But we cannot afford them both, and we have to choose which set of transfers to reduce.

Part of the solution is to reduce the burden of private transfers by reducing the rate of interest. This is a necessary step for many reasons, direct and indirect, which we will explore in detail. And indeed it is a step whose necessity even the Federal Reserve has recognized on occasion: interest rates and debt burdens fell in the late 1980s and early 1990s. Reductions in the interest rate provide short-term relief, for they make paying other bills—especially taxes—easier, and they ease the federal budget crunch affecting other vital services. But reducing the private transfer burden on a permanent basis is more difficult, since it would involve regulating the extension of private credit, which is a much more difficult proposition. Without this, the problem would not be solved, for an unregulated reduction of debt burdens is only an invitation to a greater accumulation of debt.

It is therefore likely that without fundamental reform of the underlying wage structure the public half of the transfer state will continue to give way. This is the meaning of past, losing battles for health care reform, of the disastrous 1996 battle over welfare, and of the developing battles over Medicare and social security. One cannot forge the kind of basic agreement on the terms of a social contract that the survival of social security, Medicare, and other basic protections requires on the basis of the current American distribution of income and wealth.

The rise of wage and salary inequality is in this way a development that raises deep questions about the legitimacy of the most prominent social processes of modern economic life, indeed of the system itself. It forces us to ask how much we are really prepared to leave to the market. Having placed ostensibly private wage and salary decisions on a pedestal, having set them out of bounds of normal public policy, are we ready to see the results lead to an abandonment of the poor? Of the elderly? To the destruction of the middle class?

Sooner or later, fundamental issues will have to be faced. Sooner or later, we will have to face the choice between gutting the redistributive system or fixing the distributive problem.

To fix the distributive problem, we must first understand what caused the rise in wage inequality. Chapters 2 through 4 present a critique of the explanation of rising inequality that has dominated academic discussion in America—an explanation that relates pay to the skills required by new forms of technology. I argue that inequality is not a result of rising skill differentials, expressed in the evaluations of a free and efficient market for labor. Rather, we are observing a process driven by the interaction of economic policy, economic performance, and the existing structures of monopoly power. The fundamental contribution of technological change lies in the redistribution of this form of power toward suppliers of knowledge-intensive capital goods. The contribution of weak and unstable economic performance has been to deprive everyone else, and in particular workers in consumer goods manufacturing and services, of the economic and political power that they would have needed to counterbalance the new monopolies and so to maintain their own position.

Chapters 5 through 9, in Part II, ask what the macroeconomic and policy forces are that underlie this redistribution of power and the rising inequality it has produced. These chapters include a systematic look at how the industrial wage structure has changed through time and tests of alternative explanations. To see how the process works, we must rethink how we describe the economy as a whole. I will show that a reorganization of industrial categories into three broad groups—knowledge-based capital goods industries, consumer goods producers, and pure services—can help clarify how the wage structure has evolved. This in turn permits us to see with some precision what the historical forces buffeting the industrial wage structure in the past three decades have actually been.

When we examine these forces, we shall find the fingerprints of state policy. It turns out that the main forces affecting inequality and industrial change are not mysterious irruptions of gadgetry and changing human relations. They are, in fact, directly traceable to actions of the government. The most prominent among these to the naked eye are the redistribution of tax burdens, governmental hostility to trade unions, and an indifference to preserving the real value of the minimum wage. But we shall find others more powerful and less visible, in the actions of monetary policy and particularly in the reliance on monetary policy to battle inflation, whatever the cost to working people, especially in terms of unemployment.

The thought that state policy caused much of our rising inequality leads to the idea that state policy might properly be involved in the cure. The direct approach to wage inequality is to raise the wages and improve the employment prospects of the comparatively unskilled. The simple view is that society can reduce its inequalities by regulating the gains of the rich and the comparatively successful. The simple view is that the poor can best help themselves when labor is scarce—when there is sustained and stable full employment. The simple view is that all of these are proper responsibilities of government, and a fair action program for unions and political parties. And the historical fact is that such steps are what societies interested in greater equality have always taken. This includes the United States as recently as 1996, when a Republican Congress enacted, and a Democratic president signed, a long-overdue increase in the minimum wage.

That will lead toward a discussion of the the economic policies required to bring the inequality crisis to an end. In Chapters 10 through 12, I argue that the stock issues of the modern American economic policy debate cannot deliver cures to economic inequality, and indeed have contributed to the rising inequality of the past generation. These chapters take on the conservative approach to inflation (the natural rate of unemployment), the savings-investment fetishism that preoccupies the center, and also the supply-side policies of research, infrastructure, and education favored by modern liberals.

Once we understand how and why inequality has increased and why the mainstream debate has failed to do anything effective about it, we can consider some different answers. The final part reviews these alternatives. My case, in the end, is that reducing inequality requires sustained full employment, stable and low interest rates, and reasonable price stability. The main areas demanding reform are monetary and budget policies and international economic policies. We also need new policies to take the necessary burden of inflation fighting off the back of the Federal Reserve. Direct actions to raise substandard wages, through higher minimum wages and more effective labor organization, are appropriate and not precluded by any valid economic argument. A return to a national presence in wage setting, with a more equal structure as the explicit goal of public policy, would be even better.

There is a range of additional steps, including further increases in the minimum wage, renewed investment in urban and public amenities, jobs programs, and universal health care. These measures work. If based on a national program of sustained full employment, they could form a coherent, sensible, economic policy agenda. They may be radical actions, by the tame standards of what now passes for politics in America, and by the defensive agendas on taxation and welfare that have been even the true progressive's lot for several decades. But they are not unprecedented. We have experienced sustained full employment with reasonably stable prices in living memory; our main need is not to reinvent but to rediscover the ways and means of this achievement. In any event, the important point is not whether an action is radical but whether it is needed.

The approach has to be direct, or it will not work. If the crisis of rising inequality results from policies and not from the market, it follows that policy is needed for the fix. We cannot rely on the market to sort things out, given only the thin raw material of more widely distributed college degrees. Nor can we accept the economists' nostrum, which is to leave the distributive mechanisms as they are, and then to rely on transfers and progressive taxes to mend the problem of an excessively unequal result. We cannot do this because the rise in wage and salary inequality is itself the fundamental cause of the ongoing rollback of transfer policies and of their untenable political position. As wage inequality goes up, the transfer cure becomes less and less realistic. Unless we come to grips with inequality, social security will surely go the way of welfare sooner or later.

In the end, the crisis of the Transfer State has to be met on the terrain of the wage structure, or it will not be met at all.

2

THE SKILL FALLACY

In so far as business ends and methods dominate modern industry the relationship between the usefulness of the work . . . and the remuneration of it is remote and uncertain to such a degree that no attempt at formulating such a relation is worthwhile.

—Thorstein Veblen, *The Theory of the Business Enterprise*

It was not so very long ago that the subject of income inequality rarely came up in public policy discussions. The more general topic of income distribution was also, until recently, a backwater of economic research. In 1982, as executive director of the Joint Economic Committee of the U.S. Congress, I organized hearings on the issue,[1] at the behest of the chairman of the committee, Congressman Henry S. Reuss of Wisconsin, a man far ahead of the times on this and many other things.

At our hearings, Professor Edward Budd of Pennsylvania State University reviewed the then-known facts. Inequality in the distribution of family incomes had been rising very slowly, since around 1970. So far as was known, changing family structure played a role in this development—mainly a rise in the number of households headed by unattached individuals. Changing types of income played a role: a rise in capital income, affecting the rich, and a decline in transfer income, affecting the poor. Among economic factors, the main one had been a rise in average unemployment between 1970 and 1980. Professor Budd predicted that the proposed policies of the Reagan administration would tend to accelerate developments, increasing inequality still more. The hearings attracted no attention.

23

Those 1982 hearings occurred at a turning point. As Professor Budd predicted, they foreshadowed the largest increases in inequality in fifty years. Yet it took another half-decade before the larger American academic community began to take an active interest. It was only in the late 1980s, notably in response to the work of Barry Bluestone and Bennett Harrison,[2] who were among the first to call the attention of a larger public to the issue, that the economics profession in America began to become engaged.[3] Since then, writings on the topic of inequality have proliferated. By the mid-1990s surveys were already appearing, two important ones being by Sheldon Danziger and Peter Gottschalk, distinguished experts on poverty and antipoverty policy, and by Robert Z. Lawrence of Harvard.[4]

In the new literature on inequality, the explanations of the early 1980s, based as they were on common wisdom and policy variables, play very little role. There is a new consensus, and it focuses on the changing reward to the acquisition of education and productive talent. Danziger and Gottschalk summarize the prevailing literature on the rising inequality of earnings by naming the essential conundrum as economists have seen it, which is to explain a *rising demand for skill:*

> First, no single cause had an effect that was large enough to account for the observed increase in wage and earnings inequality. . . . Second, only demand-side factors can explain why employment of skilled workers increased at the same time that firms had to pay them higher wages.[5]

The phrase *demand side* refers to the decisions of business organizations to change the number and the type of workers they hire. When employment and wages both increase for a particular sector of the economy, there must have been an underlying increase in demand in that sector. In this case, the situation is not quite so straightforward. What we are said to observe is an increase in the relative wages of workers with better educations. That is, workers with good educations are getting paid more, in comparison with workers who do not have such good educations. This shift in relative pay is known as a "rise in the rate of return to skill" or "an increase in the skill premium." When it occurs in conjunction with a parallel shift in relative employment, it may be attributed to "a shift in relative demand."[6]

The economists Chinhui Juhn, Kevin Murphy, and Brooks Pierce have conducted perhaps the most detailed study of the change in wage structures on record so far, a massive pooling of survey data from the annual Current Population Surveys of the Census Bureau for the years from 1963 forward.[7] Juhn, Murphy, and Pierce have separated out three distinct patterns of rising inequality, of approximately equal importance. One is associated with "experience"—years in the labor force, a factor whose contribution to inequality begins to rise around 1970 as older workers gain ground on their junior colleagues. The second is associated with years of education. This premium is cyclical: it rises in the 1960s, actually declines in the 1970s, before rising sharply in the 1980s. The third is labeled "unobserved skill," and is a residual unattributable to any measurable characteristic. The contribution of this catch-all category to rising inequality also begins in the late 1960s.

Taking the three factors together, we observe the following pattern. First, through the 1960s, the income distribution remains comparatively stable. After 1970, the lower half of the wage distribution—those with incomes below the median, including a disproportionate number of younger workers (and, of course, female workers)—suddenly begins to lose ground. At the median or above, things are little changed through the decade. This suggests that the effect of demand shifts in the 1970s is essentially negative; the major phenomena concern damage to the less skilled and to younger workers rather than advantages to the most skilled or to older workers as such. It is only in the 1980s that the income distribution becomes unhinged both above and below the median income; then the relative income of those with higher levels of education begins to rise. It is only in the 1980s, therefore, that one can begin to speak of the pull on the wage structure of demand for sophisticated new skills.

Overall, income inequality rises comparatively slowly in the 1970s; a falling education premium partly offsets an increasing premium for experience and that mysterious third factor, "unobserved" skill. In the 1980s, the education premium reverses direction and suddenly begins to rise. At this point all three distinct components of the rise in inequality kick in together, and the rise in inequality overall correspondingly proceeds at a significantly more rapid rate.

This is a complex pattern. It indeed suggests that no single, simple, invariant, and relentless force can lie behind the recent history of inequality. Instead, we need explanations that can account for the stability of income distributions before 1970. We need explanations that can account for a general effect in favor of older workers and against younger workers in the 1970s. And we need an explanation that can account for the relative losses—the declining skill premium—of more highly educated workers in the 1970s, alongside their strong gains after 1980.[8]

Given the complexity of the pattern and the fact that inequality begins to rise in 1970, it is a bit odd that the main explanations in the academic literature and the associated policy discussion have been relentlessly, indeed almost exclusively, focused on a single aspect of the phenomenon: the rise in the rate of return to education or "skill" after 1980. They have substantially neglected the forces affecting experience and the remaining, unexplained dimension of inequality. Although numerous authors have noted the discrepancy, very little has been done to repair it.[9]

What has caused the most recent rise in the rate of return to skill? Industrial restructuring affecting the type of jobs available? Globalization and the foreign sourcing of low-skill assembly jobs? No—at least, not according to the new consensus.[10] The new view is that the shift in demand for labor that underlies rising inequality after 1980 was a positive shift, not a negative one, and *not* caused by deindustrialization or by trade. By a process of elimination, economists have arrived at the conclusion that *technology* did it. Danziger and Gottschalk summarize:

> Technological change which raises the productivity of older and more-educated workers faster than that of younger and less-educated workers is consistent with increases in both relative wages and relative employment of more-skilled labor. If workers with more education are more productive, then firms will hire more of them in spite of their higher costs. This is exactly what happened.[11]

This is the conclusion that most professional economists in America who are concerned with the issue of inequality have now reached. As the University of Michigan economist George Johnson reports, the literature shows "virtual unanimous agreement that during the 1980s relative demand increased for workers at the high end of the skill distribution and thus caused their relative wages to rise."[12] The literature observes that when other factors are controlled for, there has occurred a rise in the incomes of those with longer and better educations—a rise in the implicit "price of skill." After coming up dry in a search for alternative explanations for this shift, technology is brought out from within the black box and credited with having been at the origin of a vast social revolution.[13]

This wisdom is not implausible on the surface. Consider the automobile from, say, the 1890s to the 1920s. It created a demand for drivers and mechanics, thus increasing the return to the skills associated with the automotive arts. It also undercut the demand for harness makers, carriage drivers, blacksmiths, veterinarians, and grooms. If the former effect was larger, the automobile was job creating; if not, it was job destroying.[14] If, and only if, the education required to master the automotive skills exceeded that necessary for the horse-and-buggy skills they replaced, the new technology was "skill enhancing" or "skill biased." But in the normal definitions of skill, which associate skill specifically with *formal* education, this is normally to be expected. Training in the fine older crafts (say, blacksmithing or harness making) is normally devolved over the generations from the formal educational system to the household or the apprenticeship; it passes from master to trainee outside of school. Only newer crafts, being by their nature less familiar, require systematic instruction. It follows that the rise of the new technologies will increase the demand for formal education and disproportionately reward those who have it.

It is equally plausible on the surface that some technological development in 1980—let's leave it unspecified for the moment—was like the automobile after 1890. If so, we need a pattern of technological change that was skill biased from 1980 onward and remains so, but that was not sufficiently powerful in the 1970s to offset the depressing effect of a rapidly rising population of college graduates on wages.

We might reasonably ask for the evidence of such a particular pattern of technological change. There is, as it turns out, little direct evidence for any such pattern.[15] That is, it is hard to find formal efforts at measurement of technological change—skill biased or otherwise—whose time pattern might be compared to movements of inequality. There is no variable labeled "technological change" in the national income and product statistics, nor is there any standard estimating technique that isolates the technical from other forms of economic transformation. Lacking this, there is no direct way to know whether recent years have seen more technological change, or less, than earlier decades.

Equally, we have no direct way to know whether it was technological change or some other factor that drove up the relative pay of more educated workers after 1980. The degree of "skill bias," like the rate of technological change itself, is an inference rather than an observation. We have only the patterns of price change: a falling skill premium in the 1970s and a rising one over the following fifteen years. Since an increasing supply of skills can be measured—or so the literature supposes—by the increasing quantity of schooling embodied in the labor force, the usual inference is that there must have been an even greater shift in the relative demand for skill after 1980 to account for the rising skill premium. Otherwise the skill premium would have continued to fall, as it did during the 1970s. But we do not have direct evidence on what that demand shift consisted of.

To make the connection between demand shifts and technological change, economists have tended to rely on case studies,[16] alongside appeals to the facts of common knowledge, to establish that we are living in an age of technological revolution, in textiles, printing, aerospace, and other areas. They present such studies and, of course, can point to this or that revolutionary development as a sign of our tumultuous times.

But how much can we rely on our perceptions, entirely outside historical context, on a matter as complex, elusive, and apparently unmeasurable as the "degree of technological change"? Case studies can be interesting and useful, yet they cannot serve as reliable guides to issues and questions that are inherently numerical. They cannot tell us that our technological age is more dynamic or transformative than previous ones. Nor can they tell whether new generations of technology actually do require greater increments of skill than previous generations. Nor can they tell us, in any way that is useful for purposes of comparison, by how much the new technologies increase the demand for skill. To answer such questions, we need independent numerical measurement of the degree and nature of technological change, and this is what our economists, on the evidence available to them, cannot provide.

This problem becomes acute when we realize that every generation for two centuries has produced case studies on the acceleration of technology in their time.[17] In our own living memory or nearly so, we have witnessed the dawn of the automobile age, the ages of radio and television, the jet age, the atomic age, the space age, the computer age, the information age—to name only the main ones. Each of these ages was greeted at the time with a sense of profound wonder. ("What hath God wrought?") Some changed daily life; others affected the mode of production. Technological change in one form or another is a never-ending cultural motif, at least in the United States, and every great technological change creates a class of beneficiaries whose incomes rise as a result. If new technology always has this effect but is producing huge increases in inequality throughout the society only now, then there must be something different about the modern age. Either the nature of technological change must have changed, or the process must have accelerated.

Surely the claim that there is something more than usually revolutionary about the most recent developments should be accompanied by systematic, comparative, historical evidence. *By how much* did the rate of technological change accelerate? Alternatively, *by how much* did technological change itself change? These questions cry out for quantitative answers, but there are, in fact, no such answers; there are only anecdote and case study.

The closest that standard economic statistics come to a measurement of the pace of technological change is the measurement of productivity growth. Productivity is the ratio of labor inputs to the value of production, usually measured over the nonfarm business sector. Its growth rate is taken by many to measure the progress of economic life. In a very general way, productivity can be seen as a summary measure of technology writ large, though many things, including changes in business organization, capacity utilization, and the composition of output across sectors, can affect productivity growth that would not be considered matters of production technology in a strict sense.

Even allowing for the loose connection between the concepts, there is an odd contradiction between the belief that the period after 1980 was one of especially rapid technological change[18] and the established measurement of productivity growth since 1973. Economists have long argued that the underlying trend rate of productivity growth slowed after 1973, from an annual average improvement of around 3 percent to less than 2 percent per year, and even to 1 percent or below by the end of the decade. Nor, by standard measures, did the rate of productivity growth accelerate again during the 1980s. Economic research has not been successful in efforts to explain the productivity slowdown, but it stands in odd counterpoint to the notion that we live in an age of unprecedented technological marvels.[19] To compound the puzzle, income distribution was more stable before 1970, when productivity growth was high, than it became after 1970, when productivity growth fell.

Among many others, Danziger and Gottschalk wrestle with this problem. Like many others, in the end they opt to emphasize the changing nature of technological change rather than an increasing rate of such change. They attempt to resolve the puzzle by arguing that the new types of technology do not actually increase productivity on average. Rather, in this view technology changes only the required proportions of skilled (and expensive) to unskilled (and increasingly inexpensive, in relative terms) workers. Thus technology "forces" change in wage structures that reward the skilled few at the expense of the unskilled many.

This solution lays the emphasis on the question of "skill bias." A particular beauty of this solution is that it does not disturb the prevailing orthodox theory of the forces underlying income distribution. Technology works, in this argument, through its effect on the productivity of individual workers and through the supply and demand for their skills. Those with the skills appropriate for the era are rewarded with rising relative wages. In this way, the power and the wisdom of the market mechanism, of supply and demand, are reaffirmed. Equally important, the economist need not fight any tiresome ideological battles in delivering an explanation of the phenomenon under study. And although the rise in inequality may be regrettable, no uncomfortable questions about its necessity need be raised. It is therefore not surprising that interpretations along these lines have caught on. Nor is it any surprise that they have proved popular with leading sectors of opinion, including political leaders, the press, and even the leadership of the technology sectors.

The idea of skill-biased change that does not raise productivity on average leaves some big questions unanswered. Why would business firms adopt new technologies if they actually took this form? The theory seems to imply that under these conditions, businesses have the option of getting the same results by continuing to employ unskilled workers using older technologies at newly lowered wages. So long as wages adjust to reflect the value of marginal products, why do firms adopt the new technologies with such enthusiasm? Even more troubling, why should (and why does) society as a whole tolerate technological change that merely creates inequality without raising even the average standard of living? I have not seen any effort by partisans of this approach to come to grips with either of these intriguing questions.

Problems of this kind have, on the other hand, prompted some researchers to take up the possibility that the paradox is an illusion, because average productivity growth has been radically undermeasured. In other words, given an apparent conflict between an inference based on theory and the evidence, they would reconcile the two by changing the data. Given that rapidly rising skill premiums imply skill-biased technological change, so the logic runs, the observation that measured productivity growth remains stagnant must be in error. It is true that problems with the measurement of productivity growth have been raised by critics for many years; they have to do with the measurement of price change in advanced manufacturing sectors, among other issues.[20] But unfortunately for this line of reasoning, the problems go back well before 1980—indeed all the way to the original turning point in the productivity series in 1973. So the proposition that unmeasured components of productivity growth suddenly turned up in and after 1980—but not before—remains an inference in search of evidence.

We are left with little to go on except the possibility that there was some particular technological change, beginning in 1980, that brusquely overturned both the established order of production and the measurement of productivity. Such a thing would, by its nature, elude capture in statistical measures; one would simply have to "know" about it by some other observational method. To focus the issue in this way actually reduces the apparent burden of evidence, since it becomes necessary only to identify a particular change in the direction of technological innovation, a particular type of new technology, that happens to possess the appropriate "skill-biasing" property and that makes its appearance at the appropriate moment in time. Thus, a quantitative dilemma becomes a qualitative one—provided the qualitative change is sufficiently dramatic to be convincing.

What can change the productivity of an individual worker, in whatever industry he or she may be found? The ageless answer is, the use of tools. The use of a tool, necessarily associated with the acquisition of a skill, is at the heart of human productivity from this point of view. The question then becomes: Is there a tool, or a group of tools, that might account in practice for a widening in the dispersion of human productivities across the spectrum of industrial and service activities and through an increase in the dispersion of productivities to an increase in the dispersion of pay?

This is the logic that leads us on to the computer. For, as it turns out, there *is* a particular technology that emerges around 1980, one that peculiarly and uniquely transforms the work environment of comparatively educated workers. Nonexistent in the preceding decade, the desktop personal computer is the quintessential device of the 1980s. It is the emblem of that time—the automobile, radio, and television of that age. It is a tool, and of a particular sort: a tool for information workers, for symbolic analysts, for typists and accountants and office managers, as well as writers and artists and publishers. In other words, computers are a tool for the educated person.

Studies of the relationship between computer use and pay have found a strong and significant statistical association between the two.[21] On this matter, evidence and theory thus apparently coincide. And in this way, an idea about the deepest source of rising inequality has crept into a prominent, if not unchallenged, position in our culture. It runs as follows. First, the use of computers requires skill. Second, the skill associated with computer use must be learned, and is more easily learned by people with better educations. Third, therefore, the addition of computers to the tool kit of more educated people is a catalytic factor raising the relative worth of skill in the labor market, an increase that begins by most measures no earlier than 1979.

Computers are certainly the most conspicuous new tool in the American workplace. They are undeniably useful. They are a convenience. Employees like them, and, no doubt, people with higher levels of formal education generally tend to like them more. Computers boost the productivity of writers, accountants, secretaries, actuaries, and graphical artists. One presumes they have little effect on the labor of ditchdiggers, seamstresses, and gardeners. And personal computers came in at about the right time, or so it seems at first glance.

But although it is certainly tempting to move from the statistical association to the marginal-productivity explanation, the question cannot in fact be settled quite so easily.

Even remaining within the framework of competitive labor markets, the hypothesis linking the spread of computers to the rise of pay for educated workers after 1980 neglects a basic question, to which, so far as I know, economists have devoted almost no systematic research. What *exactly* are the acquired skills, the educationally derived bits of human capital, whose productivity the use of computers is supposed to enhance? How exactly is computerization connected to the enhancement of skill? The answer cannot be that computers themselves are difficult machines, whose use requires an exceptional depth and breadth of training, which is then rewarded in the labor market. Computer users (as distinct from programmers) are not like early auto mechanics or early chauffeurs. Computer skills are easy to learn. Millions do it at home. Small children work on computers. Secretaries who type for a living type more easily on a computer. Accountants keep books, and clerks maintain files, more easily on a computer. Typesetting is easier on computers. Computers don't make things hard; they make things easy. The fact that e-mail is evidently the most highly rewarded of particular computer "skills"—an interesting finding of the econometrics—should perhaps suggest that computer skill per se is not exactly what well-paid computer users are being paid for.

Rather, the idea appears to be that computers extend the productivity of the underlying intellectual talent. Thus, they make typists faster, writers more vivid, artists more accessible, bookkeepers more accurate, and so on. The wages of typists with computers therefore rise relative to typists without them. Similarly, writers, accountants, artists, and editors armed with computers come to outcompete those without them. Thus, within each intellectual profession, a split develops between the computer haves and the computer have-nots. Pay of the former goes up, while that of the latter declines: skill-biased technological change.

There is undeniably in our culture a kind of cargo cult surrounding these alleged powers of the computer. It is a cult greatly abetted by the marketing of the industry itself, including a massive placement of computers in the schools. But does the use of computers for typing, graphical draftsmanship, calculation, and bookkeeping really require more "skill" in the abstract than these occupations in their noncomputerized forms? Does it really raise the value of such skills where they already exist? Common sense and personal experience suggest something different. Computers make many of these talents, which are more than routinely difficult to acquire and which, unlike blacksmithing and harness making, have remained to a substantial degree inside the formal education system, quite redundant. To the extent they do so, computers therefore reduce, rather than enhance, the aggregate skill level required for the performance of certain tasks. They have, in effect, reduced the value of older educations relative to newer ones, and made certain short and casual educations (in particular software packages, for instance) into reasonable substitutes for longer and more arduous ones.

Computers, of course, increase the *average productivity* of those who use them. The checkout clerk can clear more customers, the typist can produce more letters, with a computer than without one. But this bears no theoretical relationship to the wage and is not the argument that advocates of "skill bias" are making. In competitive theory, a worker's wage depends not on the amount of raw product that he or she can loosely supervise, but on the degree of difficulty in replacing that worker for that purpose. It depends on the amount of skill the job requires and must be paid for. Skill, in turn, is measured by the degree of difficulty involved in acquiring it in the first place. *It is the marginal product of the investment in skill that counts.* A totally de-skilled job may be part of a highly productive system without being well paid, and many are. Not many years ago, to pursue the example, checkout clerks routinely made change in their heads. This particular skill became redundant with electronic cash registers—another type of computer. The pay of checkout clerks did not improve.

This line of argument implies that the case of true "skill bias" in the effect of computers on pay is much more limited than we might at first imagine. True, there must be *some* cases. Economists of my own generation are perhaps an example. Trained as we were on cumbersome mainframe computers in the 1970s, we find that the personal computer enhances our skills quite directly, by making calculations and statistical work of all kinds faster and more accessible than ever before. We therefore do work of a kind and in quantities that otherwise we would not attempt. Personal computers in this way have valorized our educations. But such are fringe cases. It does not seem sensible to explain the fact (if it is a fact) that a checkout clerk in a computerized retail store makes more money than one in an old-fashioned small business, in a similar way, for in fact neither job requires significant skills. Nor can computerization explain the increase in the inequality of pay between, say, noncomputerized economists and computerized checkout clerks. Yet there is no doubt this type of inequality has also increased.

There are other problems with the attribution of rising inequality to computerization. Just as computerization and productivity growth are ill associated on average, the observed patterns cannot explain the observed pattern of changing wage differentials in relation to changes in measured productivity growth across manufacturing sectors. If pay were tied to the average productivity *of a sector,* we would expect to find relative pay rising in sectors with higher productivity growth. But if we examine the acceleration of rising inequality in the early 1980s, we find that it is blue-collar production workers— less skilled males in heavy manufacturing, for the most part—who suffered the largest relative wage losses at that time.[22] And yet measured productivity growth was higher throughout this period in the blue-collar manufacturing sectors than elsewhere in the economy, despite the fact that computerization was much less widespread in this sector. We are left—again—with the possibility that the relationship between pay and computerization does not run through a measurable connection to a changing value of output. If so, then whatever relationship exists between computers and pay exists not because computers have transformed those (comparatively well-educated souls) who use them into vastly more productive people, but for other reasons.

The most important and decisive difficulty in the computer story is the question of timing. For while the timing of the great rise in skill premiums and the introduction of personal computers seems fortuitously close, a closer examination reveals that the latter followed the former and therefore cannot have caused it.

Inequalities in family income and in individual earnings continued to rise through the 1980s. Yet the rise of hourly wage rate inequality actually appears to have peaked out as early as 1984.[23] All of the research on the increase in inequality by education levels is agreed, moreover, that the premiums to "education" or "skill" began rising in 1979 and reached a preliminary peak in 1985 or 1986.[24] And all researchers agree in principle that if technological change affects the wage structure in any way, the effect must operate through changes in hourly wage rates. Changes in nonwage income and family structures, which apparently continue to raise overall inequality after 1984, are not plausibly connected to marginal productivity–based explanations such as "skill-biased technological change."

The invention of the personal computer dates to 1971. The diffusion of these machines, however, came much later. In fiscal year 1980 Apple sold just 78,000 Apple II Computers, to hobbyists for the most part.[25] The IBM personal computer, aimed at a business market, was introduced in 1981. But 1982 was a recession year, and business investment of all kinds was extremely low. By 1983 there were just over 1 million personal computers installed in industry, still a quite small number; there were also just over 400,000 larger computer systems. Business investment in computers began in earnest with the recovery that year and the boom of 1984, coupled with the introduction of the IBM AT, a computer based on the 80286 processor.[26]

By 1985 the installed computer base had reached over 5 million for PCs and over 600,000 for business computer systems; the overwhelming majority of these systems were less than two years old. Retail sales of personal computers, including sales to households, reached 3 million only in 1987 and accelerated by less than half a million units per year until the early 1990s, when the pace picked up, reaching almost 6 million in 1993 and over 8 million in 1995. Retail sales of VCRs were larger than those of computers until 1988, and computers caught up with televisions only in 1994.[27]

Thus, the actual diffusion of computers occurred *after* the rise in skill or education premiums.[28] Indeed, it occurred for the most part during a time when hourly wage rates were no longer growing more unequal. Computerization also cannot account for any other part of the general rise in inequality that begins in 1970—more than a decade before personal computers reached American desktops.

Thus, the computer revolution explanation of rising inequality is deeply questionable on at least five counts. It offers no very coherent account of the precise mechanism whereby tools and education interact to produce higher marginal productivities in the information age. It can't account for the distribution of rising inequality across sectors, contrary to relative productivity movements, that apparently occurred in the early 1980s. It cannot account for rising premiums to experience and to unobserved characteristics, beginning in the early 1970s. It can't account for rising skill premiums in the early 1980s, before personal computers came on the scene in the middle years of the decade; no one suggests that the previous diffusion of mainframe computers had similar effects. It cannot account for the stabilization of relative hourly wages after 1984, a part of the story to which we shall return.

These considerations—surface implausibility, mismatch of sectors, mismatch of timing—surely dictate rejection of the computer as the great engine of inequality. If anything, the relationship between computers and pay is a case of causation running from pay to computerization, rather than the other way around. In the next chapter, we shall return to this alternative, which is fundamentally bound up in an explanation of pay that is not rooted in competitive labor markets or marginal productivities.

So if computers are not a pervasive agent of skill bias in technological change, does any such agent exist? As doubts about the computer hypothesis have multiplied, economists have been broadening their notion of what should be counted as technological change.[29] But as they move away from a specific technology and a specific type of technological change, they also lose the intuitive linkage to the concept of "skill bias" and the little bit of empirical evidence that exists linking particular technologies to pay. The center of gravity in the debate moves back toward the quicksand of pure inference. Observing a rising skill differential, it concludes that skill-biased technological change *must* have been the cause. There is no other reason than that this label fits the observation *and the model of a purely competitive labor market,* in a way that no other concept can.

Thorstein Veblen, the great turn-of-the-century economist, deplored the habit he observed in the economics of that day of simply assigning labels to things one does not understand. Veblen called the wage doctrine of his time "monocotyledonous"—having only one seed leaf—meaning that it subsumed everything into a single idea, a "metaphysics of normality and controlling principle."[30] One hundred years later, we have not escaped the problem Veblen identified. On the matter of wages, economics still insists that a criterion of valuation related to product must be applied in all important cases. The possibility that *something else* might be predominantly at work is excluded not on the ground of evidence, but because it is too horrible to contemplate. After all, if demand for skill cannot account for the rise in inequality we observe, it might not be justified. What, then, would we tell the children?

In the next chapter, we will explore a different view of the wage distribution. We will cut free from the strained and implausible ground of the supply-and-demand, competitive labor market model with its precommitment to the skill fallacy. We shall instead explore the interaction of technology, monopoly power, and macroeconomic performance in a worldview that is decidedly horrible to contemplate. But it does have the virtue of being clear, coherent, and—as we shall see through much of the rest of the book—useful in giving structure to the evidence of the historical record.

3

MONOPOLY POWER

> In capitalist reality as distinct from its textbook picture, it is
> not that kind of competition which counts but the competi-
> tion from the new commodity, the new technology, the new
> source of supply, the new type of organization (the largest-
> scale unit of control for instance)—competition which com-
> mands a decisive cost or quality advantage and which strikes
> not at the margins of the profits and the outputs of the existing
> firms but at their foundations and their very lives. This kind of
> competition is as much more effective than the other as a
> bombardment is in comparison with forcing a door.
>
> —Joseph A. Schumpeter, *Capitalism, Socialism and Democracy*

Must we see everything through the delusory prism of the
competitive model? Are we really so satisfied with the efficiency of markets? Are we so committed to the framework of marginal productivity and its implicit claim, made explicit in so much textbook
propaganda, that the distribution of income is legitimated by market forces?[1]
Are we prepared to rule the issues of power, monopoly, and financial control
off the table when we discuss the way incomes are apportioned inside the
United States? Are we prepared to disregard the many variants of imperial-
ism, colonialism, neocolonialism, and bully-boy behavior, including debt
crises, corruption, and capital flight, when we discuss international disparities in the income distribution? We impoverish the analysis when we do so.
We weaken the credibility of the case. And we undermine the correspondence between theory and fact.

37

Adam Smith would have been surprised to see monopoly power left out of the search for causes of rising inequality. Smith was greatly concerned with this topic, and wrote about it with a clarity that would serve us well today. Indeed the idea that governments *foster* inequality, through their sponsorship of monopoly power, is in fact Smith's own idea. It is the cornerstone of his attack on mercantilist trade policies, crown monopolies, licensing, and the other surviving institutions of Elizabethan economics that is at the core of *Wealth of Nations,* published in the same year as the American Declaration of Independence, itself "dedicated to the proposition that all men are created equal," as Lincoln would put it eighty-seven years later. The idea that equality and monopoly—whether of economic or political power—were hostile, irreconcilable forces was a foundation stone of economics in Smith's day.

In Book I, Chapter X, of *Wealth of Nations,* Smith first treats the sources of wage inequality that arise in the context of natural liberty:

> The five following are the principal circumstances which, so far as I have been able to observe, make up for a small pecuniary gain in some employments, and counterbalance a great one in others: first, the agreeableness or disagreeableness of the employments themselves; secondly, the easiness and cheapness, or the difficulty and expence of learning them; thirdly, the constancy or inconstancy of employment in them; fourthly, the small or great trust which must be reposed in those who exercise them; and fifthly, the probability or improbability of success in them.

But these, Smith writes, are not the major sources of inequality actually existing in the world. To the contrary,

> the policy of Europe, by not leaving things at perfect liberty, occasions other inequalities of much greater importance. It does this chiefly in three ways. First, by restraining the competition in some employments to a smaller number than would otherwise be disposed to enter into them; secondly, by increasing it in others beyond what it would naturally be; and, thirdly, by obstructing the free circulation of labour and stock [capital], both from employment to employment and from place to place.

With this result:

> It frequently happens that while high wages are given to workmen in one manufacture, those in another are obliged to content themselves with bare subsistence.[2]

Smith, in a word, blames *governments* for causing excessive inequality of wages. Governments did this, in Smith's view, by restricting the free movements of capital and labor and by distributing privileges to the rich and favored at the expense of the poor—in other words, by fostering monopoly power. The prime beneficiaries were members of the class of merchants and manufacturers, as well as craftsmen and tradespeople, who (Smith also wrote) "seldom meet together, even for merriment and diversion, but the conversation ends in a conspiracy against the public, or in some contrivance to raise prices." But the winners also included the laborers in the favored sectors, who come to enjoy high wages while those in disfavored sectors "are obliged to content themselves with mere subsistence."

Monopoly power is the power to set prices higher than marginal production cost. It is therefore the power to earn a positive economic profit—a profit higher than the rate of interest on the loans that finance business activity. Classical monopolies enjoyed this power by the law. As sole legal suppliers of such items as salt, tobacco, and spices, they could restrict sales and raise prices without fear of being undercut by upstart rivals. In the nineteenth century, large private monopolies emerged, in oil and elsewhere, through control by private trusts of key natural resources, in formal terms more or less independent of government. More recently, we have become aware of "natural monopolies," which arise in network industries like communications, electric power, and the airlines, owing to the fact that larger networks enjoy unit cost advantages over smaller ones and therefore can offer their services at lower prices as they expand, until a single network or just a small number of them come to dominate an entire industry.

Adam Smith had little concept of the kind of monopolies most prominent in our own day, which are those associated with the rise of new industries and fueled by the development of new technologies. Such monopolies arise because the new, so long as it *is* new, is usually unique. The production of novelty, when it succeeds, is the creation of a small sphere of monopoly power. So long as the novel product remains unique, it can be priced well above the cost of production. Indeed the price can often be adjusted—for example, by starting high and then cutting prices over time—to extract nearly the largest sum each customer is willing to pay. In this way, the producer earns a monopoly profit. Thus technological development has become the dynamic form of monopolism and, as we shall see, the dominant form of monopolism in the modern American economy.

The modern economy affords numerous paths to monopoly. All the older paths, such as government protection, mergers, increasing returns to scale, network economies, and war profits, remain open. Still, in today's world, technology appears to be not only the dominant and most spectacular pathway toward exceptional riches in the industrial sphere, but also the one most strongly aligned with government policy itself. Technological monopolists become politically powerful, and they lay claim to a legitimacy other forms of monopolism do not enjoy, in a society where technology has a strong hold on the popular and political imagination, so that the technologist can claim special favors from the government (for example, development subsidies or trade protection) or else win the patronage of a technologically oriented military.

It is true that the tendency for monopolies of this kind to emerge is inherent in the advance of science and technology. Although often allied with the state, technological monopolies are not created by arbitrary power. It is true that they work only when they meet a bona-fide need, providing a product or service more cheaply or quickly or better than was possible before. It is also true that technological monopolies are unstable: here this year, they may be gone the next. Finally, it is true that such monopolies arise only after the expenditure of large sums on research and development; the fact that price exceeds marginal cost does not guarantee that there will be a positive profit—only that the profit will be higher than it could have been under competitive conditions.

The word *monopoly* (like *trust, cartel,* and some others) is a fighting word in American economic history, redolent of the age of class struggle and the simple taxonomies pitting "capital" against "labor." But the point here is not to make an ethical case against technology or against monopoly power in the technology sector. The point is only that technological enterprises *are* monopolies, so long as they last. As such, they enrich the few at the expense of the many. And when they can do this with too great a success, there is a problem. Finally, in taking from Smith the thought that we should look to the "policy of Europe," or in our case the "policy of America," to explain the rise of this form of monopolism, we are at least a step ahead of the Panglossian view ("we live in the best of all possible worlds") to which Smith, like his friend Voltaire, did not subscribe.

The great theory on the relationship between technological change and monopoly power is that of the midcentury economist Joseph Alois Schumpeter. For Schumpeter, technology is first and foremost a weapon of struggle. Companies invest in research and development not to become famous, to win prizes, or to benefit humanity but to become rich. They do this by developing new products and thereby stealing markets away from their rivals. The stealing of a market is the construction of a monopoly, for it permits pricing above marginal cost and profit above the rate of interest. Thus for Schumpeter, to achieve or to retain monopoly power is the central objective of the business firm, and new technology is the main instrument to that end.

There is a vast difference between this Schumpeterian use of the word *competition,* which closely corresponds to the use of the word in ordinary business life, and the meaning of the term in textbook economics. The textbook sense of the word *competition* requires large numbers of firms, all of which are essentially identical: they produce an identical product, face the same cost curves, and sell to the same market demand. As technologies change, these textbook competitors passively absorb the new developments in the same way and at the same rate, all therefore producing each product by identically evolving means. Hence, faced with an identical selection of workers, they make identical labor-pricing decisions and pay each worker just the value of his or her output at the margin.

Pure competition in that sense hardly exists in the real world, and Schumpeter derided efforts to base analytical economics on this idea. Instead, and especially in manufacturing, competition is the search for uniqueness, and competition for uniqueness is competition to establish a monopolistic position. The important thing is not to make the same decision as everyone else, but to do something different—to be distinctive, to break down the existing market structures, to take over the niches and the fiefs of other firms. In some cases, this can be done by advertising, packaging, product differentiation, the location of a retail outlet, and other quotidian means. But none of these compare, in force and effectiveness, to successful technological change.

In the modern search and struggle for market power, technology *is* the paramount weapon. Devices such as advertising and product differentiation can protect or enhance market power, but they can hardly eliminate a determined and entrenched rival. Technological development, on the other hand, creates monopoly power. When Microsoft wins an operating system war, the whole world uses Windows—but only one company makes money on it. Thus from society's point of view, the essential form of competition—the one that effects social change and income distribution, that gives each generation its *nouveaux riche*—is the brutal displacement of the obsolescent by the novel. If and when successful, the innovator becomes a monopolist—for as long as his wits, patent protections, political lobbying, and power can persist.

Monopolies and monopoly power are actually necessary for technological development. In the textbook model of a competitive economy, competition ensures that profits are small to nonexistent. Correspondingly, there is no money in the model to finance the development of new technologies. Technology is supposed merely to happen; it descends like the general rain of heaven or a singing child in the *Magic Flute*. There are no designers, no engineers, no Bell Laboratories or Xerox PARCs in this model, for there is no money in the private sector to pay for any such things. Histories of technology that attempt to correspond to a competitive-model view of the world must be essentially accounts of the lone genius, building light bulbs and wax cylinders from collections of household odds and ends.

As Schumpeter wrote, technology is not in fact something that descends gently on the modern corporation from the outside. Technological change cannot be treated as something caused externally by the advance of pure knowledge and human understanding. It is, rather, the product that technology corporations produce. It is integral to their search for riches, the fabric of their business life. Inventions don't just happen; they are created, and for the express purpose of making money. Technological development is indeed the central internal process of capitalist change and social transformation. Said Schumpeter:

> Was not the observed performance due to that stream of inventions that revolutionized the technique of production rather than to the businessman's hunt for profits? The answer is in the negative. The carrying into effect of those novelties was of the essence of that hunt.

Monopoly rather than competition is the world in which this sort of businessperson lives. At any moment of time, the object of the game is to reap the largest possible monopoly profit from the existing situation. The fact that the grip on monopoly is unstable does not restore the pricing principles of perfect competition. Nor does the fact that huge fixed research and development costs render positive profits at the end of the day uncertain change the analytics. Win or lose, monopoly is what the game is about.

Technology firms are substantially and predominantly producers of capital and durable goods. The essence of technological development is the creation of new machines. Such machines are created in a continuous process of design and refinement, but they are purchased in waves, in the great ebb and flow of business capital investment. The rhythm of the business cycle is thus tied closely to the peformance of technology-producing firms. Such companies do especially well in the early, investment-driven stages of economic expansion. Later, as investment slows, they encounter more difficult times. When the recession hits, they are temporarily idled. But when the recovery starts, as eventually it always does, they go back to work, first and foremost building new machines for new factories to supply the consumer markets that are certain soon to begin expanding once again.

Technology-producing industries sell to technology-consuming industries, which use new technologies to install factories and produce consumer goods. The unit sales of these complex products may be very low: the world demand for new passenger jet aircraft, for instance, may be only a few dozen units a month. But technology users serve a vast market, making use not only of the newest equipment but also of all surviving equipment that was ever produced in the past. Some consumer goods industries are highly dynamic, constantly renewing their plant and struggling to update their offerings to the public (consumer electronics is an example). Others are quite traditional, much less affected by the major new technologies of the age (home building is a major example).

Consumer goods producers rarely achieve the full monopolistic advantage of technology suppliers, for they cannot afford to abandon older production lines and methods, as technology producers routinely do. Consumer goods producers therefore typically coexist with their competitors, advancing to new technologies through waves of expansion and investment that often proceed for decades without changing by very much the relative size, market share, or distinctive product characteristics of the competing firms. Core-spective stability is the overriding goal of the giant producers of consumers' goods; it is a goal that they often achieve, though on occasion they do not.

If technology is an important force in the shaping of modern monopolies, it follows by logical necessity that it must be an inequality-increasing force on the distribution of income. But the technological monopoly is different from other forms, in that the necessity of sustaining one's position over time imposes the requirement of continuous investment in research, development, design, and engineering, and this raises the question of in whose hands exactly this form of monopoly power ultimately resides. Indeed, monopolies based on technological advantage differ in important ways from those based on raw political power or massive economies of scale. Particularly, the element of monopoly power conveyed by technology is inherently fleeting. Creative destruction is a weapon, but it is also an ever-present threat; someone else may be just around the bend. The technological monopolist cannot become complacent; the search is forever ongoing for the next edge. The lease on monopoly must be continually renewed, and the struggle to do so becomes a consuming feature of the technomonopolistic life.

This situation conveys a unique and ultimate power on at least some of the workers in the technomonopolists' employ. The designers, engineers, indispensable managers, and skilled production workers have to be kept happy and hard at work, which means they have to be given, in effect, a share of the monopolistic returns. But ordinary production workers must also be treated with some compunction, since they can, in some situations, upset the work of the firm and cause lasting damage to its prospects. An unstable monopoly needs excellent working conditions for reasons that do not apply to network or resource or scale monopolists, and that need not apply either in the oligopolistic world of large consumer firms.

In this way, we should expect that the revenues of the technological monopolists make their way into the wage and salary streams of this sector. This phenomenon is strongly consistent with the idea that part of the pay workers earn reflects the imperfectly competitive nature of the industries in which they work, a part known as "industry-specific labor rents" in the literature of labor economics. That idea simply states that industries tend to share the monopolistic element in their earnings with their workforces so as to promote stability, loyalty, low turnover, and labor peace. The "efficiency wage" is a concept that economists have used to describe the payment of wages higher than competitive rates in return for performance at higher than competitive levels. Such wages will be a feature of those parts of the economy where workers enjoy de facto power over the fate of the firm.

Firms in the sectors mass-producing consumer goods are, of course, no more perfect competitors in the textbook sense than are technology producers. But they deviate from the textbook model in a different way. Externally, they are corespective; their pricing and product decisions are strongly, if implicitly, coordinated with those with whom they share the market. Internally here, capital rules, not labor and not knowledge or skill. The machinery sets the division of labor and the pace of production, and determines to a great degree (if not totally) the quality of the final product. Here the manager and the supervisor can regulate in fine detail what each worker does at each minute of the workday. Thus, the leverage of the worker here is not individual, not an intangible combination of ingenuity, energy, ability, and morale. It is rather collective: the organized power of workers generally, within the firm and in society at large, determines how the rents will be shared out.

Professional economists have not been blind to the existence of imperfect competition in its myriad forms. There are many studies of the effect of unions, monopolies, oligopolies, winner-take-all situations, and the minimum wage. Some of these have raised fundamental questions about whether labor markets can be described in terms of competitive supply and demand.[3] There has been considerable attention to the broad phenomenon of "labor rents" earned in some industries, which eventually flow in part to workers in those industries and account for a significant proportion of their pay.[4]

What has been missing from the economic research, for the most part, has been an analysis of *change* in the patterns of monopoly power. A world in which the prime form of monopoly is novelty, that is, technologically driven, monopolism is bound to be unstable. Given an unstable balance between technology producers and technology consumers, the relative strength of such powers will vary with time, as the relative strengths of firms, industries, and economic institutions in the broad sense change. This point, simple as it seems and is, remains substantially unexplored in the literature[5] and represents the major point of departure of this book.

Why a discipline with a lively sense of monopoly in its static analysis has failed to extend that perception to the body of research concerned with the evolution of income inequality remains slightly mysterious. Perhaps the presence of so many firms working so hard in the technology sector, and of so many losers alongside the handful of winners, has lulled observers into thinking of them as competitive rather than "monopolistic." Perhaps the fact that some workers grow well-to-do under the system makes it seem unlike monopoly capitalism, and especially unlike the vicious monopolistic capitalism of Marxian and post-Marxian critics. Perhaps. I offer a simpler explanation: economics possesses a coherent dynamics of models based on competitive assumptions, but none that can easily be applied to a monopolistic sector. From the assumption that pay tracks marginal productivity, it is a short step to argue that when marginal productivity rises, so will relative pay. Given this, when the observed structure of relative pay changes, it follows that the unobserved structure of relative productivities must have changed; the remaining task is merely to find out why.

In the literature, and in the particular body of research that attempts to link technological change to income inequality, the dynamics of technology have therefore been treated with competitive rather than monopolistic tools. There is no discussion of the social origins of technological change, or any explanation of why the nature of such change became "skill biased" in the 1980s where it had not been so before. According to this analysis, the computer merely arrived. Why did businesses buy them, thereby obliging themselves to hire more expensive workers, for no evident gain in productivity or profits? The explanation is silent. It is as though the employees themselves went out and bought the computers, brought them to work and set them up on their desks, raised their relative output compared to those workers not so far-sighted, and then demanded and got a redistribution of relative pay. This may work in an economics department, and so may sound plausible to an economics professor. It is not a theory with wide application to the business world.

Once the competitive assumption is dropped, on the other hand, the theoretical relationship between skill and pay tends to disappear. We then become free to investigate alternative ways of explaining how the undoubted, empirically visible relationship between education levels and pay might have evolved. Can the rising education premium be explained by shifting structures of monopolistic power?

Some simple examples show how this could happen in principle. Suppose, for example, that a political act of deregulation makes truck driving more competitive. Truck drivers' wages would fall. If a decline of tariffs and nontariff barriers opens up the free import of cheap apparel, shirtmakers' wages might fall. Here the relationship between earning and education is not spurious. From a purely personal standpoint, it is more important, after such changes, to "get a good education"—because with increasing inequality, education becomes an increasingly valuable means of escape from the afflicted sectors. But there is nothing in the changed politics of the situation that is connected to the less educated character of the workers themselves or to the work they do. A truck driver remains a truck driver, and a shirtmaker continues making shirts, exactly as before deregulation or trade liberalization. Only the pay is less.[6]

In an economy saturated by a structure of monopolies, a change in the relative market power of skilled and less skilled workers can occur for reasons not connected in any direct way to political decisions. A recent study found that oil price changes have significant differential effects on average wages across industrial sectors, so that increases in the oil price are associated with relative gains for skilled workers and relative losses for the unskilled.[7] Since an increase in oil prices happens over a very short period of time—a matter of days, typically—this is clearly not a technological change in the usual sense. Rather it represents the choices taken by firms to allocate the squeeze on their cash flow occasioned by the rise in price of an important input, in such a way that a disproportionate share of the burden falls on less skilled, less powerful, more readily expendable workers. Here the monopoly power of workers more highly placed existed before the change in resource prices; it served, in part, to protect those workers from serving on the front line as shock absorbers.

When changes such as these are run through an analysis that has been constructed from the beginning to be blind to the presence of monopoly power, these kinds of changes would, *and do,* show up in the data as "skill-biased technological change." Skill bias is thus a phrase that can account, with perfect plausibility but equally perfect meaninglessness, for many different phenomena—not merely those that are intimately tied to the productivity of particular types of work, but also reversible price and regulatory and institititutional changes that no one would ordinarily describe as being "technological." This is true because the marginal productivity pricing principle presupposes that these market imperfections don't exist in the first place; they are ruled out of the model from the beginning.

The virtue of the competitive assumption is that it is simple. The main difficulty of introducing noncompetitive explanations is the complexity of the analysis that must follow. Monopoly is diverse: it may be political, technological, or organizational. It may be based on novelty or networks or scale or rights of ownership. It may be legal or illegal; it may derive its strength from a guild or a union or a mafia. To figure out which of these forces is at work at any moment and their comparative strength is difficult enough. To figure out how they have played out through time, and in what relative proportions, is a significant analytical problem.

Still, in principle, noncompetitive explanations can resolve some otherwise baffling issues quite easily. Consider the question of computers and pay. In an imperfectly competitive world, within firms, among office workers, the provision of fast and efficient computer tools is a device for rewarding the most capable and reliable staff members, increasing job satisfaction, and reinforcing within-office status relationships. There is the simple fact, ignored in much of the research linking computers to pay, that the dissemination of computers through the workplace takes time. At any particular moment in time, therefore, workers with higher pay will generally enjoy fancier equipment. No company would dream of starting its program of computerization from the bottom up, almost irrespective of the match, or lack of it, between individual job responsibilities and the need for a computer.

Thus, so long as education is associated with rank, and so long as monopoly power and therefore discretion over wages, perquisites, and hierarchical business structures exists, we would expect an association between wages, education, and the propensity to computerize. It would be astonishing if such an association did not exist! Toys trickle down from the top.[8]

Consider another baffling issue: the relationship of inequality, technology, and trade. Suppose that manufacturing workers are divided across two general types of industry: exporters, on one side, and those competing with imports, on the other. Suppose that among the exporters, we find a larger proportion of monopolists and quasi monopolists, industries and firms with market power in the world economy. These firms will pay correspondingly

higher wages to their employees, sharing in part the monopoly rents that derive from their powerful position. Such employers will also tend to screen
their workers by insisting on greater formal qualifications, and so have a
more highly educated ("skilled") workforce. Suppose, finally, that an increase
in trade ("globalization") takes place, to the benefit of exporters and the detri-
ment of import competers.

In these conditions, the relative wage of exporters will rise, and that of import competers will fall. Monopoly power is now greater in the domestic
economy than it was before, insofar as technomonopolists command a larger
share of output and employment than they did. Inequality will therefore increase. This will happen without any changes in underlying production techniques or the mix of products consumed by either industries or consumers.
To attribute these developments to a technological change or changes in the
relative productivity of skills would be a mistake, even though to someone
confined to competitive assumptions and looking only at the domestic shift,
within broadly defined industrial categories, from import-competing consumption goods to advanced exportables, the change will look very much
like a "skill-biased" shift in technologies!

In both of these cases, if we have described particular institutional
arrangements correctly, explanations incorporating monopoly greatly simplify our understanding of an otherwise arcane process and help to bring the
evolution of inequality into much clearer and more intuitive focus. *The problem with the prevailing arguments is the competitive assumption.* If we purge
ourselves of this assumption and instead accept the world as it is, which is to
say a place of interlocking monopoly powers of one kind or another—some
"natural," some political, and some technological in nature—then phenomena that are otherwise convoluted become quite plain. We need to take one
further step: accepting that the struggle for power is a matter of constant flux.
And then we need to start on the challenging but promising task of sorting
through the patterns of observed change, to see which are the most important in modern history.

The system is rigged—and the ordinary person knows instinctively that
the "system is rigged." Nor, if she is sensible, does she object to this condition. The system has to be rigged, and well rigged at that. The rigging *supports* the system; without good rigging, the sails will collapse in a light squall.
The world may be unstable and dangerous, but the instability of competing
monopolies is like nothing compared to the world of perfect competition. It
is the difference between being out on the ocean in a well-rigged barque and
out on one's own in a life preserver. Unregulated competition forces wages

toward the level of "mere subsistence." Structures of monopoly power, on the other hand, serve the interest of employees, for whom they provide a structure of stability and a platform from which they can face the dangers and even go after a share of the spoils.

My thesis is that *unstable economic performance*—the external conditions that sometimes favor certain monopolistic groupings, sometimes others—is the main culprit that has fostered the rise of the new monopolies, raised inequality in the wage structure, reduced the share of wages in personal income, and fueled the rise in compensatory transfers. When the ocean is flat, rowboats and dinghies can join the trawlers out on the reef where the fish are running. But in a gale, the little boats sink while the large ones do not.

The distribution of monopoly power matters little in a world of stable full employment. But outside that world, in the one where we actually live, the stronger and more erratic the business cycle, the greater the swings of unemployment, the weaker through time is the bargaining position of small and competitive businesses and of unorganized production workers. Wage structures erode from the bottom. Low-wage workers are the first to give ground in hard times. Equally, an unstable economy strengthens the relative position of technology suppliers, whose boatyards thrive when stormy weather sinks older and smaller ships and creates a demand for new and bigger ones. Instability speeds the turnover of the capital stock; in this way, it creates repeated surges in demand for new machinery and new equipment. Unemployment and capital turnover are the anvil and the hammer between which a stable structure of relative wages can be beaten apart.

Thus technology suppliers, uniquely as an industrial class, benefit from economic instability. Instability accelerates technological change. Since the sellers of technology products are necessarily few, and since the buyers of technology products are necessarily many, an acceleration of technological change relative to other forms of economic activity—or, what amounts to the same thing, a slump in consumption and services relative to technological change—can only, and must necessarily, redistribute wage and salary income from the many losers to the comparative few who come out at the top of the ladder of technological competition. We therefore predict that while the structures of monopoly power are necessarily many and varied, those based on technology will emerge in the dominant position in an unstable world.

4

THE CONCEPT OF
THE WAGE STRUCTURE

In other words, the struggle about money-wages primarily affects the distribution of the aggregate real wage between different labour-groups, and not its average amount per unit of
employment. . . . The effect of combination on the part of a
group of workers is to protect their relative real wage.

—John Maynard Keynes, *The General Theory of
Employment Interest and Money*

The fundamental source of an alternative theory of distribution lies in the economics of imperfect competition and the
analysis of monopoly power. Monopoly power is a power over price. It is defined as the ability to set a price greater than the marginal cost of production,
and so to earn a return on investment. It is a degree of freedom from the
tyranny of pure competition, which punishes even the slightest price difference in the most draconian way. Monopoly and monopoly power need not
be absolute. Indeed they never are absolute—a degree of monopoly exists
whenever firms can raise prices, even a small amount, without completely
driving away all customers. On the other hand, precisely because monopoly
is not absolute, it is virtually universal. It permeates the economic system,
across industries and through time, and variations in the degree of monopoly
will be our guide to changes in the structure of wages.[1]

Monopoly power normally inheres in business firms; it derives from their
ability to produce a product for which a perfect substitute does not exist. But

monopoly power can equally be thought of as a goal for individual employees, or more precisely as something that can be captured in part by employees. People achieve positions of power inside their enterprises by distinguished performance or dogged climbing in a bureaucratic structure. When they do, they claim a reward, in the form of pay greater than the competitive rate for their particular type and class of labor. This is a share of the monopoly rent. Thus the monopoly power of a firm may be, and often is, passed through to its workers in some degree. Firms, on the other hand, can pay such a premium only if they are themselves earning at above the competitive rate. The structure of monopoly power across firms will therefore come to be reflected in the distribution of wages across firms and across the industries in which firms concentrate their operations.[2]

The sources of monopoly power are varied. Taxi drivers acquire it, on dark nights, by being the only transport available at that moment on that street. To control this type of monopolism, most cities force taxi drivers to use meters.[3] Small restaurants acquire monopoly power by diligent burnishing of their reputations; this sets them apart, creates a loyal clientele and lines for their tables, and enables them to charge a premium price for their entrees. One might think of such tiny enterprises as "purely competitive," but from a technical standpoint, this is not at all the case. So long as the enterprise itself has distinguishing characteristics, and therefore cannot be substituted perfectly by some rival, it is enjoying and profiting from a degree of monopoly power, however small. It is to the principles of monopoly, rather than to the theory of competition, that we should look for an explanation of its income.

Larger enterprises have other strategies and tactics. Consumer firms practice product differentiation and advertising. Utilities and communications companies take advantage of decreasing cost structures as their networks grow larger. Manufacturing companies seek government protection from foreign competition—a legally protected form of monopoly power. Airlines differentiate across classes of customers, discriminating against those with deep pockets and inflexible schedules. And technology firms, in the most tumultuous struggle for power in the modern economy, seek to beat each other to the next killer application.

Each of these business strategies is, from the analytical standpoint, the construction of a sphere of monopoly power. The purpose of advertising, of product differentiation, of market segmentation and price discrimination, and especially of technological change is to beat the competition. It is to create a fief, or an empire, where the competition cannot reach. It is to isolate oneself from the hypothetical brutality of textbook competition, from competition that forces price to marginal cost and eliminates economic profit. The point of the game, played in a bewildering variety of ways, is to defeat the rules of the competitive model.

As a world of rivalrous monopolies takes shape in our minds, the image and metaphor of distribution through efficient and perfectly competitive markets necessarily recede. Either relative pay is determined for each worker by a market evaluation of his or her contribution at the margin to the value of output, or it is determined by a set of rules governing the distribution of rents and by the distribution of market power across organizations. Indeed, if there exists even one monopoly anywhere in the system—just one Mobutu in the Congo—it follows that others must be averaging less than the marginal value of their output. So to concede the existence of monopoly requires that one either drop the competitive model entirely or construct an elaborate new theory (and on what principles?) that divides the world into monopolistic, competitive, and subcompetitive ("exploited") sectors.

All approaches to monopoly have this in common: they involve the organization of individuals into groups. The group that holds monopoly power is usually a business firm, organized for the particular purpose of building and selling a commodity or product; it may also be a professional or craft organization. Either way, these groups are tribal structures, practically speaking. From the perspective of its members, each group forms a reference group and a hierarchy. Individual advancement within the group tends to be slow and rule bound; the group itself regulates within-group changes. Lateral movement across groups—for example, from master chef to master surgeon—is also hard, even where skills are similar, for membership in each competing group is carefully protected by rituals of qualification and by a general presumption that newcomers start at the bottom. It follows by both intuition and necessity that the struggle in a world of interlocking monopolies is mainly a struggle of one group for gain at the expense of others.

An analysis of distribution based on widespread structures of "competing monopolists" must therefore accomplish two goals. First, it must show how the rules of allocation are established within groups—the nature of and reasons for corporate and union seniority structures, partnership ladders, professorial promotion rules, and similar devices. These devices are rules of behavior or conventions; they are also known in the economic literature as *institutions.* Second, such a theory of distribution must give an account of the historical forces that account for the relative rise and decline of different groups through time. In other words, it must provide both a taxonomy and a history of types of monopoly power, an account of institutional failure and institutional success. We shall call the combination of internal structures and the relationships between competing pyramids of would-be monopolists, at any given moment of time, the *wage structure*.

The study of internal business structures has been the province of many other writers,[4] and we shall accordingly neglect it. But there is room for a contribution to the second aspect of the wage structure, the analysis of changing between-group relationships. Moreover, it is a reasonable bet, indeed a logical necessity, that this aspect should be the more dynamic and changeable of the two. Change within groups is governed by conventions and rules; it is necessarily slow on this account, for the point of conventions, rules, and hierarchies is to slow down and regularize the process of change. Change between groups is not so governed, and accordingly has the potential for instability. The dynamics of monopolistic rivalry is therefore likely to be primarily a dynamics of change between groups, and in understanding how this dynamics works out, we can understand a very large part of the evolution of the structure as a whole.

Monopolistic rivalry is a struggle for income shares between large blocs of economic actors: business corporations, trade unions, professional organizations. But this by itself does not get us very far, for it tells us nothing about the actual group structures of the real world. How can we best give substantive content to the insight that monopolistic rivalry is a rivalry of groups? How can we tell, as outsiders looking at historical data, where lay the fault lines of twentieth-century capitalist evolution? There is an essential preliminary task. It is to determine: What are the groups?

The answer to this question is far from obvious because there is no natural unit with which to work. In between the level of the individual, who can be observed in a census sample, and that of the nation, for which aggregated income accounts exist, the social scientist faces a complex and interlocking network of self-organizing structures. The task is to organize a large mass of information about these structures, so as to reveal a manageable number of meaningful economic groups whose interaction—monopolistic rivalry—best characterizes the changing internal structure of the system. I will argue that the best way to do this is to examine patterns of performance through time. The most important forms of monopoly are necessarily organized along industrial lines. By tracing the patterns of performance of groups of industries, therefore, we can best get at the major patterns of economic change underlying the income distribution. By tracing patterns of performance in historical data, we can also best isolate the group structures that mattered most for the distribution of wages.

The definition of group structures is thus going to become the central analytical problem that we will face. This necessitates a digression, for the analysis of groups is a familiar one in the context of a quite different discussion about inequality. It is likely that many readers will be looking at this stage for an analysis of race or gender. It may be helpful to explain why such an analysis will not be found in this book.

Much of the large literature on economic inequality is focused on the categorical standing of different races, ethnicities, and genders. These are, indeed, the important social structures in the American social and political context—as perhaps religion or social class may be in other societies that define themselves along different lines of demarcation.[5] A glance at the writings spawned by *The Bell Curve* attests to the prominence of racial concerns, specifically, in the modern politics of the United States.[6]

The legacies of slavery, segregation, discrimination, and disenfranchisement exist. These legacies would exist—as they do for Americans of Jewish and Chinese extraction—even if there were no differences in the average economic status of the individuals involved, although obviously the disappearance of economic distinctions is often a prelude to the decline of social ones. No one is going to dispute that for women and for African Americans, especially, the very facts of gender and race are important determinants and predictors of income.

But this is not sufficient to make race and gender into the primary organizing principles of an inquiry into the evolution of the wage structure. The reason is straightforward: the vast majority of American workers are not minorities, and a substantial majority are not women. Most of the movement in the wage structure, and most of the increase in inequality, would have occurred in the absence of a single working woman, or black, or Hispanic citizen. It is one thing to say that white men hold most of the monopolistically rewarding positions in American society. This is not the same as saying that white men are powerful; many are not. Our problem is to identify the economic sources of the market power that some white men hold, and from which others, along with the preponderance of minorities and women, are substantially excluded.

Indeed, neither racial nor gender categorization is intrinsically economic, in the sense of being able to cast light on the reasons that the differentials across the wage structure are as large as they are or why they change through time as much as they do. Race and gender classifications are not "groups" in the sense in which a family, a company, a cartel, or a trade union is a group. That sense implies an affinity of purpose, common action, or division of labor among the members of the group. Although it is reasonable to state that African Americans share a common heritage, this in fact means little in terms of the evolution of economic inequality, and particularly not over the span of just a few years or decades. There is no grand trade union of African American workers, or of American women workers, capable of altering the large structure of economic outcomes, and the establishment of political and civil rights is connected in only the loosest way, if at all, to the structure of wages.

Thus as we seek to explain the evolving structure of economic inequalities over the past thirty years, we need to understand that racial and gender classifications are not, by and large, informative for this purpose. What these classifications mainly concern is the placement of particular individuals within a given structure. When the objective is to analyze the changing shape of the structure, something else is called for.

The distinction between structure and placement is often muddled in discussions of inequality in America, and it seems likely that one of the most prevalent policy prescriptions for inequality—support for education and for equal access to education—is based on a confusion between the two. Promoters of schooling as a cure for inequality are arguing, in effect, that fixing the initial placement of disadvantaged people or groups will have, by itself, an effect on the equality of pay in the society that results. This is a serious fallacy, and one with pernicious effects on our ability to confront the problems of inequality that America actually faces. For this reason, it is worthwhile to take some pains to separate the analysis of inequality along gender, ethnic, or religious lines, or along lines of educational attainment, from the industrial and evolutionary approach of this book.

It may help to think of the wage structure as a building—for instance, a skyscraper. A few people—chief executive officers of large corporations and banks, top professionals, athletic and film superstars—occupy penthouses on the top floor. Middle management, ordinary professionals, and the best of the small businessmen fill up the floors below them. Next come the workers, each taking a position in line with their relative pay. And in the basement (fittingly for this metaphor) we find the underclass—the unemployed, the disabled, the chronically ill, and the unfit.

The wage structure, that is, the shape of the building and the number of spaces available on each floor, is a built structure. It is a product of history, built up by the rules, institutions, and political forces that influence how the economy works. The demographic composition of the distribution of people across the floors, on the other hand, is a matter of their individual characteristics and of how these characteristics are treated. To be sure, as we rise through the building, we find fewer members of racial or minority groups, and fewer women, than on the lower floors. The advantages of education and the curse of discrimination play their roles here. Yet these forces, important though they are, are not the ones determining the height of the building or the number of places on each of the floors.

An increase in the supply of educated people, in particular, does not by itself create more spaces on the top floors. Instead, as education increases, more of the existing slots will be filled by workers of higher qualification. Since this process works from the top down, average levels of education will rise on the middle and lower floors. Positions on the topmost floors actually become ever harder to break into, and more remote. In a purely meritocratic system, they would be reserved to those whose educational attainments exceed the average by the largest amounts. More plausibly, in the society in which we actually live, they are allocated essentially by inheritance, connections, and the random processes of the lottery of life. There is no reason to think that an expanded supply of educated talent will reduce the gap between those most highly paid and the middle ranks.

As the uppermost ranks fill with increasing numbers of advanced degrees, it is a matter of arithmetic that the average wage earned by a given level of education, relative to the overall average wage, will fall. This is what economists like to call a declining premium to education or skill. The declining premium reflects the fact that more college graduates are placed in jobs that do not really require college training and were held previously by less qualified workers. But the underlying structure and relative pay across positions need not change, and generally will not change, just because the supply of college diplomas has been increasing.[7]

Like schooling in general, affirmative action is about access to comparatively privileged positions, whether unionized jobs on a Philadelphia construction site or admittance to the University of Texas Law School. Affirmative action is not about the degree of privilege that exists in the first place. Affirmative action was never designed to alter the shape of the wage structure and does not do so. It is, instead, designed for the sole purpose of opening up some of the existing spaces to people who might not otherwise have access to them.

Policies that improve the treatment of African Americans, Hispanic Americans, other ethnic groups, and women can and do change the distribution of persons within the wage structure. Such policies may work directly, by changing hiring practices, or indirectly, by opening up spaces in educational institutions that serve as gateways to privilege. As the educational opportunities open to minorities and women improve, the distribution of their incomes will come more and more to resemble the distribution of incomes for the society as a whole. This is what successful affirmative action does, and this is all that affirmative action can do.[8]

Because affirmative action addresses placement and not structure, even a successful affirmative action program is not inconsistent with rising inequality between groups. The average wage of African Americans can fall relative to that of the white population even while black representation in higher professions improves. This can happen because rising inequality generally drives down the relative wage of the majority of African American workers, who remain in occupations for whom affirmative action provides no meaningful relief or in industries that are losing ground on domestic and international markets. In fact, this is precisely what has occurred. The major changes in the manufacturing wage structure since 1970 have been catastrophic for high school–educated male workers, a category covering a large part of the African American labor force. The decline in the relative wages of this large group and its black members swamped the effect of increasing average education in the African American population.

This situation does not invalidate the accomplishments of affirmative action, but it radically undermines the viability of affirmative action as a remedy for past discrimination. As inequality increases overall, minority populations will themselves become stratified along socioeconomic lines. They will become characterized by small numbers of comparatively successful families amid much larger, impoverished populations. Since the economically successful remain eligible for affirmative action, the direct benefits of affirmative action will fall increasingly to the comparatively privileged members of minority groups—to the children of an earlier generation of professionals. This is not in itself an injustice. To the contrary, affirmative action remains necessary, for the small representation of minority groups in any pool of professional school or job applicants means that without affirmative action, racial diversity would substantially disappear from the higher professions. But the function of affirmative action under these stressed conditions becomes simply to prevent the complete resegregation of the most selective employments. It ceases to provide a significant avenue for the truly disadvantaged within stratified minority populations; in these circumstances, the existence of affirmative action loses relevance to the poor who will never enter the applicant pool for elite positions in any event.

Second, although it may be that affirmative action programs can succeed for a time in their remaining role, and for a time prevent the total resegregation of the higher professions, even this limited success almost surely cannot be sustained, for a rising degree of inequality in the larger society raises the stakes and intensifies the competition very dramatically. Affirmative action was first conceived, around 1965, under conditions of genuinely strong demand and short supply of skilled labor. The minorities and women who benefited from affirmative action were joining a wage structure characterized by declining wage and salary inequality and by the rapidly increasing availability of good jobs. Under these conditions, political opposition was minimal, for few could feel displaced by the success of those who were being assisted.

The severe crisis of affirmative action programs, leading to concerted opposition by right-wing political forces and their rejection in a referendum in California in 1996 and in court cases affecting Texas and elsewhere, has occurred under opposite circumstances, and clearly has to do with the increasing relative value of the prizes. In the *Hopwood* case, decided in 1996, four young white applicants sued the Law School of the University of Texas at Austin, claiming that they were denied admission while less qualified minorities, as measured by standardized test scores, were admitted. Why was it worthwhile for such marginal applicants, who could presumably have gone on to other law schools only slightly less well ranked, to file such a lawsuit? The answer surely has to do with the spreading out of the structure of earnings, which raises the premium associated with passing through the most prestigious and prominent gateways. (*Hopwood* was decided for the plaintiffs in a federal appeals court, and within a year new black students virtually disappeared from the University of Texas Law School.)

The conclusions here are twofold. First, although we cannot deny the importance of race and gender classifications or of educational achievement for predicting how individuals will fare in the wage structure, they are of limited use in analyzing the reasons for rising inequality in the wage structure in recent years. The major changes are not of changing race or gender relationships, or in the supply of skills, but rather of the fortunes of industries and occupations in which race and gender differences are embedded.[9] There is no paradox in rising inequality, even in rising group-specific inequality, alongside falling discrimination. There is also no guarantee that conquering discrimination will materially raise the average wage of any particular population.

Second and specifically, the economic fate on average of women and of Americans of African descent has depended, in the twentieth century, much more on general developments affecting equality and inequality, employment and unemployment (the vast changes that occurred during World War II, in particular, and the cycles of growth and recession thereafter), than on the specific struggles for racial or gender equality under the law. The future will again reflect this truth. Only a narrowing of the wage distribution in general can make possible a large reduction in the wage and earnings gap that now separates African from European Americans, or men from women, in particular.

Let's therefore return to the key question: What governs the wage structure, and how can the wage structure be made to change?

Once again, the wage structure is about the relationships between and within economic groups. Relationships within groups are, by the definition of an economic institution, comparatively stable. Relationships between groups change with the large social, political, and economic forces of the day. Our first task is therefore to define the most relevant groups, and to do so in a systematic, meaningful, and revealing way.

In manufacturing, such groups are inevitably industrial rather than matters of ethnicity, gender, or years of education. But that in itself does not get us very far. We need a way of thinking about industries, and about industrial change, that can help make sense of a large mass of otherwise confusing numbers. In other words, we need a system of classification and a system that can apply to a very complex system of differing types of process, of product, of industrial organization.

The problem with systems of classification is that they tend to be arbitrary. Firms are conventionally grouped by size, or by location, or by such characteristics as the proportion of sales spent on advertising or the percentage of revenue devoted to expenditures on research and development. And industries are classified, by the government, according to a complex hodgepodge of rules called the Standard Industrial Classification (SIC), which loosely resembles the Dewey decimal system—a highly structured and very useful filing system, but not the last word on the substantive organization of human knowledge as found on library shelves.

These schemes are based on physical characteristics—on similarities or difference of appearance. As such, they are convenient, and they may be intuitive. But with industries as with people, physical characteristics may not meaningfully distinguish entities that are different from each other from those that fundamentally resemble each other. For this reason, the SICs in particular lack analytical content. There is no particular reason, a priori, to believe that industries classed as closely resembling each other in the SIC will in fact behave in similar ways. In some cases they will, and in others they will not.

An alternative and much more sensible way to construct a system of classification is to do so on measurements of behavior. That is, instead of basing classification on physical features, we may base it on similarity and differences in performance over time. This is a principle common in other fields of science, particularly life sciences, but peculiarly unknown in economics.

Well, almost unknown. The remarkable John Maynard Keynes had, as usual, thought about this issue. Keynes emphasized that members in economic groups were linked by shared ideas, outlooks, "rules of thumb," and other psychological characteristics that govern behavior. Groups of workers form unions, and accept common contracts that govern the union as a whole, because they believe themselves to be commonly situated in the economy and therefore to share interests in common. Groups of investors stampede one way and the other, not because they all analyze the world independently and yet come to identical conclusions, but because they talk to each other, and each acts on this shared information about what the others happen to think. And as for bankers, "the sound banker, alas! [Keynes wrote], is not one who foresees danger and avoids it, but one who, when he is ruined is ruined in a conventional way along with his fellows and so that no one can blame him."[10]

The point about a shared convention, leading to a common pattern of behavior, is that the sharing of it defines the group itself. It also makes the individual member of the group, previously the focal point of all analysis, analytically redundant. Once you have the group, there is no longer much point in looking below the level of the group at the individual, because within a well-defined group, individuals are essentially similar. (An independent-minded banker would have to be called something else.) If the group is not well defined, the individuals within it will differ in important and relevant ways, and the tactic of "grouping up" will fail. So it is vital to pay attention to getting group structures right.[11] Basing them on behavior is a useful first step.

Without going more deeply into the classification problem, to which we will return, let's assume that we can devise a way to construct systematically meaningful industrial groups, so that we isolate the most important patterns of change in wage behavior. What are the forces that distinguish one pattern of interrelation in wage movements from another? Why do some wages go up and others not, under differing conditions and at different moments in time?

There is a wide range of possible influences on the between-group behavior of the wage structures, including social convention, politics, and external pressures. Taking up the example of unionism, one of the simpler cases may be collective bargaining. If it is sufficiently widespread and effective, collective bargaining may do more than move one group into a position previously occupied by another in our skyscraper-wage structure. Instead, it may actually change the way spaces on the floors are handed out. A widespread form of collective bargaining, a solidaristic wage structure, might in principle move all union members upward, into the cubicles now held by (say) small businesspeople and middle managers. Slots in the middle classes are not merely reallocated. They are actually more densely populated than they were before.

What unions fail to achieve, sometimes the government can. Minimum wage laws can move people en masse from the crowded first floor toward the second or third in our wage building. Public service employment and welfare payments can improve conditions in the basement. Job training, day care, and other employment services, on the other hand, are mainly matters of placement: they can help move some people out of the basement and toward the first floor, but only on condition that first-floor jobs are available to receive them.

Those are the easy cases. They are the kind of causes whose workings we can understand without much trouble. In the case of the minimum wage, where simple quantitative measurement is possible, the statistical influence of changes in the policy variable is apparent. But this is not the usual situation. Much more pervasive are the workings of that ubiquitous but somewhat mysterious concept of technological change.

Suppose there are some groups of people—let's call them an industry—who all work in lines of activity that are similar in some unspecified but important way. One result of this similarity is that they are all positioned to be affected by a technological change in similar ways. Think of the invention of the semiconductor. That device changed our lives, diverting vast sums of consumers' money into electronic equipment, destroying whole industries from typewriters to cash registers to the long-playing phonograph record, while creating a horde of new products, such as the personal computer, the computerized inventory control system, and the compact disc.

How can such technological change, in principle, affect the wage structure? The conventional story focuses on the consequences of technology for the production process, of both goods and services. New technologies are said to be demanding. Their deployment, it is said, requires skill. Hence, those who have such skills, or acquire them, will prosper, and those who do not will not. This is an individualist or at most a within-group story, not a between-group story, according to which the structure of wage outcomes changes only as the pattern of marginal productivities changes. But it is not the only possible story.

In an alternative version of the semiconductor tale, we might divide the world not into the skilled and the unskilled, but into the industrial winners and losers whose essential difference is that they are on opposite sides of a struggle for markets. It might be that the worker who assembles a typewriter is no less well trained, no less highly educated or professionally skilled, than a worker who plugs chips into a memory board. The typewriter worker is perhaps even better trained: typewriters have to be assembled with care!

But the semiconductor worker nevertheless displaces the mechanical craftsman. She does this not because she is more skilled, but because she is in the right industry at the right time. She is in the industry that gains in a struggle for monopoly power, when the superiority of word processors dries up the demand for mechanical typewriters and creates a large and (temporarily) inelastic demand for personal computers. Employment in the new sector will probably expand, but that is not the main point. The main point is that the newly introduced computers sell for prices far above their marginal unit cost of production. And in consequence, computer firms see their revenues augmented by a share of the monopolistic rents. If they pass this on to any of their employees—on the production line or off it—average earnings in this sector rise, while those of the typewriter-assembling craftsperson decline.

This sort of changeover—in contrast to a change in ethnic or gender composition of the workforce or the education levels of individuals—may affect the shape of the wage structure as a whole. If the computer industry is much more efficient, and much smaller per dollar of sales, than the mechanical crafts that it displaces, then the monopoly revenues will be distributed over a much smaller number of persons. Inevitably there will have occurred a redistribution, from the comparatively numerous to the comparatively few. (Compounding this, it may also be that the internal pattern of distribution of pay in the winning industries is different from that among the losers. The gains in the computer sector may go only to executives and designers, while those of the typewriter industry may flow, in an egalitarian way, to the skilled craftspeople on whom the industry relies.) For these reasons, the very shape of the building will have changed after the typewriter makers have been kicked from the fifth floor down to the basement. It is in this way, finally, that we can expect technological change to influence the structure of wages.

Another way to change the shape of the building is to close off certain floors within it. If, for example, an emergency occurs on the lower floors—a flood of imports, for example—parts of the structure may become unusable. Jobs will be extinguished. People will be displaced from the lower floors—some may have to leave the building. At the end of the day, the structure will again be more unequal than it was before. This kind of event is not fundamentally different from technological change. Both involve shifts away from established patterns of activity and the displacement, mainly downward, in the wages of certain classes of workers. And both, interestingly enough, necessarily imply a displacement of labor itself. Unemployment must rise in some sectors and industries, though eventually this may be partly or wholly offset by reemployment in others.

Whether unemployment in the aggregate rises or falls with technological change—whether technology moves in cycles—depends on how new technologies are incorporated into the productive process. In the real world, technology diffuses through the process of business investment. Investment is also the driving force behind what economists call the business cycle—the ebb and flow of activity from recession to boom to recession. Since investment is cyclical, perhaps technology is also. We should not be surprised to see a relationship between technological change, unemployment, economic growth, and inequality. In the slump, when unemployment rises, the wages of the lowest-paid workers suffer because they are the least well protected by their employers' monopolistic positions. Inequality rises. As the recovery starts, moreover, the first new jobs fall to the highly paid workers in sectors that supply investment goods—and inequality rises again.

The slump and the early recovery phases of a business cycle should therefore be associated with rising inequality. But when the economy has returned to full employment, at the peak of the business cycle, the situation turns in favor of less well paid, less powerful, and less protected workers. At the same time, the progress of new investments and the aggregate economic growth rate slow down. Existing capital is exploited more intensively, so that added employments come, not mainly in the investment sectors, but in the production of consumption goods and services. It is at such times that we should expect to observe decreasing inequality in the structure of wages. Figure 4.1 presents a simple schematization of the business cycle and its relationship to inequality in the wage structure.

Technology and trade, in other words, operate collectively on large numbers of people and directly on the structures of relative pay. They do so mainly by displacing some people from their customary employments while creating new opportunities for others. And they do so in waves, over the course of the business cycle. Moreover, in the nature of the drive for efficiency that underlies both the design of new technologies and the globalization of production, these two forces inherently tend to redistribute income from larger to smaller numbers of workers. So long as they are the dominant forces, therefore, there will be a tendency for inequality to increase.

So long as they are the dominant forces. For while technology and globaliza-

FIGURE 4.1

THE BUSINESS CYCLE AND INEQUALITY
A Theoretical View

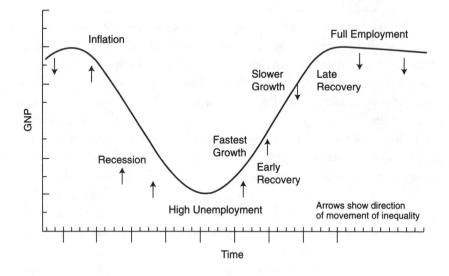

tion have long been the dominant forces, they have not always been so. The period from 1945 to 1970, though marked by vast technological change and a dominant position for U.S. manufacturing in world trade, was not a period of rising inequality. Why not? The answer has to be that other interindustrial forces offset the inequality-increasing properties of technological change and globalization. The question, then, is, What other forces? And how did they work? My contention will be that these forces can be identified, and their effects measured, once we have done a proper job of dividing industries into economically meaningful groups, so that the industrial structure, properly parsed and organized, actually reveals rather than conceals the essential patterns of variation in the structure of wages.

Yet the fate of industrial groups remains a relatively neglected question; the literature is not full of surveys of winners and losers across the industrial realm. Much of the reason for this is taxonomic—a matter of bad categories making good analysis difficult; some of it has to do with failure to develop the relevant techniques. The taxonomic problem stems, to be blunt, from the fact that economists usually just take the government's word for what an industry is. And the government is not a systematic classifier of industries. The government's SIC categories are merely a standard scheme of labels; they do not correspond to the structure of economic groups in the sense that we need. Their purpose is not to analyze, but merely to facilitate the systematic collection of data about manufacturing and service activity.[12]

Lacking a systematic approach, one that can transform arbitrary "categories" or classification codes into economically meaningful "groups" with coherent and corespective patterns of economic behavior, we have at best a muddled picture of the development and changes in the U.S. industrial structure in recent decades. And that has led to the casual but erroneous belief that little has changed in the wage structure as between industries and groups of industries. We hear a repeated refrain that the important changes are "within industries, not between industries." Of course this will be true if the boundaries are not properly drawn! On the other hand, once the boundaries are properly drawn, we will find that the principal forces affecting American wages do appear before us as variations in the interindustrial wage structure.

That industrial structures matter, that industries organize and deploy their political muscle for their own benefit, that they in fact do benefit from their organizational power and their capacity to influence public policy, should not surprise anyone who has ever walked down K Street in Washington, D.C. There is the epicenter of American political economy: the offices of the trade associations, lobbyists, and law firms that represent American companies before the executive agencies and the Congress. Those featureless glass office blocks are not, in the main, dominated by organizations like the National Organization for Women. Instead we find competing groups of rich white men, organized as the Chamber of Commerce, the National Association of Manufacturers, the Aerospace Industries Association, the Semiconductor Industries Association, and associations of truckers and steelmakers and scores of similar groups. No economist can seriously believe that the resources flowing to such places are without purpose or that the pattern of organization itself is functionless and arbitrary.

But what purposes, exactly? And in what proportions? With what relative strength? And what history of success or failure? And, above all, with what pattern of effect on the structure of American wages? If we choose a meaningful scheme for industrial grouping and a set of procedures that expose between-group variations to historical interpretation, we can move toward answers to such questions.

Part Two

EVIDENCE

5

INSTABILITY AND STAGNATION

The liberal reward of labour, therefore, as it is the necessary effect, so it is the natural symptom of increasing national wealth. The scanty maintenance of the labouring poor, on the other hand, is the natural symptom that things are at a stand.

—Adam Smith, *Inquiry into the Nature and Causes of the Wealth of Nations*, Book I, Chapter VII

Part II delves into specifics: the performance of the economy, the movement of wages, how inequality is measured, how much inequality there is, how inequality in wages has changed and exactly when it did so, and why. Readers who have no appetite for technical issues may wish to skim these chapters but should not skip them. The most important findings of this book are here, and the policy analysis that follows depends directly on these findings. Even casual readers should take note of the figures in Chapters 7 and 9, where they may find the industries in which they are themselves employed.

Chapter 5 is the most straightforward. It reviews the overall performance of the economy, the stagnation of productivity and wages, the rise of inequality in family incomes, and the rise of the Transfer State. This chapter sets the stage for those that follow.

Chapters 6 and 7 form an integrated argument about how the major parts of the manufacturing economy are best described and how they interact and behave. Chapter 6 sets the stage, with an argument about the institutional, political, and social character of the wage structure, as an alternative to the usual supply-and-demand models of wage distribution. Chapter 6 begins to give this concept some empirical content, breaking the economy into three broad sectors, which are

differentiated in very general terms by their function and their behavior: a knowl-
edge sector (K-sector), whose principal function is the production of new capital
goods; a consumption goods sector (C-sector) that manufactures goods for mass use;
and a services sector (S-sector). The first two of these together comprise the manu-
facturing sector, which has been the subject of most of the argument about the effect
on wages of technology and of trade.

Chapter 7 looks at the forces affecting industrial performance—and therefore
changes in the wage structure—within the manufacturing sector. It presents the re-
sults of statistical work that isolates the principal sources of industrial change dur-
ing the period from 1958 through 1992, as well as the relative importance of each.
Because it is possible to identify each of these sources with macroeconomic and pol-
icy variables, this chapter's analysis drives a key conclusion of this study as a whole:
that policies, rather than random or indecipherable market forces, lie behind the
principal patterns of industrial change that the American economy has experienced
over the past generation.

Chapter 8 presents measurements of inequality in manufacturing wages, in
particular a variation that is based on industrial wage data. This measurement
has the virtue of being based directly on hourly wages; it is not affected by changes
in hours, family structure, or nonwage sources of income. It has the particular
virtue of being measurable in detail on an annual basis in the United States; in-
deed (with the help of a few tricks) I'll present such measurements going back to
1920. Chapter 8 then presents a statistical exercise—multiple linear regression—
that shows that changes in this measure of hourly wage inequality through time
are very closely related to, and almost fully explained by, the movement of mea-
sures of aggregate economic performance, such as unemployment. Chapter 8
therefore makes a self-contained case for the macroeconomic foundations of the
movement of manufacturing wage inequality in the United States.

Chapter 9 extends the analysis to the services sector. It shows how some activi-
ties classed as services actually have patterns of behavior that closely follow those
found in related parts of the manufacturing complex. The remainder, which we
may call "pure" services, tend to group together; they follow a behavioral pattern
strongly influenced by the minimum wage and not greatly influenced by much
else. The real story of services wages is that there is no independent story. The pat-
terns that distinguish wages in manufacturing are also the important forces sepa-
rating the behavior of wages in manufacturing from the behavior of wages in
services. Most notable among these is the cycle of investment and unemployment.

Part II thus establishes the key themes of this book. First, I show that the pat-
terns of wage inequality and diverging industrial performance are closely related
to the large movements of the macroeconomy, to the cycles of investment and em-

ployment, and also to changes in specific variables strongly affected by public policy, especially monetary policy but also the minimum wage, trade protection, and the military budget. The pattern of effect of these variables differs across industries in ways that are related to the sensitivity of each type of industry to each particular policy, and especially to their differing degrees of monopoly power. It follows that the historical developments through which we have all lived are not, and cannot be, mere adjustments of relative pay to the changing relative productivity of skills. They are demonstrably the creatures and effects of policy decisions. From this, it follows that if policy decisions change, so too will the patterns of inequality.

We are living through a political crisis of the Transfer State: the United States has reached social and political limits beyond which it has become very difficult to squeeze the wage earnings of the working population for the benefit of those who do not earn wages. The signs and symptoms of this crisis are essentially everywhere: in the drive to cut the federal budget, in welfare reform, in the continuing debate over health care, in recurring drives to "reform" and privatize the social security system.

If the crisis of the Transfer State is a surface phenomenon, on what does it rest? The roots appear to lie in the rising inequality of wages and salaries, and in the competition between public transfer programs and service on private debts. American economic outcomes are unequal, both by global standards and by comparison with our own recent past. As they became more unequal, the burden of public transfers grew. The poor became more numerous, and the elderly were maintained at a higher standard, with respect to both pensions and medical care. The rich, for whom the whole structure of universal social programs is increasingly irrelevant, were allowed to reduce their share in payments for the system. And the middle class, struggling with the increasing burden of private debt incurred in an effort to maintain living standards, became increasingly frustrated with the burden of public transfers. None of this would have happened had the underlying distribution of wages, salaries, and wealth not become more unequal.

So we must come to closure on the causes of rising inequality in the wage structure. In the preceding chapters, I reviewed two competing explanations. One is rooted in the competitive model of income distribution and places the responsibility on new technologies that raise the relative productivity of the comparatively skilled. This answer is powerfully appealing for three reasons. First, it is backed by the authority of economic theory, holding in each case that market forces are at work to reward individuals and nations for higher productivity. Second, it provides the reassurance that good things will result in the end from the discomfiture that new technology causes. Third, it places responsibility for reacting to the situation on the individual worker, while delegitimating collective responses to the inequality crisis. The message is that one cannot oppose the march of progress or obstruct the working of the market.

Yet in its standard form, the skill-biased technology hypothesis is not coherent. It is plagued by empirical difficulties and, more fundamentally, the implausibility of the underlying marginal productivity theory of distribution on which it relies. It doesn't work in theory, and, as a quick look at the timing of the diffusion of computers and the spread of wage inequality makes clear, it doesn't work in practice either.

The alternative explanation is that new technologies act on the economy in quite a different way. Behind the alluring surface of technological revolution and economic globalization lie the old familiar forces of monopoly and economic power, of rivalrous enterprises, and competing nations, battling to extract a maximum of rents from the larger social order. These familiar forces today operate in a modern and unstable guise, insofar as the struggle for technological supremacy and the struggle for monopoly merge into one. The next questions must therefore be, How is this power created? How is it maintained? How and under what circumstances can it be brought under control?

My hypothesis is that the technology sectors perform better, relative to all the others, under comparatively unstable economic conditions. Therefore, changes in macroeconomic performance, brought on in part by actions of state policy, precipitated the changes in the balance of market powers and the increases in inequality we have observed. They did so by creating, and tolerating, greater instability, and worse average economic performance, in the years following 1970 than in the years before. Instability, stagnation, and rising inequality in their turn can be linked to the rise in transfer incomes and the political crisis of the Transfer State.

To explore this hypothesis, we need first to review the history of economic performance itself. Have there actually been changes in the macroeconomic climate? Do these changes correspond, in time and in severity, to the rise of inequality in wage structures? These questions are particularly important given the widespread opinion that the economic performance of the 1980s and 1990s was good by historical standards and that therefore the increase in inequality during this time was anomalous, a paradox, that requires a more complex explanation than would have been provided by the old-fashioned wisdom that sustained growth is equalizing while recessions and depressions are not.[1]

We can usefully begin with the broadest measure of economic growth, the gross domestic product (GDP). Figure 5.1 illustrates the course of economic growth since the trough of the 1990 recession, and compares it to the pace of economic growth in every previous expansion since 1960. The figure shows, in striking fashion, just how different the expansion that began in 1961 and ended in 1969 was from all those that have followed. The long boom of the Kennedy-Johnson years was far stronger than any since then. It also lasted longer, and produced cumulative gains in gross production more than 20 or 30 percent greater than those of its nearest competitors, the Reagan-Bush expansion of 1982 through 1991 and the Ford-Carter expansion from 1975 through 1981. The figure also shows that economic growth has been quite slow in the expansion that began in 1991 under George Bush, continuing to the present under President Clinton. By this measure, and using the business cycle timing methods of the National Bureau of Economic Research, the cumulative expansion of the 1990s is the slowest on the postwar record up to this point.

To be entirely fair, the measure of cumulative growth is somewhat sensitive to the choice of starting date. Usually recoveries begin with a bang; the most recent one did not. Part of the overall shortfall from the normal postwar standard for economic expansions is due to several quarters of near-zero growth at the very beginning of the current expansion; the shortfall would be less if the recovery were simply dated as beginning some months later. If, for example, one were to date the recovery as beginning in late 1991 rather than at the beginning of that year, then the cumulative record of growth, though shorter, would somewhat more closely resemble the postwar norm. Still, by no measure is the economic expansion of the 1990s a rapid expansion, nor can it begin to compare with the record of the previous two-term Democratic presidency, that of Kennedy and Johnson.

Another question that frequently arises when comparing business cycle expansions concerns the economic conditions at their point of departure. It might be that certain expansions look better than this one, only because they started from the troughs of deeper recessions, and therefore the economy had more room to bounce. If there were a natural tendency for the economy to return to an equilibrium state, a kind of natural elasticity to the business

FIGURE 5.1

WEAKER EXPANSIONS . . .

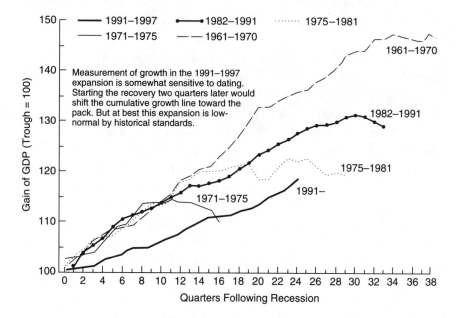

cycle, then we might find that a weak recovery accompanies a strong starting point, and vice versa.

But an examination of the record shows that this bounce-back theory is not supported by history. There is no clear-cut relationship between the depth of a recession, measured as the loss of GDP from peak to trough, and the speed of the expansion that follows. The mid-1970s and early 1980s saw stronger expansions after deeper recessions, but the 1950s, 1960s, and early 1970s saw stronger expansions after recessions that were not so deep.[2]

Instead, it appears that the fate of an economic expansion is most strongly influenced by the way in which it begins. There is a fairly consistent empirical relationship between growth in the first year of an economic expansion and growth over the four years that follow.[3] The slow beginning of the recovery of the 1990s left the evident legacy of a slow overall pace of expansion. Thus, in this respect the George Bush–Alan Greenspan partnership in the early 1990s did control the destiny of President Clinton's economic record. And Clinton's 1996 campaign claims—that the United States was experiencing the "best economy in thirty years"—were doubly ironic. The Clinton administration was in fact defending a weak record, yet one largely determined by events before it took office. (A third irony, of course, is that the defense succeeded.)

After a very slow start, with essentially no new employment creation for the first year of recovery, job growth in the expansion of the 1990s parallels the slow employment growth of the 1960s expansion. While political leaders have boasted of 10 million jobs created since 1990, this represents a growth in employment of just over 2 percent per year—a slow rate by any historical standard. As a rate of job creation, the current expansion lies far below the job-creating speed demons of the 1970s and 1980s; indeed it exhibits the slowest rate of new job creation in a generation.[4] (See Figure 5.2.)

And what of unemployment? Although much was made of falling jobless-ness in the expansion of the 1990s through early 1997, here again historical comparison paints a different picture. By the time it reached the same age, the Reagan expansion of the 1980s had reduced unemployment to almost ex-actly the same level, from a higher point of departure, and with two more years to run. It was only during the year 1997 itself that President Clinton's record on unemployment substantially improved on the Reagan expansion. And the long period of growth through the 1960s enjoyed lower unemploy-ment rates at every stage of the way, maintaining unemployment a full point below 1997 levels for three years. Thus, the employment growth of the most

FIGURE 5.2

... WITH WEAK JOB CREATION ...

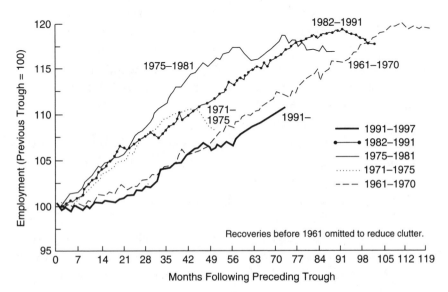

FIGURE 5.3

... MODERATE PROGRESS ON UNEMPLOYMENT ...

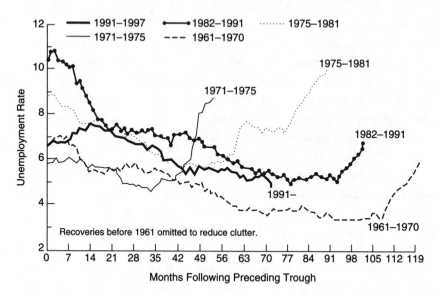

recent expansion came in the context of unemployment rates that are consonant with those of the period after 1970; the good years of the first quarter-century after World War II have not been recaptured. (See Figure 5.3.)

How is it that the economic growth rate of the 1990s was so much lower than in the expansion of the 1960s, but that employment growth in the two periods did not differ so much? The answer is the difference in measured productivity growth. From Figure 5.4, we see especially clearly the defining difference between the period before 1970 and the period that followed. Productivity growth in those earlier years typically exceeded 3 percent per annum. In the period since 1970, in contrast, it has hovered near 1 percent per year. And while in the late 1980s a number of economists began to suggest that productivity growth might be returning to the higher trend of the 1950s and 1960s, the data since then show that this hope has not been realized. There has been no productivity revival.

To summarize, the macroeconomic performance of the postwar period seems clearly to divide at the watershed of 1970. The 1960s brought high output growth, high productivity growth, and low job creation. The 1970s and 1980s saw a collapse of productivity growth, so that fairly high rates of output growth were sustained only by drawing many new workers into the labor force; in the 1990s this also disappeared, and we have been left with low rates of output growth, low productivity growth, and low job creation.[5] There remains a gulf, on the historical record, between economic performance leading up to 1970 and what came later. There is little evidence for the view, advanced by Republicans under Reagan in the 1980s and by Democrats under Clinton a decade later, that new policies had succeeded in curing the problems of instability and stagnation.

This is not the place to assess in full the deeper question of why economic performance went bad after 1970. We may merely note a wide difference of opinion on the point. Those associated with events at the time favored a model of external shocks, laying particular emphasis on the oil crises of 1973 and 1979. Those opposed most strongly to the Vietnam War pointed to a failure of fiscal policy in the late 1960s, especially President Johnson's reluctance to raise taxes as the war accelerated in 1968. Monetarist economists made much, at the time, of allegedly inflationary monetary policies, including especially the contributions of the Federal Reserve to Richard Nixon's re-election campaign in 1972. And many partial explanations exist.[6]

FIGURE 5.4

... AND MEDIOCRE PRODUCTIVITY GROWTH

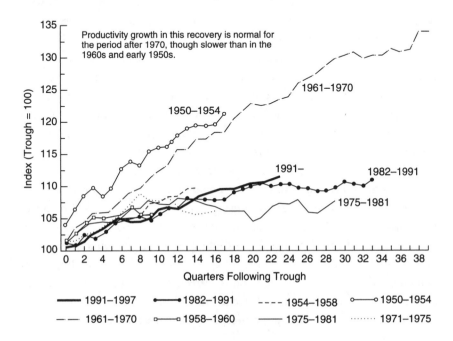

Whatever one's explanation for the turning point of 1970s, it must also account for the failure of economic growth and of productivity growth to recover in the 1980s and 1990s. Thus, explanations based on the Vietnam War or oil and other shock phenomena, perfectly good as explanations of the inflation that occurred at the time, tend to recede as candidate explanations for slow productivity and output growth. The same goes for any pattern of explanation aimed at associating allegedly inflationary monetary policies and productivity growth. Inflation, after all, came to an end in the 1980s, but slow growth persisted. Similarly, supply-side explanations rooted in the tax structure of the 1970s fall off the table in the 1980s, since tax rates were radically reformed but productivity did not recover.

We are left with three possibilities. First, there is the idea that the slowdown in productivity and output growth after 1970 is inexplicable, a force of nature that economics is powerless to understand. This is the position to which quite a number of frustrated students of the phenomenon have retreated, but it is obviously not very satisfying. Second, there is the possibility that our economic measurements are entirely wrong, that the slowdown of productivity growth is a statistical artifact, and that our perception of declining improvement in economic performance after 1970 is an illusion.[7] Although this is an intriguing hypothesis and not without interesting advocates, we are obliged at this point to leave it to further investigation.

Third, there is the possibility that the policymakers of the 1960s were doing something right—something that the policymakers of the 1970s, 1980s, and 1990s all consistently rejected. In that case, the wounds of the past three decades would have to be diagnosed as self-inflicted, as disasters that could have been avoided but were instead accepted for political reasons.

The obvious candidate for this unthinkable possibility is Keynesian economic policy. Presidents Kennedy and Johnson were committed to full employment. They both pursued high growth—and our evidence on the importance of early growth spurts suggests that it was Kennedy's actions in this regard in the early 1960s, and not the Vietnam War, that were most important. They both fought to hold the line on inflation with direct intervention in wage settlements and price setting—policies that succeeded, myths to the contrary notwithstanding—as inflation slowed in 1968 despite full employment. These policies were all consistently rejected by their successors, or else employed for only short periods of time immediately surrounding presidential elections. If this interpretation is correct, the essential point is that instability and stagnation became de facto national economic policy after 1970, and this explains why stability and prosperity have never been restored.[8]

For those who were working, growth in the real value of the average wage, after adjustment for inflation, measures the course of change in living standards. As with productivity, history in this area shows a sharp break between the high-wage-growth expansions of the 1950s and 1960s and the no-wage-growth expansions after 1971. Before 1970, real wages tracked the growth of productivity and production in the economy overall. After 1970, they ceased to do so. Here again the expansion of the 1990s shows its kinship to the more recent period, and its failure, so far, to break out of the poor-performance mold cast a quarter-century ago. Real wages did not grow at all through the first four years of the 1990s; only with unexpectedly rapid economic growth and falling unemployment in 1996 was there any sign of progress. By mid-1997 cumulative improvement in real wages had exceeded the records of the 1970s and the 1980s by a few percentage points, but it remained less than half of what had been accomplished by the comparable phase of the Kennedy-Johnson expansion, that is to say, by 1965.

Real wage growth fell sharply below measured productivity growth after 1970 (even though the latter also slowed). Does this mean that workers have

FIGURE 5.5

REAL WAGES AND PRODUCTIVITY

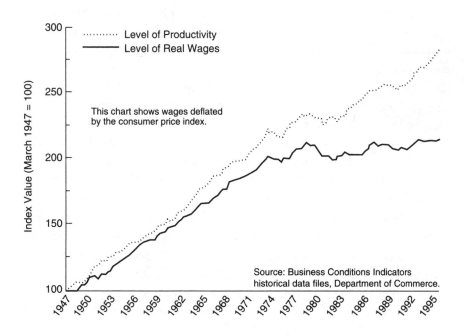

lost ground to other claimants on economic income? One interesting answer to this question hinges on the distinction between the *consumption wage* and the *production wage*. The consumption wage is the purchasing power of earnings in terms of the goods that workers purchase for their own use; the production wage is the wage of workers adjusted for changes in the price of commodities that they produce.[9] (If you work at Boeing, your consumption wage, like everyone else's, is your basket of groceries and your rent; your production wage is the fraction of one of those airplanes you might be able to purchase.) A basic fact about American manufacturing workers is that they produce advanced capital goods—computers, aircraft, machinery, instruments—in disproportionate quantities, a fact that reflects the leading position of American technology in the economic development of the planet. A good many of these advanced American products are sold on foreign markets to pay for our national imports of consumption goods.

Unfortunately for the average American worker, the relative price of these capital goods—relative, that is, to the price of goods in the consumption basket—has been falling in recent years. This is partly because of the intense drive for monopoly through technological change in the capital goods sector—a war of each against all in which the gains are large but transitory and the struggle for advantage is all but eternal. As a result, American production wages have continued to rise, roughly in line with productivity growth, and therefore wages have not declined dramatically in relationship to profits. It is consumption wages—living standards—that have been stagnant or falling. It may be cold comfort to the workers, but if we could live inside jet engines and eat microprocessors, the problem of American wage stagnation *on average* would be less severe than it is.[10]

When it comes to measuring the evolution of living standards through time, there are unavoidable elements of paradox, ambiguity, and uncertainty. These have to do, first of all, with the measurement of price changes. Many consumer goods that are commonplace now, from compact disks to color television to computers, did not exist a generation ago or were immensely expensive. The quality of a fair number of services, including jet air travel and long-distance telephony, not to mention coronary bypass operations and kidney dialysis, has also changed dramatically. The real value of such changes is often not properly captured in the economic measures used to adjust for changes in price. Because many aspects of improved product quality simply cannot be measured, they are like an unseen price decline.

The presence of unseen price declines in many products would imply that past measurements of inflation are overstated and that past measurements of the growth of real output and real wages are correspondingly understated. The rate of improvement of real living standards must therefore have been higher than we have been able to measure. Correspondingly, it would follow that the average family was poorer in the distant past, relative to the present, than comparisons based on official statistics would show.[11]

Thus, though measured median real wages have hardly changed, it is still very probable that today's median income household eats better, drives a safer car, lives in a more comfortable home (much more likely to have, for example, central air-conditioning), is healthier, and lives longer than thirty years ago. And by most measures, the country was dirtier and more dangerous in 1966 than it is today. It is also true that nonwage compensation has risen and that the quality of some services provided outside the wage package, such as health care, is markedly better today than three or four decades ago. (On the other hand, the quality of some public services—parks and mass transit in New York City, for instance, and congestion on the Santa Monica Freeway— has surely deteriorated over the same time.)

But whether unmeasured quality improvements can account, in whole or part, for the slowdown in measured productivity and real wage growth after 1970 remains doubtful. It would have to be shown that biases in price measurement increased after 1970, due to an acceleration of unmeasured quality improvement and other sources of inflation overcounting. It is possible that some acceleration did occur, most notably with improvements in electronics and very rapid reduction in prices of electronic goods (including computers after 1980), and perhaps more broadly with an increase in product diversification and "complexity."[12] But it remains unlikely that such developments fully account for the slowdown in measured productivity growth. It is even more unlikely that they could be credited with reversing it, silently, in the most recent decade.[13]

In general, the official statistical history of the postwar years remains standing in spite of the problems inherent in long runs of economic statistics. This history tells us that the turn of the decade at 1970 was a watershed for economic growth, productivity, and employment. In the years before, full employment truly prevailed. Productivity growth was high, as was the growth in real wages and living standards. Employment growth was low, but this reflected the stability of demand for employment: employment growth was enough to absorb the natural increase in the labor force and a steady increase in the proportion of women wishing to work. After 1970, however, the picture changed dramatically, and for the worse. Economic growth slowed, as did growth of productivity. Many new workers were accommodated in employment in the expansion of the 1980s, but only at dramatically reduced rates of wage gain.

Equally, nothing yet overturns the official picture, according to which the 1990s expansion is of a piece with the years since 1970 and not those before. The slow growth of productivity continues. The slow growth of average wages also continues. There is little basis for the claim that economic performance in the 1990s has been strong by any reasonable standard.

With stagnation of real wages, there has been a rise in the components of income that are not directly linked to current productive activity. The squeeze on wages and proprietors' income as shares of all sources of personal income is illustrated in Figure 5.6, which presents the proportions of personal income attributable to different sources, decade by decade from the mid-1940s. Through this period, wages and salaries have remained the major source of personal income. But their share in the total has declined from a high of more than two-thirds in the 1950s to about 59 percent so far in the 1990s.

Proprietors' income fell even more sharply. The share of this item in total income has fallen in half over forty years, from about 15 percent of all personal income in the 1950s to just over 8 percent in the 1990s.[14] The decline of proprietors' income tells us about the kind of society we have become: apparently less entrepreneurial and less hospitable to the family or small business operation now, in relative terms, than we were a half-century ago.

What has taken the place of wages and proprietors' incomes in total personal income? Not corporate profits, at least not the private distribution thereof. (Corporate profits rose sharply in the 1990s but do not enter personal income unless they are distributed.) Dividends from the stock market were about 3.3 percent of total income forty and fifty years ago, and they remain at about that figure today. Certainly capital gains, the appreciation in value of existing assets, is a major development increasing the wealth of the richest Americans relative to the middle class, and this reflects the valuation of corporate profits not distributed to stockholders. Capital gains are concentrated among the very top percentile of the income distribution, but they are not recorded as income in the national accounts data, and so fall outside the purview of Figure 5.6.

Instead, the winners are of two kinds: receivers of interest and receivers of transfer payments from the government—principally the elderly. Each type of income has added ten full percentage points to its share of personal income in the last half-century. Interest payments have increased from around 3 percent to a range of 13 to 14 percent of total personal income, depending

FIGURE 5.6

THE SQUEEZE ON WAGES

Shares in Personal Income

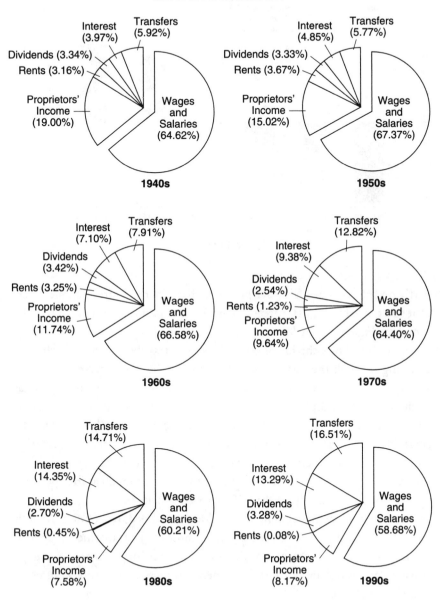

Based on averages of quarterly data, by decade.

FIGURE 5.7

THE SHIFT TO TRANSFERS AND INTEREST

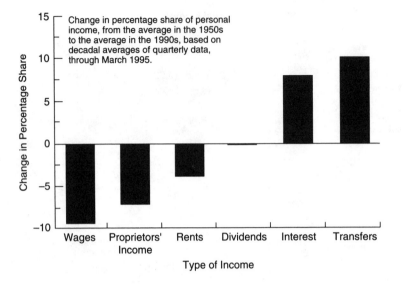

partly on interest rates. Transfer payments have increased from about 6 percent to a range of 15 to 16 percent, depending in part on the condition of the economy. Figure 5.7 illustrates these trends.

Figure 5.8 shows the history of interest and transfer incomes. Both were climbing through the 1950s and 1960s. But as the figure makes clear, they diverged in the 1970s. Economic recessions boosted payments to individuals in the form of unemployment insurance, and after social security payments were indexed to inflation in 1972, that inflationary decade helped raise the share of income going to senior citizens. Interest payments, on the other hand, remained on their previous path until 1979, when the vast increase in interest rates pushed them up within a few years by as much as four percentage points of income, from 8 to 12 percent. Finally, in the late 1980s the share of interest payments in income suddenly declined, reflecting a diminution of debts at the end of the decade and, most of all, a sustained decline in interest rates. Unfortunately, new debts have been fueling the most recent expansion, and the share of interest payments in income may soon resume its increasing pattern.

Figure 5.9 shows transfer incomes by type. By far the largest is the rise in personal interest payments—equal alone to just about the entire governmental transfer sector. Among governmental payments, the largest category and

FIGURE 5.8

THE GROWTH OF THE TRANSFER STATE

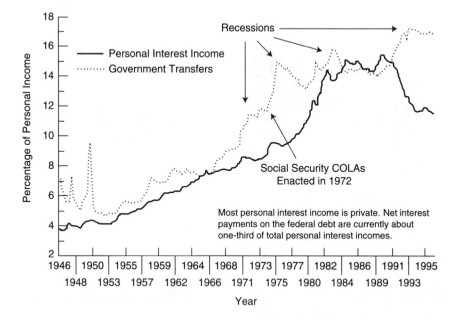

the greatest growth has been in social security proper: retirement payments to the elderly and survivors' benefits to their dependents, plus health insurance (Medicare). Other governmental transfers, including prominently supplemental security income (SSI), are the second largest category and the second largest gainer. All other sources of government income, including unemployment insurance and welfare, are comparatively small. Veterans' benefits tend to decline as a share in national income as wars recede into time.

Taken together, these numbers tell a disturbing story. The story begins with overall economic performance. The stagnation of aggregate wages stems from the stagnation of economic activity after 1970; slow wage growth in the current economic expansion stems from slow economic growth since 1991.

Second, and equally important, economic instability has increased. From 1960 through 1970, there were no recessions. From 1970 through 1992, there were five. In no period have we enjoyed economic performance as strong as that of the 1960s; in no period have we enjoyed growth as long; in no period have we enjoyed growth as stable.

Third, as a clear result of instability and stagnation, the share of pay in personal compensation has declined. This is not a simple story of rising prof-

FIGURE 5.9

TRANSFERS BY TYPE OF INCOME

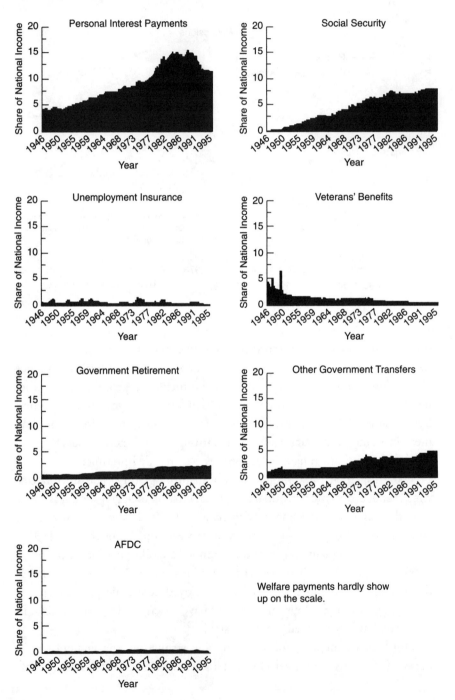

its and falling wages. Rather, both wage incomes and profit incomes have been crowded by rising transfers and rising interest payments, and each of these is once again the product of larger economic forces. Rising public transfers occur because need increases when unemployment and economic instability strike and because the wage base to support a given set of needs declines. Rising interest payments occur because of increasing debt and rising interest rates. The rise of the Transfer State, in which interest and social security sum to nearly 30 percent of personal income, is an artifact of policy and performance.

So what is the relationship of these developments to the inequality of incomes? These trends are reflected in a comprehensive measurement of family income inequality prepared by the Bureau of the Census. This is the Gini coefficient, a statistic that measures the cumulative departure from equality across an entire distribution of income. The Current Population Survey, which today has a sample size of around 60,000 households, permits reliable calculation of inequality in family incomes back to 1968. Using sketchier data sources, official estimates of this measure have been calculated back to 1947.

The Census Bureau's measure of family income inequality usefully confirms that inequality was approximately unchanged from the end of World War II until about 1970. More precisely, inequality in family incomes shows no strong trend over this time. Inequality declined during the Korean War and early 1950s, ticked upward in recessions, but then declined again as the economy recovered. Beginning in 1969 or 1970, however, the picture changes. Inequality, as measured by the census numbers, starts to rise. It continues upward through the 1970s and then, at an accelerated rate, in every year of the early and mid-1980s. Only in 1988 or 1989 do the increases stop, but after just a few years of stability, they resume.[15] Figure 5.10 illustrates these movements.

In a loose analysis of turning points and trends, Figure 5.10 supports the view that economic events underlie the great increases in inequality of the past generation. We can detect the equalizing force of full employment in the late 1960s. The transition to instability that produced rising inequality after Richard Nixon took over from Lyndon Johnson in 1969 is clear. So are the huge increases in inequality that followed the recession and 10 percent unemployment of the early 1980s. And we can see at least some slowdown in the rate at which inequality got worse after the economy recovered from that cataclysm.

But these movements are only suggestive. To see more precisely what the linkages are and how they have worked out, we need to deepen our analysis.

FIGURE 5.10

INEQUALITY OF FAMILY INCOMES

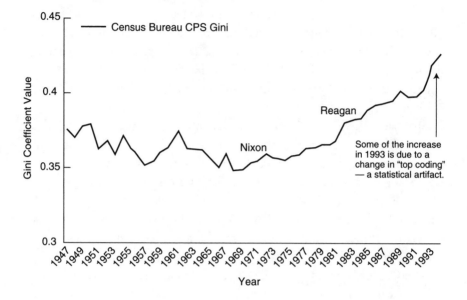

The next chapters explore patterns of industrial change and the movement of inequality in wages, first in the manufacturing sector and then between manufacturing and the much larger services sector. They will bring us closer to an appreciation of cause and effect in this complicated matter.

6

THE THREE-LEVEL ECONOMY

> The essential point to grasp is that in dealing with capitalism
> we are dealing with an evolutionary process.... Capitalism...
> is by nature a form or method of economic change and not
> only never is but never can be stationary.... Since we are deal-
> ing with a process whose every element takes considerable
> time in revealing its true features and ultimate effects, there is
> no point in appraising the performance of that process *ex visu*
> of a given point of time; we must judge its performance over
> time, as it unfolds through decades or centuries.
>
> —Joseph A. Schumpeter, *Capitalism, Socialism and Democracy*

The drive to monopoly power, so obvious to Adam Smith and Schumpeter, has been nearly obliterated from the conscious-ness of modern economics insofar as the evolution of inequality is concerned. An essential step toward restoring it is the identification of who the new mo-nopolists really are and how they operate in the modern context. When this is done, if it is done correctly and if the underlying premise is not mistaken, then the importance of changes affecting industries and groups of industries, as distinct from changes operating at the individual level, will become more apparent. The more accurately chosen the structure of industrial groups—that is, the better the taxonomy or system of classification—the more ex-planatory power will be attributed, correctly, to the operation of forces affecting such groups.

I proceed in two steps. The first is to present a conceptual structure of in-dustries: a stylized breakdown that tries to distinguish the principal types of industry in the American economy. Stylized taxonomies are very common in the literature, and some of them, such as Robert Reich's distinction between "symbolic analysts" and "routine-production" and "in-person services," have gained considerable popular acceptance.[1] Reich's taxonomy is not far different from mine, but with two distinctions. First, I will be classifying industries rather than individuals, because the data and also to a great extent the economy itself are organized that way. Second, in what follows it will be possible, broadly speaking, actually to reclassify the standard industrial categories according to the stylized types. In other words, unlike many other analyses with purely conjectural grouping schemes, this one applies to the real world.

As a first step, imagine a national economy entirely closed to trade. Such an economy will have three basic types of activity in it. Some workers, perhaps a fairly small number, will be employed as machine makers. Highly skilled, they build the instruments that others use and develop the technologies that lead from one generation of machines to the next. We can call them K-workers, where K stands for knowledge, or equally, for "capital goods." K-workers are those who produce airplanes and machine tools and who write software, as well as the architects and engineers and some of the other professionals who give shape to the society in which we live. They include Reich's symbolic analysts, and then some.

We can often usefully distinguish between the truly irreplaceable knowledge workers, those who actually control the keys to the kingdom, and their production-line subordinates within the knowledge-based industries. Depending on the nature of the production process, the latter may, or may not, be in a position to share the bonanza of a technological gold strike. But the K-sector as a whole is the conceptual entity to be reckoned with, right down to its janitors and secretaries in many cases.

A larger number of workers will be employed using the machines designed in the K-sector. They will produce the goods that the whole population actually consumes: food, shelter, clothing, transportation, and entertainment. They will do so in factories using machinery accumulated over the years from the K-sector output. Some of their equipment will be new, some older, some on the verge of retirement. We can call these workers, the machine users, the C-sector, where C stands for "consumption goods."

The C-sector, which includes much run-of-the-mill machinery and intermediate goods production as well as all of the mass production of consumer goods, is no monolith. Some factories are new, technologically advanced, up and coming, and profitable. Others are old, run down, overstaffed, costly to maintain, and barely able to turn a profit. Some C-sector factories employ directly the armies of clerks, janitors, and secretaries they need to support their productive operations—and pay these service workers wages scaled to the C-sector norms. Others contract out their service functions and perhaps pay less for these easily replaceable supporting workers.

This description of diversity within the C-sector is offered at the level of the factory, but it can be extended to the full range of companies and of industries as well. Companies are groups of factories. Industries are groups of firms. At each level of grouping up, we will find differences of efficiency, unit cost, market power, and potential profitability at each level of demand. (To use a fancy phrase from a new branch of mathematics, fractal theory, we can say that these entities are "self-similar at different scales.") The C-sector is highly heterogeneous.

Finally, there will be a large group of workers who use little or no capital equipment, and who do not produce machinery or goods and are not employed by companies that do. These are the services workers, the S-sector, who live by their labor alone. They are the janitors, clerks, cashiers, secretaries, hairdressers, nurses and orderlies, masseurs and masseuses who in the actual economy of the United States make up 80 percent of the working population, often employed in companies specialized to the provision of services and the distribution of goods.

Now consider the wage structure in this highly stylized economy. There will be a tendency for wages in the K-sector to be quite high, relative to all the rest. Why? Because the K-sector is the sphere of modern monopoly power—temporary, tenuous, and volatile though it may be in many cases. The K-sector is also the sphere of innovation and luck. K-sector outcomes are a lottery—winner-take-all on a huge scale.[2] Schumpeter described the phenomenon with acuity:

> Spectacular prizes much greater than would have been necessary to call forth the particular effort are thrown to a small minority of winners, thus propelling much more efficaciously than a more equal and "just" distribution would, the activity of that large majority of businessmen who receive in return very modest compensation or nothing or less than nothing, and yet do their utmost because they have the big prizes before their eyes and overrate their chances of doing equally well.[3]

This is the arena of the rat race, the shakeout, the scramble for technology and the big score. Firms cannot afford to lose their top staff; the staff is the firm. They therefore bid up the wages of their workers, from the top down. Our most famous business wonder-boys of this half-century, from

Robert Noyce to William Gates, have operated in the K-sector. But the phenomenon extends down to the level of engineers, designers, and marketing wizards who permeate this sector, who view themselves as professionally mobile and competitive, whose motivation for participation in economic life is partly because it offers a chance at the big score.[4] And it goes on down the line to the production workers as well, for such firms cannot afford the disruption or even the standard inefficiencies and turnover of an unhappy, underpaid labor force.

At the other end of the spectrum, the S-sector worker has very little leverage over her wages. Workers are easily replaced, the necessary skills are acquired in a few days, turnover is high, and the sector is the last resort of all those who might be displaced from higher-order occupations. S-sector workers are not upwardly mobile. In a pure market economy, Malthusian forces would dictate that S-sector wages would decline to the bare minimum of subsistence. People who are desperate for work cannot be picky about their wages.

Civilized economies do not, in fact, allow this to happen. Instead, civilized societies universally set standards, by one means or another, to ensure a decent minimum. Minimum wages are one way that this is done in America. The social safety net is another. In modern Europe, minimums include free public health care and higher education, alongside a plethora of urban public services. Trade unions can extend the market power of C- and K-sector workers to employees in the S-sector who have no market power of their own. In many countries, restrictions on the right of employers to dismiss their employees create a kind of artificial leverage for S-sector workers. In the final analysis, there is no market determination of S-sector wages, because market forces push these wages down to politically determined social minimums, and the social minimums effectively determine what those wages are. The way to bring down S-sector wages is to undercut the minimums themselves, *politically, by weakening the social protections of the S-sector workers.* Thus the S-sector worker has an economic destiny governed by the relative power of organized working people in the political system.

But what about the workers in the C-sector? Potentially, their wages do depend on the economic fortunes of the companies they work for. That potential may or may not be realized. Unlike those in the K-sector, C-sector companies are not obliged by self-interest to raise wages in good times. Generally they'd rather not. Production workers in the C-sector can be replaced—something that is much harder to do when a firm's reputation depends on the perception of quality in its workforce. But on the other hand,

C-sector firms may be forced to raise wages, if their workers are well organized and insistent and the conditions are right.

Thus the C-sector is the scene of a struggle for income shares whose outcome is not strictly determined by either markets or politics. The outcome will depend on tactics, strategies, the balance of forces, and larger economic conditions. It may be determined on a company-by-company basis, with a wide distribution of winners and losers, or it may be coordinated to a greater or lesser extent across companies, either directly or indirectly through the action of the unions.[5]

How can a firm in the C-sector fight off a wage increase at a time when profits are high? One way is to threaten workers with technological change. Each firm and each industry in the mass production sector is an amalgam of older and newer factories and facilities. Typically, the older a factory, the more labor it requires to produce a given output and the higher the unit labor cost. Conversely, new factories are more automated, requiring less labor per unit of output. So the threat to modernize, to automate, or to relocate is not an idle one. Workers in older factories may be well aware that their future employment depends on not pushing too far for higher wages, for that may push their employers to automate away their jobs.

The effect of a new, labor-saving technology is to weaken the bargaining position of production workers in the C-sector, who are at risk for their jobs. In the first instance, the C-sector firm wins in this confrontation. The production workers will make concessions, in the hopes of persuading management to hold on to the older factory a little longer than it might otherwise do. One can imagine that to some extent nonproduction employees—supervisors, managers, and executives—will gain some of what the production workers lose.

But even the C-sector executives cannot be the largest winners in this process. At the end of the day, when the threat of a new technology is made real, they have to buy the technologies with which they confront their workers. The firms and their workers who sell technologies to the firms producing consumption goods hold the trump cards in this game of technological chicken. The workers within those industries who are truly irreplaceable— the highly paid, salaried professionals and the tiny elite with profit-sharing and stock options—hold the highest trumps of all.

Technology is therefore hardly the benign, impersonal force of so much modern writing, an immanence operating smoothly and uniformly on the destiny of individuals, independent from the business cycle and fluctuations in unemployment. Quite to the contrary, *technology, like everything else of real importance, is a political force,* deployed for tactical and strategic advantage by those who control it. Its implementation has winners and losers.

What happens when we reopen our hypothetical economy to international trade? First of all, it is perfectly apparent that (like technology) trade affects the K- and the C-sectors in radically different ways. Generally the knowledge workers in the K-sector cannot be replaced from Hong Kong or Thailand or the Dominican Republic. The industries they work in do not exist outside a small number of the most advanced countries. Indeed, the products of the K-sector will be sold worldwide, proof of their comparative irreplaceability. Equally, aspiring K-sector workers from developing countries must come to the advanced countries in order to work—and for the most part they do.

C-sector workers, at their best, are only as competitive as the factories in which they work; for them technologies are largely fixed by the designers and engineers who establish how the plant will run. Within broad limits, factories can be moved; more precisely, they can be torn down in one place and reconstructed in another, according to a different and usually superior blueprint. Some, like garment sweatshops, are entirely footloose and easily set up in backwaters the world over. Others, like automobile assembly plants, require substantial and reliable infrastructure available in only a limited number of places. In some, the threat of relocation has been reduced for political reasons—reasons like national security or trade protectionism. But the basic fact remains: factories can be moved across national frontiers; workers, as a rule, cannot be.

If the potential relocation of factories is to countries with lower average wages than in the job-losing country, then the threat of expanded trade is exactly like the threat of technological innovation. Job loss through relocation—or indeed to a growing foreign-based competitor—is just the same as job loss through automation. And indeed, as many companies have discovered, the two can be combined. That new factory in Chihuahua can have both cheap labor and modern tools, working together to undermine the bargaining power of the workers left behind in Dayton.

As a result, we have a developing asymmetry in the advanced economies. The K-sector becomes larger over time as trade expands, and K-sector goods dominate exports. The domestic C-sector tends to shrink, and C-sector goods dominate imports. K-sector wages rise, while the power of workers in C-sector firms diminishes. Both technology and trade strengthen the K-sector at the expense of the C-sector, not because they "enhance skills"—workers in the C-sector can be just as highly skilled as anywhere else—but because they strengthen the monopoly position of K-sector firms, and because they weaken the bargaining power of C-sector workers. Since the C-sector is vast and the K-sector is comparatively small, the result is an upward distribution of income.

To summarize: In the K-sector, firms need workers, and knowledge workers have an advantage. Wages and salaries, especially salaries, in this sector drift upward under competitive pressure and in consequence of expanding trade. In the S-sector, workers are vulnerable, insecure, and desperate for their jobs. Wages in this sector tend to drift downward, unless sustained by political and social pressures. In the C-sector, wages depend on the balance of power between companies and workers. This in turn depends on worker organization, the larger social and political climate, and the potential twin threats to employment of modernization and trade.

It is now time to measure, and then to explain, the pattern of change in industrial performance in America. If this stylized taxonomy is roughly correct, we should expect to find three broad patterns of wage change through time: a group of winners, associated with technology suppliers (K-sector), a group of service providers with broadly declining relative wages that follow political trends (S-sector), and an intermediate group influenced by a range of historical pressures on industrial demand (C-sector). We will never get a clean or exact partition of the real world into our ideal categories; one cannot move from a coarse and highly aggregated data set to a perfect classification of every person. But the point is not to achieve the unachievable, but to see how close we can get, to explore just how much our available information can tell us about the world in which we actually live.

We begin by taking a fairly complex structure of industrial data, organized by the government in the usual way, and reorganizing it into a relatively small number of groups. The purpose of this exercise is to help us see what we are doing and to deal with a very basic problem in the analysis of industries: What, precisely, is an industry? The word *industry* denotes a collection of economic activities; it represents a taxonomic category, a scheme of classification. But if the scheme in actual use does not distinguish between entities that are truly different, or identify and group together entities that are truly similar, then the grouping won't be very meaningful or useful for understanding what is going on in the world.

Which definition of industry should one adopt? The important thing is to design a classification scheme that efficiently organizes the information available. Ideally, we should search over all the possible classifications and choose the one that most effectively separates observations into distinct groups, chosen in such a way as to give the strongest test of the research question we are attempting to investigate.

For example, suppose you have started by assuming that change across industries does not matter to the wage structure. It is always possible, by well-chosen misaggregation, to confirm this hypothesis, to find some ordering or stratification or pattern of aggregations of the data according to which industries do not matter. A mishmash classification, averaging winners together with losers, will lack cross-group differentiation. But the results in that case are meaningless.

To achieve a meaningful test, we need to test the hypothesis that industrial groupings do not matter against that scheme of industrial classification that gives the strongest support to the counterhypothesis: if industries truly do not matter, there should exist no classification scheme—or, at least, no economically meaningful scheme—according to which they do.

The task then becomes that of discovering the strongest, most meaningful pattern of classification in the data set. No arbitrary or purely traditional classification scheme—among them, the SIC—is likely to meet this test. These schemes are descriptive, not analytical; they exist to facilitate the collection of data, not their interpretation; they are not built on any consistent analytical principles. A systematic classification scheme, one that follows a thought-through set of classification principles, usually ought to do a better job—provided, of course, that the principles and method are sound.

I have argued that industries should be classified according to their behavior. The essential element in a scheme that attempts to do this is a measure of industrial performance through time. Such a measure needs to be consistently available in highly disaggregated form. It needs to be sensitive to many different forces, including technology and trade. And it needs to hold roughly similar meaning over the full spectrum of manufacturing activity, so that the measure can be compared from one industry to the next.

In principle, one might suggest the use of industrial profits as a measure of performance. But economic theory, useful in this case, tends to discourage this. Theory suggests that capital markets smooth the flow of profits across industries, so that even persistently successful industries are unlikely to show persistently high profit rates through time. Instead, theory predicts that successful industries will expand more rapidly and experience higher capital valuations—in the financial markets, something that our industrial data sets unfortunately do not measure.

The use of production worker wage rates as an organizing principle is a more promising possibility.[6] Our rent-seeking, monopoly-sharing view of the wage process suggests that wages will rise when industries do well and stag-nate when they do badly. Even secretaries, janitors, drivers, and other service employees, whose skills are wholly transferable from one industry to another, are more likely to get a raise if they happen to work in a thriving industry than in a slumping one.[7] Thus, patterns of change in average wages across in-dustries can be, in principle, an effective tool for classification of the indus-trial structure.

But the changing average hourly wage of production workers has an obvi-ous drawback as a measure of industrial performance. It omits information on payments to salaried employees, who are not paid on an hourly basis. In many industries, the benefits of improved performance may flow dispropor-tionately to salaried workers, and the more "advanced" an industry, the larger the nonproduction employees are likely to bulk in total payroll. So it would be useful to devise a performance measure that captures the relationship be-tween production work, on the one hand, and total industrial earnings, on the other.

After several experiments, a colleague and I developed a measure that does a strikingly good job, and that is uniformly available for every industry, at every level of disaggregation, for every year in our data (1958 to 1992).[8] This is a measure of *total employee annual earnings per production worker hour by industry.* We'll call this the P-measure.

The virtues of the P-measure as a practical measure of industrial perfor-mance, easily computed from large data sets, became clear as we worked with it. In an environment where large corporations like to pay dividends in a sta-ble stream—a pattern of behavior that much of U.S. industry follows—total employee earnings will closely resemble industrial value-added. Total payroll or earnings divided by production hours is therefore closely related to indus-trial productivity, and its change is closely related to industrial productivity growth. Thus the P-measure is a good measure of how an industrial grouping is performing in principle as well as practice.[9]

Many different forces will affect the P-measure, including productivity growth but also changes in market power and position. An improvement in technology should raise total output, and total earnings, per hour spent on production. But so will a decision to move a production plant across the bor-der to Mexico. Assuming that nonproduction workers (managers, sales, R&D, and so on) are paid on average more than production workers (a safe assumption!), both effects will tend to raise earnings in the United States rel-ative to U.S. production hours. Similarly, a stronger monopoly position, or one better protected from foreign competition by trade tarriffs or quotas, may cause earnings per hour to go up. So too an increase in sales to a protected market.

On the other hand, shifts in the allocation of earnings *within* an industry, say from production workers to nonproduction workers or vice versa, do not affect the P-measure, though they would (misleadingly) affect a measure based on production worker wages alone. And since these shifts may occur because of external pressures—the strengthening or weakening of unions or federal wage standards, for instance, or of collective bargaining—they are not related to industrial performance and we don't actually want them in the P-measure. The P-measure thus nicely captures the industrial forces that may affect wages, profits, and employment, while leaving out redistributive forces that do not operate along industrial lines.

Armed with this yardstick, let us tackle the industrial structure. Changes in the P-measure through time measure changes in industrial performance. If two groups of firms experience the same pattern of gain and loss, improvement and deterioration, over a long period of time, that can only be because the wide range of forces affecting the economy through history affects both of these groups in essentially similar ways. Given a long history, we can infer that the groups themselves are essentially similar in some underlying and important aspect of their operations.

The use of history and behavior for classification is a very common, even standard practice, in other scientific disciplines where taxonomy matters. Confronted with a rock or a fossil, one of the first things a geologist or a paleontologist will do is to date it. The age of the specimen tells an enormous amount about the kind of thing it is: it cannot be too closely related to rocks or fossils that came millions of years later or millions of years before. The best-known use of these techniques has been in the study of the paleontology of dinosaurs, with revolutionary consequences for our understanding of those creatures in recent years.[10] Similarly, an epidemiologist or a clinical diagnostician will make a record of the course of symptoms of a patient and compare the course of the symptoms with the known histories of disease, in an effort to aid diagnosis or identify a mutant strain.

Economists have little tradition of classification of this kind. They are rather like the Linnaean botanists, who classified by superficial resemblance without any sense of evolution. Or they are like the doctor who examines only his patient's current symptoms, but never asks for an account of those of yesterday or the day before. Such botanists long since disappeared, and such doctors would not generally have a successful medical practice. But economists, who do little field or experimental work, have become accustomed to accepting the Dewey Decimal–like classification schemes of government accountants, without inquiring too closely into how well, or how poorly, such schemes fit the purposes of economic research.

To break out of this pattern, and to do so within the resources of a lone researcher, I too begin with a list drawn from the SIC. What I did with it, on the other hand, was unconventional. Using a list of 139 standard industrial categories,[11] I first computed the P-measure—total employee payroll per hour of production work—for each of these industries, for each year from 1958 to 1992. I next transformed this raw measure into its annual percentage rates of change, from 1959 forward. This gives a thirty-three-year history for each industrial category in the original scheme.

The next step is to ask what the relationship between these paths, or patterns of industrial performance, has been. Where two paths are similar, we form a group. Where they are distinctly and persistently different, it is likely that the underlying industries will be assigned to different groupings in the end. This is not an either-or process, of course. Rather, between each pair of observations in the original data, there is a greater or lesser degree of similarity in performance over time. What we must do is compute the relative degree of similarity across all pairs of groups[12] and organize the data to reveal the whole complex structure of similarity and difference that the original numbers possess.

This is a process that requires a great deal of computation and would be impractical without a systematic procedure and a fast computer. The procedure is cluster analysis, a technique for detecting similarity and difference. With it, we are able to bring order to our otherwise long and inchoate list of names of industrial categories, to reduce that list of 139 to a much smaller, much more coherent, and on the whole more meaningful collection of groups.[13] The technical details of our cluster analysis are discussed in the appendix to this chapter at the end of the book.

Table 6.1 shows the breakout of 139 three-digit industrial categories into seventeen industrial groups. The groups are given descriptive labels as follows: Aircraft and Communications, Chemicals, Photographic and Electronic Equipment, Bikes and Precision Equipment, Oil, Ordnance, Grains and Paper, Steel and Heavy Equipment, Construction Supplies, Machinery and Building Equipment, Cars and Metals, Printing, Low-Technology Consumer Goods, Food and Clothing, Women's Apparel, Homes-Pottery-Wool, and Tobacco-Hats.

TABLE 6.1

INDUSTRIES GROUPED BY PATTERNS OF PERFORMANCE

Short Name	SIC	Text
Low-tech Consumer Goods (LTC)	224	Narrow fabric mills
	244	Wood containers
	284	Soaps, cleaners, and toilet goods
	301	Tires and inner tubes
	306	Fabricated rubber products, n.e.c.*
	314	Footwear, except rubber
	323	Products of purchased glass
	339	Miscellaneous primary metal products
	373	Ship and boat building and repairing
	387	Watches, clocks, watchcases, and parts
Bikes and Precision Equipment	375	Motorcycles, bicycles, and parts
	382	Measuring and controlling devices
	385	Ophthalmic goods
Food and Clothing	201	Meat products
	202	Dairy products
	206	Sugar and confectionery products
	209	Miscellaneous food and kindred products
	221	Broadwoven fabric mills, cotton
	222	Broadwoven fabric mills, man-made
	225	Knitting mills
	226	Textile finishing, except wool
	227	Carpets and rugs
	228	Yarn and thread mills
	229	Miscellaneous textile goods
	232	Men's and boys' furnishings
	234	Women's and children's undergarments
	239	Miscellaneous fabricated textile products
	249	Miscellaneous wood products
	285	Paints and allied products
	311	Leather tanning and finishing
Chemicals	208	Beverages
	211	Cigarettes
	262	Papers mills
	263	Paperboard mills
	271	Newspapers
	281	Industrial inorganic chemicals
	283	Drugs
	286	Industrial organic chemicals
	287	Agricultural chemicals
	322	Glass and glassware, pressed or blown
	324	Cement, hydraulic
	355	Special industry machinery

Short Name	SIC	Text
Machinery and Building Equipment	259	Miscellaneous furniture and fixtures
	265	Paperboard containers and boxes
	282	Plastics materials and synthetics
	289	Miscellaneous chemical products
	308	Miscellaneous plastics products, n.e.c.*
	325	Structural clay products
	342	Cutlery, hand tools, and hardware
	343	Plumbing and heating, except electric
	344	Fabricated structural metal products
	345	Screw machine products, bolts, etc.
	347	Metal services, n.e.c.*
	349	Miscellaneous fabricated metal products
	354	Metalworking machinery
	356	General industrial machinery
	358	Refrigeration and service machinery
	361	Electric distribution equipment
	362	Electrical industrial apparatus
	363	Household appliances
	364	Electric lighting and wiring equipment
	394	Toys and sporting goods
Homes, Pottery, Wool	223	Broadwoven fabric mills, wool
	245	Wood buildings and mobile homes
	326	Pottery and related products
Oil	252	Office furniture
	291	Petroleum refining
	295	Asphalt paving and roofing materials
Aircraft and Communications	366	Communications equipment
	372	Aircraft and parts
Cars and Metals	329	Miscellaneous nonmetallic mineral products
	335	Nonferrous rolling and drawing
	336	Nonferrous foundries (castings)
	346	Metal forgings and stampings
	369	Miscellaneous electrical equipment and supplies
	371	Motor vehicles and equipment
Women's Apparel	233	Women's and misses' outerwear
	238	Miscellaneous apparel and accessories
	393	Musical instruments
Grains and Paper	203	Preserved fruits and vegetables
	204	Grain mill products
	205	Bakery products
	207	Fats and oils
	254	Partitions and fixtures
	261	Pulp mills
	267	Miscellaneous converted paper products
	273	Books

(continued)

TABLE 6.1 *(continued)*

Short Name	SIC	Text
Steel and Heavy Equipment	331	Blast furnaces and basic steel products
	332	Iron and steel foundries
	333	Primary nonferrous metals
	341	Metal cans and shipping containers
	351	Engines and turbines
	352	Farm and garden machinery
	353	Construction and related machinery
	374	Railroad equipment
Ordnance	348	Ordnance and accessories, n.e.c.*
	379	Miscellaneous transportation equipment
Tobacco, Hats	214	Tobacco stemming and redrying
	235	Hats, caps, and millinery
Construction Supplies	242	Sawmills and planing mills
	253	Public building and related furniture
	327	Concrete, gypsum, and plaster products
	334	Secondary nonferrous metals
Printing	236	Girls' and children's outerwear
	275	Commercial printing
	278	Blankbooks and bookbinding
	279	Printing trade servies
	359	Industrial machinery, n.e.c.*
	391	Jewelry, silverware, and plated ware
	399	Miscellaneous manufactures
Photographic and Electronic Equipment	367	Electronic components and accessories
	386	Photographic equipment and supplies

Special cases (outliers)

Cigars	212	Cigars
Tobacco	213	Chewing and smoking tobacco
Fur	237	Fur goods
Logging**	241	Logging
Periodicals**	272	Periodicals
Publishing (miscellaneous)	274	Miscellaneous publishing
Greeting cards	277	Greeting cards
Petroleum and coal**	299	Miscellaneous petroleum and coal products
Rubber and plastic footwear	302	Rubber and plastic footwear
Footwear cut stock	313	Footwear cut stock
Leather gloves	315	Leather gloves and mittens
Luggage	316	Luggage
Handbags	317	Handbags and personal leather goods
Leather, n.e.c.*	319	Leather goods, n.e.c.*
Computers**	357	Computer and office equipment
Audiovideo**	365	Household audio and video equipment
Missiles**	376	Guided missiles, space vehicles, parts
Search and navigation	381	Search and navigation equipment
Medical**	384	Medical instruments and supplies

Short Name	SIC	Text
Probable misclassifications		
	395	Pens, pencils, office, and art supplies
	231	Men's and boys' suits and coats
	243	Millwork, plywood, and structural members
	251	Household furniture
	276	Manifold business forms
	396	Costume jewelry and notions
	328	Cut stone and stone products

*n.e.c. = not elsewhere classified.
**indicates used in inequality calculations.

Most of these groups are recognizable as cohesive, internally at least somewhat similar, and mutually distinct. In some cases, such as the inclusion of beverages and cigarettes (and possibly newspapers as distinct from other printing) in the chemicals grouping, the classification scheme has analytical force. In others, the results may look surprising at first, less so on reflection. For instance, girls' and children's outerwear seems oddly assorted with printing, and far removed from other garment trades and even from the larger body of women's clothing.[14] But what are girls' and children's outerwear, if not—prints? Too, the similarity of aircraft and communications equipment manufacture is at least suggestive: both of these industries are highly concentrated, and both supply advanced goods to operators of networks.[15]

A few clusters (Homes-Pottery-Wool; Tobacco-Hats) are evidently grab-bags of miscellany. Not every parallel path in history is linked by organic necessity, yet even here, the fact that these products are all made substantially by hand may explain their similar patterns of industrial performance through time. The bicycle-motorbike grouping includes measuring and controlling devices (actually, a larger industry) and ophthalmic products for no reason known to me. Pens and pencils associate with food and clothing, and there is no clear reason why men's suits should align with cars. A few small categories such as toys, cut stone, and musical instruments also turn up where they might not be expected.

No classification scheme based purely on numerical techniques will ever satisfy every critic. But this is unnecessary. The scheme does not need to be perfect; it needs only to be good for a purpose. And this one is successful for the purpose we seek, for it succeeds at distinguishing between major modes or processes of production. One can pick at it here and there, but from this standpoint, it makes only a few incontrovertible mistakes, and most of these involve minor industries with few employees. Compared to the arbitrary accounting categories of the SIC, this scheme is characterized for the most part by intuitive good sense. And because it is based systematically on a common measurement and classification technique, it has what the standard schemes lack: a rationale. For this reason, I have resisted the temptation to "fix" even the more obvious "errors," except in some very minor cases where they would merely clutter the table. Rather, I present the whole classification scheme as it emerged from the computer, in the belief that, warts and all, the internal consistency of these groupings will strike the fairminded reader as impressive.

In addition to the seventeen groups, we have another nineteen individual industries, whose performance on the P-measure so deviated from all of the others that they could not be grouped together under the same principles of numerical similarity. Some of these outliers are evidently similar to each other: a number are drawn from different aspects of the leather trades, and others are part of the tobacco industry. A few are spun out from printing: periodical and miscellaneous publishing and greeting cards. A half-dozen others are simply idiosyncratic, full stop: computers, missiles, search and navigation equipment, logging, audiovideo equipment, medical supplies. In what follows, we treat the large idiosyncrasies as special cases and ignore the smaller ones.

Let's take a step back and ask, Do these classification results tell us anything directly about how differences in industrial performance occur? In general terms, I think they do. An impressive fraction of industrial categories are grouped together according to the nature of the production processes that they employ. Thus, chemical processes are strikingly uniform, in their patterns of industrial performance through time, over a wide range of differing types of product. Food and textiles—processed agricultural products—fall into a single closely knit pattern. The exceptions are grains and paper, which are processed on a strikingly larger scale and are grouped together, perhaps for that reason. Machinery resembles other machinery more than it resembles anything else. Here the exception is in the case of particularly heavy machinery, which resembles iron and steel. Car manufacture resembles (and probably dominates) a range of forging, stamping, and foundry sectors; printing and plating seem to be grouped together. In all of these cases, the dominant principle appears to be commonality of process rather than similarity in final market or the particular nature of the final product.

Table 6.2 presents information on employment for the seventeen groupings plus computers, missiles, logging, audiovideo, medical equipment, and periodical publishing. The machinery sector, cars and metals, and the group of ordinary (low-tech) consumer goods producers are among the largest employers. Chemicals, steel and heavy equipment, aircraft and communications, food and clothing are all smaller, in the range of a million workers apiece. The groups covering photographic and electronic equipment and the manufacture of computers are smaller still.

The table also tracks the evolution of employment across selected major groupings through time. Its most prominent feature is the very sharp decline in employment in three large groups from the late 1970s through the early 1980s: machinery and building materials, cars and metals, and steel and heavy equipment (which together lost over a million workers). Low-tech consumer goods have lost as much employment as the car-and-metals group-

TABLE 6.2

EMPLOYMENT BY INDUSTRIAL GROUP, SELECTED YEARS
(In Thousands)

Year	1958	1970	1980	1992
Machinery and Building Supplies	2595.4	3418.8	3824.2	3439.7
Food and Clothing	2325.2	2475	2312	2088.6
Cars and Metals	1690.8	2105.2	2184.7	1959.2
Chemicals	1397.9	1598.9	1688.1	1476.2
Printing	730.8	914.6	1127.1	1257.5
Grains and Paper	878.6	874.7	875.5	1059.4
Steel and Heavy Equipment	1317.8	1555.5	1543.8	815.5
Aircraft and Communications	860.3	1110.3	1146.7	786.7
Low-tech Consumer Goods	758	812.4	811.8	657.1
Electronics and Photographic Equipment	258.1	452.3	612.5	607.3
Construction	462.6	426.3	440.3	385.6
Women's Apparel	436.4	498.2	542.1	352.7
Bikes and Precision Equipment	146.4	201	276.3	314.2
Computers	121.6	221.7	381.4	248.6
Medical Supplies	41.7	77.6	129.8	263.3
Missiles	248	212.7	140.7	149.3
Oil	192.6	172	187.3	168.4
Periodicals	66.7	77.1	77.8	116.7
Homes-Pottery-Wool	122.9	142.6	126.2	105.9
Ordnance	56.5	211.5	117	109.8
Logging	71.7	76.1	96.5	83.8
Audiovideo Equipment	73.9	108.4	87.5	
Tobacco-Hats	50.4	29.3	29.1	25.6

ing, but more smoothly over time. In very modest contrast, employment in printing and in electronics has been on an upward trend, while that in computers rose in the early 1980s before falling in the second half of the decade. Overall, employment in manufacturing declined by about 3 million workers from 1979 through 1992.

Figure 6.1 summarizes employment trends in manufacturing over the entire period from 1958 through 1992. This was a time when overall employment in the economy nearly doubled, from 65 to 118 million persons, equivalent to a reading of 1.8 on the horizontal scale of this diagram. In comparison, manufacturing employment has grown very little during the four decades since Dwight Eisenhower left office. Major industrial sectors, such as food and clothing, consumer goods, women's apparel, home building, aircraft and communications, and oil, have fewer employees than they did a generation ago. Chemicals and cars and metals have scarcely more. A few big losers include steel and heavy equipment, missiles, and the tobacco group. (Some of these changes, perhaps, are not to be regretted.)

Overall, the shift in employment shares across industries does not appear

FIGURE 6.1

EMPLOYMENT CHANGE, 1958–1992

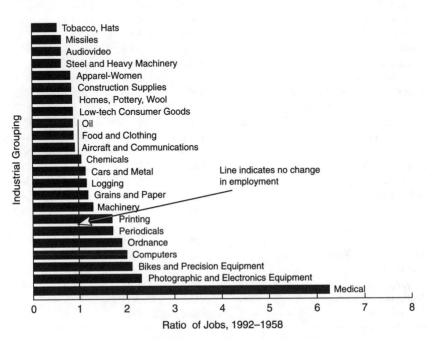

to be closely related to our measure of industrial performance. The largest declines in employment are not in the sectors with the highest rates of productivity growth. Equally, some of the slower-growing groupings, such as chemicals, have fairly high rates of productivity growth, while in others, such as steel, the relative rate of change of productivity seems to have been comparatively slow.

The greater part of employment changes is therefore probably due to shifts in the composition of demand, changes in technology, and displacement by imports. The major employment growth in manufacturing has been very strongly oriented toward information processing: computers, electronics, and printing and publishing among them. But there are also demand shifts straightforwardly related to changing patterns of consumption. Medical equipment, a small sector with a sixfold increase in total employment over thirty-five years, outstrips them all, a fact that doubtless reflects the rising expenditures of Medicare, Medicaid, and private insurance plans on health care, especially for the elderly.

So how well did these industrial groups do? Figure 6.2 presents the cumulative change in the P-measure over the thirty-four-year period, for each of the seventeen major groupings and all nineteen of the special cases. This figure gives a comprehensive and numerically precise relative ranking of American industrial performance. From it, we can read the names of the winners and losers in the industrial structure, in order, and gain some sense of the difference in degree of cumulative performance gain between them.

At the top of the performance ranking are computers—no surprise there—followed by missiles and search and navigation equipment. Aircraft and communications rank high, as do chemicals, photographic and electronic equipment, bikes and precision instruments, and medical supplies. Here, broadly, are the most knowledge-intensive elements of the K-sector. Lower down on the list we find the heavy industrial and agricultural sectors: steel and machinery, grains and paper, industrial machinery, cars and metals. These are better classified as mass-produced durable goods, whether purchased primarily by consumers, by business, or for export. Lower still come the strictly-for-the-consumer goods-producing sectors: low-tech consumer goods, food and clothing, women's apparel. Footwear and furs come along at the bottom.

A few (tiny) special-case industries provide some interesting perspectives. We observe the very high relative performance of various tobacco-related sectors (close to chemicals, where the largest single element of this industry, cigarettes, is to be found). Handbags and luggage are characteristic examples of

FIGURE 6.2

INDUSTRIAL PERFORMANCE, 1958–1992

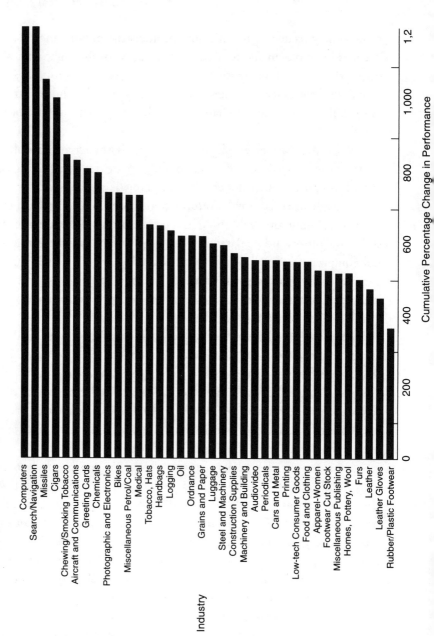

product transformation over a generation, as leather gave way to nylon and other synthetic fabrics, hard shell suitcases to soft shoulder bags.

Figure 6.3 provides some historical perspective on changing industrial performance for selected clusters. The graph shows that the great divergence across clusters is of recent vintage. Through the 1960s, productivity in most American industries rose at comparatively uniform rates. Only in the 1970s do large gaps between the winners and the losers begin to appear. In the 1980s computers begin their ascent to the stratosphere, when compared with the performance of all other sectors. The graph reveals the improving relative position of aircraft and communications in the early 1980s, and the slumping position at the same time of the steel and machinery sector. Steel and machinery began the decade on a par with chemicals and ended it on a par with the cars and metals and food and clothing clusters. Rubber and plastic footwear, a trivial industry, is included to show the lower bound of U.S. manufacturing performance.

Once again, what does this broad-brush comparison of industrial performance tell us? In the most general terms, it suggests that industries that produced advanced equipment of many different kinds did very well in the

FIGURE 6.3

INDUSTRIAL PERFORMANCE THROUGH TIME

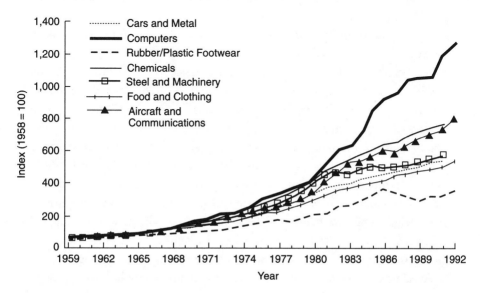

United States over the past forty years, while industries producing hand goods did poorly. Between these extremes, we find the broad spectrum of consumer goods and industrial machinery sectors, with processed goods toward the top of the range and hand assembly toward the bottom. There are exceptions to this generalization—tobacco and greeting cards, as we have seen—but they tend to be minor.[16]

The historical pattern of Figure 6.3 tells us that the great divergences in industrial performance revealed in the sweeping summary of Figure 6.2 are not universals of history. They are in fact comparatively recent. From 1958 through 1970, virtually all industries show remarkably compressed and nearly equal performance trends; there is little divergence that can be characterized on technological or any other grounds. It is only after 1970 that the great dispersions open up and the K-sector begins its rise in comparative terms. Only after 1970. The question immediately arises whether divergences in industrial performance and the great increase in inequality of wages that also begins around 1970 may be linked.

So if the K-sector has, since 1970, outperformed the C-sector in terms of changing payroll per productive hour—essentially a measure of the change in value-added per hour—does this translate into actual employee earnings? Not surprisingly, the answer is yes. Figure 6.4 presents the relationship between industrial performance, measured over the whole span from 1958 through 1992, and the growth in the average annual earnings of all employees in each industrial grouping. The figure reveals a phenomenon that we will meet several times: a two-part or split pattern in the relationship between performance and pay.

Notice first the industrial groups at the top of the diagram—those whose growth in nominal average annual earnings over the thirty-four years exceeds about 6.5 times and whose industrial performance has improved by a factor of seven or more.[17] This group includes computers (on the far right of the diagram), missiles, aircraft and communications, photographic and electronic equipment, bikes and precision equipment, chemicals, and medical supplies. For this group, the relationship between changing industrial performance and the improvement in total employee earnings is nearly horizontal. While average earnings gains per employee are higher here than elsewhere, they top out below a value of 7.5. Performance gains, on the other hand, frequently exceed eight times and range as high as thirteen. Overall, the variation in performance change for this meta-grouping of manufacturing industries is far greater than the variation in the change of average employee earnings.

An almost opposite pattern characterizes the remaining industrial group-

FIGURE 6.4

EARNINGS AND INDUSTRIAL PERFORMANCE
1985–1992

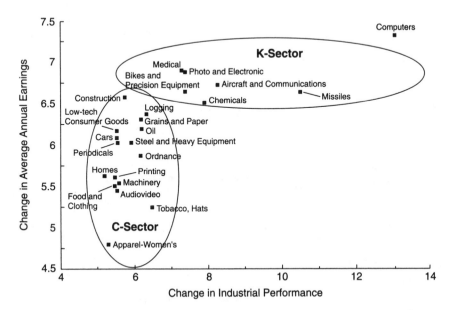

ings, whose nominal performance gain is less than a factor of eight and whose average nominal earnings gain is less than a factor of 6.5. This set of groups, from construction, logging, oil, and grains and paper at the top of the diagram, to women's apparel at the bottom, experienced a much narrower range of performance improvement that tends to be a much better predictor of total earnings variation.

The set to the upper right is our knowledge economy. It is a set of industries that have performed well, hence a high general level of average earnings gain. But beyond this, it is also the set of industries that are transforming themselves most rapidly over this time, a transformation visible in these data mainly as an increase in the proportion of salaried, nonproduction workers they employ and the resulting rightward distribution of these industries across the chart. The set to the lower left is our consumption sector. It contains the industries mainly producing mass consumer products and standard industrial supplies. Here the share of nonproduction workers in total payroll has been rising much less rapidly, if at all. This comparatively low rate of transformation, in most parts of the C-sector, explains the relative uniformity of performance rankings in this part of the diagram.[18]

FIGURE 6.5

WAGES AND INDUSTRIAL PERFORMANCE, 1958–1992

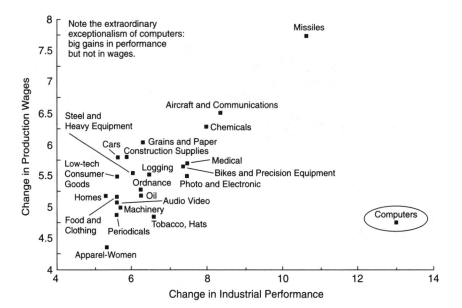

While Figure 6.4 is based on the average earnings of all employees for each industrial grouping, including salaried and nonproduction employees, Figure 6.5 narrows the focus to the relationship between industrial performance and the wages of production workers. As the theory of industry-specific labor rents predicts, production workers share in the performance gains of their industries. Here, indeed, an approximately linear relationship is very clear: missiles, aircraft and communications, and chemicals at the top on both measures, women's apparel at the bottom, and the rest spread out in between.

The difference between the two figures suggests that the distinction between the K-sector and the C-sector mainly affects *the share of total pay earned by nonproduction workers.* The distinguishing feature of the K-sector is a sharp increase in this share: between 1970 and 1992, it rose from 50 to 56 percent of payroll in aircraft, from 55 to 66 percent in communications, from 47 to 57 percent in electronic components, and from 50 to 80 percent—a huge jump—in computers. By contrast, in a typical C-sector industry, such as motor vehicles, the share of total payroll going to nonproduction workers was both much lower and more stable. In the motor vehicle sector, it actually fell from 24 to 23 percent.

This shift in K-sector payrolls is a combination of two things: an increase in the relative pay of nonproduction workers and an increase in the proportion of total employment off of the production lines. Of these, the first is to be found throughout all branches of manufacturing; there is a rise in relative pay of salaried workers that does not appear to be strongly industry specific. The second is the thing that really distinguishes the K-sector. The proportion of nonproduction workers in total employment was below 40 percent in almost all sectors in 1958. By 1992 it was characteristically around half even in such large K-sector groupings as aircraft, and considerably higher than that in some others. This was partly due to a rise in the absolute numbers of nonproduction workers, and partly to a decline in the production component, some of which was caused by internationalization of production processes in this sector. Thus nonproduction employees rose from 42 to 48 percent of employment in aircraft from 1970 to 1992, from 32 to 40 percent in electronics, from 45 to 53 percent in drugs, and from 45 to 64 percent in computers. In motor cars, the proportion stayed constant at 19 percent, a figure typical for the C-sector.

K-sector production workers started out in 1970 with wages that were a relatively high fraction of those of their own salaried colleagues. This premium was about twofold in such low-wage, labor-intensive manufactures as women's apparel, food and clothing, and footwear, but within a range of just 20 to 40 percent for high-wage, salary-dominated groups such as aircraft and communications, chemicals, and publishing.[19] Over the years from 1970 to 1992, the premium paid to nonproduction over production workers rose in most of American industry, and by very similar amounts—generally 10 to 20 percent. But in some parts of the K-sector, including aircraft, communications, and chemicals, it actually did not rise at all. Thus, surviving production workers in these particular high-wage industries actually did better, relative to salaried workers, than they did in industries that did not expand their nonproduction employment. Because their sectors have done relatively well, so have they. K-sector production workers have captured part of the rents that improved industrial performance and strengthened monopoly power have earned. It follows that what has really transformed the K-sector since 1970 has been the increased relative employment of nonproduction workers, something virtually invisible in the C-sector.

Figure 6.6 compares cumulative gains in average employee earnings directly to cumulative gains in production worker wages for the period 1958 through 1992. The figure shows that for industries in the C-sector, which are dominated by production workers, changes in total earnings and changes in production wages are closely correlated. Virtually everywhere, gains in hourly production wages lagged behind the change in total earnings; the salaried classes gained on the workers. But the proportions are similar across industries; they all seem to fall just moderately above the diagonal that would indicate equal improvement, and they reflect the common increase in the relative pay of salaried workers compared to production workers. On the other hand, differences in cumulative gains across industries appear larger. The bigger gaps in this part of the diagram are between construction supplies and women's apparel, affecting production workers and nonproduction workers alike in these sectors.[20]

When we move up the stem to the K-sector, however, the correlation between gains in production wages and gains in total earnings disappears. Within the K-sector, production workers face a range of outcomes ordered along a spectrum. The spectrum runs from the most worker-friendly (missiles, so help us), to moderately so (aircraft, chemicals), to the distinctly unfriendly photo-electronics and medical groupings, and to computers, the least friendly of all.[21] Only salaried workers do consistently well in these most

FIGURE 6.6

AVERAGE EARNINGS AND PRODUCTION WAGES, 1958–1992

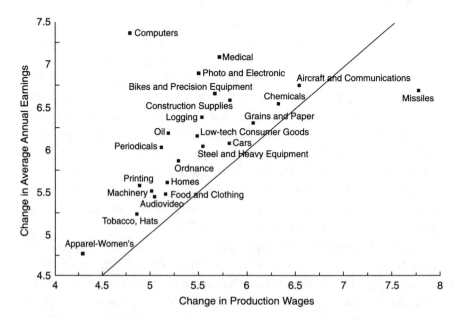

unstable, most dynamic parts of the K-sector, which appear to combine the worst features of monopolism and cutthroat competition, at least from the production worker's point of view.

This analysis teaches that the knowledge and consumption sectors of the industrial economy are not conjectures. They exist. They can be picked out of the data. Particular groups of industries can be assigned to one or the other.[22] The behavior of these two great sectors differs mainly with respect to their nonproduction workers. The internal employment structure of the C-sector appears today not very different from a generation ago. That in the K-sector, on the other hand, is totally transformed.

The concentration of this transformation of employment inside the K-sector is a telling argument against a one-size-fits-all vision of "skill-biased technological change" affecting labor demand throughout the economy. If new technologies were truly driving an increased demand for skill, then technology-using industries—the manufacturers of consumer goods—would be increasing their share of (computer-using) nonproduction employees as much as everyone else. But they are not doing this. Although nonproduction salary premiums increased in the C-sector, relative employment did not; C-sector firms appear stuck in the old-fashioned business of employing production workers to make consumption goods.

This behavior is consistent with a general shift across industries in the power of managers relative to production workers. It is not consistent with a skill-biased demand-for-labor model, which would be obliged to predict rising relative employment of skilled salaried employees in technology-using sectors. Conversely, in some parts of the K-sector, we also find that relative employment of nonproduction workers increased while their relative pay did not. This is again inconsistent with the demand-for-labor model. But it is consistent with the idea that the K-sector generally divides the benefits of its industrially based, technologically driven monopoly power between its production workers, on the one hand, and an expanding corpus of nonproduction employees, on the other. This is behavior we do not observe in the C-sector.

The notion of skill bias in technological change would thus appear restricted to those few parts of the K-sector where both relative wages and relative employment of nonproduction employees strongly increased—something that is especially characteristic of just one industry: the *production* of computers. This is a restriction on the applicability of the skill-bias notion that no economist has yet advanced or defended. And if not skill bias, something else must explain the employment transformation of K-sector industries. What else can explain it? An increase in the monopolistic power of K-sector firms, combined with a propensity to distribute monopolistic rents to those parts of the enterprise concerned with research, development, administration, financial control, advertising, and similar activities, explains it very well.

This analysis thus suggests three distinct and cross-cutting sources of increased inequality in wages and salaries. First, there is a general increase in the differential between production and nonproduction workers; this reflects a general shift in the balance of power after 1970 toward management and away from labor. Second, there is a shift toward the employment of a fairly small number of highly paid salaried employees in the K-sector; this is well explained as resulting from the disposition of increased monopoly rents earned in the sector.

Third, for those production workers who survive in the K-sector, alongside their far more numerous colleagues in manufacturing at large, the evolution of wages has depended heavily on the dispersion of industrial performance. The K-sector industries dominate on the performance measure, and the relative wages of production workers in this sector have improved to a comparable extent. But why? How is it that patterns of industrial performance, which were so very similar across industries for the dozen years before 1970, suddenly and radically diverged in the twenty-two years that followed? Can we pick out the precise moments that this occurred, and to whom? Can we identify the particular patterns of interindustrial divergence in performance that evidently lie behind the final realignment of production wages and the great splitting of the K-sector from the C-sector? Can we, in other words, isolate the forces of history that drove this upheaval? I believe all of this is possible; indeed it is the next phase of this study.

7

THE PATTERNS OF
INDUSTRIAL CHANGE

The discovery, and useful application of machinery, always
leads to the increase of the net produce of the country . . . [but]
the opinion entertained by the laboring class, that the employment of machinery is frequently detrimental to their interests,
is not founded on prejudice or error, but is conformable to the
correct principles of political economy.

—David Ricardo, *On the Principles of Political Economy and Taxation,*
3d edition, Chapter XXXI

L et me recap the analysis to this point. First, we identified a set
of distinct industrial groups, based on similarities and differences in industrial performance through time. We identified a broad relationship between capital goods providers, capital goods users, and service
providers, to help guide our expectations about the relationship between industrial performance and wages. We showed that these distinctions are useful
in interpreting the performance of industries and the behavior of both earnings and wages across industrial groups. Particularly since 1970, the U.S.
manufacturing sector has evolved in ways that strongly differentiate the technology providers from technology-using industries in practice, mainly because performance was better in the K-sector and also, as theory predicts, the
monopolistic earnings from this superior performance flowed to nonproduction workers in the K-sector, sharply and especially increasing their relative
numbers.

But while all of this is suggestive, it falls short of a systematic approach to finding the sources of industrial change. We have learned, for instance, that production workers in the aircraft and communications sectors did comparatively well mainly because the sector within which they worked did comparatively well.[1] We have seen that this pattern of increasing dispersion in industrial performance begins around 1970, which is in line with the larger increases in measured inequality of wages and incomes. But we have not yet come to grips, precisely, with the causes of this change or with how it played out over time.

This chapter presents a study of the evolution of the American industrial structure from 1958 to 1992, of the sources of difference in industrial performance across groups. Of these, it turns out, the four most important appear to be the cycle of business investment, the scale or volume of consumption, trade protectionism, and military procurement.

Our task is to examine the driving forces behind the divergence in industrial performance that, as we have observed, hit the U.S. economy following 1970. What caused the industrial structure, whose performance up to that point had progressed more or lessly evenly and consistently across industrial groupings, to break apart?

Remember that our economic groups are internally as similar as possible, yet externally they are as different as they can be made to be. This is a useful property, for it enables us to focus on the variations in industrial performance *between* our major groupings, while ignoring the smaller variations *within* each of these groups.[2] The variations between groups are the basic forces that, because they affect the different industrial groupings systematically and in differing ways, account for most of the dispersion in industrial performance that we have observed.

Four such forces account for just over 60 percent of the total variation.[3] The first eight figures in this chapter make the case for identification of these four forces. In each case we have two types of reinforcing evidence. The first is a kind of score: How important was the force in question, in relative terms, to each industrial group? By looking at this pattern of *canonical scores,* we can often make an educated guess about the nature of the thing we are looking at. Indeed, the scores can be plotted against total performance change for each grouping, or against changes in wages or average earnings, in ways that powerfully reveal not only the relative importance of each force for each group of industries, but also the contribution of that force to the overall pattern of divergence in industrial performance.

I name the first and most important force "technology." Figure 7.1 presents the reasons. On the vertical axis we see the cumulative performance change of American industries, from 1958 through 1992, measured by the P-measure and ranked as they are from computers at one extreme to home building at the other.

On the horizontal axis we have the group scores for each industry in terms of the first force ("canonical root"), which accounts for 24 percent of the variation in between-group industrial performance over the thirty-four years. Notice that aircraft and communications equipment are at the top of the pile. Computers, medical supplies, missiles, and electronics rank high, followed by chemicals, grains and paper, and then by a mass of less dynamic clusters. Ordnance, substantially unchanged since World War II, and home building (likewise) bring up the bottom of the list. My case that this force reflects the main patterns of technological change is based substantially on commonsense evaluation of this ranking of relative scores.

The figure illustrates that a high ranking on the technology force is associated with strong industrial performance over time. This reflects two things: the fact that the movement of this force accounts for nearly a quarter of all variations in industrial performance, and the fact that the association is positive. Not all industrial performance is accounted for by a strong ranking on this force. Something else, some other pattern of forces, is clearly at work in

FIGURE 7.1

TECHNOLOGY AND PERFORMANCE, 1958–1992

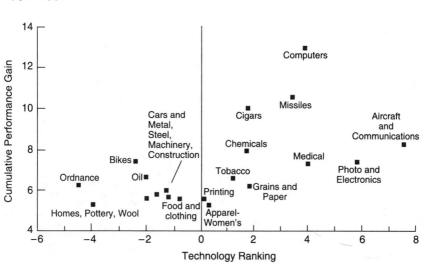

the performance of the computer sector, for example. The same is true, less importantly, of missiles, and in the trivial case of cigars, both of them strongly affected by the peculiar global politics of the cold war. But a common pattern of movement through time clearly does explain a lot of the variation in industrial performance, and it is therefore interesting to ask what that pattern of movement through time corresponds to in history.

The second type of evidence addresses this question. It is a close match between the pattern captured by a canonical root and particular historical time series. Figure 7.2 compares the technology force to a measure of change in investment over time.[4] The close correspondence is not accidental. Investment is the way in which new technologies are incorporated into the capital stock and into economic life. Thus a close correspondence between these two series is exactly what one should expect, if the hypothesis linking the first force to the progress of technology is correct.

Technology is multidimensional, and I do not claim that all aspects of technological change are wholly encapsulated in the single ranking of Figure 7.1. But the pattern of Figure 7.2 does seem to capture the essential flow and ebb of new technologies into new investment and into the capital stock. It

FIGURE 7.2

TECHNOLOGY AND INVESTMENT

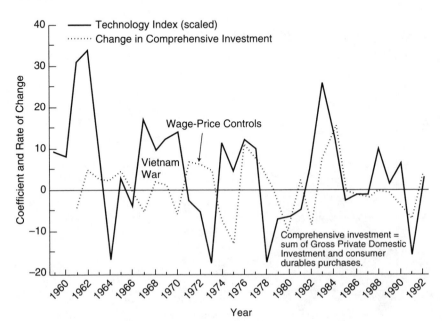

FIGURE 7.3

CONSUMPTION AND PERFORMANCE, 1958-1992

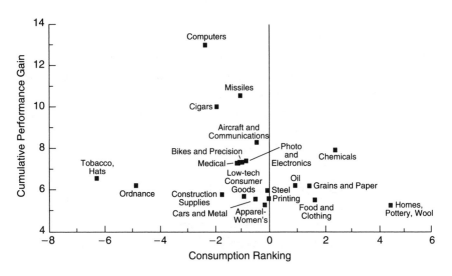

therefore provides a way to give precise measure to two phenomena: variation in the uptake of technological progress through time and the relative importance of technology across industries. It shows, beyond reasonable doubt, that the cycle of investment is the cycle of technological uptake.

The second force accounts for an additional 14 percent of the variation in industrial performance across clusters.[5] Figure 7.3 ranks our major groups and a few outliers according to their scores on this force. The high scorers here are very different from the previous diagram: homes, chemicals, food and clothing, grains and paper, and oil. The low scores, as before, go to ordnance and to tobacco and hats.

Figure 7.3 differs from 7.1 in another striking way. This time, there is little clear association between a high score and the cumulative performance of the industry, but overall the association that exists seems to be negative. Industries that were strongly responsive to this force did not do well, the reason being that the force itself was comparatively weak, and grew weaker as the period progressed. The contrast between the first and second forces through time is thus a contrast between a winning and a losing pattern of performance.

In contrast with the technology-intensive and investment-sensitive rankings of the first force, the second appears to be picking up the force of variation in consumer demand. The industries that score high tend to be producers of basic consumer goods (housing, food, clothing, gasoline). With the exception of home building, they also tend to be continuous-process industries, whose basic method of operation consists of moving a liquid or granular product through pipes. The performance of such industries, measured by earnings per production-worker-hour, will be particularly sensitive to fluctuations in demand, since it requires nearly the same number of production hours to operate a distillery at a low volume as at a high one.

Figure 7.4 compares the time pattern of variation on this force to the annual change in the consumption of nondurable goods and services over the same period of time. The patterns are once again close. It appears that the forces making for variation in the consumption of nondurable goods and services are indeed the forces driving the variation in this second pattern of industrial change.

For this reason, I have associated this force with the scale of operation of the economy as a whole and have named it "consumption." As Figure 7.4 shows, the growth of consumption was much more robust in the late 1960s than at any time since. Consumption growth has been falling off for over a

FIGURE 7.4

CONSUMPTION SPENDING AND PERFORMANCE

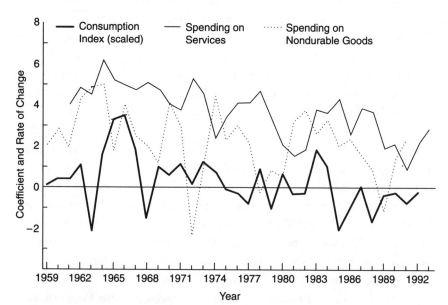

FIGURE 7.5

PROTECTION AND PERFORMANCE

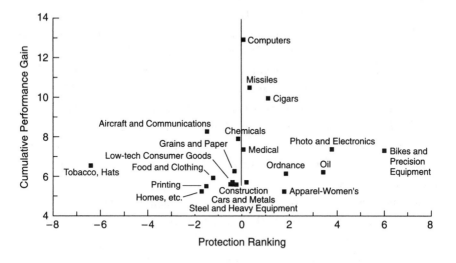

decade, since reaching a small peak in the year of the Reagan reelection boom, 1984.

The third force adds another 11 percent of explanation to the variation in interindustrial performance. Figure 7.5 compares scores on this force, once again.

The industries scoring highest on this index include motorbikes, electronics, oil, ordnance, and apparel. What do these groups have in common? The answer, I believe, is that they have all benefited to an unusual degree from policies of restriction on international trade. Apparel was first protected in the 1960s under the multifiber agreement. Oil was protected until the early 1970s by import quotas and in the 1970s by the effects of Project Independence, Richard Nixon's plan to insulate the country from the power of the Organization of Petroleum Exporting Countries (OPEC). Motorbikes benefited in the 1980s from special trade protection to ensure survival of the premier American manufacturer, Harley-Davidson. Ordnance is purchased domestically for national security reasons. And since the mid-1980s electronics has been the object of intensive and continuing government intervention, to restore the technological vitality of the sector, and to secure an increased market share for the American industry in Japan.

For these reasons, the third force is labeled "protection." It appears to be a crude index of the effectiveness of nontariff barriers to international trade. Its time pattern traces the ebb and flow of the value of protectionism strategy over the past three decades, with high points in the 1960s and 1980s and a short but sharp peak in the mid-1970s.

What determines the changing value through time of trade protection to the workers in strongly protected industries? A reasonable possibility is the exchange rate. The force of protection is most strongly felt during periods when the value of the dollar has been high, as it was during the 1960s and 1980s. At such times, the competitive pressure of imports hits hardest, placing downward pressure on the wages of import-competing industries that are not protected. It is therefore at such times that protectionist policies have their highest value for those industries that are the beneficiaries of strongly protective policies.

It is not easy to find appropriate time-series data with which to evaluate this conjecture. Among other things, the Dallas Federal Reserve's broadly based trade-weighted real exchange rate (RX101) is available only for years after the mid-1970s. Figure 7.6 presents a comparison of the third force with a longer but less satisfactory series: the trade-weighted exchange rate of the

FIGURE 7.6

PROTECTION AND THE EXCHANGE RATE

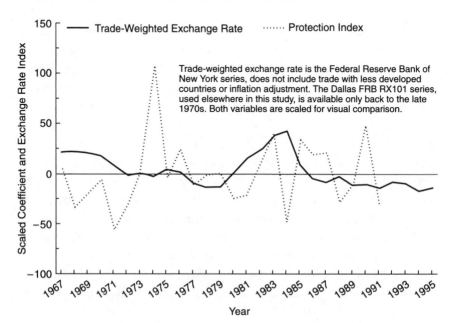

FIGURE 7.7

PROCUREMENT AND PERFORMANCE

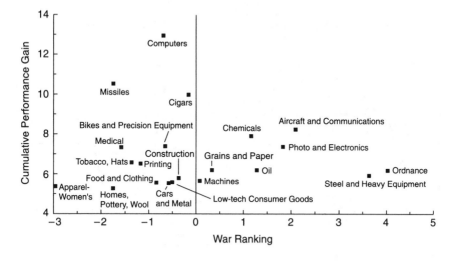

dollar computed with respect to the major industrial trading partners of the United States, readily available back to 1967. The match is far from perfect; nevertheless, the sharp rise in both series in the early 1980s, and several other co-occurring turning points, suggests that a relationship is not out of the question. The odd behavior of the third force in the early 1970s is perhaps partly explained by the wild shifts in direct trade policies in that period, including export controls in 1971–1972 and the oil-independence drive on which Richard Nixon embarked in 1973–1974; this is of course also the moment when the modern flexible exchange rate system took shape.

The fourth force accounts for a bit less than 10 percent of the variation in industrial performance. The high-scoring industries are ordnance, chemicals, oil, steel, electronics, and aircraft. Homes, medical supplies, and apparel score among the lowest. Figure 7.7 illustrates this pattern. Figure 7.8 compares the time sequence of this force to the obvious candidate cause: the pattern of federal expenditures on the military. The two comparisons leave little doubt: the fourth force on industrial performance is military procurement.[6]

Together, the first four forces account for about 60 percent of all the variation in industrial performance in American manufacturing industry, as measured across this particular sorting of industries into groups. There are another four forces that are significant in a statistical sense, but they contribute little to the explanation, in part because they capture distinctive

FIGURE 7.8

DEFENSE ROOT AND DEFENSE PRODUCTION

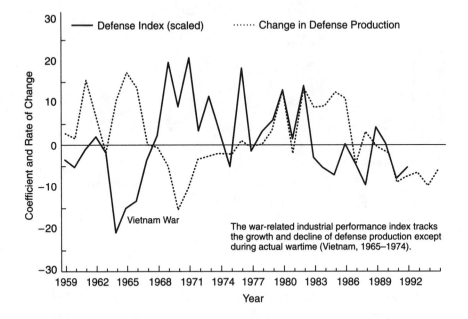

The war-related industrial performance index tracks the growth and decline of defense production except during actual wartime (Vietnam, 1965–1974).

movements of only a few small industries. (Ordnance, a truly idiosyncratic industry, ranks high on several of these.) It seems fair to conclude that in investment, consumption, protection, and war, we have the four most important forces determining differences in the way industries have performed in America since 1958.

We may next examine the cumulative effect of these four forces—how they played out not just from one year to the next but as the years unfolded. Figure 7.9 presents a way to do so. In this figure, I convert the annual pattern of raw coefficients into a cumulated variable that resembles an index number. Thus the effects of past impulses are preserved and carried forward as the series advances in time.[7]

The figure reveals that the even and consistent progress of American industry in the first decade of the period under study was made possible because all four of the principal forces advanced together during that time. Technology advanced alongside consumer spending, which increased under the spur of tax cuts, economic growth, and the War on Poverty. The cold war kept the war industries healthy. And trade protection relieved competitive

FIGURE 7.9

FORCES ON INDUSTRIAL PERFORMANCE

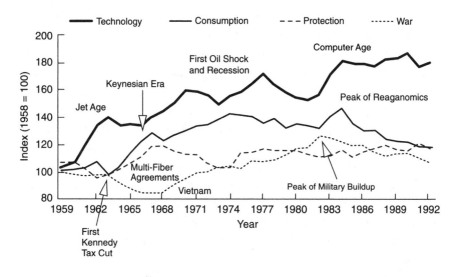

pressure on the weakest sectors, of which at that time apparel and oil were leading examples.

After 1970, however, technology is the only major force with a consistently positive effect on the performance of American industries. The progress of technology comes in great waves, each lifting the most technology-intensive industries (the K-sector) to a new crest—with the last such crest coming in the investment expansion of the Reagan-era boom.

After the mid-1970s, decline sets in for the next two most important forces. The growth of consumer spending tails off, under the impact of repeated recessions and episodic increases in the prices of oil and food and in the interest rates on which housing finance depends. The Reagan tax cuts of the early 1980s create a partial revival in the consumer sectors, but it is neither strong by historical standards nor long-lasting, and the decline that follows is sharp and unrelieved. After the high-water mark of the multifiber agreements, trade protection becomes inefficient and of diminishing importance—though it is still valuable to a small number of strongly protected industries when the massive overvaluation of the dollar hits American manufacturing in the early 1980s.[8] After the Vietnam War, arms exports and a military buildup keep the defense sectors going for another decade, but by 1984 these industries are also beginning a decade of decline.

As a result of this divergence in forces, the synchrony of industrial performance across industrial clusters breaks apart and is never restored. Instead, we have the pattern of separation observed in the figures. Industries strongly based on knowledge and on the monopoly power of new technology and oriented toward global as well as domestic markets continue to perform well. In 1959 about 4 million workers were employed in civilian manufacturing industries that rank highest on the technology ranking (chemicals, aircraft and communications, photographic and electronic equipment, computers, grains and paper); by 1992 this number stood at 4.4 million, not a small number. On the other hand, total employment in the United States in 1992 came to some 120 million, so the effect of a redistribution toward the K-sector must truly be a massive funneling of income from the many the few.[9]

Thus we see what specifically causes industries to gain or lose relative position. Responsiveness to the investment cycle, variations in consumption, the exchange rate, and variations in military expenditure are the first four factors that distinguish between the winners and the losers on the American industrial scene.

Once again, we have looked at the sources of change through time in American industrial performance. And what have we found? We have found the traces of the main macroeconomic and policy changes of the past generation. These are, first and foremost, the heightened instability and more rapidly churning business cycle brought on mainly by unstable monetary policy—by the actions of the Federal Reserve—in the years following 1970. Second, we find the effect of slower growth, and the squeeze on American wages and living standards, turning up in a pattern of poor performance for industries most sensitive to consumption demand. Third, we have found the effects of trade protection, albeit strongly affecting a handful of industries, which fluctuate with the exchange value of the dollar. And finally we detect the traces of military spending on industrial performance.

Macroeconomic and political causes of change in wage inequality are mediated, at the industry level, by the filtering and polarizing forces of technology, scale intensity, trade sensitivity, and war. Government policy did not determine, for the most part, which industries would be most strongly affected by which forces. But neither can the industries themselves, once they have chosen a particular path of development, escape from the circumstances that government policies create. And in recent times, three of the four major forces have been losers. Only investment has been a winner in the industrial performance sweepstakes, and this accounts for the vast relative success of the K-sector firms over the past twenty-five years.

FIGURE 7.10

TECHNOLOGY AND EARNINGS GAIN, 1958–1992

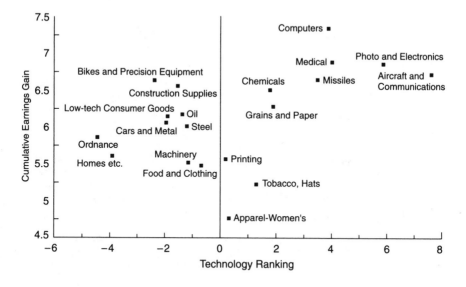

There remains one task, which is to place our analysis of changes in industrial performance in relationship to changes in earnings and pay. Figures 7.10 through 7.13 compress this task into a sequence of graphs, each showing the relationship between a force determining industrial performance and the change in average production worker pay for that industrial group.

I provide separate charts relating the technology-investment factor to earnings and to average wages. Figure 7.10, which associates this factor with the change in total payrolls, makes an unmistakable point: *the relationship is not linear.* Instead, the diagram has a backward and sideway S shape. There is a small group of industries, including computers, aircraft and communications, photographic and electronic equipment, and chemicals, that ranks highest on the technology index and also enjoys the highest rates of increase in total employee compensation. This *is* the K-sector. But when one slips below the technology scores associated with the knowledge industries, there is a range in which the relationship between our measure of technological intensity and earnings turns negative. This is true over a very wide section of the C-sector, incorporating a majority of manufacturing employment.

This diagram illustrates the harsh side of the technological era in which we live: the fact that technology is not a gentle mist descending from heaven to the benefit of all. It is instead a competitive weapon, with which one set of eco-

FIGURE 7.11

TECHNOLOGY AND WAGES, 1958–1992

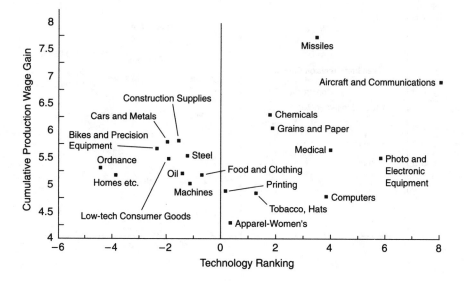

FIGURE 7.12

TRADE PROTECTION AND WAGES, 1958–1992

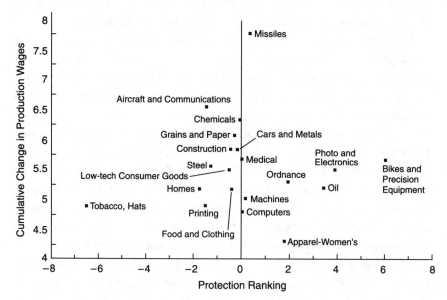

FIGURE 7.13

PROCUREMENT AND WAGES, 1958–1992

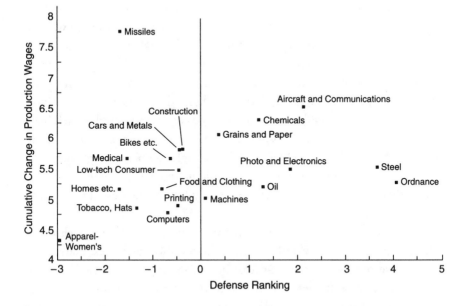

nomic organizations wrests markets and incomes from another. In our time, this weapon has been deployed with ferocity. The knowledge workers in the knowledge industries—a tiny number of very successful people—have been big winners in this struggle. Production workers in the C-sector have, comparatively speaking, been losers. Those in industries that are comparatively competitive, and therefore renovate their equipment more quickly, suffer a greater transfer to the equipment producers of the knowledge-intensive sectors.

Thus, when the printing industry moves from hot type to computer type-setting, production worker hours decline and the performance of the industry as a whole is enhanced. This accounts for an association between investment and performance in that industry, and therefore for a relatively high score on the technology index. But the earnings of production workers are not enhanced by these performance gains. To the contrary, the more the printing industry shifts to computer-based technology, the weaker the position of the printers themselves becomes, and the lower the gain in their wages.[10] Since printers of the old style are far from being unskilled, this is far from being the "skill-biased technological change" of academic folklore. It is instead old-fashioned automation and technological obsolescence—something that may be good in the end for society as a whole but definitely not for the affected workers.

Moving on through the diagrams, we can see that the relationship between technology and production wages is much less definite. Particularly in the cases of computers and electronics, strong sectoral performance was not passed along to those on the production line. Although we know that variations in consumption were the second strongest factor affecting wages from year to year, I have omitted a diagram relating consumption to cumulative wage change, since over the period as a whole, the relationship is not very strong. This is attributable to the fact that the consumption index itself has a period of strength, in the 1960s, followed by a long period of oscillation and decline. Over the full period taken all in all, high-volume, strongly demand-sensitive industries like oil and chemicals did neither better nor worse, on average, than batch processing and assembly-line industries like cars and machinery.

The pictures become more distinct, once again, when the eye travels to the effects of trade protection and war on production worker wages. Here, positive associations meet the eye, at least in certain ranges of the rankings. Industries that score highest on the protection ranking do not enjoy high overall rates of production worker wage gain. Nevertheless, it does appear that within the range of relatively protected industries, a higher score is associated with a better wage position. Demand factors are evidently at work: industries and their workers don't press for protection in the first place unless they need it. With defense-oriented industries, the association is even clearer: selling to the government is good business for workers. The position of the missile industry, with the best production wage record (despite an inverse association with the military budget), illustrates this point to perfection.

The forces of protection and military spending, not very visible to economists, are indeed just as present in the data as they appear to be to ordinary people in real life. In particular, strong association with the military has been clearly associated with high levels of hourly production wages. It is not surprising, and not irrational, that vast political energies are invested into protecting and preserving these lifelines, however inefficient and even damaging to economic performance as a whole they may be. It would be good, indeed, to forgo protectionism and dismantle the unneeded incubus of the national security state. But for workers to take an interest in some other way of raising wages, it will be necessary to demonstrate that something else can be made to serve their interests equally well.

8

INEQUALITY, UNEMPLOYMENT, INFLATION, AND GROWTH

> The general movement of wages are exclusively regulated by the expansion and contraction of the industrial reserve army, and these again correspond to the periodic changes of the industrial cycle.
>
> —Karl Marx, *Capital*, Volume I, Chapter 25

High inequality is a fact of life in America today. But to know this fact is not very useful, unless we have data that can tell us just when, and by just how much, and under just what influences inequality increased. It would also be useful to know just when, and under what circumstances, a rise in inequality slows down. And it would be very helpful to know when and how inequality has been reduced in the past.

This chapter seeks to answer these questions. First, it presents a procedure for measuring the increase in inequality specifically in hourly wages in manufacturing and compares the results with more conventional measures. Second, it analyzes the changes in this measure of inequality. As it turns out, the causes of rising inequality are mainly *macroeconomic*. Although tied up with technology, they are not driven by movements of technology. Rather, the movement of wage inequality through time can be explained almost entirely by a small number of causes, to which different industrial groups and social institutions respond in different ways. Of these, unemployment is the most important. Inflation, growth, the exchange rate of the dollar, and the minimum wage play lesser but significant roles, as do the policy forces, like the interest rate, that influence the movement of these variables.

Because these causes are all themselves reversible—they can go up or down—my hypotheses have predictive and even prescriptive value. They can explain declines in inequality in the past, and they can lead to a prescription for reducing inequality in the future.[1]

For many purposes—such as tracking the evolution of black-white or male-female wage differentials through time, or measuring the "return to education" or to age in the wage structure—the Current Population Survey (CPS) is the data set of choice. We visited the census measure of family income inequality in Chapter 5. Yet the CPS has limitations when it comes to analyzing the cause of changes in the structure of hourly wages across industries and occupations, mainly because households and even workers themselves are not the best source of information about the exact nature of industrial employments.[2] For a study of trends in industrial pay scales, we need data that are more tightly focused on industries themselves.

Several studies have isolated changes in the distribution of wage income, separating wages specifically from other sources of income reported in the CPS. These studies give a general picture of the wage structure's evolution through time. One particularly massive (and valuable) study traces movements in the relative income of each percentile in the distribution of wages. In this way, it confirms the radical transformation that occurred after the turn of the 1970s:

> The increase in inequality between 1963–65 and 1969–71 was quite modest overall. . . . In the six years from 1969–71 to 1975–77, workers at or below the tenth percentile of the wage distribution lost about 7 percent relative to the average . . . and workers in the upper quartile gained about 3–4 percent on the average worker. The changes from 1975–77 to 1981–83 are slightly larger, particularly at the extreme upper percentiles. . . . Over the most recent period (from 1981–83 to 1987–89) . . . workers at the lowest percentiles lose about 7 percent relative to the mean, and workers at the highest percentile gain about 7 percent.[3]

The implication is that all population groups and levels of the wage distribution shared in real wage gains in the 1960s; the rising tide raised all boats. During the 1970s, those below the median suffered sharp losses; the rowboats sank while the yachts floated. During the 1980s, losses below the median continued, only now accompanied by equally large gains among those who were already in the top half of income earners. The rowboats went to the bottom; the yachts morphed into Zeppelins and floated off into the air.[4]

Another study has provided snapshots of inequality in family earnings through time, also taken from the CPS.[5] The snapshots are taken by calculating ratios, between earnings at various percentiles of the income distribution—the tenth, twenty-fifth, seventy-fifth, and ninetieth—and the median position. They again confirm that inequality began to rise with a decline in the position of the bottom half of the wage distribution during the 1970s. They also show that the rise in inequality accelerated in the 1980s, when the bottom dropped out for the lower half of the distribution while the relative position of the uppermost groups dramatically improved.

CPS studies dominate the literature on inequality. The Annual Survey of Manufactures (ASM), which we have been using to analyze industrial change, has not been used at all in inequality studies so far. These data are based on establishment (factory) surveys and contain no individual-level detail. The survey is therefore not useful for examining questions of race and gender, age or education, or about the composition of families or nonwage sources of income. But the information in the ASM is based on worker pay. It contains information about hourly wages for production workers by fine industrial category, as well as annual earnings for all employees, including those on salary. From this standpoint, the ASM offers (in clumped form) the kind of information with which a study of wage inequality in manufacturing should properly be concerned. It has distinct advantages if the goal is to examine movements in the interindustrial structure of pay.

Moreover, as a data source for manufacturing, the survey of manufactures has three particular advantages. First, it is comprehensive, a census and not a sample; most of the manufacturing sector is covered. Second, the data are disaggregated in great industrial detail; in fact, there is much more industrial detail than one needs. Third, data are available at substantially the same level of detail for a long period of time: from 1958 to 1992. And as compared with information from a household survey, ASM industrial classifications are likely to be more consistent across time. It will generally be true that a factory is classified in the same way from one year to the next (unless the factory actually changes industries or the government itself changes the classification scheme). In contrast, error rates in industrial classification in the CPS are very high.

So, bearing in mind that this is only for the world of manufacturing, how can we use the ASM to look at inequality in hourly wages?

There is a statistic known as Theil's T (for the econometrician Henri Theil, who devised it) that measures the dispersion, or degree of inequality, among any set of numbers. Theil's T has an interesting property that the Gini coefficient doesn't have. If the underlying data are organized into groups, T can be decomposed, or broken up, into the part of inequality that falls between groups and the part that occurs within groups. The sum of the two parts will equal the measure of total inequality for the whole set of numbers.

The ASM is an excellent source of data on a particular set of group structures: all industries in the manufacturing sector. An industrial classification scheme, after all, is just a way of imposing a group structure on what would otherwise be a long and chaotic list of factories. That being so, we can compute the between-industries part of the Theil statistic from the ASM.

What good is that? It is true that such a measure misses most of the inequality that is out there. It is measuring only the inequality between averages of wages by industrial category, and not the inequality within any industrial group. T' ("T prime"), the measure of between-group inequality, is a (very low) lower-bound estimate of the full measure of inequality, T. We cannot use T' to measure the level or total amount of inequality in the wage structure at any moment of time.

But the ASM is available for every year, and in a consistent format so that particular categories are generally maintained from one year to the next. We can therefore compute T' for a sequence of years, with some confidence that, whatever the resulting statistic actually measures, it is a consistent measure from one year to the next. Thus, the *movements* of T' contain information. My argument is that they are a very reasonable way to approximate movements in the larger, unobserved inequality of hourly wages. In general, when the dispersion of average wages increases throughout the economy, the effect will be felt both within groups and between groups. Movements detected across groups will therefore usually reflect increases or decreases in inequality that are also going on within groups. In other words, so long as we are interested mainly in movements of inequality, and not in calculating or comparing levels, we do not lose much information by basing our analysis on industry-level data.[6]

Within the flood of data about manufacturing that are available from the ASM,[7] it turns out that it is not necessary to work at the lowest possible levels of aggregation and with the greatest numbers of subdivisions. A great many industries involving similar processes or similar products behave through time, for practical purposes, in highly similar ways. For instance, we have seen how virtually all of the chemical industries, including essentially chemical processes such as those involved in producing beer, soda, and cigarettes, resemble each other more closely than they do anything else in industry. And many subdivisions dealing with apparel are similar to the point of being indistinguishable on the basis of measurements of performance. So are many machinery industries.

All in all, I have found it convenient to reduce the industrial categories that make up the industrial structure of the United States for the period 1958 to 1992 to seventeen major manufacturing groups and another nineteen outliers or individual cases that don't group well with anything else: thirty-six entities in all.[8] Of the outliers, only a half-dozen are large enough to make a difference, so in the end we work with seventeen plus six, or twenty-three, distinct industrial groups. These cover the overwhelming bulk of manufacturing employment in the period under study.

A measure of hourly wage inequality, of T', between these twenty-three industrial groups is depicted in Figure 8.1. This will be our basic measure of changing inequality in the hourly wage structure of manufacturing in the United States. It is a summary measure of the interindustrial changes discussed in Chapters 6 and 7, but with the important difference that these changes are now weighted by the relative employment of each industrial group. The movements of this series therefore reflect changes in the inequal-

FIGURE 8.1

INEQUALITY IN MANUFACTURING WAGES

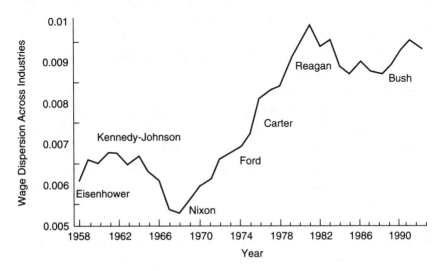

ity of manufacturing wages as experienced by the typical worker in the manufacturing sector.

By this measure, inequality in the manufacturing wage structure was roughly stable for the first half of the 1960s, before plunging sharply in the second half of the decade. Beginning around 1970, wage inequality began an inexorable fifteen-year rise. This rise comes to an end around 1984. After that point, wage inequality in the United States declines a bit and then stabilizes—near the highest values of the whole period—only to rise once again in 1991–92.

How good is this measure? One way to get an idea is to compare it to the Census Bureau's calculation of inequality among family incomes for the same years. The simple correlation coefficient between the two series is .77—meaning that the two series move together 77 percent of the time. This is a remarkable number, considering how different the two measurements are. The Census Bureau's measure is based on a household survey of family income, covering all sectors of the economy. Ours is based on an establishment census of hourly wage rates, restricted to manufacturing. And the computations are quite different in mathematical form. Yet a change in inequality in one series is closely reflected in changing inequality captured by the other.[9]

One significant difference between the two series occurs toward the end of the time frame. After the mid-1980s, family income inequality continued to rise. The inequality of hourly wages, on the other hand, which had risen sharply in the early 1980s, stabilized at a high level in the second half of the decade. We have already seen the implication of this finding, which is corroborated in at least two other recent studies, for the argument that the diffusion of computers might be behind the rising inequality of wages.[10] A rise in family income inequality that does not correspond to a rise in wage inequality must be due to other factors, including increasing inequality of nonwage incomes and changing family structures.

Hourly wage inequality is the issue we wish to examine here. We have found a way to measure—albeit approximately—the movements of such inequality within manufacturing over a long time frame. We note that these movements closely mirror movements of inequality in the economy as a whole, suggesting that the real interest of the series extends beyond the phenomenon that it actually measures. The next task is to explain why this series behaves as it does.

My lead hypothesis is that macroeconomic events will largely determine the movement of a wage inequality measure through time. In a world of organizations—firms, industries, and unions—with greater and lesser degrees of market power, we should expect that events will differentiate the strong from the weak. Those with the strongest positions will be least affected by all sorts of external difficulties; those with the weakest positions will be most affected. But the same is also true, in reverse, of favorable events: institutions and organizations with monopolistic power take less advantage of good news than do weaker, more responsive entities. Since market power also means a high position on the scale of incomes, it follows that adverse macroeconomic events will tend to increase inequality in the wage structure, and favorable events will tend to reduce it.

Few economists have been interested in testing these ideas; macroeconomic phenomena appear in most studies of inequality mainly as "controls" for the movements of the business cycle—as factors to be removed before the "underlying" determinants of rising inequality can be uncovered. This is an understandable instinct: the idea that macrophenomena drive distribution is, after all, in flat opposition to the predictions of a competitive, market model of labor supply and demand. Indeed, it stands in opposition to the basic division of economics into "macro" and "micro," according to which the distribution of income is a microeconomic, market-based phenomenon.

There is no reason, under the supply-and-demand model, why the state of the macroeconomy should make any difference to relative pay. Each worker should get paid just exactly the value of his marginal product. The market, in a balancing act between consumer preferences and technological possibilities, determines what that value is. Aggregate unemployment, or inflation, or the rate of growth should make no practical, systematic difference to anyone's pay, and certainly not to the range of the pay scale, to the distance separating the top from the bottom. If they do, something must be very wrong with the competitive model.

There is much at stake in a statistical exercise that looks for effects of macroeconomic variables on the structure of hourly wages. One theory, with heavy backing from professional economists, predicts that no such effects will be found. A dissenting view predicts that such effects will be commonplace, even determinative. Both views cannot be correct at the same time. Nor can their underlying models be equally valid.

This is not merely an issue that separates neoclassicals from Keynesians. (Typically, a neoclassical is an economist who believes that the macroeconomy is substantially self-regulating, whereas Keynesians believe it is not.) Most self-described Keynesians nowadays stay away from microeconomics. They have made their peace with the marginal productivity distribution theory and would not expect relative pay to be strongly affected by macroeconomic variables. A finding that such effects exist would upset the modern Keynesian orthodoxy as much as the neoclassical. It would suggest not just separate spheres for macro and micro, but that macroeconomic conditions (unemployment, inflation, growth) actually determine microeconomic conditions (such as relative rates of pay). It is a heresy beyond heresies to make this suggestion.

But let us follow the path suggested by our own model and view of the world. Good econometric practice is to specify and describe in advance the variables that one expects to influence the variable one is trying to explain. Then one conducts a computerized exercise—multiple linear regression—that fits the explanatory series to the explanandum. The results tell whether the theory was a good one.

Here are the variables that I predict may account for the movement of inequality in the structure of hourly wages. They are chosen, in each case, for the same specific reason: they reflect forces in the macroeconomy that are known to influence the relative strength of well-organized and monopolistic as against poorly organized and competitive sectors. They are: unemployment, inflation, economic growth, the exchange rate, the minimum wage, and several brief episodes of direct governmental control over wages and prices.

Rate of civilian unemployment. A high rate of unemployment, we ought to expect, produces more pressure on wages in low-wage, weakly organized, and competitive industries than in high-wage, strongly organized, and cartelized or monopolistic sectors. Rising unemployment therefore undermines the position of low-wage workers, while leaving earnings structures in the higher strata alone.

Rate of consumer price inflation. Some workers are protected against inflation through cost-of-living adjustment (COLA) clauses in their contracts. Others are not. Protected workers tend to be unionized; COLAS are a feature of a typical strong union contract. As a rule, unionized workers enjoy higher wages than many others who are not unionized. Conversely, workers unprotected by COLAs tend to be less well paid and unorganized. Thus, like a rise in unemployment, a rise in inflation drives a wedge between the strong and the weak, and so raises inequality in the system as a whole.

Rate of economic growth. This one is a little bit trickier. Since growth is a good thing, we might superficially expect that a high rate of growth reduces inequality, while a low rate of growth increases it. But the actual pattern of effect may depend on the relative wages of those sectors of the economy most highly affected by swings in the growth rate. If high rates of growth boost employment in the highest-wage sectors, such as construction, the rate of growth could have a positive relationship to inequality, even though the lower unemployment that growth produces eventually brings inequality down.

Real exchange rate of the dollar. The influence of the dollar reflects the difference in market power of industries that export and industries that compete with imports. The former, dominated by such activities as aircraft, computers, chemicals, and communications equipment, tend to be monopolistic. The latter, including apparel, toys, sporting goods, and automobiles, tend to be highly competitive. Thus, a rise in the exchange rate should increase the spread between high-wage exporters and lower-wage import competers, raising inequality in the wage structure.

This effect may seem nonintuitive to many readers. In principle, a rise in the dollar's exchange rate makes exports expensive and imports cheap. It therefore hurts all kinds of manufacturing industries and their employees: both those that export and those that compete with imports. But, and here is the key point, the effects are not symmetric, because the composition of the two types of industry, exporting and import competing, is not similar. The United States is, by and large, an exporter of advanced goods. We export aircraft, computers, pharmaceuticals, and machinery. In these industries, we enjoy a degree of worldwide monopoly power challenged only by a handful of producers in other advanced countries. When the dollar goes up, many export sales happen anyway.

Some markets are lost to competitors: Airbus takes sales from Boeing; Komatsu takes sales from Caterpillar. But these effects, while important, are not as strong as in industries that compete with imports. Import-competing industries tend to be mass-production consumer goods industries, such as automobiles, consumer electronics, and clothing. When the dollar rises, U.S. producers in these industries face intensified competition in the U.S. domestic market from producers around the world. Foreign producers can gear up to supply the U.S. market, and in the years following 1981 they did flood our market with imports. As a consequence, U.S. workers in these sectors suffer intense pressure on their wages.

Workers in export-intensive industries earn more, on average, than import competers. Since they are also less vulnerable to the effects of changing exchange rates, a rise in the exchange rate hurts low-income workers more than it hurts workers at the top of the wage structure. In this way, appreciation of the dollar increases inequality in the United States. And depreciation, a decline in the value of the dollar that raises the competitiveness of mass-production industries in the United States as compared with the rest of the world, might be expected to have the opposite effect. That is, a depreciation of the dollar might, after a time, reduce the inequality of the wage structure, by strengthening import-competing U.S. workers relatively to their exporting cousins.[11]

Real short-term interest rate. High interest rates, like high exchange rates, hurt competitive industries more than monopolistic ones, for the fairly simple reason that competitive industries cannot finance themselves easily with long-term bond debt. They are hence more vulnerable to interest rate fluctuations, and we should expect a rising real interest burden (that is, after adjustment for inflation) to tend to increase inequality in the wage structure.

Minimum wage.[12] The minimum wage is particularly important to women workers, and when the value of the minimum wage was high, inequality among women workers, as well as between women and men, was lower than it later became.[13]

Wage-price control policies. The dramatic examples during this period were the Nixon wage-price controls of 1972–1973 and the period of wage-price guidelines under President Carter's Council on Wage-Price Stability (CWPS) in 1979–1980.

Putting all of these possible explanations to the test, and simultaneously, is the function of a multiple linear regression. The results are presented in Table 8A.1, which to avoid clutter has been relegated to the Chapter 8 appendix, located in the back of the book. To show that the results do not depend strictly on my particular measure of inequality, I ran the equation three times, using three different measures, including my own and two from other sources.[14]

Unemployment turns out to be a key variable: it has a significant, positive effect on inequality in all three measures and is the variable with the largest effect on the measure of wage dispersion in the manufacturing wage structure. The stratifying effect of unemployment is pervasive through time and throughout the economy. Unemployment also strongly affects the distribution of family incomes—as one might expect because low-income people are at higher risk of unemployment. But the finding that unemployment drives the hourly wage structure is apparently quite independent of the simple movement of people into and out of jobs.

Inflation, as it turns out, also has detectable effects on American wage inequality in manufacturing. Inflation is not good for equality in wages. This effect was felt strongly in the supply-shock years of the 1970s, when the most heavily unionized manufacturing employees did comparatively well, while wages among the unorganized generally sank into stagnation. In more recent years, inflation has not been strong enough to be a significant force on the wage structure. And because unionized contracts with COLAs are such a small part of the larger economy outside of the manufacturing sector, we find that inflation affects our inequality measure only within the manufacturing sector. The effect is not strong enough to be significant when more broadly based measures of inequality are brought into play.

The *rate* of economic growth also has an effect on the wage structure. As suggested earlier, this effect at first sight actually appears perverse. The direction of the effect is to *raise* inequality: the more rapid that economic growth is, other things equal, the greater the degree of inequality in the wage structure. But on reflection, the explanation is not difficult. Economic growth is most rapid just at the beginning of a business cycle expansion, when unemployment is high and the general level of economic activity remains depressed. Growth slows down when unemployment is low and the economy is operating near its capacity. And when growth is rapid, the greatest effects are felt in the industries supplying investment goods to the economy—construction and machinery and transportation equipment, for example. These are industries that pay higher-than-average wages. Thus, the surge of growth at the start of an economic expansion tends to widen the gap between high-wage and low-wage workers.

Next, the foreign exchange rate of the dollar turns up as a probable cause of rising inequality. Importantly, the effects of the dollar's exchange rate on the wage structure are felt only after the great surge of trade beginning in 1981. At that time, the dollar's value rose by some 60 percent in real terms, and a fundamental change in the importance of trade to the domestic economy occurred. It is necessary to work carefully with the data to find this effect, and given the power of other forces it is only weakly significant in the statistical sense. But, unlike the effects of inflation and economic growth, our measure of dollar overvaluation persists as a significant force on inequality, when one extends the analysis to the structure of family incomes taken in the large.

From this evidence, we may infer that there is probably a link between trade and inequality. But the final cause of rising inequality isn't expanded trade itself. Rather, it lies in the policy actions that raised the value of the dollar, prompted a huge increase in manufactured imports, mainly from low-wage countries, and therefore put asymmetric pressure on lower-wage import-competing manufacturing workers. These policy actions include the big tax cuts and large deficits that stimulated growth after 1981. But first and foremost, the responsibility for precipitating these events lies with monetary policy, with the very high interest rates imposed by the Federal Reserve under Chairman Paul A. Volcker, beginning in 1979 and greatly increased again in 1981. Trade may be a good thing, but a well-managed expansion of trade that did not crush import-competing workers all of a sudden would have been better for inequality than what actually occurred.

The interest rate has some direct effect on inequality in the wage structure; periods of high real interest rates coincide with periods of rising inequality, notably in the early 1980s. But in the end this direct effect seems less important than the effects of unemployment and the exchange rate, and the reasonable inference is that the main effect of high interest rates on wage structures runs *through* the effect they have on unemployment and on the dollar. For this reason, we eventually removed this variable from the model. Still, when one takes direct and indirect effects together, the results do suggest that the real interest rate, and so the conduct of monetary policy, is a major underlying cause of rising inequality in the wage structure.

Second to last, we find that the value of the minimum wage makes an important difference to the overall measure of inequality in the manufacturing wage structure. The higher the minimum wage, the less the gap between the least well-paid of American workers and those in the middle of the wage structure. It is interesting that the effect of the minimum wage appears significant, even though the analysis reported in this chapter relies exclusively on data from the manufacturing sector. Manufacturing employs less than a fifth of the total number of workers in the American economy, and the average wage in manufacturing is well above the legal minimum. We would expect minimum wage effects to be stronger if we examine wages in services alongside manufacturing, and this is borne out by the second and third equations, whose estimates of inequality include workers in the services sectors.

Finally, we took account of two brief periods when the government of the United States exercised direct control over wages and prices. These were the wage-price controls of the Nixon administration in 1972–73, and the compact negotiated with the leadership of Amercian labor by the Carter Administration in 1979–80. There is evidence that Nixon's controls, imposed in late 1971 as his re-election campaign took shape, may have worked to reduce inequality in the wage structure; the Carter program, which was undertaken in an atmosphere of anxiety over inflation and yet lacked any compulsory authority over prices, may have inadvertently added to inequality in those disastrous years. But in the final analysis we could not clearly identify a separate effect for these policy episodes, and we therefore removed them from the model.

Leaving the interest rate aside, our five macroeconomic forces—unemployment, the exchange rate, inflation, economic growth, and the minimum wage—account for nearly 90 percent of the variation in wage inequality over time. This is a very high degree of explanation by the standards of economic research.[15]

We can conclude the following:

First, if we have to pick one, the single most important statistical determinant of changing inequality in the modern American manufacturing wage structure is surely the movement of the rate of unemployment. This old conclusion, known in its essentials to economists decades ago (well known, in fact, even to Karl Marx, as the quotation at the start of this chapter shows), remains substantially valid, notwithstanding the vast literature since then devoted to finding effects from technology, trade, and other possible causes.

Second, the huge increase in the real value of the dollar after 1980 may have driven a significant international wedge, apparently for the first time, into the wage structure. Before that time, the exchange rate did not affect wages very much. Afterward, it probably did. Globalization matters, but mainly because we have pursued globalization in ways that generated a structural overvaluation of the trade-weighted dollar. We could have had globalization—though at a slower pace—without this policy-generated calamity for the wage structure.

Third, the minimum wage affects the overall structure of wages and incomes. Raising it is an effective means of reducing inequality overall. This effect is stronger in data covering all family incomes than in data covering only manufacturing wages, which is not surprising since the minimum wage is more strongly felt outside the manufacturing sector.

Fourth, growth and inflation have effects on the wage structure, but these are not strong enough to show all the way through to the structure of incomes as a whole. The same is true of effects attributable to episodes of control and regulation over wages in the past.

Fifth, the fact that almost 90 percent of the variation in manufacturing wage inequality as measured by this series can be accounted for by these variables leaves little else to discuss. There is little left over for other forces, such as changes in education or the supply of skill, to explain.

The measured importance of unemployment does not mean that technology is unimportant. Rather, it moves us away from a benign view of the role of technology as "skill enhancing," and back toward the old-fashioned argument that technological change is mainly aimed at saving labor. When unemployment rises due to the scrapping of an old plant, the wages of workers in technology-producing sectors remain stable, while those in technology-

FIGURE 8.2

INEQUALITY IN THE WAGE STRUCTURE, 1920–1992

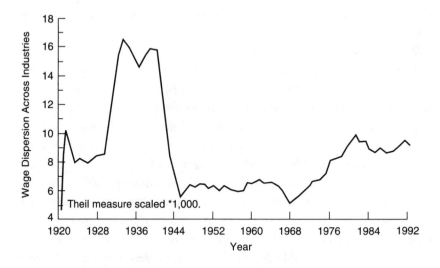

consuming manufactures tend to drop. Only in periods of long and sustained high employment, when workers gain leverage on their employers, do the technology consumers tend to recover and inequality in the wage structure declines. Such a relationship could account well for the sharp rise in wage inequality in the early 1980s, as well as for the stabilization of inequality thereafter as unemployment declined.[16]

Let's now step back, and expand our historical horizon. Using some of the same methods to measure inequality in the hourly wage structure, it is possible to construct a prewar history of American wage inequality, dating back to 1920. Figure 8.2 shows this roller-coaster ride; details of the data and calculation are in the appendix to this chapter (at the back of the book).

The time pattern is easy to narrate.[17] From the end of World War I, inequality rose sharply in the slump of 1920–1921. Then inequality fell again, and remained stable until the end of the 1920s. In the main, this was because of the relative prosperity of the American farmer after recovery from the slump of the early 1920s, alongside rapid industrial growth that kept all manufacturing wages growing closely apace, one with another.

All of this came to an end, with astonishing swiftness, in the Great Crash of 1929 and the Great Slump of 1930. Inequality soared, and stayed very high for a decade—higher, in fact, than at any subsequent time.

World War II brought inequality down. In the short space of four years, inequality fell more than it had previously risen through the Great Depression. And then came the miracle of the postwar era: inequality virtually unchanged for another quarter-century. It is a reasonable conclusion from this that World War II created, all at once, the middle-class wage structure of the American midcentury.

Inequality did rise again somewhat, in the period 1958 through 1960, years of back-to-back recessions. But it then stabilized in the early Kennedy and Johnson years and began falling from 1966 through 1968—the time of the Great Society and also of the escalation of the Vietnam War. By 1968 or 1969, inequality in the United States was apparently lower than at any other time since the First World War. The United States of 1970 was truly the middle-class society by then-existing world standards. But it did not last. Beginning in 1969 inequality started to rise, and continued to increase sharply for fifteen years. By 1984, overall inequality had risen toward, if not quite to, the levels of the Depression era.

After 1984, for the remaining years of our sample, the picture is not quite so gloomy. Inequality remains very high, but it does tend to level off. Indeed, virtually all measures of inequality that I have seen, even those that report inequality continuing to rise, appear to show a slower rate of change after 1984 than before. By all measures, nevertheless, levels of inequality remain high compared to the postwar norms. Though if my long-term measures are correct, *inequality* as of 1992 remained *below the appalling levels of the Great Depression in the 1930s,* it was nevertheless higher than in any other time since World War I.

Is there a single strongest driving force behind these ups and downs? The answer is depicted in Figure 8.3, which matches hourly wage inequality to the unemployment rate over this entire time. The fit is both remarkable and consistent. Movements of the unemployment rate alone account for 79 percent of all variation in wage inequality over this time. Other forces are to be reckoned with, to be sure, and 79 percent falls short of being a complete model. But changes in unemployment are overwhelmingly the main thing. It is, above all, the low rates of unemployment in the 1920s, during World War II, and in the late 1960s that bring inequality in the wage structure down. Nothing else in our history has had a comparable effect.

It is true that our postwar analysis had pointed to a range of measures—macroeconomic and political—that would necessarily be part of a concerted effort to reduce inequality in the wage structure. A depreciation of the dollar would help. So would a rise in the minimum wage. Policies that control infla-

FIGURE 8.3

INEQUALITY AND UNEMPLOYMENT, 1920–1992

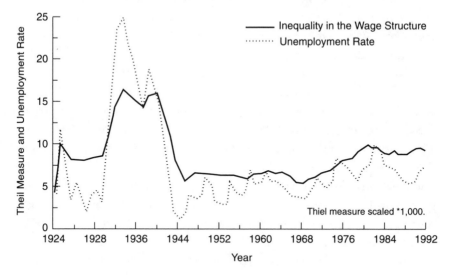

tion without resort to unemployment, high interest rates, or dollar appreciation would contribute. *But sustained full employment is the essential step on any serious agenda.*

Now we know that when unemployment is high, inequality rises. And when unemployment is low, inequality tends to fall. This, along with the other factors already considered, brutally undermines the competitive market model under which relative wages are not affected by macroeconomic conditions. But it also raises a question. Is there a threshold rate of unemployment, above which inequality is likely to rise and below which inequality is likely to fall?

The question can be explored statistically by looking at the *change* in inequality, year by year, against the level of the unemployment rate. A simple computation reveals that the change in inequality will equal zero, on average in this century, when unemployment averages about 5.5 percent. When unemployment is below 5.5 percent, inequality is likely to fall. The fact that measured inequality began to show distinct declines in the autumn of 1996, just as unemployment fell to 5.1 percent, is no surprise. When unemployment is above 5.5 percent, inequality is likely to rise.

A 5.5 percent rate of unemployment may therefore be called the *ethical rate of unemployment* for the United States over most of the twentieth century. For those who are concerned with inequality, it should be an article of policy that unemployment be kept below this value.

The ethical rate of unemployment can be contrasted with the so-called natural rate of unemployment, sometimes called the nonaccelerating inflation rate of unemployment (NAIRU). Many economists employ the natural rate argument to place a policy floor under the unemployment rate, lest inflation accelerate out of control. Estimates of the NAIRU have fluctuated inconsistently in recent years, but with many placing it at or a bit above the very same 5.5 percent. Here is a wicked irony: economists have argued that we must keep unemployment above the level at which it might reduce inequality. In this way, our inflation paranoia has placed the intellectual weight of the economics profession firmly on the side of a more unequal America. Yet if we care about inequality in America, a 5.5 percent rate of unemployment should assuredly be a ceiling, not a floor.

9

SERVICE WAGES AND
THE INVESTMENT CYCLE

The labourers, when driven out of the workshop by the machinery, are thrown upon the labour-market, and there add to the number of workmen at the disposal of the capitalists. . . . And even if they should find employment, what a poor lookout is theirs! Crippled as they are by division of labour, these poor devils are worth so little outside their old trade, that they cannot find admission into any industries, except a few of inferior kind, which are oversupplied with underpaid workmen.

—Karl Marx, *Capital,* Volume 1, Part IV, Chapter 15

So far we have restricted our focus to manufacturing, itself subdivided into technology-producing and technology-using sectors. But what of services? What of that third estate, so often left out of account?

The services sector is vast. It is also diverse and inchoate, a diffuse collection of disparate lines of work. Service workers range from gas station attendants to engineers, retail clerks to roofers, garbage collectors to computer data processors. Over 80 percent of employment in the American economy, 95 million workers by a recent count, is officially classed as service providing.

And services are also the terra incognita of the economy. Because they do not produce a physical product, the physical productivity of the service worker cannot be measured. For this reason, many of the preoccupying questions in the study of manufacturing cannot be addressed. There is no distinction between "production workers" and "nonproduction workers" in the services sector. Hence, there are no data to distinguish production from nonproduction wages. For the most part, we also lack data on international trade in services. Indeed the very exercise of industrial classification in the services sector lags behind that in manufacturing, so that the data that we do have, covering such very basic matters as employment and earnings, were often not available in disaggregated form until the early 1970s or in important cases even more recently than that. Thus, one cannot conduct a long-term analysis of trends in services at the same levels of detail or precision as the data on manufacturing permit.

Nevertheless, partly because of data sets only very recently published, we do have annual data from 1973 through 1994 on both average hourly pay and employment in over eighty subclassifications of the services sector. Merging these with hourly wage data for production workers in our seventeen major groups of manufacturing industries (and the half-dozen principal outliers), we can assemble a reasonably representative table of wage trends in the U.S. economy. This data set covers over half of all workers, systematically excluding mainly certain personal services and entertainment subsectors, and the government sector. So if we cannot quite get a complete picture of the service world, we can at least get a majority view.

A systematic look at the rates of change of average earnings in each of our services and manufacturing groupings reveals a fundamental fact: the modern wage patterns of the American economy are split into two. There are two distinct patterns of wage evolution over this time, dividing the employed labor force into two distinct major groupings. Finer subdivisions, though they exist, are much less important. Figure 9.1 reports and illustrates this schism. It can be read as a kind of organizational chart for the manufacturing and services sectors, based on the patterns of change in hourly wages over the years from 1973 to 1994. Entities listed close to each other have similar patterns of wage evolution, and conversely.[1]

On the right-center branch of the tree, we find virtually all of manufacturing employment. But we also find a significant number of service activities whose wage patterns through time appear to track those in the manufacturing sector. The time path of earnings in the hospital and the health and casualty insurance sectors, for example, closely mirrors that in the manufacture of medical supplies.[2] Earnings among car dealers fluctuate alongside earnings in the cars and metals manufacturing group. The variations of earnings in several advanced utility sectors (gas, telephone, electricity) resemble the variations in earnings in industries producing energy, including the mining

FIGURE 9.1

PATTERNS OF WAGE CHANGE IN SERVICES AND MANUFACTURING, 1973–1992
Cluster Analysis Using Ward's Method and Euclidean Distances for 108

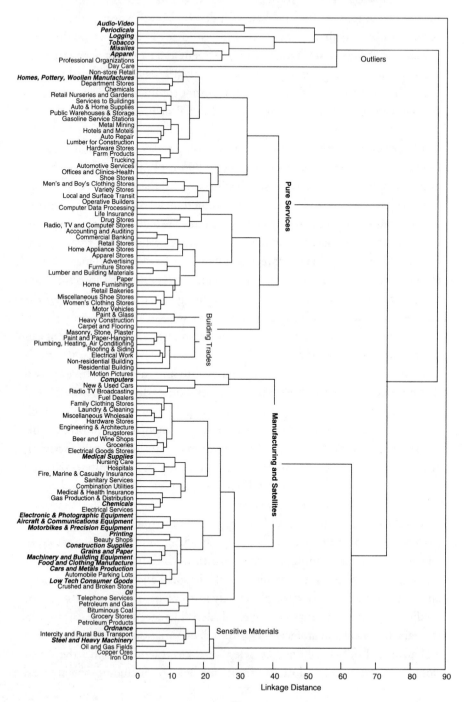

sectors. Even a few specialized retail sectors, grocery and drug stores in particular, appear as manufacturing satellites alongside their associated manufacturing sectors, foods and pharmaceuticals.

On the center-left of the diagram, we find a gigantic array of activities whose earnings do not track the fluctuations of earnings in manufacturing. This branch includes virtually all of retail sales activity. It includes hotels and motels and transportation. It includes banking and accounting services. It includes the craft activities associated with building: carpentry, roofing, plumbing, masonry, and so on.

This admittedly complicated diagram reveals in a very simple way the great divide that splits the American economy. It is a division that corresponds with striking accuracy to the theoretical divisions of Chapter 6, with the C- and K-sectors on the right of the diagram and the S-sector on the left.[3]

In the first group, we find all activities significantly associated with technology or the accumulation of physical capital, that is, with the production of capital goods and the production of goods for mass consumption. These include many activities classed formally as services but in fact closely associated with manufacturing. Services like utilities and the provision of health care, it turns out, are essentially inseparable from the provision of the goods (power grids, medical supplies) with which they are associated. They are thus not really services, but indispensable adjuncts to the production of goods, satellites of the manufacturing process.

In the second group, we find the S-sector proper. This is a range of activities for which the accumulation and depreciation of capital, the change of technology, and the flow of production itself are much less important. This group includes most of retail, construction trades, and purely personal services, as well as banking and accounting. It includes several industrial groupings formally classified as manufacturing in government statistics: home building, pottery, wool garments, women's apparel. It is telling that these are known to be, in substantial part, craft activities rather than modern manufacturing proper.

Two other groupings deserve brief notice. On the far right of the diagram is a small group of industries mainly involved in mining and energy products: iron ore, copper ore, petroleum products, and ordnance (!). We may call this the sensitive-materials sector; wages here will be shown to vary with sensitive-materials prices. On the far left is an odd lot of idiosyncratic cases: day care, professional organizations, tobacco, logging, and periodical publishing.

Figure 9.2 presents the pattern of employment in the two major groups over the past twenty years. The figure reveals several striking facts. First, total

FIGURE 9.2

MANUFACTURING AND SERVICES
Official and Estimated Employment

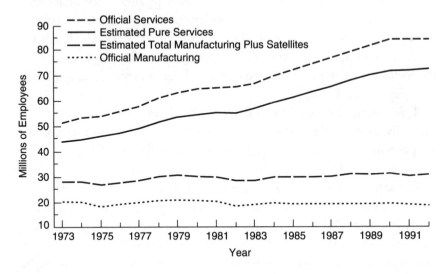

employment in manufacturing, when combined with industries classed as services but allied with the manufacturing sector, is more than half again larger than the official manufacturing sector. By official estimates, the manufacturing sector contained only about 18 million workers as of 1994, down from about 20 million in 1984. Our best estimate is that the total employment in manufacturing and its near satellites was actually about 30 million in 1994, and virtually unchanged over the preceding decade. The drop in employment in manufacturing proper was more than offset by a gain in satellite activities.[4]

In short, it is true that 80 percent of employment is now in the official services sector. But that number masks the sizable degree to which certain service jobs are linked to manufacturing. The *manufacturing-dependent* part of employment is actually at least 25 percent of the total and has not declined substantially if these estimates are correct.

Manufacturing occurs in conjunction with services. You could not have a medical supply industry without hospitals, or hospitals without insurance. You could not have telephones without linemen, cars without car dealers, or pharmaceuticals without pharmacists. The issue is where to draw the line. At the factory gate, as the official statistics do? Or at the boundary that divides work specifically associated with a goods-producing sector from work that is not industrially specific, such as general-purpose retailing or banking? I take the second position. The line between manufacturing and services should be drawn much further over into the official services sectors than the official statistics allow.[5]

By this larger definition, the total volume of manufacturing plus satellite employment over the past decade and a half has been approximately stable, after a substantial increase in the late 1970s. There have been some fluctuations, including a fall in the early 1980s and a recovery by the second half of the decade. But much of the apparent decline in manufacturing employment in the United States, of deindustrialization, appears from this perspective to have been a statistical nonevent. Rather, large drops in certain types of employment within manufacturing (notably, in heavy equipment, steel, cars, and machinery) were offset in the aggregate by gains in satellite sectors (notably, health care and related activities).

Second, after allowing for job redistribution across activities within manufacturing and its satellites, it remains true that virtually all net job creation in the past twenty years has occurred in the pure services sector. Using official data for services industries and subtracting out those components identified as satellites of manufacturing, we have a gain of nearly 30 million jobs over two decades, from 43 million in 1973 to 72 million total employees in 1992.

Average wages in the services sector are low. They were just $3.40 per hour in 1970, and only $10.70 per hour—all sectors counted—in 1994. In real terms, this is a decline of about 11 percent over the quarter-century. The dispersion of wages within the services sector is also low, and, to the extent we can measure it, the inequality of wages within the services sector has changed little over a generation, when compared to inequality within manufacturing or between manufacturing and services.[6]

What then is the major force that drives the pattern of wages in the C/K-group to be so distinct from the pattern in the S-group? On theoretical grounds, we would surely expect the answer to be related to the main thing that separates manufacturing activity from service activity: *the use and transformation of physical capital equipment.* Investment marks the phases of this transformation and the main force that affects manufacturing far more than it affects services. When physical investment is strong (by both businesses for equipment and households for appliances and other durables), so will be the demand for labor in the goods sectors and especially in the sectors producing machines with which goods are produced. And so wages in those sectors will improve. There is no reason to expect this effect to spread beyond the sectors that are directly concerned with manufacturing activity, into services lacking any particular tie to the production of goods.

FIGURE 9.3

WAGE CHANGE AND INVESTMENT
Manufacturing over Services, 1973–1992

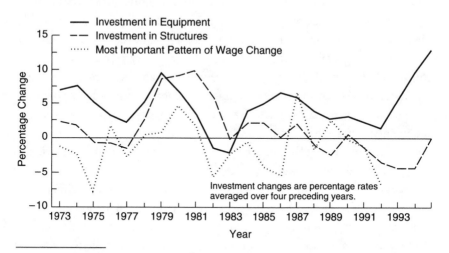

Note: The patterns of wage change in Figures 9.3 to 9.5 are the first three canonical roots of a discriminant function that separates the independent components of between-group variation in manufacturing and service wages over time. See the appendix to Chapter 7 for technical details.

Figure 9.3 tests this proposition. It presents the time pattern that best distinguishes the evolution of earnings in manufacturing from that in services and compares that pattern to two others: the movement of investment in structures and the movement of investment in equipment.[7] The physical resemblance of the lagged investment series to the pattern extracted from the earnings data is remarkably strong. A simple rule: when physical capital investment increases, the relative earnings of employees in manufacturing eventually follow. But these effects do not carry over to the S-sector, where the vast majority of American workers are employed.[8]

What other forces affect the wage structure, when manufacturing and services are included in the analysis together? Figure 9.4 shows the next most important, accounting for about 20 percent of the remaining 38 percent of wage variation: change in sensitive materials prices. The industries most helped when materials prices change include copper and iron ore production, as well as the steel and heavy equipment industries, oil and gas fields, petroleum products, and ordnance—industries that either produce sensitive materials or most readily pass on price increases in their inputs to their customers.[9] Those hurt by rising materials prices include such entities as new and used car dealers and furniture stores, perhaps reflecting the fact that

FIGURE 9.4

WAGE CHANGE AND MATERIALS PRICES
Manufacturing and Services, 1973–1992

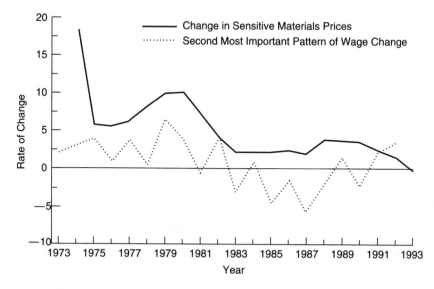

households hit with higher energy bills defer capital purchases, especially of energy-using equipment like automobiles.

A third force accounts for most of the remaining variation—for 13 out of 18 percent. It is presented in Figure 9.5, alongside the annual fluctuations of investment in business equipment—one of the two series shown in Figure 9.3, but this time without any time lags. The correspondence is once again very close, and this relationship is perhaps the most interesting of them all.

This tells us that there is a group of industries—not a very large group—where wages respond *immediately* to fluctuations in the demand for business equipment. Theoretically, we know what to expect. This should be characteristic of industries where employees have clout. Such industries, in turn, are likely to be found in the knowledge-intensive sector, in the K-sector. Wages in such industries get a double-kick from an upturn in investment: immediately because of their presence at the leading edge of technology and again with a lag because of their membership in the larger spectrum of manufacturing as opposed to service business.

When we examine the industries whose earnings are most responsive to the short-term flux of equipment investment, what do we find? The leaders include motion pictures, combined utilities, computers and computer data processors, hospitals, pharmacies and medical insurance, gas producers,

FIGURE 9.5

EQUIPMENT INVESTMENT AND THE K-SECTOR

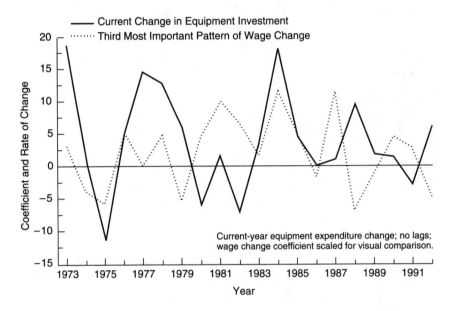

chemicals, radio and television broadcasting, and aircraft and communications equipment producers.[10] It is a telling grouping, suggesting once again that the existence of a K-sector is no theoretical abstraction. Table 9.1 presents the twenty-five highest- and fourteen lowest-scoring classifications on each of the three separate causes. Industries ranking high on this third criterion numbered about 9 million employees in 1973; this number rose to over 12 million by 1992, or from about one-third to perhaps 40 percent of the total employment in manufacturing and its near satellites.

Looking next at the levels and changes of average wage rates across all of these sectors, we can document the very striking degree to which the divergent performance of these large sectors has contributed to the breaking apart of the wage structure after 1973.

In 1973, there was a difference of less than 5 percent between average production worker wages in manufacturing and satellite services and average hourly compensation service activities not so associated. This is, and was, essentially a negligible number. By 1994, however, the gap between average earnings in the two sectors had risen to become a chasm of over 30 percent! This is the difference between an average hourly earning of $13.40 in the manufacturing sector and its satellites taken together, and an average of about $10.00 in pure services. It is enough to play the major role in the rise

TABLE 9.1

INDUSTRIES RANKED BY CANONICAL SCORES
Annual Change of Hourly Earnings, 1973–1992

First Root:	Second Root:	Third Root:
HIGH SCORES, ASSOCIATED WITH:		
Lagged Investment	*Materials Prices*	*Current Equipment Spending*
1. Day Care	Intercity and Rural Bus Transport	*Motion Pictures*
2. *Audiovideo Equipment**	Copper Ores	*Combination Utilities*
3. *Missiles*	Iron Ores	*Computers**
4. Tobacco	Oil and Gas Fields	*Hospitals**
5. Periodical Publishing	Ordnance	*Gas Production and Distribution*
6. Logging	Grocery Stores	*Chemicals**
7. Professional Organizations	Petroleum Products	*Computer Data Processing*
8. Apparel	Steel and Heavy Equipment	Iron Ores
9. *Telephone Services*	*Audiovideo Equipment*	*Electrical Services*
10. Construction Supplies	Low-tech Consumer Goods	Automobile Parking
11. Printing	Petroleum and Gas	Bituminous Coal Mining
12. Grains and Paper	*Telephone Services*	*Radio TV Broadcasting*
13. *Bikes and Precision Equipment*	Logging	*Telephone Services**
14. Oil	Groceries	*Medical and Health Insurance*
15. *Medical and Health Insurance*	*Motion Pictures*	Petroleum and Gas
16. *Combination Utilities*	Trucking	*Drug Stores and Pharmacies*
17. Gas Production	Life Insurance	Crushed and Broken Stone
18. Fire, Marine and Casualty Insurance	Nonstore Retail	Beauty shops
19. New and Used Car Dealers	*Medical and Health Insurance*	*Aircraft and Communications Equipment*
20. Machinery	*Drug Stores and Pharmacies*	Fire, Marine and Casualty Insurance
21. *Electronic and Photographic Equipment*	Grains and Paper	New and Used Car Dealers
22. *Aircraft and Communication Equipment*	Automotive and Home Supply	Ordnance
23. Cars and Metals	*Aircraft and Communications Equipment*	*Bikes and Precision Equipment*
24. *Motion Pictures*	Paper	Grains and Paper
25. Bituminous Coal Mining	Metal Mining	Metal Mining

(continued)

TABLE 9.1 *(continued)*

First Root:	Second Root:	Third Root:
LOW SCORES		
95. Motor Vehicles Parts	Local Surface Transit	Shoe Stores
96. Automobile Repairs	Furniture for Homes	Radio, TV and Computer Stores
97. Plumbing, Heating, Air-Conditioning	Residential Building Contractors	Home Appliance Stores
98. Homes, Pottery, Wool	Commercial Banking	Intercity and Rural Bus Transport
99. Lumber for Construction	Motor Vehicles	Day Care
100. Service to Building	Accounting, Auditing	Carpeting and Flooring
101. Furniture for Homes	Radio, TV Broadcasting	Retail Baking
102. Electrical Work	Periodical Publishing	Roofing and Siding
103. Trucking	Apparel—Women	Nonstore Retail
104. Life Insurance	Computer Data Processing	Logging
105. Gasoline Service Stations	Beauty Shops	Office—Clinics and Other Health Practitioners
106. Automobile Services	New and Used Car Dealers	Residential Building Contractors
107. Grocery Stores	Furniture Stores	Periodical Publishing
108. Operatives—Building	Operatives—Building	Petroleum Products

*Italicized entries indicate industries generally thought to be knowledge based.

of inequality in the wage structure, particularly given the vast expansion of pure-service employment during that time.[11] As it turns out, our measure of wage-structure inequality, drawn from manufacturing alone, is very highly correlated with the rising difference between manufacturing taken as a whole and pure services. Once again, the same forces are at work across and within groups.[12]

Table 9.2 sorts our industries by the overall degree of earnings gain over this period and reveals the core pattern of winners and losers in the wage structure. At the top of the pile, we find the medical-industrial complex: hospitals, insurance, medical supplies, with nursing care a bit behind. Not yet the highest paying of all sectors, these have come a long way on the explosion of demand for medical care and the explosion of health costs in the past quarter-century. Next we find the technological beneficiaries of the information age: computers, electronics, communications, movies. In roughly the same league we find the energy sectors: petroleum and gas (but not coal). There then follows the long list of core consumer manufacturing and an even

TABLE 9.2

INDUSTRIES WITH HIGH AND LOW HOURLY REAL EARNINGS CHANGES, 1973–1992

Winners	Percentage Change in Real Earnings per Hour	Losers	Percentage Change in Real Earnings per Hour
Hospitals	25.5	Roofing and Siding	−34.6
Fire, Marine and		Electrical Work	−33.7
Casualty Insurance	22.3	Carpet and Flooring	−32.6
Medical and Health		Masonry, Stone, Plaster	−32
Insurance	19.9	Paint and Paper Hanging	−32.5
Medical Equipment		Plumbing, Heating, Air	
and Supplies	19.2	Conditioning	−31.9
Petroleum and Gas	16.2	Residential Building	−30.6
Bikes and Precision		Grocery Stores	−28.3
Equipment	15.6	Heavy Construction	−27.2
Computers	14.3	Trucking	−26.3
Iron Ore Mining	13.0	Petroleum Products	−24.6
Nursing Care	11.5	Nonresidential Building	−24.0
Professional		Operative Builders	−23.2
Organizations	11.3	Intercity and Rural Bus	−23.1
Combination Utility		Services to Buildings	−23.0
Services	10.9	Gasoline Service Stations	−22.0
Ordnance	10.7	Department Stores	−21.3
Motion Pictures	10.6	Retail Bakeries	−20.8
Telephone	10.4	Paint and Glass	−20.3
Computer Data		Paper	−20.2
Processing	10.4	Lumber	−19.2
Gas	9.8	Household Appliances	−18.8
Electronics and		Local and Suburban Transit	−18.0
Photographic		Furniture Stores	−17.7
Equipment	9.2		
Electrical Services	9.0		
Aircraft and			
Communications	8.9		
Life Insurance	7.9		
Chemicals	6.7		
Oil	5.2		
Drugstores	2.9		
Grains and Paper	2.6		

longer list of retail, repair, maintenance, and services establishments. Bringing up the rear, we find the construction and home repair trades: carpentry, plumbing, electricians, roofers, and so on. Once the highest paid of all services activities, this sector has done poorly since the early 1970s, no doubt victim of the massive decline in residential home building since that time.

In the period since 1973, investment and investment above all has driven the interindustry wage structure. This is true within the manufacturing sector proper, and it is true between manufacturing and services, once the two are properly demarcated.

The story of services, therefore, is that there is no separate story. Industries associated with capital investment, with the production of capital goods and particularly with the production of new technologies, have done comparatively well in modern times. Industries and activities that rely on any other source of prosperity, whether it be consumer demand or the national security state, have done poorly. The bottom has fallen away for the noninvestment sector.

The implications of this finding go well beyond the analysis of the sources of rising inequality. They suggest that an entire civic mantra, on the virtues of saving and of investment and on the deficiencies of American society in this regard, has been misleading as both diagnosis and prescription. *Comparatively speaking,* we have not in fact lacked for investment. Therefore we cannot have lacked for the saving required to finance investment. To the contrary, private business investment is the singular activity that the American economy has continued to pursue, willy-nilly, at a high rate and in a state of frenetic self-renewal, within a general environment of stagnation and decline. We lack for everything else that accompanied rising private investment in the period from 1946 to 1973: rising living standards, rising wages, falling poverty, increased employment in the high-wage, nonmanufacturing sectors such as government itself, and especially for the public investments that raise collective living standards and provide amenities that every citizen can enjoy. Thus, the floors that society had formerly placed under wages in the S-sector have been progressively eaten away.

It is impossible to square this picture with the prevailing image of a country afflicted by declining savings and private consumer profligacy, though that image is relentlessly touted by a certain school of policy advisers and their allies in academic economics. The evidence presented here contradicts it. What we see from the movements of the wage structure leads to the opposite conclusion. Investment is the activity that has survived and prospered, at least in relative terms, in an otherwise declining economy.[13] And those in position to profit from spending on investment equipment have done well, almost alone among manufacturing workers, in the distribution of wages.

A surfeit of investment! An excess of technological change! But, on reflection, how could it be otherwise? Private business investment is the source of the technological revolutions to which we are repeatedly subjected. These revolutions would be hard put to occur in a society that was not investing; indeed they would not and could not occur in such a society. They therefore fit oddly into the picture of a savings-starved, investment-short, happy-go-lucky culture with which we are constantly fed. Investment brings us technology. And these technological revolutions are themselves the instruments of a massive transfer of wealth, away from technology users and toward technology producers. This pattern of transfers, following the rhythms of the business cycle and of the unemployment rate, is an ultimate source of rising inequality in wages.

But, one may ask, aren't the comparative gains of the manufacturing sectors and particularly of the knowledge-based industries due to their superior productivity performance? Isn't this just the proper working of a market system? Haven't things always been this way?

The answers are surely yes, but then no, and no. Certainly the technology sectors and the goods-producing sectors below them enjoy high rates of productivity growth, compared to pure services. They always have. This is in the nature of activities that use technology and capital: they can change, and they do change, with the progress of technique and the renewal of equipment.

There is nevertheless no necessary reason, no dictate of economic logic, why a rapid rate of productivity gain inside a sector should necessarily lead to proportionately higher relative wages *in that sector.* The rule that real production wages track productivity growth applies only at the most aggregate level, to the averages for a society as a whole. It does not apply to the internal distribution of income.[14] In a different institutional setting, the result might as easily have been a generalized catch-up to rising manufacturing wages and an accompanying general rise of the level of prices—a mild and steady inflation. Or we might have seen falling prices for manufactured goods and a stable structure of nominal wages. In that case, the benefits of higher manufacturing productivity growth and new technologies are spread through the society rather than being concentrated on the technology generators and goods producers.

Such institutional settings are not merely hypothetical. They are part of history and have occurred at other historical moments in the United States as well as overseas. They were in fact the prevailing pattern during the first generation following World War II. They remain the pattern, to a very substantial extent, in Northern Europe. What has happened in the United States since the early 1970s is therefore historically and politically specific. To put it most briefly, politics and history govern our fate.

WE CAN now round out our analysis of the rise in inequality of wages and salaries in the United States that began in the early 1970s. We have seen that the explanations so far offered—that technology did it or that trade did it—are at best partial and inadequate. Although technology did play a major role in the income transformation of the past two decades, the role of technology cannot be fitted into the model of a competitive labor market. That framework offers a distorted idea of what technology is. It is biased toward the computer at the expense of the full array of other technologies undergoing almost equally rapid change. It has no comprehensive measure of technological change that can be matched to the rise in inequality that has occurred. It offers no foundation for the belief that technology should have changed in such a way as to produce higher inequality after 1970, when it did not do so before that date.

What emerges from this analysis is the industry-specific and policy-dependent character of the technical revolution. Some industries design, make, and sell capital goods. These industries—whose exact boundaries are broadly but not precisely captured in my industrial classifications—hold the cards in the game of technological winner-take-all. Workers in these industries are defined to be the workers with scarce and valuable "skill." Outside these sectors, in the realms of machine-using mass production and pure service activities, there is comparatively little that workers can do, as individuals, to enhance their position. Working "smart" here is an illusion: the number of winners in a winner-take-all lottery is necessarily a small fraction of those who would like to play. "Technological revolution" is a game that only a few can win.

Once the increase in dispersion in manufacturing wage and salary incomes is measured with satisfactory precision on a year-to-year basis, it can be substantially explained. Macroeconomic developments and policy measures—changes in unemployment, the rise in the dollar's exchange rate after 1980, economic growth, inflation, and the minimum wage—can all be shown to have had significant effects on increasing inequality in manufacturing wages. This exercise removes the mystery behind the movements of inequality in the manufacturing wage structure. And a similar story holds for the larger movements of wages between manufacturing and services, though here an even greater explanatory weight must be laid on the investment cycle.

What remains to be explained is *why* the movements of the macroeconomic variables took the form that they did. And this we have now also done. We have shown that what happened was a collapse of the political forces that had previously supported mass consumption. Up until the early 1970s, a broad-based improvement of living standards by working Americans had been achieved through a range of means working in parallel and including high volumes of output and employment, trade protection, and government expenditures on national defense. This is what disappeared. The worker's state, it would seem, did not just decline and finally collapse in the Soviet Union. Rather, a much more powerful, much more successful one also fell into decay, over the same period of time, in the United States.

From the end of World War II until about 1970, the pressures of creative destruction on the wage structure were under control, for the United States pursued policies of full employment, reasonably steady economic growth, and rapid actions to prevent or end recessions. These were accompanied through the 1960s by an explicit policy of wage discipline and solidarity. All workers in the society came to expect an average increase in real compensation approximately equal to the average national rate of productivity growth. This was the "guideposts" policy. Its intent and effect were to squeeze the wage structure, gradually reducing differentials between professions and jobs. The squeezing was promoted by a low unemployment rate (3.5 percent by 1969), a steadily rising minimum wage ($6.50 in 1994 purchasing power by 1968), a strong union movement in alliance with the governing party, and a War on Poverty whose intended effect was to strengthen the poor in their struggle for jobs and incomes.

After 1969 the government took a different turn. Wage-price guideposts were abandoned, freeing business firms to raise prices. Macroeconomic policy became dramatically unstable, creating and tolerating recession in 1970 to tame the inflation that the end of price restraints produced. An investment tax credit further boosted the investment sector. In 1973, OPEC raised oil prices, partly to finance enormous purchases of American arms, and monetary policy again responded with high interest rates and unemployment. The pattern repeated at the end of the decade following the revolution in Iran, with a short recession in 1980 and a deep one in 1981–1982.

Through this time, full employment, protectionism, and later national security expenditures were progressively stripped away, and though there were occasional election year booms, the first in 1972 and the second in 1984, consumption expenditures fell with the declining average real wage. After 1980, the dollar went up, and imports flooded in. Minimum wages fell sharply in real terms. All of these changes had the effect of breaking down the structures of solidarity that had held the American middle class together for the first quarter-century after the end of World War II.

The new instability of macroeconomics gave a powerful boost to investment and technology, both in absolute terms and as compared with consumption. With each recession, waves of older factories disappeared. With them went the hard-won, high-paying jobs of the traditional blue-collar workforce. But with each recovery, firms faced an imperative to replace lost capacity, and to do it in the most cost-saving, labor-saving, technologically advanced way available at that moment in time. Waves of layoffs were followed by waves of investment. But the new investments were never designed to relieve the distress of the previously unemployed. They were designed instead to substitute entirely for them, and this they accomplished.

At the same time, incomes policies were abandoned. The idea that all society should benefit equally from national productivity gains was replaced by an ideology of the market, in which winner-take-all and the devil-the-hindmost. Minimum wages were allowed to fall in real terms; safety net social expenditures came under assault. There began a cult of the entrepreneur, laying great stress on the wonders and virtues of new technology but no accompanying concern for its fantastic propensity to redistribute existing income and wealth from the many to the few. The technology-producing sectors, which had been present all along (but tamed) in the old Keynesian economy, began their drive for an ever-expanding share of incomes. And they succeeded, at the expense of the middle-class society that America once was, not long ago.

What was left was a technology empire. In that empire, a comparatively small number of firms and their salaried employees, plus a fair number of independent professionals, could reap the rewards of an immense predatory raid on the previously existing structures of production. The weapons in that raid are selected and even deployed by the victims themselves. But participation is involuntary nonetheless. "Invest or die" becomes the creed in every industrial activity under technological assault. The consequence is an enrichment of the technology producers, a weakening of the technology buyers, a successive displacement of C-sector workers into the S-sector. Ultimately, the losers end up in debt or on the dole, in the ever-less-welcoming arms of the Transfer State.

In presenting this story, one might be drawn to the idea that the rush to new technology as such was at fault.[15] The rebuke of Luddism haunts this argument, just as the protectionist urge lurks behind the trade-did-it position. But neither technology, properly measured and accounted for, nor the expansion of trade *in themselves* brought on the rise in inequality of which the country was the victim. They were merely the battering rams with which the old structures were knocked down, with technical revolution in the senior and the high dollar in the junior position.

Behind the battering rams, behind the decisions to use them in this way, behind the creation of the situations in which they could be used in such a way, were political figures and policy decisions—decisions, for example, to tolerate unemployment. The economy is a managed beast. It was managed in such a way that this was the result. It could have been done differently. It was not inevitable even given the progress of technology and the growth of trade. It was, in a sense, done deliberately. That is the real evil of the time.

Part Three

HERESIES

10

THE NAIRU TRAP

The Conservative belief that there is some law of nature which prevents men from being employed, that it is "rash" to employ men, and that it is financially "sound" to maintain a tenth of the population in idleness for an indefinite period, is crazily improbable—the sort of thing which no man could believe who had not had his head fuddled with nonsense for years and years.

—John Maynard Keynes, *Can Lloyd George Do It?*

If we want a more equal wage structure, we need a low rate of unemployment. Other conditions would help: a still-higher minimum wage, a more competitive value of the dollar, general price stability. Nevertheless, a low unemployment rate—say, 4 percent or lower, and sustained for a long period of time—is the essential thing. This is the principal way to equalize the playing field between sellers of technology and those who must buy it, and so to turn the American wage structure from a bloody battleground back toward a model of middle-class solidarity.

Is this possible? Can we return to full employment and stay there? Most professional economists would say no. At a minimum, they would argue that persistent low unemployment would generate an unacceptable increase in inflation. Many would argue that unemployment below 5 percent or so would produce accelerating inflation—a fast track to hyperinflation. This is the "accelerationist hypothesis," associated with the idea of a natural rate of unemployment.

The concept of a natural rate of unemployment, or nonaccelerating inflation rate of unemployment (NAIRU), has more or less ruled American macroeconomics for about twenty-five years. It has its origins in a remarkable 1968 presidential lecture to the American Economics Association by Milton Friedman, perhaps the most influential such lecture ever given. Not by coincidence, macroeconomists in the years since have mostly abandoned research into the problems and costs of unemployment, and for the most part have become a potent voice against policies directed at reducing the rate of unemployment. So long as this brand of economics remains influential, it is unlikely that much will be done about unemployment or about the high rates of *underemployment* that develop when open unemployment is high and good jobs are scarce.

This chapter presents the case for no confidence in Friedman's idea and its successors over the years, an argument for discarding the NAIRU as a basis for policy. First, I will argue that the theoretical case for the existence of a natural rate of unemployment is not compelling, and never was compelling. Second, the empirical evidence for the accelerationist hypothesis is weak, and it has become much weaker in the past decade. There is little basis for the fear that inflation accelerates quickly once unemployment falls below some threshold level. Third, the record reveals that attempts to estimate the location of the NAIRU or natural rate have been, on the whole, a professional embarrassment, a sequence of repeated failures. This has been more than just a series of missed guesses, of cases where the unemployment rate went down and inflation didn't rise as predicted. Rather, there has occurred a failure of the economics profession even to agree on the basic methods by which one would set about finding the natural rate. Fourth, I will argue that adherence to the concept of the natural rate as a guide to policy has major social costs but negligible social benefits; it amounts to a device for turning the economics profession into apologists for those social forces that do not want full employment. The risks of dropping the natural rate hypothesis are therefore minor, except so far as those particular interests are concerned. If we are wrong, the error can be corrected, and not much will have been lost.

Before Friedman's lecture, most American economists accepted the famous "stable Phillips curve" as the best concise statement of the relationship between unemployment and inflation. In concrete terms, they expected that a lower unemployment rate would be associated with a higher rate of inflation. For example, they might expect that a 5 percent unemployment rate would yield a 2 percent rate of inflation, while a 3 percent unemployment rate (full employment by any standard) might yield inflation of 5 or 6 percent per year. Critically, they expected these relationships to be stable. Three percent unemployment might be associated with inflation of (say) 5 or 6 percent. It would not be the cause of inflation rates rising from year to year, from, say, 6 to 8 to 10 percent and continuing on upward. Likewise, high unemployment would cause low, but again stable, inflation; it would not be the cause of steadily declining rates of inflation, perhaps leading to falling prices.

Thus, the Phillips curve presented policymakers with an inflation-unemployment trade-off and a resulting menu of policy choices. But it was a menu that they could live with. Liberals could argue for a lower rate of unemployment, at the cost of a slightly higher rate of inflation. Conservatives could argue for accepting a higher rate of unemployment, in return for a closer approach to price stability. What both camps shared was an underlying analysis of the choices involved. They agreed that the choice was fundamentally stable. While they might disagree on the appropriate policy, neither conservative nor liberal could accuse the other of making an error based on faulty theory or of embarking the economy on the road to ruin.

Friedman changed all of that. His device was very simple. Friedman asked, What happens if rational economic actors come to understand the Phillips curve? Won't they then make a correct forecast of the consequences for inflation from falling unemployment and adjust their price expectations accordingly? Won't that lead to a ratchet effect in the inflation rate, in which yesterday's expectations become incorporated in today's demand for higher wages and higher prices? In this way, Friedman introduced what economists call an "expectations function" into the equations describing the Phillips curve. Henceforth, the inflation rate would depend both on unemployment and on *past inflation expectations.*

In Friedman's model, efforts to drive the unemployment rate down would lead workers and businessmen to expect a higher rate of inflation. They would therefore raise their demands for wages and price increases. This would cause the short-run Phillips trade-off between unemployment and inflation to "shift upward." Every given level of unemployment would now be associated with a higher rate of inflation than had been the case before. And once economic agents again realized that this had happened, they would again react, raising their price and wage demands yet again, so long as unemployment remained "too low."

The expected rate of inflation would come to predict the actual rate of inflation—and the process of inflation acceleration would stop—only when unemployment is held at an equilibrium value, a value that did *not* induce expectations of accelerating inflation. This is the value that Friedman called the natural rate of unemployment. By definition, the long run is a condition of the economy when expectations are satisfied, and therefore conditions do not change. Friedman's natural rate of unemployment was thus a long-run equilibrium in this sense.

Friedman was drawing the distinction between the short run, when variations of unemployment could affect inflation, and the long run, when by construction unemployment could not vary. Efforts to reduce unemployment below its natural rate equilibrium would appear successful in the short run but would soon generate accelerating inflation whose intolerability would force a retreat to the natural rate.

This argument swept the field, giving conservatives a virtual monopoly on both innovation and respectability in macroeconomics for perhaps the following fifteen years. Friedman's policy lesson was plain. It was foolishness to pursue full employment, that hoary goal of federal policy since the Employment Act of 1946, except by measures on the "supply side" that might enhance human capital or "make the markets work better." The simple-minded but successful policies of the 1960s, which had reduced unemployment below 3.5 percent while maintaining inflation below 6 percent, despite a shooting war, were rejected as though they had harbored an unsuspected virus. Even those who had designed the policies of the 1960s became defensive about them in later years, so great was the stigma of theoretical error they carried in the wake of Friedman's speech.

Yet Friedman's approach is open to questions that were not widely raised at the time, questions that remain essentially unanswered decades later. First among these concern the shortcomings of the Phillips curve itself. The Phillips curve had always been a purely empirical relationship, an inference from the data of economic history. It had been adopted by the Keynesians of the day, because their theoretical model had no effective way to predict the rate of inflation. (James Tobin once elegantly described the Phillips curve as a set of empirical observations in search of a theory, like Pirandello characters in search of a plot.) The Phillips curve plugged the hole in a simple but effective way, and for the first decade after it was introduced (in 1960), it seemed to be a remarkably effective forecasting device.

Milton Friedman accepted the Phillips curve as a valid model *in the short run*. He supplied no theory for a short-run Phillips curve; he simply affirmed that such a relationship would "always" exist. He did this, as a matter of logic, because he had to; the theoretical logic of the natural rate of unemployment itself depends in a critical way on the validity of the Phillips curve in the short run. If the Phillips relationship fails empirically—that is, if levels of un-

employment do not in fact predict the rate of inflation in the short run—
then the construct of the natural rate of unemployment also loses meaning.[1]
This empirical issue, which is more troubling than most suppose, will be discussed later. For the moment, it is sufficient to note that a theoretical argument that rests on a purely empirical, atheoretic foundation is likely to run
into trouble sooner or later.

Friedman surely sensed the difficulty. For while his core argument was
macroeconomic and dependent on the short-run Phillips curve, he also
phrased a version of it in *microeconomic* terms, in terms of the basic economics of supply and demand. According to this alternate version, the real wage
adjusts so that the amount of labor firms wish to hire comes exactly to equal
the amount that workers wish to supply. The natural rate of employment
(and, implicitly, unemployment) is then simply the equilibrium point of this
market. If policy attempts to push unemployment lower than the equilibrium, money wages and money prices start chasing each other skyward.

The two versions are quite distinct. The main line of Friedman's argument
concerned a long-run Phillips curve based on sticky wages and slowly adjust-
ing expectations; it left the possibility open that some short-run policy interventions to reduce unemployment might succeed. The notion of an
aggregate labor market pointed the way toward the radically right-wing economics that dominated macroeconomics in the 1980s. This model took the
idea of a "natural rate of unemployment" to new extremes. Friedman put it
this way:

> At any moment of time, there is some level of unemployment which has the
> property that it is consistent with equilibrium in the structure of *real* wage rates.
> . . . The "natural rate of unemployment" in other words, is the level that would
> be ground out by the Walrasian system of general equilibrium equations, pro-
> vided there is embedded in them the actual structural characteristics of the
> labor and commodity markets. [emphasis added]

Such a labor market is pure and perfect in all the ways that a neoclassical
economist of the late nineteenth century—Leon Walras in Friedman's in-
structive reference—would have liked to believe. It is free of money: it has no
money contracts and no "money illusion," meaning that workers see through
the dollar value of their paycheck to the underlying basket of consumption
goods it will buy. Thus, workers cannot be fooled into neglecting the
prospects for inflation, which might lead them to think that their pay is
worth more than it is. Employment is purely a function of the real wage, acting on the marginal physical productivity of labor (the basic force underlying

the demand curve) and the marginal disutility of work (the basic force underlying the willingness to work).

In such a market, economists say, nominal shocks can have only nominal, not real, effects. This means that if you simply inject money into the system, you get an effect on prices but not on output. Money (for which one may as well substitute "macroeconomic policy") is neutral, perhaps even in the short run. Friedman's formulation states that persistent unemployment below the natural rate must lead through the labor market to rising real wages—to money wages rising more rapidly than prices. Rising real wages must then dampen the willingness of firms to hire new employees, engendering a return to the natural rate of unemployment.

Inflation enters the picture only insofar as employers try to push up prices to keep the real wage from rising. But this proposition cannot succeed, under the terms of the model, so long as unemployment remains below the natural rate. Money wages must catch up to rising prices, and the only recourse for employers is to push prices up once again. Thus, in this version just as in the other one, Friedman's formulation led to accelerating inflation if governments are so foolish as to try to keep unemployment below the natural rate.

This story is pre-Keynesian in all its essentials; every bit of it could have been articulated before John Maynard Keynes published *The General Theory of Employment Interest and Money* in 1936. And the essential theoretical objections to it were set forth by Keynes in that book.

First, Keynes argued that labor supply and demand cannot be modeled in terms of the real wage, for workers care about relative wages as well as real wages. They care about how much their neighbors and colleagues are earning, not merely about the purchasing power of their own wages. This means that workers bitterly resist cuts in their money wages, which are almost always particular rather than general in effect, while they do not resist small rises in the cost of living that erode the real wage. Keynes argued that for this reason one could not model the labor market as an "equilibrium in the structure of real wage rates." Both money wages and prices affect real wages—but in sharply differing ways.

Second, and more seriously, Keynes argued that workers cannot actually negotiate for their own real wages. This is because of an interdependency between money wages and the price level. If workers accept a cut in their money wages, the firms they work for will observe a reduction in their costs. The result will be a cut in the prices of products that those firms produce. But this will feed back into the consumption basket of the workers: goods they purchase will be cheaper. The result: the real wage will not fall, in response to a cut in money wages, at least not by nearly the same amount as the money cut.

The mechanism for the adjustment of real wages in the labor market therefore cannot work along the principles that the classical economists (and, in 1968, Milton Friedman) proposed. The labor market cannot achieve an "equilibrium in the structure of real wage rates." Even if workers as a group would like to accommodate their employers, Keynes argued, by working for less, they find themselves incapable of achieving this result. Wages are cut, demand falls, inventories stock up, and firms will cut prices in order to move the merchandise. Once that happens, real wages go back to where they were before, and the workers, while better off individually, have done nothing to increase employers' willingness to add new workers to the labor force.

These two objections fatally undermine the concept of the labor supply curve. Hence they take apart the very construct of an aggregative labor market. You can't have a labor market without a supply curve for labor. There is no getting around this difficulty: markets require supply and demand. If part of the market model is irreparably inconsistent with the facts, you cannot rely on market adjustments to deliver pleasing equilibrium results.

If there is no aggregative labor market in any sense meaningful to economics, then theories based on shifts in real wages clearing labor markets will fail to hold. From a proper Keynesian perspective, the correct response to Friedman's second formulation of the natural rate hypothesis would have simply been, "Sorry, but at the aggregative level the 'labor market' is a misconception; it doesn't exist." Keynesians in 1968 should have insisted that aggregate demand for output, and not supply and demand for labor, determine employment, and that therefore only the first Friedman formulation, that of expectations plus the Phillips curve, was worthy of serious examination. Friedman's second formulation was simply a failed metaphor, unsuitable for use as the foundation of a theory.

A further line of objection to Friedman's theory of the natural rate also has its roots in Keynes. Is long-run equilibrium really a good guide to macroeconomic policy? Friedman's NAIRUvian long run and the more strictly classical natural rate, based on rational expectations, are certainly beguiling; they have a logical charm and evoke the appreciation economists reserve for clever argument. But are they relevant? Information may be asymmetric. Competition may be monopolistic. Nonlinearities and even chaos are possible. In such cases, the long-run equilibrium may be undetermined or incalculable or beyond achievement. The future may be inherently unpredictable. And workers may very well understand that in a world of rational indifference, of a principled refusal to compute, surely the short-run relationships and policy actions are what matter. As Keynes famously made this point: "In the long run we are dead."

Even the Chicago economist Robert Lucas has made the argument that the long run is only a sequence of steps which each occur in the here-and-now.[2] If short-run policies necessarily fail, which is Lucas's position, then you must live by the long run. But if short-run policies actually work, it is fruitless to look that far ahead, and what you have to do is work from one short run to the next. This is the position of Keynes. The gulf between Lucas and Keynes is unbridgeable, but the point on which principled conservatives and liberals must agree is that one must choose one construct or the other. It is impossible to think clearly about economic policy problems if you spend your time trying to split the difference, to divide the world into mutually noncommunicating spheres by basing policy in the short run on one set of considerations and policy in the long run on others.

These objections are far easier to make in retrospect than they were in 1968. Mainstream American Keynesians of the late 1960s were committed to the Phillips curve.[3] Yet they could also hardly deny a role for expectations, or that expectations must be satisfied in the long run. In their own interpretations of Keynes, they had also already resurrected the aggregate labor market, literally over the dead body of the master. They were thus in no position to react to Friedman by citing Keynes or by repudiating the fallacies inherent in a model that combined Keynesian and anti-Keynesian thinking.[4]

Let us now consider some evidence. Figure 10.1 shows the short-run Phillips curve in the 1960s and beyond.[5] The data are monthly moving averages (over twelve months) of inflation and unemployment, with yearly labels inserted at midyear. At a glance, Figure 10.1 does resemble a shifting set of short-run Phillips curves. For example, one can pick out a curve in the lower left for the 1960s, and another curve in the upper center representing the late 1970s, after the second oil shock. But on average, taking the data as a whole, there is only a very modest inverse relation between inflation and unemployment. The range is very wide, with much horizontal movement. Moreover, the main upward thrusts are contributed by a fairly small number of inflationary months—in the late 1960s, 1973, and 1979. These upward thrusts happened at very different levels of unemployment, sometimes low and sometimes quite high, and it is hard to see any unifying or consistent theme relating them to the rate of unemployment.

Equally important, the figure is not symmetric.[6] Leftward movements,

FIGURE 10.1

INFLATION AND UNEMPLOYMENT
Monthly Moving Averages, 1961–1997

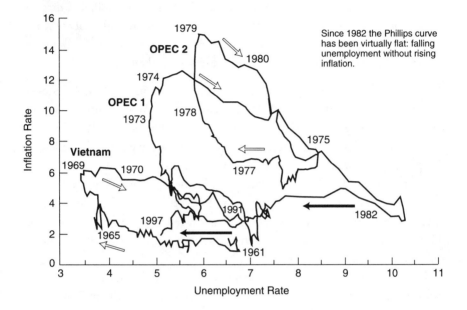

when unemployment is falling, are substantially horizontal. In each expansion from the late 1960s to the mid-1990s, inflation rose little as unemployment fell. However, rightward movements as unemployment rises do result in a fall in inflation. Recessions are indeed disinflationary, as no one disputes. Thus, one can get Phillips-type patterns very easily by looking at times when unemployment is rising, but when unemployment is falling, the figure gives very few hints of where and when inflation will strike. If there is a natural rate of unemployment running through the diagram in Figure 10.1, where is it located, exactly?

In a 1997 article that fairly represents the state of the art in estimating NAIRU, the leading practitioner reports NAIRU estimates for 1994 with mean values just below 6.0 percent, with some variation when different measures of inflation are used. But the 95 percent confidence intervals—the statistical margin of error—around these estimates range from 2.8 to 7.7 percent! Such a band by itself makes the NAIRU useless for policy purposes; one might say that with such friends, critics are superfluous.[7]

When, as an alternative strategy, the studies have allowed the natural rate to move, it has shifted considerably. According to one study:

> The natural rate of unemployment is estimated to have increased steadily from 3.5 percent in the mid-1960s to a peak of 7.25 percent in 1980, and then to have fallen back to about 5.75 percent in 1988. . . . Thus, roughly half of the increase in actual unemployment rates from the mid-1960s to their peak in the early 1980s can be attributed to increases in the natural rate.[8]

Thus, as the real unemployment rate moves, the apparent NAIRU moves in its shadow. Estimates of the NAIRU were at 6 percent or so for the overall unemployment rate following the recession of 1990, and as late as 1995 many still insisted on that number. Currently, they have generally fallen to 5.5 percent or lower.[9] Yet unemployment has already fallen below 5 percent, with no perceptible effect on inflation. As in the past, the present estimates and reestimates seem largely a response to predictive failure. We still have no theory, and no external evidence, governing the fall of the estimated NAIRU. The literature simply observes that inflation hasn't occurred and so the previous estimate must have been too high.[10]

It is often necessary to revise a parameter once or twice in the light of new information. Differences of specification are also normal in the early stages of scientific inquiry. But to hold to a concept in the face of twenty years of unexplained variation, predictive failure, and failure of the profession to coalesce on procedural issues is quite another matter. If professional economists want to be taken seriously on the NAIRU, they have to come to agreement. Yet agreement on even the present location of the NAIRU or its confidence interval remains far away. Nothing remotely resembling the unified policy view of the 1960s Keynesians, with their commitment to the pre-NAIRU Phillips curve, exists today.[11]

Speaking politically, the natural rate hypothesis has served a conservative cause. Ever since Friedman's speech, orthodox macroeconomics has virtually always leaned against policies to support full employment. In spite of stagnant real wages, it has virtually never leaned the other way.

For the radical conservatives, this must be forgiven: the logic of their case imposes opposition to all policies affecting employment through aggregate demand. But for the more pragmatic NAIRUvians, who believe that demand policy may have an appropriate role in engineering "soft landings" at the NAIRU, these statistical games seem to be a matter of curiously irrational, systematic error. Some economists have been more eager to raise their estimate of NAIRU than to cut it. The NAIRU, like the wage rate, is downwardly sticky.

When a higher NAIRU accompanies higher unemployment, it cuts against the case for a policy of expansion, since a higher proportion of the existing unemployment is seen as necessary to preserve stable inflation. When unemployment is falling, a downwardly sticky NAIRU bolsters the natural caution of many economists concerning pro-growth policy intervention. In consequence, policymakers are almost *never* presented with a clear case, based on natural rate analysis and supported by a consensus of NAIRU-adhering economists, for a pro-employment policy. This pattern continues right up to the present; some economists who a few years ago insisted that the natural rate was 6 percent now insist on 5.5 percent, or perhaps 5 percent. Lower estimates will be forthcoming, after the fact, if unemployment continues to fall and inflation does not increase. But by then it will be too late, and potential gains from having the estimates in hand now will have been lost.

Economics has in this way talked itself out of a role in solving the central macroeconomic problems of unemployment and stagnation. Taxonomy in the least useful sense of that term—the empty art of labeling existing unemployment as "structural," "frictional," or "cyclical"—has substituted for the development of theory bearing on action. The theories that have developed reinforce the message implicit in the taxonomy chosen: once frictional, structural, and cyclical unemployment are allowed for, there is truly nothing left to be done. The cost of unnecessarily high unemployment itself must therefore, to some extent, rest on the conscience of the economics profession.[12]

We have seen, in earlier chapters, that high measured unemployment reflects conditions that have pernicious effects, not just on the unemployed but throughout the structure of wages and incomes. This simply calls further attention to the pervasive evil of excessive unemployment. The conditions that produce unemployment also work to split the wage structure. They undermine the middle-class character of society and separate the comfortable from the poor. The relationship between unemployment and inequality is therefore an additional reason for devoting intellectual and material resources to the pursuit of full employment. It also makes it reasonable to ask that advocates of speed-limit theorems and natural rate hypotheses prove their cases convincingly and in a unified way, something that in three decades they have not done.

Can economics live without the natural rate of unemployment? Surely the measure of scientific maturity lies in a willingness to match theory with evidence, to discuss anomalies with an open mind, and to move on when it is appropriate to do so. Occasionally this may mean reconstructing one's thinking from the ground up.

In fact, the case for basing anti-inflation policy primarily around the rate of unemployment was never persuasive—not in 1960 when the short-run Phillips curve came onto the American scene, not when Friedman introduced the nearly vertical version he called the "natural rate." The evidence since that time weighs further against drawing implications for policy from either confection, and equally against drawing implications from modern versions. One need not object to the NAIRU as a purely mathematical or statistical construct. The problem comes when one is asked whether to raise interest rates, *today*, based on the fact that the actual unemployment rate has dropped below the estimate of such a rate in someone's model. The uncertainty and dissensus among the best economists working on this issue, and the persistent failure of inflation to accelerate in recent years despite transgressing past NAIRUs, should make this an easy call. It is only necessary that the working body of professional economists finally face this problem and make their judgment, liberating us all from an unnecessary and insupportable intellectual barrier to the return to full employment.

11

THE NEW VICTORIANS

The new rich of the nineteenth century were not brought up
to large expenditures, and preferred the power which investment gave them to the pleasures of immediate consumption.
In fact, it was precisely the *inequality* of the distribution of
wealth which made possible those vast accumulations of fixed
wealth and of capital improvements which distinguished that
age from all others. Herein lay, in fact, the main justification of
the Capitalist System. If the rich had spent their new wealth
on their own enjoyments, the world would long ago have
found such a regime intolerable.

—John Maynard Keynes, *The Economic Consequences of the Peace*

In his first, great and angry essay, *The Economic Consequences of
the Peace,* the young British economist John Maynard Keynes
wrote in 1920 that the economy of nineteenth-century Europe had been sustained by a "double bluff." A small number of the very rich were allowed to
earn a great share of national income, because instead of spending it for their
own pleasures, they took on the obligation of saving, investing, and choosing
the direction and the scale of social progress. Because they did so, they were
perceived by the workers as performing a necessary social function. The rich,
in their turn, accepted this obligation not from altruism but selfishly: their
idea was that through accumulation, they could ensure the prosperity of their
own children.

In truth, both sides were in the grip of illusion. On one side the "laboring
classes accepted from ignorance or powerlessness, or were compelled, per-

suaded, or cajoled by custom, convention, authority and the well established order of Society into accepting" only a small share of the "cake that they and nature and the capitalist classes were cooperating to produce."

> And on the other hand the capitalist classes were allowed to call the best part of the cake theirs and were theoretically free to consume it, on the tacit underlying condition that they consumed very little of it in practice. The duty of "saving," became nine-tenths of virtue and the growth of the cake the object of true religion.

The illusion especially gripped the wealthy, for they had freedom of choice. Unlike the workers, they could, in principle, consume at pleasure, yet they did not, preferring to save for old age or for their heirs. But, as Keynes pointed out, "this was only in theory." For the moral imperative to save and accumulate transcended death and generations: "the virtue of the cake was that it was never to be consumed, neither by you nor your children after you."

The system thus depended on a current and a continuous disinclination by the wealthiest citizens to consume. Lest the bluff be called and the workers assert their claim to a large share, the same obligation, the same restraint, the same modesty had to be passed along down to the final generation. This possibility disappeared after 1914: *"The war has disclosed the possibility of consumption to all and the vanity of abstinence to many."*

World War I shattered faith in eternal progress; the rich lost confidence in themselves and in the security of their role. They abandoned their active responsibility and sought instead either to protect their financial positions by remaining liquid or through stock market speculation, or else to enjoy the fruits of wealth in consumption. Either way, both the accumulation of capital and the growth in living standards slowed down. And in the meantime the workers, having seen the vast capacity for consumption made evident by the war itself, refused from that point forward to refrain from demanding a larger share for themselves.

The old institutions and the economy they sustained collapsed. New methods of achieving the old objectives were required. It took until the end of World War II for this to happen, particularly in Europe, although the New Deal ran a laboratory for experimentation in the United States. And for a generation following World War II, the role of the wealthy was assumed, in essence, by the state. Social security systems and large-scale public investments, including military spending, closed the loop between savings and investment that had failed to close during the interwar period and the Great Depression. This was a great success, and it ensured almost continuous growth and full employment for a generation. It turned out that a social arrangement of a middle class led by its government was quite as feasible as, and more stable than, the old division of the world into capitalists and proletariat, kept alive in the rhetoric of the Marxist powers. Indeed the cold war contributed to the success of the system, for it put the elites in the democracies on notice that their middle classes had better conspicuously outperform the rise of living standards in the communist world. This they achieved, and the Keynesian system thrived in Europe and in the United States.

The wealthy were dispossessed of their power, but they never reconciled to the system, especially not in the United States where, unlike much of Europe, industrial capital remained almost wholly in private hands. And so the rich campaigned against the system. After 1969, for a variety of reasons, they tasted success and gradually returned to a controlling political role, from which they began to force the state to withdraw from the responsibilities that the new system had required of it. The long campaign continued over the 1970s, achieving small triumphs on capital gains taxation in 1978, with the appointment of Paul A. Volcker to the Federal Reserve Board in 1979, and with President Carter's commitment to balance the budget in 1980. It culminated in the election of the rich man's government of 1980. The Reagan Revolution completed what the Nixon administration had only begun, and tentatively: a massive reduction of taxes on the richest Americans, a massive increase in their interest incomes, and a start on the demolition of the welfare state.

So the rich triumphed. Yet they did so without resuming their former positions of social obligation, without resuming their former posture of industrious restraint. And therefore they failed to recreate either the dynamism of the late nineteenth century or the illusion of their own indispensability. A patina of legitimating economic argument, known as supply-side economics, laid the ground for Reaganism by claiming there would be an enormous rise of saving, investment, and work effort, that these would be "unleashed" just as soon as tax codes were rewritten to improve the structure of incentives.[1]

Nothing of the kind occurred. Tax rates were slashed, on both incomes and capital gains. Work effort among the upper classes did not improve. Interest rates were multiplied, which in theory should have raised the propensity to save. But instead there was a consumption binge, one that occurred strictly among the wealthy, who enjoyed almost all of the net income gains of that period and almost all of the increase in living standards.[2] The price they paid was to expose themselves to the country as the irresponsible people that in fact they were.

Supply-side economics nicely illustrated the distinction between an ethos and an exercise in propaganda. It was slick, clever, and certain to fail, an exercise in bad faith from the beginning. And in truth the ordinary rich, as distinct from their propaganda artists, are not really to blame. They had few alternatives, except to take the money and run. They could not have reassumed social leadership if they'd wanted to. Nineteenth-century industrialism could proceed from individual initiative only because it occurred at nineteenth-century scale, vast though it seemed at the time. The scale of accumulation that is routinely required today to support the current mass consumption that we have since come to expect lies far beyond the capacity of purely private economic institutions to assume and sustain the risks.

To put it another way, at the scale of the modern economy, the collective action problem is present in acute form. The Victorian wealthy were truly a tiny class, geographically concentrated, and subject to an intense social discipline that enabled them all to share, with minor exceptions, in the prevailing ethos of accumulation. The accumulating classes in the United States today are spread over the entire continental expanse of the country, and their prevailing attitude is hedonistic, libertarian, and selfish. So long as a significant fraction of the wealthy defect from an ethos of saving and accumulation, so long as they do not, in fact, invest, the resulting low rates of growth guarantee that the exercise will not be profitable for the remainder, the small number of technological virtuosos always excepted. Virtue does not pay unless all practice it; to restore the true religion in the 1980s would have required an Inquisition, and one was not forthcoming.

The supply-siders left an ideological vacuum. Since their collapse, there has existed no frank statement of a doctrine asserting bluntly that private control of private assets, concentrated in a tiny elite of the population, should become again the sole criterion for voice in economic affairs. And yet the alternative propositions are also so weak that this precise position has prevailed in practice. The roles of the state as engine of accumulation and as stabilizer of consumption seem to have been nearly forgotten—though the state continues to play that role in important ways, including the budgets for social security and national defense. The government's role in ensuring a fair and equitable pattern of income distribution is remembered only by conservatives and only, by them, with contempt. There is a common ground on the unchallengeable authority of markets that now stretches, with differences only of degree, from the radical right to the mainstream liberal. The poor are voiceless, the middle class marginalized; in the new theology of economic governance, only dollars vote, and only the rich have them. Thus we have essentially recreated in disguised form the myth of the indispensable capitalist leader.

Backing up this de facto social order, in the nearest thing we have today to a supply-side doctrine, is a stale religion of the virtues of saving, of thrift, of accumulation—a kind of reborn Victorianism for the masses. Legions of writers castigate Americans for an allegedly low national savings rate, for overconsumption, for profligacy. They urge hard work, abstinence, self-reliance, the acquisition of skills, and faith in the fairness of the private market outcome. Most of all, they urge financial prudence and provision for the future, by each household individually and by the government on behalf of the whole. The movement for a balanced budget is the public sector manifestation of this creed; the preacherly exhortation to "work, save, and invest" is the manifestation of it in the private realm.

The problem with this revived liturgy of national self-improvement is that, unlike the old Victorianism, which was a creed meant for the rich alone, the new one is directed at an audience incapable of responding in any substantial way. Half or more of American households accumulate nothing; the lower middle class and below live from month to month. For the majority of the remainder, accumulation takes the form of a house and a mandatory retirement plan, neither of which they control. The bottom 80 percent of American households controlled just 6 percent of total financial wealth in 1989; the top 20 percent controlled 94 percent, and the top 1 percent controlled nearly half. Indeed, the share of the top percentile had risen over five full percentage points between 1983 and 1989.[3] This reflects the fact that all new saving in this time accrued to the very wealthy, and largely as the result of changes in policy that they themselves engineered, namely tax reduction and increases in interest rates.

There is, in effect, no way for average Americans to raise the national rate of savings even if they were inclined to do so. In a social and political order controlled by the financial interests of the wealthy, increases in net financial resources will be concentrated in the hands of the wealthy. Policy virtually guarantees it. Should wages rise, the Federal Reserve produces a higher rate of interest. On one hand, workers are then threatened by unemployment, while on the other the wage gain is siphoned to the creditor classes in the form of higher interest payments. Should government revenues rise, tax cut proposals focused on capital gains immediately follow. These measures are presented as instruments of macroeconomic policy, but in fact the underlying motivation is much simpler. It lies in the straightforward ability of those who control the political process to ensure for themselves the largest possible share of the dividends of growth.

Average Americans may find this depressing, but there is a bright side: the argument that we should be worried about our inability to generate new savings is also flawed. There is no shortage of savings in relation to income or GDP. In the 1980s, as it happens, gross investment was slightly higher, as a share of GDP, than it was in the 1960s. Findings of a decline in savings and investment rely on the concept of *net investment,* which is calculated after the estimated depreciation of equipment has been taken out. Because there has been a shift in the composition of investment, away from structures and toward machinery (particularly computers), depreciation has risen. This is what caused net investment and net savings to decline.[4]

The shift toward faster depreciation and hence lower net savings is itself just another manifestation of the relative rise of the technology sectors. With a relentless process of change in the technical capabilities of information processing and a debilitating increase in the real costs of construction (due to high interest rates), of course businesses have shifted their pattern of purchases toward rapidly depreciable goods. How could they do otherwise? Yet somehow an artifact of business necessity, brought on by unstable and repressive economic policies, has been turned into a moral parable for the middle class. It is a neat case of blaming the victim.

The real problem is not a shortage of savings, but a shortage of income from which higher levels of all types of economic activity might be financed. In the real world, a rise in savings by the middle classes would be a disaster for the wealthy, and it is the last thing they actually want. For, with declining accumulation by the public sector, combined with a failure of the new Victorians to behave in practice as the old ones did, we have to ask: Where has the circuit of consumption and spending been closed? How has the demand for business investment been maintained? The answer is plain: by an increase in debt finance at the level of the household, that is, by the very dissaving that the new Victorians claim to deplore. The new rich have closed the circle by lending, and very aggressively, what they could not consume or invest themselves to the embattled middle.

Instead of a return to the industrious patterns of late Victorian life, we have seen the growth of an economy characterized by distorted and unsustainable financial relations. The rich set an exemplary consumption standard. Meanwhile, middle-class American households are not merely unable to save; they cannot even maintain their existing consumption patterns on cash incomes. And so the middle classes have resorted to borrowing on the most massive scale, absorbing back as credit the financial accumulations of the wealthy. Debt has become a hallmark of the American masses—in both the private life of the household and the public sector, where it was a conservative

Republican administration, in the early 1980s, that resolved the contradiction between a financier's monetary policy and the requirements of reelection by running the largest public deficits in history.

It follows that the relationship between the middle and the wealthy—between the middle represented by households and the government and the wealthy by banks and the bond market—has taken on the embittered colors of the debtor-creditor interaction. Correspondingly, the economic interests of those to whom debtors owe money become their prevailing political interests as well. At low interest rates, expanding debts can be sustained for a long period of time. But low interest rates are sustainable politically only if the creditor classes agree to a low return on their capital. A higher interest rate policy, for which modern creditor interests ("the bond markets") are continually militating, is essentially a signal of their unwillingness to do this. And at high interest rates, the cycle of lending and repayment grows shorter, and the specter of bankruptcy looms larger. High interest rates squeeze the private household sector, through revolving credit, small business loans, and adjustable mortgages, and they squeeze the state, by raising the flow of net interest payments on the debt relative to other uses of taxpayer funds. By squeezing the state, they indirectly squeeze the household again, and so further raise the tension between government and private household that marks the politics of our time.

Exhortations to the public at large to save are substantially cosmetic, but the same cannot be said when the discussion turns to public policy. The doctrine of a savings shortage takes its public form and enjoys its policy impact in this discussion. Indeed this discussion deploys the greatest illusions in the hall of shadows and mirrors known as the American economic policy debate.

As a matter of history, the federal government of the United States has been in deficit continuously since 1970. The budget deficit rose above $100 billion per year in 1982 and remained above $150 billion for every year but one after 1983. For the recession year of 1991, the budget deficit exceeded $300 billion for the first time in history; it remained above $300 billion in 1992. With economic expansion and deficit reduction policies in the 1990s, however, the deficit declined. It fell back into the range of $100 billion in 1995–1996. In the electoral campaign of 1996, both parties campaigned on the theme that the budget should be balanced—having agreed to a timetable that, if implemented, would bring the budget into balance by the year 2002. In this way, the political system sought to bring closure to a long-running morality tale—the salvation of a lost soul, perhaps, or the recovery of a deficit alcoholic.

The seldom-put but interesting question is, Why? For what purpose are we intent on the effort of balancing the budget?[5]

It is easily shown that the deficit depends on economic performance. Figure 11.1 illustrates the relationship, using the ratio of the deficit to GDP. The arrows indicate the start of each postwar recession. The figure shows that, in every case, a falling economy generates a large increase in the deficit. And a rising economy produces, in every case, a fall in the deficit, though it took until the late 1990s before this improvement came close to restoring budget balance.

But to show that economic performance *depends* on the deficit, that a policy of cutting deficits per se is always or even generally a good thing, is much harder. Indeed there is no simple way to show this. Instead, this is something that we believe, if we believe it, strictly as the result of a chain of theoretical arguments involving deficits, saving, investment, and growth.

Advocates of budget deficit reduction conceptualize the budget deficit as a draw, by the government, on the pool of national savings—as a drain on resources available for capital investment. With a diversion of capital resources toward public consumption (via spending increases) or private consumption

FIGURE 11.1

RATIO OF GOVERNMENT DEFICIT TO GROSS DOMESTIC PRODUCT

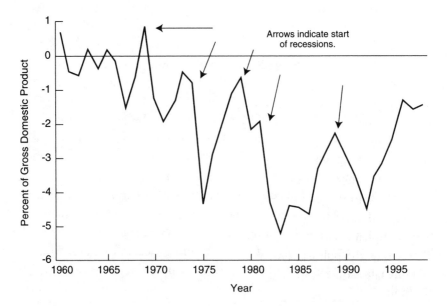

(through tax reduction), available savings must fall. If savings are reduced, the argument goes, investment must be correspondingly less. The capital stock will then be smaller than it would otherwise be. With a lower resulting stock of physical capital, productivity must be lower than would otherwise be the case. With lower productivity, the economy cannot produce the per worker output that it might otherwise be capable of, and living standards must necessarily be lower than they could be.

It is remarkably difficult to find an authoritative statement of this credo under the signature of a professional economist, perhaps because it is remarkably hard to substantiate in detail. But we may find a distilled version of it in official policy documents. The Congressional Budget Office (CBO) has provided, on many occasions of which the following is one example, a succinct summary of the established belief:

> Reducing the budget deficit continues to be an important focus of attention because it will increase national saving. In fact, reducing the deficit is the most reliable way to improve national saving. Over the long run, a permanently higher rate of saving would stimulate new investment, increase productive capacity, lower real interest rates, and raise the nation's standard of living.[6]

In fact there are very great, and unresolved, weaknesses in the theory and evidence on which a policy of unremitting deficit reduction is based. It requires that deficit reduction proceed without reducing private incomes, even though the expenditures that are cut are part of private incomes, as are the taxes that are raised in the pursuit of deficit reduction.[7]

The usual rebuttal to this point has been that deficit reduction reduces interest rates, and so stimulates demand for business investment. But the problem with this, as the Federal Reserve proved in the months from February 4, 1994, through the middle of 1995, is that there is in fact no necessary link between cutting deficits and lowering interest rates. Congress cut the deficit sharply in 1993, on the expectation that stable low interest rates would result. The Federal Reserve then doubled the short-term rate of interest. Long-term interest rates also rose, and the notion of any link between deficit cutting and interest rate reduction was decisively nullified.

The CBO was itself ambivalent about the actual effects of deficit reduction, as a review of its analytical work shows. In September 1993 Congress had just enacted President Clinton's massive five-year deficit reduction program. But there had been few if any other changes in the economic outlook between September and the preceding March. Thus, the CBO's midyear update provided an unusual opportunity to evaluate the effects of a large, multiyear deficit reduction program taken almost in isolation from other policy and external changes. CBO's September report began on an upbeat note, celebrating the legislative achievement of the previous month:

> In early August, the Congress passed and the President signed the Omnibus Budget Reconciliation Act of 1993—a major package of tax increases and spending reductions. Enactment of this legislation has significantly brightened the budgetary outlook for the next several years.[8]

CBO then noted that in the short term, the effect of deficit reduction is to "dampen" economic activity, although, to some extent, reductions in long-term interest rates may offset the dampening effect. Over the long run, however, CBO's outlook was positive, because "reducing the deficit increases national saving and spurs economic growth in the long run."

With this in mind, one may turn to CBO's numerical estimates of the effect on real GDP of the Omnibus Deficit Reduction Act. These are reproduced in Table 11.1.

Two facts about these predictions are especially striking. First, the difference between them was quite small: CBO foresaw a net change of only 54 billion 1987 dollars in real GDP, spread out over five years, as a result of the deficit-cutting law. This is less than 1 percent of GDP in any one year. Second, *the predicted movement was in the wrong direction.* Net declines in real GDP of $69 billion in the first four years outweighed a net gain of only $15 billion in the fifth year. And this fifth-year net gain was so small, and so remote, that it would have been well within the forecast error of any econometric model looking one year ahead, let alone five.

CBO also foresaw virtually no effect of deficit reduction on unemployment or inflation, and made no quantitative claims about the effect of deficit

TABLE 11.1

CBO MEDIUM-TERM ECONOMIC PROJECTIONS, SEPTEMBER 1993

(Billions of 1987 Dollars)

Real GDP	1994	1995	1996	1997	1998
After the cuts	5,190	5,330	5,476	5,620	5,755
Before the cuts	5,204	5,354	5,497	5,628	5,740
Difference	−14	−24	−21	−8	+15

reduction on savings, investment, and productivity growth. Indeed, in a special box on rising productivity growth in September's study (p. 20), CBO declined to make any link to budget actions, arguing instead that "the recent increases in productivity growth are likely to be temporary."

Thus CBO was telling Congress, in September 1993, that Congress was, by reducing the deficit, buying nothing that could reliably be measured. All economic benefits, to the extent that they existed at all, were over the forecasting horizon, more than five years into the future. And there was a measurable cost, of $54 billion in the first five years. One might as well say that in passing the deficit reduction law, the country sacrificed $54 billion of real goods and services for the sole purpose of feeling better about its fiscal and financial morals.

The Federal Reserve's 1994 actions, moreover, raised the most serious questions about the viability of future policies aimed at deficit reduction and budget balance. What confidence can Congress or the American public have that such policies will be permitted to have any reducing effect on interest rates and hence any beneficial effect on economic performance? And if the case for deficit reduction does not rest on the promise of lower interest rates, then on what premises does it rest?[9]

Massive deficit reduction occurred in October 1993. On February 4, 1994, short-term interest rates began to rise. Three months later, the long-term interest rate was higher in both nominal and real terms (inflation being actually lower) than it had been at the time of the election in 1992. And each full percentage point increase in interest rates added up to about $30 billion per year, over time, to the deficit itself. Indeed, the Federal Reserve had within ninety days already added over $100 billion to the cumulative 1994–1998 budget deficit, wiping out one-fifth of the progress made in the deficit reduction bill of 1993.[10]

This history contradicts the idea that reducing the budget deficit necessarily leads to lower interest rates, even when economic conditions are otherwise almost entirely stable. Without the promise of lower interest rates, the notion of an increased supply of savings is essentially meaningless, for it is on lower interest rates, and through lower interest rates an expansion of output, that the translation of savings into investment depends. The budget deficit and the interest rate are controlled by different centers of power, and unless the president, Congress, and the Federal Reserve work together explicitly for this purpose, there is no reason to believe that lowering budget deficits will produce lower interest rates, nor will it raise investment, savings, or productivity growth, and certainly not living standards, in either the short run or the long.

What then should policy on the deficit be? We need an answer that is independent of mumbo jumbo about national saving, and I propose the following:

Congress and the administration should manage the budget to meet our public purposes, including especially to maintain full employment, while preserving the good credit of the United States.

It is theoretically possible that nations spend themselves and borrow themselves into oblivion. But the evidence shows that the United States is not close to any such fiscal crisis as the millennium closes. Congress as early as 1982 began to repair the excesses of President Reagan's first year. President Bush, to his personal credit and political cost, pressed for deficit reduction in 1990 and accepted higher taxes to that end. President Clinton worked effectively in 1993 to end the epoch of ever-rising deficits, did considerably more on that score than fiscal stability actually required, and did so without achieving the lower interest rates that were supposed to have accompanied deficit reduction. Currently U.S. deficits are the lowest in the advanced industrial world and the ratio of public debt to GDP is stable or even falling. It will probably remain so as long as economic growth continues. Only a recession, or a catastrophic tax cut, can unhinge the fiscal stability achieved in the 1990s.

The right policy from this point forward, especially in the pursuit of a more equal wage structure, is therefore to stabilize the economy—not the budget—and to choose a mix of public and private investments and human welfare and services programs that best meets the actual needs of our present and future population. To achieve and sustain full employment may or may not require increases in the budget deficit at some time ahead. That will depend on whether a sustained policy of low and stable interest rates can achieve the objective on its own. This is a point on which the world is inherently uncertain, economists can differ, and time will tell. The essential thing is to establish the order of priority in economic and fiscal objectives. Even if the fiscal stability and good credit of the United States was once seriously endangered, the time for single-minded concentration on deficit reduction is long past.

Suppose then that we adopt a simple rule of thumb for the budget, consistent with the basic objectives that full employment be reached and held, public purposes be met, and the good credit of the United States be preserved. Let this rule be: Hold the ratio of public debt (in the hands of the public) at or below the present level of about 52 percent, so long as the unemployment rate stays below 5 percent. This may not be the best of all possible rules. But in our ignorance of the world and in the disorder of our economics, it has two important virtues. First, it will certainly preserve the good credit of the United States. Second, it does not impose draconian tax increases or cuts in social security, national defense, and public investment that are not otherwise called for on the merits of those decisions.

Having accepted this rule, and assuming that full employment can be maintained with debts and deficits at this level, let us inquire whether substantial policy changes are required to achieve a stable debt-to-GDP ratio. The answer is that changes may be necessary, but in only one area in the short and medium run, and that area is, once again, *monetary policy.* For just as monetary policy tends to hit the wage structure through the unemployment rate and the exchange rate, so it hits the government's financial position through the interest rate.

Figure 11.2, prepared in 1994, illustrates the extraordinary sensitivity of the debt-to-GDP ratio to the projected level of interest rates. The middle line presents the CBO estimate of this ratio through 2004, as of January 1994, under the interest rate assumptions that seemed reasonable then.

The upper curve provides an approximate calculation of the situation six months later in the summer of 1994, following the interest rate moves that

FIGURE 11.2

RATIO OF PUBLIC DEBT TO GDP WITH DIFFERENT INTEREST PATTERNS

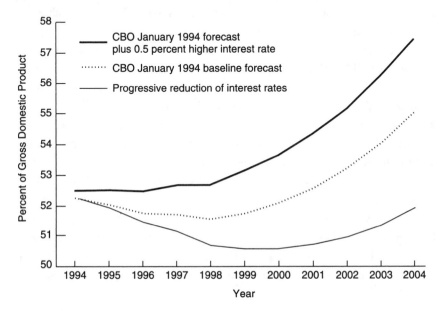

began in February. I based this calculation on the conservative assumptions that rising interest rates would add 0.5 percent to the average interest cost facing the federal government and that they would have no other effects on the budget or the economy. The consequence of this small adjustment is that the debt-to-GDP ratio no longer falls even in the short run, and starts to accelerate toward historic heights in 1998. Under this scenario, it is not too much to say that Congress would have faced a budgetary crisis by the end of the decade—absent the further steep cuts in the budget that occurred in 1995–1996, the end in 1995 of the Federal Reserve's campaign to raise rates, and the stronger-than-expected economic performance, which was due to stronger exports and some other unexpected factors.

The lower curve, finally, shows the effect of a progressive but very slow reduction in average interest costs, of 0.125 percentage point per year—one full percentage point over 8 years, leading to an overall reduction in average effective net interest costs from 5.8 percent to 4.6 percent by 2004. That kind of reduction might have been a reasonable result of the actions Congress took in 1993. The figure shows that under this assumption, the debt-to-GDP ratio would continue to fall until the year 2000, and thereafter does not rise even to 1994 levels before the estimating period expires in 2004.

Some further fiscal actions to stabilize the debt may be needed someday, just as bigger deficits may someday be needed to fight off a rise in unemployment. Neither action is needed now. Indeed no action may be needed for almost a decade—not until well into the next millennium—*provided* that monetary policy cooperates and the financial system does not buckle for some other reason.

The decision to pursue a balanced budget, taken by the president in the heat of the 1996 electoral campaign, was therefore unnecessary and even foolish, except for the obvious politics of the matter.[11] Truly, we ought to acknowledge that the goal of a balanced budget—a deficit arbitrarily fixed at zero—ought not to be achieved at all. There is no reason why the federal government of the United States should become the only major government on earth to forgo the issuance of net new debt as a matter of principle. And the effort to achieve this pointless objective runs a huge risk. The depressing effects of tax increases and spending cuts on output, employment, and therefore revenues may overwhelm their direct effects on the budget, producing lower growth and larger deficits. Alternatively, the failure of the government to anchor the acquisition of financial assets by households through the creation of safe government bonds creates a risk of instability in the private financial system, even if banking institutions succeed in financing economic expansion without help from the public sector in the short run.[12]

The absurdity of single-minded budget balancing becomes even clearer when one realizes that the political path to budget balance lies through sharp cuts in actual expenditures and actual investments. It lies in buying fewer services and capital assets that might actually contribute to the making of a better and richer society both today and down the line. Relief for the poor, or for immigrants, or the elderly is the most visible victim of this pattern of thinking, but so too are investments in housing, roads, museums, libraries, and schools. In return for this definite and actual sacrifice of pie-today and ovens-for-tomorrow, budget balancing promises pie-in-the-sky. We have talked ourselves into the bizarre situation where an increase in suffering today is celebrated as a down payment toward less suffering by the same people tomorrow. Even more peculiar, a cut in investment—say, of funds to repair a bridge or build a school—is thought of as a contribution to potential investment, through a long chain of reasoning that runs from lower deficits to higher saving and higher private capital spending. This a triumph of pure theology, since the exact same economic action—the exactly identical bridge or school—would be counted an investment and a celebrated accomplishment if undertaken in the private sector for private profit. The sacrifices are real; the gains are evanescent, as the forecasts of the government's own agencies clearly show.

In sum, more saving relative to income is not the highest macroeconomic priority. That being so, we do not need to balance the budget. By the same reasoning, we also do not need tax "reforms" that would replace progressive income taxation with exemptions for savings. If there is no shortage of savings but rather a relative shortage of purchasing power and public capacity, then tax policy should move in the other direction—toward more progressive income taxes and higher, not lower, rates on saved incomes and capital gains. There should be a reduction of sales taxes in favor of property and income taxes at the state level, not the present movement in the other direction. Schemes to prefund social security or Medicare—for example, by running payroll tax contributions through the private capital markets—are equally counterproductive. Indeed, by making the value of the implicit social security wealth of the public dependent on stock market prices, the government might undermine one of the strongests bulwarks of steady mass consumption that exists. What we need instead is gradually to expand the support that these programs provide to the private consumption of relatively low-income people who depend on public pensions and health care, and to maintain and expand their role as counterweights to the increasing concentration of private wealth and incomes.[13]

In the last analysis, we cannot recreate the "unstable psychological conditions" of the late nineteenth century, in which the drive for social improvements was in the hands of captains of industry, and we shouldn't want to try. The effort to do so, given the scale of the modern economy, is destined to fail. The double bluff cannot be restored on either side. The working population in the long run will not accept it, and will find a voice eventually that expresses their resentment at being told to do so. On the other side, the wealth owners of today have been spoiled for the task of governing by a century during which that function fell into professional and bureaucratic hands. Returning power to them will not return them to the state of thrift and hard-driven industry that, at least in the eyes of sympathetic observers, formerly enabled them to use it. What will happen is the development of a perverse system in which the wealthy come clamoring to the government for protection, support, and subsidy, while never setting out on the large-scale investment enterprises that are supposed to be the result of a policy that caters to their interests. Meanwhile, the middle classes embark on a financially ruinous, debt-driven effort to emulate the consumption habits of the wealthy, for which no proper basis in accumulation, or in the distribution of claims on society's productive powers, or in public investments has been laid.

12

LIBERALS STUCK ON
THE SUPPLY SIDE

The assumption that a Government will maintain full employment if only it knows how to do it is fallacious. In this connection, the misgivings of big business about the maintenance of
full employment by Government spending are of paramount
importance.

—Michal Kalecki, *Political Aspects of Full Employment*

Old-fashioned Keynesian macroeconomics collapsed in the
United States around 1970, with the demise of full employment policy and the revival of the natural rate doctrine among academic
economists. These were defining events, for they brought the once-towering
influence of liberal economists to an end. And because the liberal economists
not only fell from power but also came under a withering conservative assault
inside the academy, this group virtually disappeared from active political life.
The views of the liberals, though still seen occasionally on the op-ed pages,
ceased to matter. Since that time, no aggressive Keynesian has held a high political position in America; no president, no treasury secretary, no chairman
of the Federal Reserve or even of the Council of Economic Advisers has been
a consistent and effective advocate of full employment.

The collapse of the liberal economists left political progressives, the liberal
wing of the Democratic party, with a huge gap in the structure of beliefs that
had previously supported their ideas. To be sure, the ideas themselves remained, for they did not come from economics in the first place. American

liberalism is philosophically pragmatic; it reasons mainly from history, and not from economic theory. Thus, American progressives have tended to believe that the New Deal, the civilian administration of World War II, the New Frontier, and the Great Society were the great moments of modern times. At those moments, government intervened to save a collapsing, endangered, or stagnant economic system, raising living standards, equalizing opportunities, relieving suffering and injustice. Reasoning from this experience, liberals generally believe that the major political tasks facing America involve the completion of the New Deal and Great Society projects—for instance, the creation of a system of universal health care or the expansion of jobs, housing, and urban programs. They would hold these beliefs, and continued to do so, even without help from a liberal wing of the economics profession.

But in Keynesianism as it existed before 1970, economics had a theory that made sense of the liberal agenda and the historical facts on which it was based, placing them in the context of macroeconomic policies that either did, or did not, produce full employment. That being the case, political progressives and liberal economists could form an alliance, and did so. And when Keynesianism collapsed as a political force, this linkage disappeared. All that remained was the understanding of history that had motivated progressives in the first place. The question of how progressives should justify themselves in economic terms has been bedeviling American liberalism ever since.

After 1970, progressives seeking support from economic theory could now point only to an odd assortment of small ideas. There were theories of imperfect competition, justifying antimonopoly action. There was a theory of "public goods" to support certain kinds of public investment. There was a theory of "externalities," justifying some kinds of social and environmental regulation. If these ideas had a unifying theme, it was "market failure"—a concept that taken alone was completely untenable within the economics profession. "Let the markets work!" was the reply of respectability, not only from the right, but also from the remaining liberal economists, a traumatized group one might call the ex-Keynesians. And so attempts by progressives to develop agendas based on industrial policy, regional policy, urban policy, economic development policy (the list could go on) were ferociously resisted by their former allies. The fact was, the liberal economists had lost their nerve.

Displaced from public life and baffled by events, the ex-Keynesian academic economists turned inward and sought to find their bearings in economic policy mainly through attempts to explain the mysterious slowdown of productivity growth after 1973. But this was another debacle: the economists made a hopeless mess out of that endeavor. Eventually the exercise disintegrated into incoherence, with nothing to show for it—no consensus view and no coherent policy prescriptions. The rump of liberal economists therefore not only failed to ally with progressives on traditional aspects of government's role. They also failed to come up with any credible alternative productivity, growth, or employment agenda of their own. Still less could they assemble a political coalition and produce policies that could be linked in any demonstrable way to favorable economic results.

The ex-Keynesians were neutralized intellectually and politically by the mid-1970s and quite unable on either score to counter the real enemies of economic progress, the cut-taxes-for-the-rich supply-siders and high-interest-rate monetarists who joined forces during the late part of the decade. Otherwise respectable *and liberal* economists were reduced to repeating catechistic formulas: more saving and more investment, achieved by deficit reduction, would be good things. This was New Victorianism, the same sort of stuff that had gone down in history as the intellectual content of Hoover Republicanism after 1929 (or, in Britain, the infamous "Treasury View" of that same year). The reactionaries ran away with the debate, setting the stage for a decade of high unemployment, upward redistribution, and wholesale attacks on the welfare state both before and after the watershed election of 1980.

In this way, a fiasco of their own making removed the ex-Keynesians from the political picture completely for most of the 1980s. Yet while it left the reactionaries holding political power, it also set the stage for the reemergence of political progressives, who were for the most part not economists and certainly not orthodox ones. Such figures as Robert Reich, Ira Magaziner, Robert Kuttner, and Lester Thurow (the one bona-fide economist in the group) struck out on their own, developing a new argument around the theme of "international competitiveness"—a liberalism that was unabashedly addressed to building up the "supply side" of the American economy. To the dismay of many academic economists, who one suspects would have liked to inherit the influence their elders once wielded over policy, this group has been setting the liberal policy agenda ever since.

The competitive internationalists emphasized three main policy objectives. They strongly favored labor training, education, adjustment assistance, and other programs that help workers move from one job to the next. They supported public investments in infrastructure, on the ground that these assist in the international competitiveness of the economy. They supported a combination of research and development assistance to advanced enterprises, alongside efforts to open foreign markets to American products, for the same purpose of enhancing competitiveness and in the hope, ever the crutch of supply-siders, that the benefits will trickle down. Indeed these formed a triad of initiatives, a holy trinity of modern American supply-side liberalism: research, education, infrastructure.[1]

As a political matter, competitive internationalism was a startling success. Because they were unabashed about meeting the needs of certain elements of American business, the new progressives found that they could harness the forces of crude nationalism to their cause. The high trade deficits and decline of high-wage manufacturing at that time boosted their issues. Book sales took off; media stars were born. More important, beginning with Gary Hart and continuing with Bill Clinton, leading Democratic politicians realized that they could sell competitiveness policy to certain branches of industry, notably aerospace and electronics. Thus, they could, and did, help to forge the winning political coalition in the 1992 and 1996 elections.

Prominence breeds criticism, and the MIT economist Paul Krugman has assailed the competitive internationalists, citing defects in their arguments and the risk that the policies they advocate will be combined with a resurgence of trade protection.[2] But the real legacy of this line of argument does not lie in a major change in American trade policy. Few of the competitive internationalists are avowed protectionists; on the trade front, they mainly favor negotiating expanded U.S. access to closed foreign markets, steps ostensibly calculated to increase trade rather than to reduce it and that orthodox economists generally support. And the larger political agenda of competitive internationalism is remarkably tame. It does not challenge, directly or indirectly, the governing role of conservatives in the larger economic policy or the existing structures of income and wealth. None have ever become aggressive critics of monetary policy, dissidents from the pro-savings consensus, or strong advocates of full employment.

I do not wish to belittle the goals of the supply-side liberalism that the competitive internationalists advance. Expenditures on education, training, research, development, and infrastructure are, in some fundamental sense, good things. People, knowledge, and physical places are usually improved by acts of investment. Also, there are cumulative forces. Educated parents bring up educable children. Scientific and technical knowledge builds on prior stores of knowledge. New infrastructure can enhance and improve upon the old; new facilities in old places combine quality of function with the layered grace that makes places habitable. Countries that support their schools, universities, research institutes, and cities cannot be choosing unwisely in some larger sense.

Still, does supply-side liberalism add up? Taken in the context of economic policy as a whole, which includes de facto acceptance of a natural rate of unemployment and New Victorian attitudes toward the budget,[3] what can it accomplish? Can it raise average living standards effectively? And can one change the new structures of inequality by working with this set of policy tools? Indeed, are high levels of expenditure on research and development, on infrastructure and on education tenable in a larger context of slow growth, fiscal austerity, and the pressure to privatize that stems from increasing inequality? Or does the true relationship work in the other direction, so that societies that are more egalitarian find themselves willing and able to make consistently larger investments in education, training, infrastructure, research, and other public goods? And if this is so, are the liberal supply-siders in fact caught in a contradiction, which leads them to foster desires for public programs that the economic conditions they tolerate effectively make it impossible to achieve?

Let us take up the elements of the competitive international agenda in turn. Support for technology development, because it runs through the advanced private business sector, is the most powerful leg of the triad. And academic economists have long agreed that technological advance is the major component of economic growth and rising average living standards. Economists therefore have largely joined the supply-side liberals in general support for rapid technological change. The academic economists who have objected to specific technology policies—and at times they have done so vociferously—have done so mainly on grounds of doubt as to the competence of government in choosing precisely which sorts of projects to support and a preference for leaving the choices to private corporations.[4]

For the sake of argument we can concede the virtues of technology itself and also that, for good or ill, technological development will tend to follow the financial channels dredged by government programs. What happens to inequality? We know the answer. Technology-supplying industries can reasonably be described as transient monopoly profiteers. They extract income from purchasers of technology; they redistribute income to the sellers thereof. Since the buyers in these markets inevitably outnumber the sellers, and since income levels are higher among technology producers than among technology consumers, it follows that high levels of business investment embodying technological innovation work, as a matter of general principle, to unequalize the structure of wages and incomes.

This implies that government support for research and development cannot be thought of as a wage or income leveler. The effect of such policies on the income distribution almost certainly works the other way! To be sure, government R&D and export assistance helps American companies penetrate foreign markets. It may increase their market share, improve their technological competitiveness—and enable them to pay higher wages. But who benefits from these policies? The number of workers who work directly in export-oriented, high-technology manufacturing sectors is small—not over 6 million in toto by a generous count, double that if we add in all plausible parts of the services sector. And, as we have seen, the main beneficiaries of the technological revolution are the nonproduction workers in the technology-generating firms: an even smaller group. They are the primary direct beneficiaries of support for technological change, and they are already comparatively well paid. The accelerated diffusion of technological products is good for their producers, but it is plainly not in the financial interest of those caught in the gale of creative destruction.

Many would argue that technology products help ease inequality, if not in their production, at least in their consumption. As Schumpeter observed long ago, the achievement of capitalism did not lie in producing silk stockings for queens, but in bringing them within the reach of shopgirls in return for steadily decreasing effort. As Schumpeter also points out, Louis XIV himself would have envied the patient of any modern dentist. Nowadays, computers that could crack the codes of the German army fifty years ago or target the missiles of the cold war are routine household possessions. So are the capacities for musical reproduction of a fair symphony hall and instant communications around the world.

Physical possessions such as these do tend to trickle down. They also accumulate over time, so that yesterday's luxuries (televisions, telephones, flush toilets, central heating) eventually become part of the everyday expectation even of low-income households. As new technologies become old, their prices fall in both relative and absolute terms, and they become available to low-income people at substantially lower prices than were first charged to and paid by the comparatively rich. In this way, technology products may reduce absolute poverty and raise living standards in very concrete ways, by bringing themselves within reach of ever-larger parts of the population as time goes by.[5]

The idea that consumption equalizes underlies such otherwise bizarre ideas as Speaker Newt Gingrich's otherwise inexplicable suggestion of a tax credit to provide laptop computers to welfare recipients and President Clinton's call for universal access to the Internet in the schools. But let's not kid ourselves: What kind of laptops and what kind of Internet access would be provided? The best and the latest? The state of the art? Or something that is either inferior and out-of-date at the moment of delivery or else destined to become so in a very short period of time?

A moment's thought about this question uncovers a basic fact about consumption experiences in rich but radically unequal societies: consumption of like products is scaled by income level. The design, features, and price structures of new and used cars, television sets, computers, and even clothing adjust themselves to the income structure of the population; the society is fed, clothed, transported, and computed in proportion to its means.

This scaling of consumption creates a class structure defined partly by the technological level of one's consumption. It is a value of mass-market consumerism to diffuse technology products right down the scale of incomes, yet this does not create equality in the social structure. A consumer society does not deny food and clothing, transport and entertainment to its poor. What it does, instead, is create vast and invidious distinctions in the quality of the goods that people enjoy and in the quality of the larger environments in which they live. The distinctions fall between the durable and the flimsy, the option loaded and the basic model, the new and the old, the fancy and the plain. And at the very bottom of society, the absence of such goods comes to define deprivation. Just as automobile have-nots and telephone have-nots defined extreme poverty in parts of the United States two decades ago, information have-nots are becoming a class of the new poor.

In sum, the inherent tension between technology and equality in the structure of production and incomes is not reversed by consumer effects. Although there is surely a role in general terms for science and technology policy under liberal governments, these policies do not bring about a fairer and more just social order. The immediate effect of more rapid technological change is just the opposite: to increase disparities across the social spectrum. It follows that while science and technology policies surely have a place, to make them into the centerpiece of a progressive agenda is absurd.

While support for science and technology is a relatively new position for liberals, civilian public works expenditure is the historical cornerstone of liberal interventionism. But here the progressive internationalists and liberal supply-siders have abandoned an obvious argument of public good in exchange for a nebulous one of private benefit. It has always been possible to make the case that a strong base of social investment powerfully equalizes the social structure itself. Roads, water, sewer, power, and communications systems are all durable public consumption goods. The same is true of sidewalks, public parks, even the municipal golf course you may pass in the morning on the way to work. The same may be true of a public university campus or a fine courthouse in the village square. We share these amenities; they enter our sense of psychological well-being whether we make direct use of them or not. As such, they form part of the minimum standard of living in a community. The defining characteristic of Parisians, after all, is that they live in Paris, the densest center of fine public amenities in the world. As such even low-income Parisians enjoy a standard of living that is high in some respects when compared to, say, even the wealthier residents of Cicero, Illinois.

The new progressives make an entirely different claim for public works spending, one that removes it from any connection to equality and instead situates it under the rubric of competitiveness and economic performance. Renaming it "infrastructure" (as I too have done on many occasions), they argue that such public spending contributes in definite ways to the productivity of the private business economy.[6] The jobs created directly, by doing the work, are immaterial to this argument. So are the benefits to private citizens in the form of amenities that enrich their enjoyment of life. What matters, instead, is how the finished work contributes indirectly to cost reduction and increased output in the business sector, to productivity and to profit. In other words, the case for public works is recast into an instrumental one. From being a prominent necessity of civilization in their own right, state expenditures are reduced to a supporting role, and to a fairly minor supporting role at that.

These arguments are not totally without a sphere of application. Airports and seaports are classic examples of publicly provided facilities for private business use. The interstate highway system and the national information highway are routinely cited as public initiatives in the support of economic competitiveness; they have had far-reaching effects on the demand for trucks, cars, and computers. And no doubt public power projects, from the Tennessee to the Columbia Rivers, have contributed mightily to economic development in their respective regions, particularly in the decades that followed their construction during the New Deal.

Yet the evidence for a relationship between the trend of such investments and the productivity growth of the national economy since 1970 is thin, and the direction of causality is unclear. Statistical relationships do show the bare fact that average measured productivity growth declined during the same years that saw cutbacks in gross public investment. But what is the connection between these events? Which caused which? Did investment cutbacks cause the productivity crunch, or did declining growth and productivity lead to budget crises that caused investment cutbacks? There is not, in this extensive econometric literature, much that could be called a structural analysis of the nature of the dependency between private economic productivity and public works expenditure.

This should not be surprising, for minor reflection shows that the vast bulk of neglected public works in America would be at best tangential to business needs. Advanced, export-oriented American manufacturing enterprise is not seriously hamstrung by infrastructure problems. What it has traditionally needed—roads, rail, electricity, and water service—it has gotten. Boeing is not short of runways from which to launch its planes, nor is Silicon Valley suffering brownouts. The Houston ship channel is an ugly mess, but it safely accommodates the 5,000 or so ships that use it every year. Phones (a private utility) work well in this country. What is missing is investment in such things as public libraries, parks, city streets and sidewalks, urban mass transit. Big business gets the infrastructure it needs, and for the rest neither demands great improvements nor suffers unduly when spending is cut back.

At the margin, both advances and cutbacks in public spending on capital projects fall on less powerful constituencies. It is mostly consumers and workers who hit the potholes on the road to work. It is people who breathe air, drink the water, and boat on the rivers and lakes. It is children who attend the schools—a very large proportion of the physical plant in public hands. It is, of course, citizens and consumers who enjoy the national parks. All this has little to do with international competitiveness or with the measurement of national productivity growth. This explains why business interests are not in the forefront of demands for higher infrastructure spending and why these items were the first to fall in the face of conservative opposition in the Congress.

We are left to suspect that the supply-side argument for infrastructure spending is an illusion that has succeeded in deceiving mainly its proponents. The idea seems to have been that socially and culturally useful public projects could be piggy-backed on top of the well-provided essentials. Such a political logic tracks, to some degree, the strategy behind the use of national security arguments to support the interstate highway system (the National Defense Highway Act), the federal student loan program (the National Defense Education Act—a response to Sputnik), and even the National Endowment for the Arts.[7] But business interests do their own thinking on these matters, and in this instance they made the cold but correct calculation: the costs of going along with an "infrastructure boom" exceed the benefits to them.

At the same time, the infrastructure angle has distorted the case for public works, away from the objective of creating something of value for the larger community and toward that of increasing the flow of indirect subsidies to business. In this way, one is driven, with some reluctance, to conclude that the adoption of a supply-side argument has actually undermined the cause of a public investment agenda, by depriving those who would truly benefit of the political vocabulary they need, and at the same time shifting the burden of advocacy onto the shoulders of economic constituencies that are not, in any major way, interested in seeing that the job gets done.

Something similar happened with education. The public believes in education—or has believed in it—as a defining feature of citizenship in America. Education creates a degree of equality in the most indirect way: by creating citizens who believe that they are entitled to a certain fair share of the American heritage and are prepared to use political as well as economic means toward obtaining that share. But supply-side arguments have put this good thing at risk, with an unremitting stress on the purely private, individual, and competitive aspects of the educational experience and by subsuming the whole endeavor under an argument that raising investments in education will materially improve how the American economy performs on the international stage.

There is no doubt that American schools can use more money. But will the provision of such resources, if it can be achieved, matter much for the *average* level of American economic performance? Are American schools a drag on economic productivity? Can we get to a higher sustained rate of economic growth, and a material improvement in national living standards, merely by pumping up the resources we devote to education?

That question turns on whether there is a shortage of skilled labor in the United States, a shortage not being met by our colleges and universities. Despite all the ruminations about "skill bias" in the patterns of technological change, there is no such shortage. To the contrary, our economy is full of highly educated and skilled people. It remains short of jobs for those people, as every college counselor and every coordinator of a training program knows. This cannot be surprising. In a country where business interests have such a huge influence over education policy as here, it would be bizarre if high schools, colleges, and universities were undersupplying business markets. They aren't, in fact, undersupplying such markets. They are merely working to ensure that the structure of educations reflects the developing, and increasingly unequal, structure of incomes and wealth.

Equally, there is no point, in an economic calculus of the reward to education, in "wasting" resources on those who will never in any event rise far above the minimum wage. There is no point, from the business perspective, in creating overeducated applicants for miserable jobs. Such people make bad workers. They are unhappy, frustrated, and difficult to control. What the existing economy needs is a fairly small number of first-rate technical talents, combined with a small superclass of managers and financiers, on top of a vast substructure of nominally literate and politically apathetic working people. Does this sound familiar? Educational systems do not determine economic structures. In a system governed by a calculus of business benefit, they are determined by those structures, and in our case as the economy becomes more unequal, we can expect the dispersion of educations to follow suit.

One might draw a link between the hegemony of the economic calculus in education policy and the poor political track record of such national institutions as the Endowments for the Arts and the Humanities. These are, in a larger sense, educational institutions, insofar as they support, or are supposed to support, the development of a free culture. But they lack altogether, and will never acquire, the larger economic role that is constantly being attributed to the public schools and the universities. The result is that, without any strong political underpinning, they are treated as special interest expenditures and become intensely vulnerable to narrow political attacks. Contrast the situation in France, where no one supposes that the vast, and widely supported, public expenditures on arts and theater have anything to do with GNP growth or the trade balance or any purpose beyond the propagation of culture and national entertainment.

The unpleasant conclusion is that the liberal mainstream, spearheaded in recent years by competitiveness progressives, has been spinning illusions in all the areas where it has tried to have an impact, trying to find a useful and utilitarian niche in an unaccommodating, business-dominated world that is brutally skeptical of the nonutilitarian. Expanded spending on education and public works is desperately needed but not for the reasons given and not of the kind specified under those reasons. We need to expand investment in cities and schools precisely to provide the equalizing consumption experiences and political expectations that the private economy is not providing, precisely to defy and not to accommodate the influence of business needs on the social structure. If progressives are interested in these goals, they must find a language in which to defend them for the sake of the people themselves, for the sake of culture and society and democracy, and for the sake of civilization. Otherwise progressives will continue to find themselves in reliance on disinterested allies; they may be invited to the parley, but they will never be given the gavel. And they will continue to lose the budget battles when the chips are down.

To make the budget battles winnable, additional public resources must be created and on a very large scale. This cannot be done so long as the larger structures of natural rate employment theory and New Victorian fiscal notions remain superimposed over the public's need for services, amenities, and educational and cultural facilities. The liberal supply-siders deserve respect for seeking to defend certain important priorities in difficult times. But in the larger picture, they do not offer a viable way forward. As a precondition for success on the supply side, there is no alternative to a proper insistence on sustained full employment and reasonable price stability, that is to say, to Keynesian goals achieved by Keynesian means.

Part Four

POLICIES

13

INTEREST RATES AND
THE CENTRAL BANK

The justification for a moderately high rate of interest has been
found hitherto in the necessity of providing a sufficient in-
ducement to save. But we have shown that the extent of effective saving is necessarily determined by the scale of investment
and that the scale of investment is promoted by a *low* rate of
interest. . . . Thus it is to our best advantage to reduce the rate
of interest to that point . . . at which there is full employment.

—John Maynard Keynes, *The General Theory of Employment,*
Interest and Money

We come now to Lenin's question: What is to be done? If
progress against inequality requires sustained full employment alongside reasonably stable prices, together with a more competitive
dollar and a higher minimum wage, how can all of these things be achieved?
In this final part, I argue that we need, first and foremost, a monetary policy
committed to full employment, through the straightforward mechanism of
low and stable interest rates. To ensure price stability, an important goal that
should never be left to the central bank alone, we need a wider range of supporting policies, including some specifically designed to help prevent supply
shocks and wage-price spirals. And to keep the U.S. economy on an even keel
in a world of trade, we need a commitment to the growth and prosperity at
least of the major U.S. trading partners, especially in this hemisphere and in
Asia.

Interest rates permeate the great puzzle of inequality. We have seen that unemployment is tied intimately to the inequality of wages. Interest rates have a determining impact on the rate of unemployment. The exchange rate of the dollar has come to affect the dispersion of wages. It was high interest rates that drove up the dollar in the early 1980s and created this situation. We have also seen that interest rates themselves are closely associated with the distribution of interest income, because interest payments became such a major component in the incomes of the wealthiest American families through the 1980s. Finally, we have seen that interest rates dominate efforts to reduce the budget deficit, and hence over public investment, public consumption, and employment. To lower unemployment, to preserve a competitive dollar that does not destabilize wages, to check the unearned incomes of the rich, and to preserve the fiscal stability of the government—for all of these purposes, low and stable interest rates are essential.

To address the inequality crisis we therefore need a low interest rate, sustained for a long time. We need, in effect, to freeze the interest rate, as low as we can get it, for as long as we can manage. And so we arrive at the question any reasonable person would ask. Is such a thing seriously possible?

This is no easy question, for it has been a given since 1953 that the manipulation of the interest rate is a necessary element—indeed the the central element—of a properly functioning monetary policy.[1] The prior existence of a different system has been substantially forgotten, and now the architecture of a low–interest rate economy needs to be thought through from the beginning. We need to contemplate the process whereby the United States sets monetary policy, to ask whether there might exist alternatives, of both policy and decision-making structure. Do we have to do things the way we are doing them now, and with the consequences we observe? What is the proper function of the rate of interest, anyway?

This question requires a detour into the economics of the rate of interest, a subject that is scholastic even by the tolerant standards of the economics profession. The interest rate is a price. But of what, exactly? Is it the price of capital? Of time? Or of money? And is it set in a market, by supply and demand? Or is it set in some other way?

Elementary textbooks typically reflect the classical view that the interest rate is set in a market for "capital," a market that balances the "supply of saving" with the "demand for investment." Saving reflects the thriftiness of the public and their responsiveness to the interest-price of saving; savings are said to rise when higher rates of interest raise the rate of return. The demand for investment reflects the physical productivity of new capital investment; investment is said to increase when a lower interest rate makes less physically productive activities economically profitable. These forces produce a supply curve that slopes upward and a demand curve sloping downward; together they equilibrate saving and investment and regulate the quantity of the capital stock.

But there are difficulties with this formulation, analogous to the difficulties with the metaphor of an aggregate labor market. What "capital" actually is, and what might be meant by its "quantity," are elusive. There is no actual economic institution as the "capital market," in which such stuff is bought and sold. The theory lacks a process. It lacks a mechanism. Indeed it lacks a commodity to go along with the idea of the interest rate as the price of capital: actual physical capital consists of an infinite variety of machines, inventory, and materials in process. The very elusivity of these notions signals that the theory is not connected in an operational way to the economy. Indeed, were interest rates entirely determined by the private interactions of savers and investors, it would be hard to understand what the Federal Reserve thinks itself to be doing.

A less mystical explanation needs to be rooted in markets that exist, markets that have physical locations, routine trading, and quoted prices for commodities that actually change hands. The markets for money, for bonds, for equities, and for foreign exchange meet this description in a way that the metaphor of a physical capital market does not. A reasonable explanation should also incorporate the role of policy and policymakers, for policymakers surely do exist, and it would seem peculiar if a theory of the interest rate took no account of them at all.

The task for the policy economist thus merges, to some degree, with that of the political scientist. It is in part to ask what motivates monetary decision makers to act as they do. It is to ask whether the motivations and actions are appropriate or could be different. And if obstacles arise to the implementation of a superior policy, it is to find ways to overcome them.

One way to think about monetary policy and interest rates for practical purposes is simply to note that the Federal Reserve's policymaking Open Market Committee meets once every six weeks and makes a command decision about one particular rate of interest. This rate is the shortest-term rate of interest in the American market, the rate for the most liquid single asset traded in American finance: overnight reserve loans between commercial banking institutions, otherwise known as Federal Funds. The Federal Funds rate is the rate of interest that the government effectively controls. The Open Market Desk of the New York Federal Reserve Bank can intervene in the shortest-term money markets to ensure that Fed Funds are priced exactly as the government wishes, and it does so.

What happens in the rest of the financial markets, whether the auction for ninety-day Treasury bills, for ninety-day commercial paper, for six-month or one-year notes, or for long-term bonds, is essentially an adjustment to the action of the Federal Reserve in the short-term markets. Longer-term assets have a degree of capital risk: the price of a ten-year bond will fall when interest rates rise, and investors need to be compensated for holding such a long-term asset. Likewise, private securities are riskier than public debts, because there is a chance that the entity behind them will go bankrupt. For these reasons, longer-term and private assets usually command higher interest rates than short-term government debts; the term structure of rates reflects the relative illiquidity and capital risk of longer-term securities.[2]

Longer-term assets also generally react slowly to a movement in short-term rates; rates on longer-term securities usually rise and fall less than the corresponding movements of the short-term rates. The reason is that the demand and supply of long-term instruments depend not only on the short-term interest rate today, but also on the expectation of how short rates will move in the immediate future. Typically, though not always, investors view a drop or increase in short rates as a temporary phenomenon; hence long-term rates react only partly to the rise in short rates. Occasionally a sharp rise in short rates drives this class of interest rates above the rates on long-term assets (inverted yield curve), but this is something that happens only rarely. Figure 13.1 illustrates the modern history of short- and long-term interest rates, and makes very clear the close nature of their relationship. The closer in term and liquidity the asset is to overnight interbank loans, the more closely the interest rate on that asset must track the Federal Funds rate.

The implication of this argument is that whatever motivates the Federal Reserve Board and its policymaking arm, the Federal Open Market Committee, will necessarily be the driving force behind the movement of the larger structure of interest rates in the United States. This raises the profile of the political science issue and brings us to the puzzles with which this chapter is mainly concerned. First, what does motivate the formation of monetary policy? Second, what should motivate the formation of monetary policy? What, in other words, is the proper role of the central bank?

The least useful of all places to look for the guiding force behind monetary policy is to the law. The statutory goals of Federal Reserve policy are the same as for the entirety of the United States government, and they are set out in the Employment Act of 1946, as amended by the 1978 Humphrey-Hawkins

FIGURE 13.1

INTEREST RATES
The Basic Tool of Monetary Policy

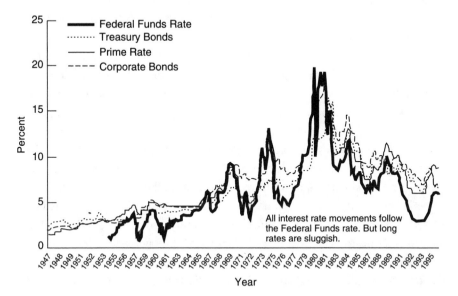

All interest rate movements follow the Federal Funds rate. But long rates are sluggish.

Full Employment and Balanced Growth Act. Both laws are quite clear that the principal objective of economic policy is to maintain a high level of employment and production. "Maximum employment, production and purchasing power" was the clarion language of the 1946 act; "Full employment, balanced growth and . . . reasonable price stability" was the otiose and bureaucratized 1978 version. In both cases, however, the intent of the lawgiver may have been clear, but, especially since 1978, the effect of the full employment statute has been mainly to illustrate the gulf that exists between the law and the actual exercise of power in the case of the Federal Reserve.

As a matter of history and practice, the modern charter of the Federal Reserve was written in the early days of October 1979. Returning from a calamitous international meeting in Belgrade, chairman Paul A. Volcker of the Federal Reserve Board announced his intention to fight the inflation that year at whatever price it might cost. Volcker's announcement was couched in technical terms, as a decision on the part of the central bank to target the growth of money rather than the level of interest rates, but its meaning was nevertheless straightforward: no interest rate would be considered, by itself, as too high. There followed a rapid run-up in interest rates and a short recession in the second quarter of 1980, compounded by the imposition of credit controls in March of that year. The Federal Reserve relaxed briefly, but when Ronald Reagan won the 1980 election it embarked on an even sharper and more prolonged run-up of interest rates in 1981–1982. This provoked the most severe recession of the postwar period, with unemployment surging to nearly 11 percent by the end of 1982.

The result was an economic disaster of the first order, going far beyond the unhappy effects of unemployment on the unemployed. The dollar rose in real value by 60 percent, rendering American products uncompetitive on both world and domestic markets. At the end of the summer of 1982, Mexico's financial crisis erupted, setting off a depression in Latin America that lasted nearly a decade and destroying in the process one of North America's most promising export markets. Entire sectors of the American manufacturing economy collapsed, never to return, including both comparatively backward sectors involved in the hand assembly of consumer goods and fairly advanced sectors producing industrial machinery and capital goods. High interest rates destroyed the financial viability of the savings and loan industry in the United States, precipitating a wave of gambling on real estate that ended in mid-decade with the collapse of the savings and loan industry and, with it, a major bulwark of housing finance in America. With collapsing tax revenues compounded by vast tax cuts, the federal budget deficit ballooned, creating a perception of financial crisis in Washington itself, which took a decade of fiscal austerity and rising taxes to unravel.

For all of this, inflation did decline. Whether it would have done so anyway is by now a moot issue. Justifiably or not, the Federal Reserve received credit for conquering inflation and substantially escaped blame for the carnage inflicted on the economy as it did so. What was left over, like the ring on the bathtub, was a general consensus that the Federal Reserve had the responsibility to fight inflation, by whatever means and at whatever cost, and irrespective of any other objective laid down by law. This was the real change in the climate surrounding monetary policy between the days of Arthur F. Burns and those of Alan Greenspan. Under Burns, chairman under Presidents Nixon and Ford, the Federal Reserve had inveighed against inflation. But Burns nevertheless accepted that other branches of government had responsibilities in the matter, always insisting that policies of wage restraint, budget deficit reduction, competitiveness, and antitrust had legitimate anti-inflation roles. Under Volcker, the Federal Reserve in effect declared that all other elements of anti-inflation were either useless or in default of their responsibilities; therefore the Federal Reserve alone would take on the job. The fig leaf of controlling the money stock was dropped within a year, but the Federal Reserve has never since given up its grip on the sole responsibility to fight inflation.

This reallocation of powers after 1979 gutted the Full Employment and Balanced Growth Act. And the new division of labor was not challenged effectively by any other branch of government. Congress and the executive were, for the most part, quite pleased to have the inflation monkey off their backs. The situation set up an imperative for the Federal Reserve. From the perspective of the central bank, inflation cannot, under any circumstances, be allowed to rise. If inflation did rise, that would be seen, by the terms of the Federal Reserve's own construction of its mandate and the rest of the government's abandonment of the field, as a failure of monetary policy. The Federal Reserve would then have to give up on its monopoly of anti-inflation policy, and in that case the reasons for its autonomy within the government would come into question.

We have slipped into a situation that would make sense under only two conditions. First, it must be true that inflation is "everywhere and always a monetary phenomenon," as the leader of the old-time monetarists, Milton Friedman, famously put it—that inflation is always caused by excessively easy Federal Reserve policy and never by external factors, such as war or shocks to major commodity prices, such as oil. Second, it must be true that the most efficient means of fighting inflation is always the old-fashioned mechanism of raising interest rates, slowing economic growth, driving up unemployment.

Neither condition holds. Not even the Federal Reserve Board itself actually believes that inflation is always caused by errors of monetary policy. The Federal Reserve is well aware that inflation can originate from many sources, of which the most common are the pressures of war or revolution on the worldwide systems of production and exchange. This fact is readily documented from the careful attention paid to widely disparate inflation indicators in official Federal Reserve documents, such as reports to Congress, and from the simple fact that if the Federal Reserve ever did believe any such thing, it would not have needed to abandon monetarism in 1982. The Federal Reserve also knows well that measures of money and measures of price change need not be closely related. The linkage between known parameters of monetary policy—growth of various measures of the money stock—and inflation has grown so loose and elastic in recent years that very few Federal Reserve officials seriously consider direct measures of monetary control to provide useful guidance into the future course of inflation.

It is also untrue that the sole use of monetary policy provides an efficient

cure for inflation, and doubly untrue that the wider world has come to believe this. The United States is among only a handful of countries whose
monetary authorities actually profess to believe any such thing. In countries
that have truly battled high inflations over the past decade, notably in Latin
America, Eastern Europe, and Israel, the successful strategies have always involved elements of wage-price coordination, exchange rate stabilization,
monetary reform, and other policies designed to permit price stabilization to
occur without forcing a depression of the real economy.[3]

These policies have been proven to work—as they did when applied in
earlier periods of U.S. history.[4] So why are they not also part of the policy ar-
senal here? Only because of the new division of labor: the instruments involved are not part of the discretionary authority of the Federal Reserve. It is
only a combination of ethnocentrism, ahistoricism, and this vested interest
that permits authorities in the United States, the United Kingdom, and a few
other countries (New Zealand is an unhappy example) to assert that effective
anti-inflation strategy consists solely of vesting responsibility for the price
level in an independent central bank.[5] The price we pay for this is a commitment to very low rates of growth, since the only way to make effective the
power of monetary policy over the inflation rate is to keep the economic
growth rate low.

If the Federal Reserve does not believe that inflation stems only from
monetary factors and errors of monetary policy, which it doesn't, it follows
that it has no business assuming sole responsibility for fighting inflation and
that the acceptance of such responsibility can only lead to serious trouble.
Suppose, for instance, that inflation were to rise as the result of some *nonmonetary* shock, such as an increase of oil prices. What should the Federal
Reserve do in that instance? Experts can debate this question, and some will
argue that because an oil shock is like a tax increase, the appropriate policy is
to offset it, by a reduction of interest rates. But the construction of the Federal Reserve's mandate as solely focused on fighting inflation makes this an
impossible choice. Oil price increases raise prices generally. That's inflation.
Under the sole-responsibility standard, the response must be an increase in
interest rates, whether such a thing is good for the economy or not.

Even stranger things happen should the Federal Reserve try to focus on a
specific measure of inflation, such as the consumer price index (CPI), as
economists Dimitri Papadimitriou and Randall Wray have recently argued.[6]
A very large part of the CPI comprises housing costs, and inflation in this
area is not actually measured directly but rather inferred from the very narrow segment of housing that transacts in the rental market. When interest

rates rise, it is more difficult for people to buy homes, and one consequence is that home rentals become more expensive. The CPI, as a mechanical matter, picks up this effect and amplifies it back through the housing sector, so that it reports a significant increase in the rate of inflation. In this way, a rise in interest rates to fight inflation, or the "threat" of inflation, can actually cause measured inflation to appear to rise, validating the Federal Reserve's unfounded worries![7]

In February 1994, the Federal Reserve fell into one of many possible traps. Apparently taking its anti-inflationary job too seriously, it started raising interest rates even though there was no evidence of any tendency for inflation to rise. Short-term rates doubled before the authorities began to have second thoughts. No inflationary pressures ever emerged.

The 1994 experience is more complex than I have just indicated, but the conclusion is correct: the Federal Reserve's assumption of the role of sole anti-inflation fighter has been a mistake.[8] This assumption of authority has imparted to monetary policy a bias against growth and a tendency to react to visions of phantoms. It has created a situation in which the vision of a phantom can lead to a reaction that produces the image of the phantom itself on the government's inflation radar screen—all without the slightest foundation in real events. And it has isolated the Federal Reserve, and the United States, from the experiences of a wide world of policies that actually can, and do, fight inflation without sole reliance on interest rates, creating unemployment, and increasing inequality.

We return in the next chapter to the question of what, if anything, might be done about this. For the moment, however, we need to establish that while "fighting inflation" is indeed the sole publicly acknowledged macroeconomic policy role of the central bank in the United States, it is by no means a complete explanation for the actual course of policy. And in fact there may emerge a substantial contradiction between the Federal Reserve's role as sole inflation fighter and its deeper, more fundamental role as guarantor of the stability of the banking and financial sectors.

The macroeconomic dimension to monetary policy is far from being the whole of the story. There is a microeconomic or, more precisely, a political dimension, for the most part hidden from view. It has to do with the system of credit and banking, and with the balance of power and the distribution of income between creditors and debtors, which is to say between the wealthy and the middle class.

The monetary system of the United States relies on the commercial banking industry to create liquidity for industry and enterprise, and has effectively vested in that industry the sovereign right to coin money—through the creation of new bank deposit—reserving for itself only the authority to "regulate the value thereof." This creation, in the aggregate, of new money is a major basis of bank profitability. Banks make money mainly from the spread between loan rates and deposit rates. The modern form of seignorage—the sovereign's profit on the coinage of precious metals—is the commercial bank profit on a newly created deposit and loan, made possible by an increase in central bank reserves and made profitable by a sufficient difference between the cost of funds and the loan rate of interest.

Banks are essentially fixed-cost operations. Their administrative, staff, and overhead costs are not closely related to the volume of transactions they undertake. The sine qua non of bank profits is therefore demand for loans at a sufficient spread to cover the fixed costs of bank operations. If loan demand is light, the spread must be higher. If the spread is too low, banks may be unwilling to lend in spite of loan demand. It follows that the Federal Reserve exercises extraordinary and nearly direct influence over bank profits, for its policies effectively set prices for the banking system, as well as influence the conditions of demand.

Banks are classic aspirants to the top of the capitalist pile. A poor or even a middle-class banker would be unheard of, even unworthy of trust. In a society with rising inequality, therefore, target rates of return for banks rise as rapidly as necessary to preserve their relative positions. And this has dramatic implications for the behavior of the banking system, for it does not follow that every financial institution can do equally well in an economic environment that is producing a smaller number of big winners and a larger number of small losers.

Partly for this reason, as long as twenty years ago, bank profit expectations came to be driven not by the average of what the economy could deliver over the medium or long term, but by some examples of selectively high performance within the banking industry itself. Flying high became the standard against which the average itself was to be judged. A culture of speculation began to develop within the financial sector, driving up required returns for successful bankers. As the average expected returns rose to levels that could in the nature of things be earned only by a few, there followed an increasingly wild pursuit of speculative investments, herd movements into and out of assets. The particular types of assets changed from one cycle to the next, from the real estate investment trusts of the 1970s, to Third World debt, to real estate development again in the 1980s.

The result by the late 1980s was a casino mentality in the economy at large, and an exhausted financial sector, with several large institutions that would have been bankrupt had they been forced to mark their asset values to market price. The collapse of the savings and loan institutions, with a half-trillion dollars in ensuing capital losses, was a serious enough crisis in itself, but only emblematic of the larger phenomenon.

The savings and loan crisis could be, and was, handled at enormous public expense by congressional legislation. But the larger problems of commercial banks, much more central to the perception of the integrity of capitalism itself, could not be handled in this way. These problems had to be dealt with by creating economic conditions under which the survival and recovery of the large institutions could be arranged below the table, so to speak. For this, only the resources and powers of the Federal Reserve would be sufficient.

An early and extremely conspicuous indication of the scale of the problem and the determination of the Federal Reserve to preserve existing financial relations came with the 500-point drop in the stock market in October 1987. Following this event, monetary policy entered a period of full-bore financial stabilization, essentially engaging in unlimited support lending to threatened financial institutions. The rescue worked, but there remained many years of rebuilding and subtle restructuring in front of the commercial banking sector before normal business operations could resume.

The trick was largely achieved by producing and maintaining a very big spread between rates on deposits (the cost of doing business for banks) and the interest rate on loans and investments. As the recession of 1989–1990 took hold, this was achieved by driving down the rate on deposits, which is tied to the short-term interest rate, and taking advantage of the fact that long-term interest rates do not move as rapidly as short rates do. The Federal Funds rate was driven downward in stages in 1991–1992, and spreads rose. But, importantly, banks also lowered their prime lending rates, while rates on long-term corporate bonds and U.S. Treasury bonds fell much more slowly.

The result is depicted in Figure 13.2: from 1991 through 1993, the spread between Federal Funds and prime rose to about three percentage points, but the spread between Federal Funds and long-term bonds rose to over five percentage points, a postwar record. This meant that banks could make money by borrowing short and buying bonds, and that is exactly what they did. This was a pure gift from the government: the opportunity for extraordinary financial returns for nonperformance. The banks could buy a high-grade corporate bond or government security at no essential risk, finance the purchase with their depositors' money, and shore up their balance sheet on the difference between interest paid and interest earned.

FIGURE 13.2

INTEREST RATE SPREADS COMPARED TO FEDERAL FUNDS RATE

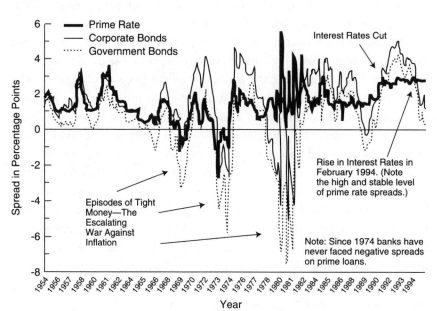

Meanwhile the economy recovered. This meant that the demand for loans on the part of business enterprises, which was naturally depressed during the recession, began to pick up. But the banks were unwilling to lend! From the bank perspective, making a risky commercial or industrial loan, at the prime rate or slightly higher, could hardly be justified when a high-grade and risk-free investment was available at essentially the same rate of return. This was the "credit crunch," widely reported and discussed at the time.[9]

Figure 13.3 illustrates the relationship between demand and supply for bank business loans during this time. The figure shows the relationship between nominal gross national product (GNP) and commercial and industrial bank lending. As the figure illustrates, the relationship is extremely close—most of the time. Thus, the level of nominal GNP is a good measure of the demand for bank lending—most of the time. The great exception to this rule begins in 1991, when the Federal Reserve embarks on an aggressively antirecessionary policy of cutting interest rates. Contrary to all predictions of competitive theory, the banks simply stopped making new loans to business (and also, not incidentally, to consumers). In relation to the value of GNP, which

FIGURE 13.3

THE CREDIT CRUNCH

GNP and Commercial and Industrial Bank Loans, 1973–1997

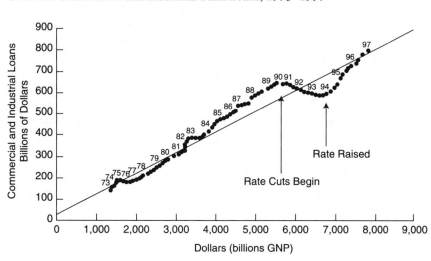

is to say after taking account of the recession, loans in both categories dropped sharply. By 1993, the banks were ready to relent on consumer loans, which are highly profitable. But business lending, tied to the prime rate, they would not expand.

The situation was inherently temporary, for although long-term interest rates move more slowly than do short-term rates, they do eventually adjust. And through 1991–1993, the long-term bond rates declined. This was not, as commonly claimed at the time, owing to progress on the federal deficit, but entirely a predictable adjustment to the prior decline in short-term rates. As short-term rates stabilized after 1992, it was only a matter of time before bond rates adjusted and the extraordinary replenishment of bank balance sheets from long-term, secure investments became impossible.

What to do? In 1993, the Federal Reserve worked to slow the adjustment of long-term rates, by sending clear signals, in congressional testimony and press statements, that the climate of low short-term rates could not be and would not be sustained. But this too could work only for a time, and it had a cost: banks, anticipating a rise in short-term rates, saw that they would lose future income if they met commercial and industrial loan demand at prevailing business loan rates. By waiting, on the other hand, they would assure themselves much higher profits on such loans, and in the meantime the bond markets provided a ready and lucrative haven for bank cash. Thus the credit crunch as experienced by ordinary business borrowers intensified: they could not get loans from their banks.

Many press observers argued that the resolution of the credit crunch would require lower interest rates and easier credit conditions. But in this case, the supply of bank reserves was not the problem. What we had instead was a mismatch of financial instrument pricing, engineered by the Federal Reserve for the purpose of replenishing bank coffers—and a huge speculation, in return, by the banking sector on the future course of interest rate policy. A stable short-term interest rate, maintained resolutely over a long time, would have resolved the problem in due course, since long-term bond rates would have continued to fall and the premium on unproductive investments would have disappeared. But this would not have met the demands of the banking sector for extraordinarily high profits on new business loans.

Ultimately, on February 4, 1994, the situation was resolved: the Federal Reserve started raising short-term interest rates, eventually doubling them over eighteen months. Bank business lending rates immediately rose by comparable amounts, preserving the spread between the prime rate and the bank cost of funds. But long-term bond rates were once again sluggish, and in consequence the bond spread disappeared just as business loans became highly profitable once again. The effects on bank business lending were dramatic: after falling for three years up to February 1994, including through the first two years of economic expansion, bank business lending immediately turned around and began to grow at very rapid rates. Figure 13.4 illustrates what happened.

This history illustrates some very pertinent facts about the conduct of monetary policy. The Federal Reserve does see itself as the sole guardian against price inflation and is prepared to raise interest rates sharply when inflation threatens, producing recession and unemployment (as it did on a grand scale in 1979–1981 and on a lesser scale in 1988–1989). But when inflation is not a problem, the evident motivations of monetary policy are substantially different. At such times, the claim that policy is "fighting inflation" is merely a useful cover for the pursuit of other objectives. In particular, the claim in 1994 that the Federal Reserve was launching a "preemptive strike" against inflation had no substance. What was involved, instead, was a complicated maneuver to restart bank business lending on terms that were sufficiently lucrative for the banking industry to accept. The fundamental fact is that the Federal Reserve, which is itself in part owned by the private commer-

FIGURE 13.4

BANK LOANS AND INVESTMENTS

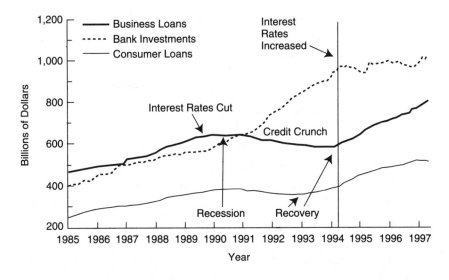

cial banking system, conducts monetary policy to support the pecuniary interests of that sector whenever there are not overriding contrary considerations. It has done so consistently since the early 1970s. Finally, the Federal
Reserve was constrained in no serious way by the high drama of budget
deficit reduction that was going on at the same time. Even though that
drama was presented to the public as holding the promise of steadily lower
long-term interest rates, it was essentially irrelevant to the motivations of the
central bank.

The interplay between monetary policy and fiscal strategy, and between
monetary policy and banking policy, makes plain that the idea of an apoliti-
cal monetary policy is essentially an illusion. Monetary policy is inherently
political, not just in its effects on the larger society but in its direct and year-
to-year effects on the budget-making decisions of the president and Congress. The real issue concerns the terms of the political relationship between
the Federal Reserve and the rest of the government.

The creation of the Federal Reserve system in 1913 had removed monetary policy from American politics—an eight-decade hiatus now slightly
longer than the whole life span of the Soviet empire. In the absence of battles
over money, fiscal Keynesianism waxed and waned. But now, with purely fis-

cal Keynesianism dead and buried, progressive forces have no alternative but to return, as democrats in Russia have done, to the issues of the pre–Federal Reserve era.

Ultimately, we need to redesign an economic system where working Americans have reasonable incomes in relation to their need, and reasonable access to credit—at reasonable and stable interest rates. If a moribund banking sector and a bank-captive Federal Reserve cannot provide this, then the political process must be called back into action.

The changing of interest rate policy, a necessary but not sufficient condition, is in a legal sense the most easily achieved part of this problem. Congress has the power to change Federal Reserve policy if it chooses. The Federal Reserve is *not,* under the Constitution, a fourth branch of government. It is an agency created under the constitutional provision that *Congress* has the power to "coin money and regulate the value thereof." It is, in the term of art, a *creature of Congress.* Although Congress has delegated the administration of monetary policy to the Federal Reserve, it is under no legal or constitutional obligation to observe a hands-off policy under all circumstances or indefinitely. Congress can set policy for the Federal Reserve if it wants to.

Congress can, of course, order a change in Federal Reserve policy by passing a law. It has done so, for example, by writing the general objectives of "maximum employment, production and purchasing power" into the 1946 Employment Act and "full employment" alongside "reasonable price stability" into the 1978 Humphrey-Hawkins Full Employment and Balanced Growth Act. To attempt to enact a new law now, however, is probably unwise. Statutes are for the ages, not the sensible step to remedy a short-term problem of policy incoherence. Also, it is not a good idea to enact laws one is not prepared to enforce.

There is an alternative to passing a law, albeit less constitutionally clear-cut. This is for Congress to place a directive on monetary policy into a concurrent resolution. Concurrent resolutions, such as the annual budget resolution, do not require the president's signature. They therefore lack the force of law. But they have been acknowledged—in repeated (reluctant) testimony to Congress itself by past chairmen of the Federal Reserve Board—to be binding in principle on the Federal Reserve. A concurrent resolution would be binding in practice partly because the board is a creature of Congress and partly because, should the board defy a congressional policy directive, Congress retains the power to invoke the more serious sanction of public law.

Congress has in fact taken this step twice in recent history. In 1975, in House Concurrent Resolution 133, Congress directed the Federal Reserve Board to conduct policy "so as to lower long-term interest rates." And in a continuing resolution at the end of 1982, Congress ordered that monetary policy "achieve and maintain a level of interest rates low enough to generate significant economic growth and thereby reduce the current intolerable level of unemployment."

Such intervention is strong medicine, suitable only for serious illness and short-term use. The previous two cases, in 1975 and 1982, differed importantly from the present. The patient (the economy) was sicker, and the treatment was exceptionally cautious. Did the Federal Reserve obey? Policy was consistent with the directive in both cases, but we do not know, in fact, whether the language in either resolution wrought any changes relative to what policy would otherwise have been.

Occasional intervention by Congress in the direction of monetary policy can be useful, but experience teaches that it is a measure for only occasional use. Over the longer run, what the Federal Reserve system needs most is a restructuring of its internal voices, so that routine pressures for interest rate stability are stronger. This requires looking hard at the way the institution itself is built.

It can be said without fear of contradiction that the Federal Reserve is the most ridiculous of all government agencies, the platypus of institutions, a bureaucracy designed by a committee, governed by an odd hybrid of public governors and private presidents, the latter spread out along lines of economic and political power (four on the East Coast, three in the upper Midwest, two in Missouri, one each in the South, Southwest, and West) prevailing in 1913.

The Federal Open Market Committee, which votes on interest rate policy, is among other things a flagrantly unconstitutional body. The voting participation of regional Federal Reserve Bank presidents who are formally beholden to their private bank directors and not "appointed by the President with the advice and consent of the Senate," as the Constitution of the United States requires, is improper. And as a practical matter, the entire system remains largely an insular white male club, equally unencumbered by the budget process and the Freedom of Information Act, responsive to no constituency below the top 1 percent of the income distribution.

Faced with this, progressive proposals have historically been modest. In bills introduced in Congress over the past decade, isolated members of the House and Senate have sought to abolish the Open Market Committee, constituting the bank presidents instead as a nonvoting Open Market Advisory Committee (a proposal by Congressman Lee Hamilton and Senator Paul Sarbanes), or alternatively to make the bank presidents into presidential appointees (a proposal by Congressman Henry B. Gonzalez). Congress also sought to place the system under the budget, to broaden its base of appointees, to expose its internal debates to external review.

These small and useful steps now need to be integrated into a larger program of restructuring, in part to repair the constitutional flaws in Federal Reserve structure, in part to repair the actual flaws in the flow of information and pressure to the Federal Reserve's decision-making structures. We need, for example, a system of districts that reflects the distribution of population and economic activity at the beginning of the twenty-first century, not that at the end of the nineteenth. How can such a major change be accomplished?

An answer to this dilemma may lie in the concept of sunset review. Many states have a process whereby the enabling statutes governing agencies of government undergo periodic review, with open public input, and must be reenacted if the agency is to survive. This process provides a powerful lever for agency modernization, for consolidation and elimination of redundant functions, and one that can operate with some independence from the gridlock of interests that settles in on a legislative committee structure.

A sunset review of the Federal Reserve, amounting to the reinvention of the central bank, would necessarily start by redrawing the lines of the regional Federal Reserve districts, and no doubt expanding the number of districts to reflect the increased size and diversity of the economy. But this would not make the regional Federal Reserve banks truly regional. For that to happen, it would be necessary that they become accountable to the polities of their regions. One way to achieve this would be to eliminate the current banker domination of the boards of directors of the regional Federal Reserve banks and to make those directors, instead, appointees of the governors of the various states comprising a region, in rough proportion to state populations. In this way, for the first time, the Federal Reserve would become in a true sense a federal institution.

The second substantial area of reform would concern voting rights on the Federal Open Market Committee. If the regional Federal Reserve banks were reconstituted under gubernatorially appointed boards of directors, then the constitutional problem would remain. Presidents of the regional banks, not being advise-and-consent appointments of the president as required by the Constitution, could not properly vote on monetary policy. But they could form an advisory committee, which could, if it desired, render a recommendation to the board of governors of the Federal Reserve system at each meeting. Indeed such a system might better balance regional and national considerations than the one that currently exists, in which an awkward pattern of annual rotations determines who actually gets to vote at any particular meeting of the Open Market Committee.

The third critical issue concerns accountability. Under the Constitution and any conceivable rewriting of the law, the Federal Reserve would and must remain a creature of the Congress, subject to the reporting requirements of the Congress and to such policy directives as Congress may choose to make. Congress, and not the president, therefore can and should insist that the Federal Reserve build monetary policy around the context of the fiscal decisions of the Congress and that it report on this relationship explicitly in its semiannual reports to Congress. Today, there is no formal requirement that the Federal Reserve even consider budget strategy and actions in justifying monetary actions, but there is no reason why such a process should not be a routine feature of monetary accountability.

The fourth and final major issue concerns Federal Reserve openness and accountability to the public. In this area, there is much to gain, and almost nothing to lose, by a radical experiment. Why not simply put a camera in the Federal Reserve's chambers and broadcast its meetings to the world? Nothing in the records of past meetings, to my knowledge, suggests that any matters of national security, safety of sources and methods, proprietary information related to private corporate entities, or any other properly secret matters are discussed in the parts of the Open Market Committee meetings devoted to decisions about the interest rate. What is discussed—the news, macroeconomic modeling, issues of economic theory—can and should be open for everyone to hear. A video camera would greatly demystify these proceedings.

Beyond reform of the Federal Reserve, it is apparent that the underlying political economy of the commercial banking sector in the United States also needs to be addressed. The time may come when even the wit and resources of the central bank will be unable to prevent a clash between the needs of the economy, the priorities of the elected government, and the culture of the financial sector from coming out into the open. That topic, however, truly lies beyond the reach of this book. We must keep to our subject, and move on to the next question. If the Federal Reserve is to be removed from the anti-inflation front lines, what do we put there in its place?

14

INFLATION CONTROL
WITHOUT UNEMPLOYMENT

Ultimately, some form of third major macroeconomic control instrument is necessary, in addition to monetary action through interest rates and fiscal action through income generation, if full control is to be exercised over three major macroeconomic variables: the rate of inflation, the level of employment, and the division of the product between current consumption and provision for the future. While with a sufficient dihedral, one can fly a plane in good weather and make gentle turns with a rudder and elevator, it was the Wright brothers' invention of wing warp, later realized as ailerons, that allows landing in a cross-wind without disaster. If value-added warrants won't do the trick, it is up to economists to devise something that will.

—William Vickrey, 1996 Nobel Laureate in Economics

This book began as an inquiry into the origins of the inequality crisis. It has become in part a tract on the reform of monetary policy. We have found that the main causes of rising inequality—unemployment, an overvalued exchange rate, high interest rates, and debt peonage—all are linked to a structure of policymaking, at the center of which is the delegation of stabilization policy and inflation control to the Federal Reserve. Even fiscal policy depends essentially on the conduct of monetary policy for its appearance of success or failure.

For this reason, calls to change the way the United States conducts monetary policy should be at the heart of our political economy. Without a change of monetary policy, in the form of a sustained, determined, and credible movement toward low and stable interest rates and the restructuring of the Federal Reserve to make such a policy possible, even concerted efforts to reduce economic inequality cannot succeed. To put it the other way around, any concerted effort to reduce economic inequality, whether by raising low wages, controlling high salaries, increasing progressive income taxes, or simply running a high-employment economy, can be defeated by a central bank with the power and the motivation to raise interest rates.

A responsible argument to change the mandate of the central bank cannot stop at the case for low interest rates. One has also to answer: What would you do about inflation? Who would take responsibility, if not the Federal Reserve, for ensuring reasonable stability of prices? What means and mechanisms might be made available for this task? In other words, if we are going to tear down a system in which the final word on anti-inflation strategy is delegated to central bankers, what are we going to put in its place? This chapter provides a series of suggestions.

One possible answer is that we should do nothing. If we examine the modern history of inflations in the United States, it is plain that serious inflation is almost always and everywhere a wartime phenomenon. The peak pressures on price levels in this century are matters of the world wars, Korea, Vietnam, and two upheavals in which the United States did not play a direct role: the 1973 Arab-Israeli conflict and the 1979 Iranian revolution, followed by the Iran-Iraq War. Inflationary pressures otherwise have been minor. It is also quite possible, though it cannot be proved, that the inflation occasioned by the conflicts of the 1970s would have subsided when the conflicts did, that supply-shock inflation would have abated on its own, even if none of the harsh actions to control inflation that were taken by U.S. monetary authorities had been taken.

With the era of globalized trade in manufactured goods that began in the late 1960s and accelerated sharply in the 1980s, the superficial case for doing nothing grows even stronger. In a global economy, the capacity of forces internal to the United States, such as trade unions or bottlenecks in the supply of critical materials, to generate inflation in the United States has been greatly reduced. Equally, as we saw in Chapter 10, the (Phillips curve) argument that a lower rate of domestic unemployment would necessarily generate inflationary pressures has lost much of its power in recent years. Open economies properly treat the prices they pay and receive on international markets as external facts of life. As the number of these prices multiplies, in relation to all national transactions, inflation must be a global phenomenon or a nonexistent one.

If inflation is not a present danger, except as part of a global phenomenon over which national policies can enjoy relatively little leverage, then one can reasonably question whether anti-inflation "vigilance" should hold its present privileged place in the hierarchy of economic goals. The hazards of anti-inflation policy—unemployment, loss of competitiveness in international markets when the dollar is overvalued, financial instability when interest rates are maintained too high, and the economic inequality to which all of these forces contribute—are all more easily documented and more readily observed than the contingent costs of a little more inflation itself. So the extreme proto-Keynesian position, that the risk of inflation ought simply to be ignored, should not be dismissed entirely out-of-hand. On a sober assessment, one can defend an accelerationist strategy on conservative, risk-versus-benefit grounds.

Still, reality intrudes. I don't in fact think this is satisfactory. One cannot expect the see-no-evil position to prevail. Inflation anxieties are endemic to the system of finance capitalism, and the reasonable goal of a policy reformer cannot be to obliterate them. The policy reformer can best hope to find some useful ways and means of mitigating the anxieties and thereby to defuse the costly and dangerous interventions to which they usually lead. If one plans to step on the gas, seat belts and even air bags are sensible precautions. In this way, institutional reform of anti-inflation policy may help to make it possible to pursue the objectives of higher employment, lower interest rates, a more competitive exchange rate, and greater economic equality more aggressively than one could otherwise hope to do.

It is also fairly clear that the drastic measures sometimes employed in the past—the wage and price controls of World War II, the Korean conflict, and the latter days of the Vietnam War—cannot form part of a nonmonetary anti-inflation agenda in a globalized economy in peacetime. A serious effort to rethink the allocation of responsibilities for economic objectives has to search for a stable set of institutional arrangements, a pattern of interactions that may plausibly endure. Drastic measures by their nature are fit for emergencies only. They can be enacted only in crises and will be abandoned soon after.

So what's left? We have ruled out sole reliance on tight money and high interest rates; we have, in effect, taken the anti-inflation mandate out of the hands of the Federal Open Market Committee. We have discounted the modern usefulness of comprehensive price control. And we have rejected the option of declaring that the problem does not exist. Have we painted ourselves into a corner?

In fact, we have simply narrowed our focus so that the remaining options can come into view. And in this area what the United States needs today is not so much radical policy innovation, as reasoned learning from the world outside. There have been over the past decade, around the world, quite a number of working models from which to learn. Anti-inflationary systems that do not cost vast and sustained unemployment exist. Some of their features can be adapted to the American case. Many of these have been worked out under conditions substantially more unstable than prevail in the United States; they are battle tested and more likely to work here than in their countries of origin. They can be described generally as heterodox approaches to inflation control.[1]

One example from which the United States could learn is that of Germany—provided one knows how to distinguish social realities from convenient propaganda. The German Bundesbank has a reputation as an indomitably independent central bank and formidable inflation fighter. This reputation is not undeserved. In fact, German anti-inflation policy is singularly effective, with lower inflation and less macroeconomic volatility than in the United States. But the mechanism does not at all resemble the American–Federal Reserve approach to inflation control, which has relied on macroeconomic volatility for its effect. Instead, the Bundesbank operates through German social institutions to achieve a low-inflation result at a much lower social cost.

As close students of the German case know, the Bundesbank is not a monetarist institution, dedicated to inflation control through the brutal mechanisms of monetary targeting, swashbuckling adjustment of interest rates, and indirect pressure on the credit markets. (Given Germany's position at the center of the European monetary system, the Bundesbank cannot in fact afford to be a source of such instability on a routine basis.) Instead, the Bundesbank exercises its authority in a more subtle and effective way, at least partly through interactions with trade unions and the mechanisms of the German wage structure.

Anti-inflation policy in the Bundesbank style works—when it does work—through an exercise of intimidation and countervailing power in a setting of repeated interaction between powerful players.[2] The workers of Germany's highest-paid and most competitive industries—specifically, the metalworking unions—know that their situation depends critically on maintaining a reasonable value of the deutsche mark on international markets. They are, after all, exporters, and if the German exchange rate goes too high, their industries will be severely hurt. They also know that the Bundesbank can, if and when it chooses, drive up this value by raising the German interest rate. They know that such an action can be an effective way to mitigate inflationary pressures in the short run; the Bundesbank will take this step if it has to.

It is therefore in the interest of these key German workers to choose a rate of wage increase that does not provoke the Bundesbank into a retaliatory course of action. If the system works, then Germany passes through a cycle characterized by pay restraint at the top of the wage structure. And when Germany's best-paid workers are so restrained, the entire wage structure remains in line; workers below the top ranks take their cues from the leaders. With all of this working smoothly, inflation from domestic German causes remains necessarily low.

The key elements in this mechanism are (1) the reputation of the German monetary authorities for commitment to a strategy of low inflation, (2) the solidaristic character of German wage settlements and the key position of the high-wage, export-oriented workers in this structure, and (3) the existence of at least an implicit structure of communication and bargaining between these two poles of countervailing power, with the result that (4) all parties expect German inflation to remain reasonably low and feel no need to act so as to protect themselves against a radically contrary result. When the system works, the Bundesbank does not need to respond to inflationary pressures after the fact by raising interest rates and driving the economy into recession—the situation actually faced on a regular basis by the Federal Reserve in the United States. The Bundesbank can achieve its objective by other, far less costly means.

Unfortunately, the fact that the Bundesbank can achieve its goals in a low-cost way, and that it has sometimes done so, does not guarantee a stable success for this implicit form of wage bargaining. And in fact, the Bundesbank has often practiced anti-inflation overkill, particularly under conservative governments who are unwilling or unable to strike lasting political bargains with the unions. So while the Germans have the potential, in their system, for non-inflationary full employment, the fact is that they have largely squandered this potential in recent years, leaving not only Germany but all of Europe suffering from the highest unemployment in a generation.

A somewhat different system characterizes Japanese labor relations, with equally useful partial lessons for the United States. Because Japanese unions have historically been company based and because Japan has never had a labor-led government, the power of Japanese workers has generally been much less than in Northern Europe, and their role in national governance has never been as substantial. (The surface militance of Japanese labor and, in past times, its revolutionary rhetoric have been, in part, compensating mechanisms for this exclusion from power.) The postwar Japanese economy has always been, moreover, a highly globalized exporter of manufactures and importer of raw materials; it is a price taker for the commodities it purchases and, nominally speaking, a price setter for the commodities it sells. As such, Japan cannot afford to let domestic labor costs get out of line.

An important feature of the Japanese wage structure has been an annual period of adjustment (the "Spring Offensive") during which all of the major industrial sectors press to make wage settlements within a relatively short period of time. The annual, national character of this settlement pattern means that past episodes of inflation are not necessarily built in to the future movement of wages and costs, as they can be under systems of overlapping, multi-year contracts and decentralized pattern bargaining (such as have historically characterized wage settlements in the United States).

The problem of inflation control in Japan has historically taken the form of managing external shocks, most notably in the price of oil in 1973 and 1979. Both of these events hit Japan—a major importer of Arab oil with no domestic sources of supply—very hard; initially inflation in Japan rose by much more than in the United States. But the interesting fact is that the Japanese survived the second shock with far less disruption to their domestic economy than was caused by the first. The difference? In 1973, the Japanese permitted their wage structure to become destabilized as the effects of the oil shock percolated through the economy. As a result, inflation surged, and it took several years to get it under control. In 1979, by contrast, the Japanese understood much better what was happening to them, individual sectors did not overreact or overcompensate, and the shock was past, essentially, within a year.

The German model teaches us that it is useful to have a national pattern setter for wages in at least an implicit dialogue with a dedicated anti-inflation agency of the government. The Japanese model adds a corollary: it is also useful for an open and vulnerable economy to coordinate the timing of wage bargains on a regular schedule and to break away from multiyear or overlapping patterns that can propagate shocks from one year to the next. If a large external shock does hit, it is much better to absorb it within a short period of time, to readjust and move forward, than to allow it to percolate indefinitely through the internal wage structure, causing shock and aftershock of wage-price destabilization.

Finally, we need to turn to the developing world, where most of the planet's practical experience with fighting inflation, often under extreme conditions, actually resides.

Up until about 1985, anti-inflation policies in most of the developing world followed a textbook pattern, largely originating with the conservative economics of North American universities and propagated by the International Monetary Fund (IMF). Cuts in social spending and increases in taxation were imposed to restore fiscal order and reduce public borrowing. A squeeze on credit was imposed to reduce the growth of the money supply. With fiscal and monetary austerity in place, inflation was certain to fall.

In most cases, such policies of radical austerity did reduce inflation. But they could not succeed in the long term because they could not be sustained under democratic conditions. Cuts in social spending would dramatically undercut the living standards of the poor. Increased taxes in many developing country cases were readily avoided by the middle class and the rich, and a credit crunch would send private sector firms into bankruptcy, creating economic disorder and political outcry. Within a short period of time, budget restraints and credit restraints necessarily had to be removed: the society in effect preferred high rates of inflation to the calamity imposed by orthodox measures of inflation control.

Eventually economists in a wide array of developing nations came to focus on the fact that their inflations had a large inertial character—that inflation expectations were "built in" to the system through networks of contracts and debts. This was true of wage contracts, which had to anticipate future inflation, and it was especially true of all forms of credit: future inflation was built in to loan agreements in the form of extraordinarily high interest rates. Anti-inflation policy, unless accompanied by a general rewriting of loan contracts, therefore necessarily implied bankruptcy for almost every debtor. Something had to be done about this by unconventional means. Otherwise one might wreck the economy and yet not succeed in bringing inflation down.

The solution to this problem took a common form around the world. Fiscal austerity was essential. Almost everywhere, governments had to stop fueling their own inflations by spending far beyond their ability to tax. (In many cases this proved easier than expected, since an end to inflation improved tax collections.) But rather than moving to a tight monetary policy, the heterodox plans envisaged an easing of monetary policy, in the form of a radical move to lower interest rates. This was often accompanied by a change of currency and a table of conversions that allowed debts contracted in the old currency at the old, inflation-adjusted interest rates to be paid in the low-inflation and low–interest rate environment following stabilization. Usually the exchange rate of the new currency was declared fixed, tied to a commodity basket or to the dollar—a measure that improved the credibility of the stabilization. And finally, to lock in the change in expectations, governments would impose strict guidelines or controls on wages and prices, at least until the situation calmed down and people got used to living with stable prices.

Heterodox stabilizations, like all other social experiments, had a varied record. Some worked for only a year or two; some lasted longer. Some fell apart for reasons not anticipated in the original design, some collapsed under external pressure, and some were abandoned for political reasons. Some (notably in Israel and later in Poland) enjoyed remarkable, enduring success. But compared to the orthodox, IMF programs that were the available alternative, there is no doubt: heterodox stabilizations worked vastly better than the orthodox prescription of tight money and balanced budgets. And, we have some reason to think, they also reduced inequality, whereas we know that the orthodox prescriptions increase inequality wherever they are applied.

Some interesting evidence on this last point comes from Brazil. Monthly estimates of the movement of inequality from 1976 to 1995 show that as in the United States, inequality in Brazil is broadly sensitive to macroeconomic conditions. The boom of the late 1970s reduced inequality, and the disastrous debt crisis of the 1980s vastly increased the dispersion of wages and earnings in Brazilian industry.[3] One can tell essentially the same story about this as one can for the United States: in periods of prosperity and high employment, the bottom of the wage distribution gains relative to the top; in periods of calamity, higher-paid workers are better protected.

The main effect of inflation in Brazil was on the intrayear, month-to-month pattern of inequality. When inflation was high, inequality rose sharply in Brazil from month to month. Then a year's inflation-induced increase in inequality would be corrected, for the most part, by the annual pattern of catch-up indexation. Thus a sawtooth pattern of rising inequality emerged in periods that represent the worst times of Brazilian hyperinflation. Yet there are also clear periods—in 1985, 1988, and 1994—when the sawtooth pattern abruptly levels off and inequality declines. These represent the three major periods of Brazilian heterodox stabilization: the Cruzado Plan, the Plan Vernal (Summer Plan), and the Real Plan. The effects are remarkably clear. *Heterodox stabilizations fight inflation and inequality at the same time.*

Can lessons from the experience of heterodox stabilization be applied in the United States? The answer should be: not a minute too soon. To an economist with a cosmopolitan perspective and some experience of recent developments around the world, economic policy discussion inside the United States, particularly in official circles, has a tone of backwardness and provincialism. The United States has become the capital of an orthodoxy, applying to itself the precepts of stabilization policy—balanced budgets and high interest rates—that more clear-sighted places have largely come to reject, in favor of more balanced, eclectic, and less costly schemes. It is for this reason, in part, that inequality has been rising much more sharply in the United States than throughout Europe or in Japan.

Yet one can make a case that the United States would be a promising candidate for conversion to heterodox anti-inflation policies, opening the way toward more rapid economic expansion and compression of the wage structure. Heterodox policies can work here. We can perhaps best see this by examining what the elements of such a policy, adapted to American conditions, might be.

The budget. The first element of heterodox anti-inflation policy, a stable budget policy, is already essentially in place in the United States. The country has preserved a fairly effective tax structure, and (notwithstanding alarmism by opponents of Medicare and social security) no aspect of its government expenditure is out of control. The public deficit of the United States, as of early 1998, is small by world standards. There is in fact no need for any wrenching adjustment of budget policy on stabilization grounds; budget balance is neither necessary nor desirable, but represents only the continuation of forces that have already given us a conservative fiscal position. To the contrary, there is room for an easing of budget policies, consistent with continued success of anti-inflation policy. This is the first great advantage enjoyed by the United States.

Banking policy. The fact that the United States actually enjoys a low-inflation environment means that several major parts of the usual heterodox stabilization package as usually applied are simply unnecessary here. There is not a need for currency reform or debt conversion. Instead, we are at the stage where a reduction of interest rates can be instituted essentially on its own, as an acknowledgment of the existing state of price stability. The main risk here is that of adjustment in the banking and financial sectors, which would no doubt have to undergo an orderly downsizing. (It is an interesting fact that inflation stabilizations in other countries have also tended to reduce the need for banking services.) But with a corresponding expansion of manufacturing and service activities, it is a reasonable proposition that the nation could absorb a reduction of purely financial employment.

The dollar. The combination of fiscal stability and lower interest rates, essentially the reverse of the big-deficit, high–interest rate policies of the early 1980s that led to the historic overvaluation of the dollar, would tend by itself to reduce the dollar's exchange value. Given the extreme sensitivity of low-end manufacturing wages to the dollar's value, this is a desirable and necessary outcome. The strong dollar policy, so favored by financial traders and the Treasury Department, is a disaster from the standpoint of economic inequality.

But actually getting the dollar down in the correct way is not so easily accomplished. The problem here is that the value of the dollar is a bifurcated phenomenon. After 1985, the dollar did decline with respect to the currencies of Europe and Japan. But it did not decline, nearly so much, with respect to the currencies of developing countries, notably in Latin America and along the Pacific Rim, with which the United States conducts an increasing percentage of its trade. The result has been a kind of weak-dollar, strong-dollar duality: the dollar has been low with respect to the deutsche mark and the yen, something that has been good for the competitiveness of advanced American exports (and the high wages of the workers who produce them), but strong with respect to, say, the Mexican peso or the Korean won, which has maintained the squeeze on comparatively low-wage U.S. producers of import-competing manufactures.

The essence of a solution to this problem lies in gradually strengthening the exchange rates of the low-income countries, increasing their capacity to demand American exports, and relieving the competitive pressure on U.S. import-competing industries. In other words, there is a need to return to development strategies that emphasize steady and sustained growth and recognize the responsibility of the rich countries in bringing this about. Because the structurally weak position of countries like Mexico and Brazil since the early 1980s has been related in part to their debts, a return to a worldwide structure of low interest rates would in itself contribute to this pattern of improvement. But probably more is required, in the form of an architecture of international regulation of capital flows and currency stabilization. This is a question of global or at least regional economic macromanagement, and some further discussion of it will follow in the next chapter.

Internal wage-price stabilization. The remaining element of a heterodox anti-inflation strategy inside the United States would need to be concerned with the pattern of wage bargaining and inflation adjustments—with the kind of structural relationships between groups of industries that we have explored in the central chapters of this book. If we are to replace the brutal hand of the Open Market Committee, which works only by destabilizing economic activity, by creating unemployment and punishing the poor, with something more orderly and sensible, what can the mechanism be?

The answer to this question takes us into territory I have explored in detail in an earlier book.[4] The essence of the matter is to find ways to restore an element of solidarity, national consensus, and coordination into the setting of wages in the United States, so that institutional pressures begin to work to compress the wage structure and to countervail against the powerful forces of technology and trade that are working to increase inequality. While ultimately radical measures may be required to achieve an actual compression of wages on the scale of 1942–1945 or even 1966–1969, in the interim there are quite a number of smaller steps that would help.

A higher minimum wage. The rise in the federal minimum wage in 1996 proved to be one of the great economic nonevents of the time. Though roundly denounced by conservatives as a source of inflation and a barrier to the creation of new jobs, it proved to be instead an essentially harmless measure that transferred some income from some of the nation's more voracious exploiters of low-wage workers (in particular, the fast-food franchise restaurant industry) to a significant number of their least powerful employees. No adverse effects, of any kind, were observed.

The problem with the 1996 rise in the minimum wage was that it wasn't sufficiently large. Over the previous fifteen years, the long delay between increases in the minimum wage had eroded both the value of the minimum and the number of people affected by it. In real terms, the increase to $5.15 was sufficient only to recoup about half of the lost ground, and it still remained true that only a fraction of the S-sector workforce was strongly affected.

The sensible next step in this area, then, is another increase in the minimum wage—this time, at least to restore the full real value of the minimum as of, say, 1968, which was $6.50 in inflation-adjusted values. Such an increase would sharply increase the number of people for whom the minimum wage is effective. There is no reason, of course, why thirty years later the minimum wage should not, in fact, be higher than it was in 1970 purchasing power. But a return to that previous accomplishment would be a step in the right direction and could lead in further stages to a target minimum of, say, $7.50 per hour after a few years. Even though such a step would affect many more workers than the 1996 increase, bringing the minimum to within 30 percent of the average wage in the services sector, there is still no real reason to fear that it would be either inflationary or costly in terms of unemployment.

What, then, should be the role of organized labor? Over the past forty years, as is well known, the share of American labor affiliated with trade unions has declined from about one-third to below 10 percent of the total workforce. This has mirrored the decline in the relative size of the U.S. manufacturing sector and the rise of competition in manufactures between rich and poor nations. Unions have fought this development, in defense of the high wages of the embattled worker in the C-sector, by supporting restrictions on international trade and opposing schemes for regional free markets, such as the North American Free Trade Agreement (NAFTA). Today the fight goes on, over such questions as the terms of admission of the People's Republic of China to the World Trade Organization. But labor has lost the battle on this front, and the question really must be, What to do next?

It is surely hopeless to suppose that the trend toward international manufacturing can now be reversed—that the United States can now, at this late date, retreat behind a wall of trade protection. Protection does protect; on this the record is clear. But except where protected industries recast themselves, as most of them eventually did, into more advanced industrial enterprises employing far fewer workers per unit of output, they could not have survived. The problem for workers is that even a successful remolding of an older mass manufacturing sector does not preserve the employment of the workforce who are behind the protectionist drive. The fruit of protectionism may be survival of an industry, but only in rare cases is it the long-term survival of an industry in the form useful to the workers who work there. The American C-sector, and with it the labor movement, has been squeezed between a K-sector where a small number of workers have thrived and a vast S-sector where general standards of wages have been sinking steadily for three decades.

This suggests that the task for labor must now be to focus on raising working and living standards in the S-sector, where 80 percent of Americans work, wages are low, trade is a less important constraint on wages, and minimum wages are a more important force on wage levels. Under existing institutional and political arrangements, this is a hard road: the costs of organizing in the S-sector are extremely high. Since the sector is highly competitive and individual shops tend to be small, unions are structurally weak there, and the probability of effective and successful decentralized collective bargaining in this sector is correspondingly low. It therefore makes sense for trade unions to focus their efforts on the collective devices that can be applied to the society as a whole, as well as on political measures that would ease union organization in the services sectors. In other words, it makes sense for unions to pursue their goals first and foremost as political organizations, to work to restore the climate for unionization as a step toward restoring unionization itself.

A higher minimum wage, sharply increasing the number of people at the minimum, would by itself constitute a large step toward restoring an element of national solidarity in the wage structure. For a very large number of people, many of them women and minority workers, the simple step of a further rise in the minimum wage would translate into a rise in living standards. This would focus the attention of low-wage workers on the single most effective political device at their disposal for compressing the wage structure as a whole. For this reason, I would judge, a further rise in the minimum wage is probably the most effective single organizing strategy for organized labor, which must pursue its return to a central position in American economic life in ways essentially adapted to the modern circumstances of the economy.

Minima and maxima. Is there anything sensible that can be done to compress the wage structure from the top down? Perhaps not. The small number of people at the very top and the extreme disproportion of their access to political power suggests that an overt move against the incomes of the executive class would be extremely unlikely to succeed. It is probably unwise even to propose a scheme so utterly improbable as to raise doubts about the sobriety of the other proposals on the list.

Still, as an intellectual exercise, why not imagine a general reform of enterprise law that would start things moving in the right direction? Such a reform might establish norms for the relationship between the best- and the least-paid workers in any given enterprise, with the penalty for noncompliance being a sharply increasing corporate franchise or profits tax. Such a ratio might be set, initially, at fifty to one, guaranteeing that a firm whose least-well-paid employee had a full-time-equivalent salary of $20,000 could not have a CEO earning more than $1 million, without paying a stiff penalty for the privilege. Alternatively, tax law could be employed for the same purpose, with a high progressive surtax on incomes more than fifty times the corporate minimum (an "inequality surcharge"). Over time, the compression ratio could be set to decrease, by a few percentage points per year, allowing firms the option of raising pay at the bottom or cutting it at the top, until a target ratio of, say, thirty to one were achieved. This would bring American practice more closely into line with that in Europe and other other advanced countries.

Indexing and inflation adjustment. A key element in heterodox anti-inflation strategies concerns breaking patterns whereby inflation propagates through the wage structure, via patterns of wage bargaining or formal mechanisms of COLAs. As we have seen, some countries, notably Japan, have defused this problem by coordinating the timing of inflation adjustment on an annual basis and refusing to make COLAs automatic.

In the United States as in other partially inflation-indexed societies, the mechanism of automatic adjustment to past inflation tends to increase in-equality in the wage structure. This is true because workers who enjoy access to automatic adjustment tend to be in the upper part of the wage structure. Thus they enhance their relative position when inflation is comparatively high. (The same is true for a much larger class of relatively low-income indi-viduals, social security recipients, who enjoy a federally mandated COLA of their benefits. For this reason, inflation tends to have mixed effects on the in-equality of overall family incomes, though it increases the inequality of the manufacturing wage structure.)

In recent years, however, many classes of C-sector workers who enjoyed automatic COLAs within the framework of collective bargaining agreements have lost that leverage and protection. It may be time to consider introducing a national device, something to restore an element of inflation protection while helping to seal the expectation of low and stable inflation. It may be time, in other words, to effect an institutional transfer of first-line responsi-bility for inflation control back to the elected political leadership, in the hope that assigning this responsibility where it belongs will encourage responsible use of the power.

A way to do this, set forth in detail in my earlier book, would be to give the president discretionary authority over each year's adjustment—not just in social security but in every federal and federally mandated pay, retirement, and income security scheme. A single, percentage adjustment, reflecting not past inflation but the current expectation of prospective inflation, would send a powerful signal to the wage structure of what sort of change in the cost of living to expect. If the timing of wage negotiations were also adjusted, as in Japan, so that all such discussions necessarily began when the news of the presidential adjustment was fresh, then there would come into being a pow-erful tool of macroeconomic stabilization, suitable for a large and decentral-ized economy, and capable of taking some of the burden of inflation prevention out of the hands of the Federal Reserve. At the same time, because of the inherently solidaristic nature of the mechanism, political pressures would tend to work to ensure that the vast power placed in the president's hands would not be abused. No president would survive long, giving out a nationwide inflation adjustment that was either blatantly too low or fla-grantly too high.[5]

Thus, we need to develop an equalization strategy that is simultaneously a comprehensive anti-inflation program: low interest rates, high employment, a higher minimum wage supported by a stronger union movement, a maxi-mum-minimum pay ratio, and a national prospective inflation adjustment.

Neither taxes nor transfers play the critical role here, as the idea is to bring about an equalization of economic incomes before taxes and transfers, not afterward.

Such a program would combine tested anti-inflation measures with steps to compress the wage and income structure. It would work to bring about a gradual wage compression and to make that strategy possible by making disabling movements of monetary policy much less necessary or likely. Both requirements of a successful, enduring reform would be in place. And within the broad limits of a minimum wage and a national schedule of wage adjustments—stipulations no more restrictive than much modern regulation in any case—the underlying structure of a free peacetime economy would be left entirely intact.

15

INTERNATIONAL FULL EMPLOYMENT

From all parts of the civilized world come complaints of industrial depression; of labor condemned to involuntary idleness; of capital massed and wasting; of pecuniary distress among business men; of want and suffering and anxiety among the business classes. . . . This state of things, common to communities differing so widely in situation, in fiscal and financial systems, in density of population and in social organization, can hardly be accounted for by local causes. . . . Evidently; beneath all such things as these, we must infer a common cause.

—Henry George, *Progress and Poverty*

Our analysis thus far has restricted its focus to the phenomenon of inequality in the wage structure of the United States. But the United States is part of a global economic system, and Americans have become, over the decades since the Vietnam War and the oil shocks, conscious of their vulnerability to forces that do not appear to originate in national policy. A work that suggests an essentially national approach to the problem of economic inequality, as this one does, must confront the suspicion that the problem now lies beyond national control, that global forces and the imperatives of international markets will overwhelm national decisions, efforts, and policies.

What's more, the principal prevailing explanations for rising inequality—trade and technology—are inherently universal, rather than national, in nature. Everyone trades, and the diffusion of technology is indifferent to international frontiers. This presents an opportunity for cross-checking the validity of the prevailing explanations. One can ask whether the apparent effects of technology and trade on economic inequality are also universal or whether national experiences differ in this regard. If it turns out that national experiences do differ, and for reasons apparently associated with national policy, that may undermine universalist theories of rising inequality and reinforce confidence about the possibility of national action.

No broadly based international comparison of the evolution through time of economic inequality has yet been published.[1] A major obstacle has been a shortage of data. Unlike measures of gross output, inflation, and unemployment, measurements of inequality are not part of the standard statistical output in even the most advanced countries. Only a few countries—the United States, Sweden, and the United Kingdom are among them, as well as Brazil—have managed to assemble as much as a single summary time series on the inequality of household income (the United States is the leader in this area, with an annual series going back to 1947, as we have seen).

For many other advanced countries, the state of the art in the measurement of inequality rests on sample surveys taken at long intervals—perhaps every five years, perhaps just once or twice in the period since 1970. In many cases these have been converted to an internationally comparable measure of inequality of household incomes by researchers based at the Luxembourg Income Study.[2] Yet although the Luxembourg researchers have produced work of great value, this approach has limits. We cannot really learn very much about causal forces in the evolution of inequality unless we can obtain consistent data through time, at least on an annual basis.

Our good fortune, on the other hand, is that there exists a large body of annual data on industrial wages and earnings. Every industrial country, and a great many developing ones, maintain such data. In recent years the Organization for Economic Cooperation and Development (OECD) has produced a systematized, electronic version of this information, known as the Structural Analysis (STAN) database, which provides annual information on average earnings for about forty distinct industrial categories, for over twenty OECD member countries, for the years going back in most cases to 1970 and up to 1994. The STAN data are easily adapted to produce approximations in the movement of earnings inequality for all of the countries concerned.

Figure 15.1 presents estimates of the interindustry dispersion of annual earnings for all the countries represented in the STAN database, for all years with sufficient usable data. Although these numbers are estimates and ap-

FIGURE 15.1

INEQUALITY IN THE OECD, 1970–1992

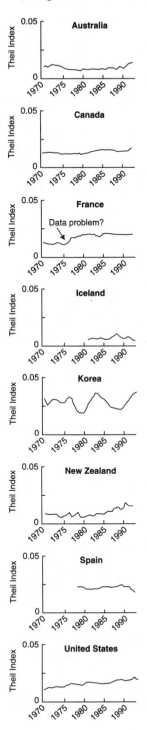

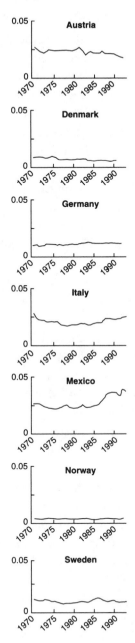

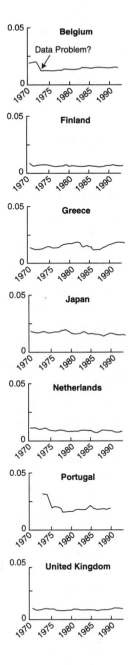

proximations and directly measure earnings rather than hourly wages, they nevertheless greatly multiply the extent of available information in the field of national inequality statistics. And where the correspondence of these measures to annual measures of income inequality per se can be checked, the correlation has invariably proved high and positive—from about .5 in the cases of the United Kingdom and Sweden to around .9 between series measured from different wage and income data sets in the United States.

There are some problems with the data.[3] Overall, however, the series appear broadly in accord with the stylized facts of the time and place. We observe that increases in inequality in Northern Europe appear quite low; in solidaristic Scandinavia, wage structures have been almost undisturbed. In France in the 1970s, a known time of turmoil and rigorous austerity policy, inequality increases, as it does in Greece; however, in both countries inequality stabilizes after socialist governments take power in the early 1980s. In Canada, the United States, Mexico, and New Zealand, there are sharp increases in inequality, especially toward the end of the period; free market liberalizations were a feature of policy in all of these countries. In Portugal following the revolution in 1974, inequality declined sharply. The same happened in Spain, less sharply, under the socialist government a decade or more later. A very few countries, notably Denmark and Austria, show steadily declining wage dispersion over the period. For Italy, the U-shaped pattern corresponds closely to recent findings of a deliberate Italian wage compression, comparable to Sweden's, in the 1970s.[4]

This *tour d'horizon* leaves an unmistakable impression: movements in the dispersion of earnings have common elements across countries, but also patterns of strictly national variation that appear related to politics and policy. We should not fatalistically accept that the inscrutable market bears responsibility for rising inequality. Rather, national governments retain some degree of control over the dispersion of their own wage structures, even though all participate in the evolution of technology and the growth of trade.

Although these measures of the change in inequality probably provide a reasonable measure of historical developments inside each country, the measurements are not strictly comparable across countries.[5] It would be useful to make such cross-country comparisons.

Fortunately, there are benchmark measures of inequality designed to be comparable across countries—from the Luxembourg Income Studies, now available for scattered years for at least thirteen countries of the OECD's twenty-two. It is therefore possible to benchmark our estimates using the Luxembourg numbers, sliding each measure of earnings inequality up or down until it matches the Luxembourg index for a known year.[6] Doing so produces a roughly useful series of numbers that are comparable both across countries and through time. Estimates of these mixed-method inequality co-efficients are presented in Table 15.1.

These data permit us to ask whether the relationship documented in Chapter 8 between unemployment and inequality in the United States also applies to other nations. I propose to do this in a simple way: by computing correlation coefficients between inequality and unemployment for each country through time. A positive correlation, consistent with the U.S. experience, would indicate that when unemployment rises, so does inequality in the earnings structure. A negative correlation, which might be predicted by a textbook economic model, would suggest that rising inequality helps labor markets to adjust to changing technological conditions, and so produces lower rates of unemployment.

When one runs this analysis with the raw data (from Figure 15.1), Germany, France, New Zealand, Canada, Australia, the United States, and Greece show a positive correlation between inequality and unemployment. Denmark, the Netherlands, Austria, Japan, Belgium, Finland, Norway, and Sweden show a negative correlation. For Italy, Spain, and the United Kingdom, the correlation is essentially zero.

This would seem to be a mixed picture, but it turns out that there is a technical issue in our measurement that has a strong effect on this particular relationship, as well as on the measurement of the rise in inequality in several countries. This is the change in the structure of employment itself. The inequality measures of Figure 15.1 are based on underlying employment weights for the forty-odd industry group that are allowed to vary from year to year, according to actual shifts in the composition of manufacturing employment. This "variable-weighted" measure of earnings inequality permits accurate tracking of changes in earnings dispersion in the manufacturing sector, but it introduces a bias into measures of the change in the structure of wages per se in some countries. The reason is that there is a systematic association in some countries between changes in the composition of employment and changes in unemployment.

In countries affected by the bias, as unemployment rises, people who are further away from (presumably, below) the mean of the wage structure are more likely to lose manufacturing jobs. This means that they will be displaced into services or into unemployment, and will disappear from the STAN data set. In these cases, the wage structure in manufacturing takes on an artificial equalization, simply because low-wage workers are dispropor-

TABLE 15.1

GINI-EQUIVALENT MEASURES OF WAGE INEQUALITY

	Austria	Belgium	Canada	Denmark	Finland	France	Germany	Italy	Netherlands	Norway	Spain	United Kingdom	United States
1970	0.248	0.311	0.255	0.408	0.251	0.200	0.203	0.318	0.342	0.261		0.331	0.200
1971	0.222	0.317	0.252	0.420	0.203	0.195	0.197	0.260	0.344	0.260		0.306	0.216
1972	0.208	0.325	0.256	0.414	0.222	0.176	0.189	0.245	0.326	0.231		0.319	0.231
1973	0.203	0.188	0.253	0.356	0.229	0.187	0.194	0.241	0.329	0.236		0.322	0.240
1974	0.224	0.191	0.243	0.356	0.211	0.197	0.210	0.229	0.342	0.240		0.289	0.238
1975	0.226	0.195	0.235	0.421	0.205	0.172	0.214	0.243	0.314	0.246		0.327	0.244
1976	0.224	0.193	0.240	0.353	0.198	0.193	0.218	0.233	0.275	0.233		0.267	0.266
1977	0.219	0.201	0.240	0.313	0.184	0.272	0.222	0.199	0.267	0.219		0.283	0.281
1978	0.215	0.199	0.238	0.318	0.184	0.275	0.211	0.200	0.265	0.208	0.308	0.290	0.278
1979	0.217	0.212	0.222	0.288	0.212	0.294	0.223	0.192	0.266	0.216	0.313	0.280	0.277
1980	0.215	0.214	0.225	0.271	0.188	0.301	0.223	0.197	0.258	0.222	0.295	0.297	0.287
1981	0.236	0.215	0.242	0.275	0.182	0.330	0.219	0.202	0.263	0.228	0.293	0.300	0.296
1982	0.228	0.213	0.272	0.301	0.168	0.325	0.225	0.202	0.257	0.217	0.286	0.310	0.301
1983	0.191	0.220	0.293	0.273	0.174	0.309	0.234	0.205	0.288	0.225	0.287	0.311	0.303
1984	0.208	0.226	0.305	0.261	0.193	0.296	0.250	0.197	0.299	0.246	0.304	0.301	0.298
1985	0.200	0.237	0.309	0.239	0.194	0.321	0.239	0.214	0.276	0.262	0.311	0.298	0.293
1986	0.200	0.230	0.313	0.247	0.202	0.312	0.229	0.221	0.256	0.245	0.306	0.304	0.293
1987	0.208	0.238	0.302	0.257	0.190	0.313	0.243	0.225	0.252	0.247	0.308	0.300	0.314
1988	0.182	0.237	0.287	0.274	0.164	0.315	0.232	0.254	0.273	0.257	0.321	0.308	0.340
1989	0.193	0.234	0.281	0.247	0.187	0.314	0.234	0.259	0.282	2.247	0.332	0.315	0.343
1990	0.184	0.224	0.266	0.260	0.199	0.315	0.234	0.255	0.282	0.227	0.315	0.317	0.340
1991	0.171	0.233	0.286	0.269	0.223	0.308	0.224	0.255	0.254	0.233	0.308	0.343	0.343
1992	0.159	0.230	0.342		0.214	0.313	0.231	0.269	0.244	0.226	0.259	0.322	0.364

Source: STAN database and LIS. Theil statistics are computed by the author from the OECD STAN data base. Gini coefficients are from Christopher Niggle, "New Evidence from Luxemburg Income Studies."

Note: Probable data errors for Belgium, 1972–1973, and France, 1976–1977.

tionately dropping out of the sampling frame. This source of bias is very small for the United States, so that in the U.S case, it matters little whether one adjusts the measure for changing structures of employment. But the bias is quite substantial in a number of other countries, particularly smaller ones. The largest country for which the problem is serious appears to be the United Kingdom, and as a result the degree to which earnings inequality has risen in the United Kingdom appears to be substantially understated by the measurement reported in Figure 15.1.[7]

The bias can be removed, yielding a measure of wage dispersion affected only by changing average within-industry wage rates. This is done by fixing employment weights in the calculation of the inequality statistic, and so, in effect, "freezing" the structure of employment as it was in 1970. The resulting inequality estimates show only the effects of changing earnings per worker; these are correlated to the unemployment rate for each country in Figure 15.2. The results are striking. When compared with the uncorrected calculation the correlation through time between inequality and unemployment now switches from negative to positive in eight cases. In only one case, Greece, does the relationship flip the other way. In other words, when we consider only the rising inequality of relative earnings, and not partly offsetting reductions in low-wage manufacturing employment, the verdict that rising unemployment leads to greater inequality becomes very strong—not quite unanimous, but nearly so.

What accounts for the presence of an employment effect on earnings inequality in some cases but not others? The countries that show this measurement bias (Norway, Japan, Italy, Finland) appear to be marked by a certain dualism in manufacturing, and in particular to have strong and relatively stable, high-wage export sectors; in some cases they also have substantial sectors, such as apparel, dominated by part-time female employment. In such countries, unemployment seems to hit lower-wage manufacturing workers especially hard, even as their relative earnings fall. This would diminish the weight of such workers in overall wage dispersion, and so account for an overall bias toward equality in the variable-weighted inequality measures for such countries.

Large economies that sit, so to speak, at the center of their own economic basin, among them Germany, France, and the United States, tend to show a positive correlation with unemployment on both inequality measures. So do the Anglo-Saxon economies generally, other than the United Kingdom itself: New Zealand, Canada, Australia—and again, the United States. In these countries unemployment may be more nearly an equal opportunity proposi-

FIGURE 15.2

INEQUALITY AND UNEMPLOYMENT
Correlations Through Time

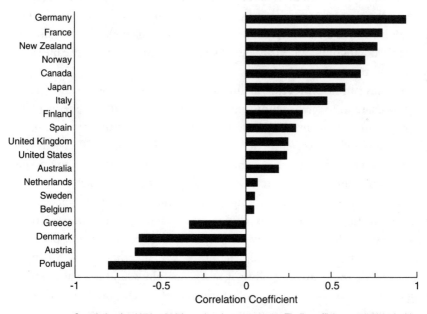

Correlation for 1970–1992 based on between-group Theil coefficients calculated with fixed 1970 employment weights. This eliminates distortion due to correlation of unemployment and changing composition of employment in some countries.

tion. This in turn may be because reductions in hours, and a corresponding fall in earnings per worker, in the relatively low-wage industries may be a more common way of distributing the burden of slack demand to low-wage workers in these economies than in some of the others.

Another revealing procedure is illustrated in Figure 15.3, which presents the correlation ratios across countries between the level of unemployment and the level of inequality, measured each year for the thirteen countries for which Luxembourg-benchmarked coefficients have been computed. This figure answers two fundamental questions involving international comparison of the level of inequality across countries. First, do countries with less inequality have more unemployment? And second, how has this relationship changed over time?

The figure shows that there was a time, back in the early 1970s, when low-earnings-inequality countries, notably the United States in those years, suffered high unemployment compared to fully employed but less equal

Europe. But that negative association disappeared with the first oil shock and the mid-1970s recession. Since then, the relationship has always been positive, and it has become more positive as unemployment rose throughout the OECD. The meta-correlation between the time series of correlation coefficients (dark line) and the OECD· unemployment rate (thin line) is .89, unquestionably an impressive value.

Thus, time-series and cross-section analyses lead to the same conclusion. There is a positive association between levels of unemployment and inequality. When unemployment rises, so does inequality in earnings. And as overall unemployment goes up, countries with the highest unemployment experience the largest increases in inequality.

We can indulge one final exercise with this data, also highly revealing: to search for international patterns in the movement of inequality and unemployment. We use the annual rate of change of inequality and the annual rate of change of unemployment. With either variable, the effect is to compose a taxonomy of nations, based on the closeness of their historical behavior regarding first inequality and then unemployment.

Figure 15.4 presents the tree diagram showing the association of movements of inequality across countries.[8] Its geographical patterns emerge with great clarity. There is a North American pattern of (rising) inequality, to

FIGURE 15.3

UNEMPLOYMENT AND INEQUALITY
Correlations Across Thirteen OECD Countries

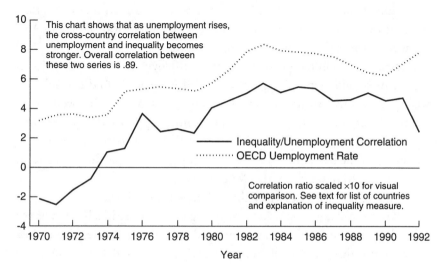

which the United States, Mexico, and Canada all belong, and which has also influenced earnings structures in Japan. Over on the right side of the diagram, we see a similar North European orbit, including Austria, Norway, and the Netherlands in close association with Germany, and, a little further out, Greece. Sweden and Finland form a Scandinavian pair in some association with the North European block; France is a bit more separate still. The United Kingdom, Italy, and Denmark appear closer to the North American pattern of wage inequality. Finally, Korea, Australia, and New Zealand each follow patterns of their own, not closely tied to any other country in this sample.

Figure 15.4 suggests that even though national political events can be picked out of individual country series, broadly speaking the dispersion of earnings structures is a transnational affair. It appears to be strongly influenced by geographical propinquity, trading patterns, and perhaps other forms of transnational association. The existence of a Central European and a North American inequality basin, so to speak, is an especially striking finding. Small countries can influence their own fates so far as wage structures are concerned, but they cannot altogether control them.

Transnational patterns also characterize changes in unemployment, as Figure 15.5 illustrates. But the patterns are different. Once again there is a North American basin (unemployment data for Mexico are hopelessly unreliable and were not used). But now the United Kingdom joins the Netherlands, Germany, Sweden, and Finland in a North European cluster. And there is a distinct South European cluster, including Italy, France, Belgium, Spain, Greece, and Austria, but also Japan. This cluster has a behavior of unemployment rates that appears closer to the American orbit than to the North European one, and indeed more resembles the American pattern than the North European countries resemble each other. Norway, Portugal, Australia, and Denmark are the outliers on this one.

Overall, intercountry fluctuations of unemployment are about twice as large as intercountry percentage variations of inequality.[9] And it would appear that earnings structures and business cycles operate in overlapping basins. The earnings structures of small countries appear to be quite tightly linked to their near neighbors, with Central European norms radiating out over much of the rest of Europe. As for unemployment, the North American pattern seems to rule most of the Western world.

A principal conclusion one might well draw from this exercise is that patterns of transborder economic relations—regional internationalization, if not full-scale globalization—are both longstanding and irreversible. The United States cannot dissociate itself from Mexico, Canada, and Japan, any more

FIGURE 15.4

PATTERNS OF CHANGE IN EARNINGS INEQUALITY, 1971–1992

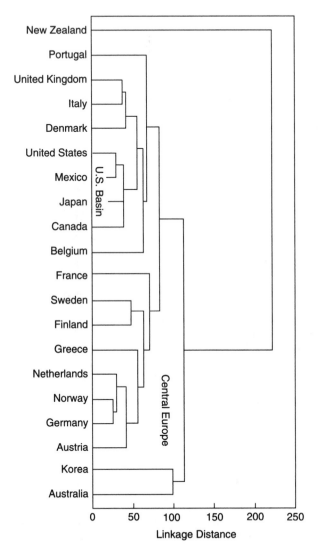

Source: OECD STAN database, 1971–1992.

Note: The figure depicts the clustering of the paths through time of change in an interindustrial Theil measure of inequality of annual earnings. The clustering of Ward's hierarchical minimum variance method on a measure of Euclidean distance between these paths. See the appendix to Chapter 6 for details.

FIGURE 15.5

PATTERNS OF CHANGE IN UNEMPLOYMENT, 1961–1993

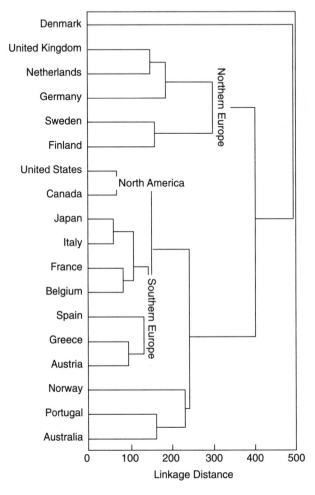

Source: OECD historical statistics, 1961–1993.

Note: The figure depicts a clustering of the paths of change of unemployment through time, using Ward's method and a Euclidean distance measure. See the appendix to Chapter 6 for details.

than Germany can operate outside the context of Europe. Patterns run strongly not only through the international transmission of movements in aggregate demand, so that countries related by propinquity and trade suffer from contemporaneous movements of unemployment, but also through movements in the earnings structure, so that linked countries suffer closely related variations in inequality.

These patterns of association are of very long standing. They do not date, in North America, from the 1994 start-up of NAFTA or in Europe from the 1992 creation of the single market. Rather, they run the full length of the present evidence, which goes back to 1970, and in all likelihood originated well before that. Economic integration is a fact of borders, trade, and population movements; it can be neither created nor undone by legal arrangements. This suggests that proposals to return to a high degree of trade protection, for example, by reversing the NAFTA or the European Union, are unrealistic: they do not address the integration that existed beforehand.

At the same time, the data strongly suggest that each major economic basin—and, importantly, the North American basin seems to include Japan—has a center. One of the centers is in Germany, and the other is in the United States. It is the national policies of the large countries that are the strongest influence on patterns of inequality and unemployment in their smaller neighbors. While it is possible even for small countries to compress their earnings structures if they strongly wish to do so, the climate under which they pursue such policies depends greatly on the pressures emanating from the centers of their respective economic basins. It is far easier for Greece, say, to maintain its earnings structure in the orbit of Germany than it is for Mexico to do so in the orbit of the United States.

On this evidence, one may sympathize with the voters of, say, Denmark or Norway, who rejected full legal integration with a larger Europe from fear that the influences of German policy on their national destinies were already far too large. But the debate that actually shook the United States in 1993 over NAFTA took the odd turn of arguing that freer trade with Mexico would increase inequality in the United States. In fact, inequality in the United States was, and remains, the product of American policy decisions; it is the Mexicans, not the *Norteamericanos,* who have to fear the actions and influence of their neighbors.[10] Meanwhile, the much greater relative equality of Germany, compared to the United States, shows that it is possible for a large country to pursue solidarity and equality, to survive and thrive at the center of an economic basin, and to foster, by so doing, the survival of much higher degrees of equality in its near neighbors than might otherwise be possible.

And while European unemployment remains far too high, this evidence cuts against the simple view that joblessness could be cured there by allowing inequality to rise. More flexible labor institutions in, say, Germany could easily mean higher inequality throughout Central Europe without any major relief for the unemployed. On the other hand, an expansionary policy, coupled to a return to the social-bargain approach to inflation-fighting, might relieve unemployment in Europe while actually strengthening the relative equality of European earnings structures.

The essential conclusion from this analysis is that the reduction of inequality and unemployment in the global economic system remains the task, and the prerogative, of the largest countries. And the United States, which led the way toward higher levels of global inequality beginning in the early 1980s, has a special obligation to lead the way back. Otherwise the entire zone of North American influence, including no doubt much of Latin America as well as the Pacific Rim, stands to become a polarized and unstable region, lagging far behind the relative and fairly enduring good order of Europe.

Do the regional patterns of inequality and unemployment have implications for the design of an equality-supporting American policy? I believe they do. In addition to attending to its own inequality crisis, U.S. policy needs to take an increasing share of responsibility for the stable economic development of the region, and this is true even if one considers only the narrow self-interest of the United States itself. Otherwise the structural overvaluation of the dollar inside the sphere of greatest American influence will undermine the achievement of a higher degree of equality in the United States. And although we have not explored deeply the effects of immigration and other regional issues, greater instability in our near neighbors will surely undermine stability at home by that channel as well.

A major element in the rising inequality and economic instability of the North American basin has been very wide fluctuations in currency values, including calamitous crashes in the real value of the Mexican peso relative to the U.S. dollar. These are due to a combination of unstable internal policies in both countries and extreme liberty in the flow of speculative finance between the two. Tamping those flows, perhaps by taxing currency and other speculation, and restoring both long-term stability and a higher underlying value to the peso (and perhaps also the Canadian dollar), are significant neglected elements of U.S. responsibility toward its neighbors.

The long debate over the NAFTA in the United States was unfortunately focused on symbolic and political issues rather than on the economic relationship between the United States and Mexico as it actually exists. Integration of these two North American giants is a long-standing fact, made inevitable years before NAFTA by the oil crisis, the debt crisis, and the restructuring of the Mexican industrial economy that followed. Under the *maquiladora* system, manufacturing trade between Mexico and the United States was already substantially free; exports from the United States to Mexico, for instance in automobiles, were burdened by higher tariffs than manufactures flowing north. The free trade arrangement could also make little difference on matters of labor and the environment, serious and enduring problems in any event.

The Mexican government, being much more aware of these facts than the U.S. public, did not pursue NAFTA as a means to gain North American market access. The true purpose was more subtle. Along with Mexico's accession to the General Agreement on Tariffs and Trade (GATT) in 1986 and its joining of the OECD, NAFTA was part of a strategy to "graduate" Mexico from the Third to the First World.[11] The benefits of such a transition were thought to lie in more stable access to capital markets and therefore in an end to Mexico's periodic crises of confidence and peso devaluations. The strategy supposed that a financial stabilization, guaranteed in effect by the umbrella of NAFTA, would permit Mexico to resume a path of steady economic development and escape from the cycles of instability and stagnation that have afflicted Latin America since the 1970s. This was a worthy goal, but one that lay beyond Mexico's capacity to achieve.

The political debate over NAFTA in the United States was a humiliating reminder to the Mexicans of their continued Third World status in North American eyes—degrees from Harvard, Yale, Stanford, and MIT notwithstanding. But what followed was even worse. The Mexican elections of 1994 were a financial disaster for the country, as the governing Institutional Revolutionary party (PRI), beset by the rebellion in Chiapas and the mysterious assassination of its first candidate, borrowed fantastic sums, guaranteed in dollars, on the short-term international financial markets. After the elections, a collapse was inevitable, and one promptly occurred, forcing the U.S. Treasury to extend an embarrassing bailout loan, partly to prevent the collapse of U.S. mutual funds that were overextended in Mexico. In this way any conceivable long-term stabilizing effects of the NAFTA were squandered. It is fair to say that the way out for Mexico today lies only through a thoroughgoing internal reform, including the end of one-party rule. Whether even drastic democratic reforms can make Mexico into the full partner of the United States and Canada that successful North American development requires remains to be seen; much also depends on whether the rich pair in this menage à trois are prepared to make the very large physical capital investments that successful Mexican development requires over the long run, as well as to stabilize and discipline the flows of speculative finance within the North American region. But once again the issue is not whether a solution is radical, but whether it is needed.

International government exists today—formally in Europe, less formally in the vast economic region centered on the United States. In Europe, free-market ideology and a conservative desire to Americanize the earnings structure run into persistent resistance from populations who favor retaining the great social democratic accomplishments of the postwar generation. This is the meaning, surely, of 1997's swing to the left in both Britain and France, following a similar movement in Italy the previous year. Whether a unified Europe can overcome its great problem, which is unemployment, while maintaining the comparative solidarity of its social structure is an enduring challenge. What seems clear, however, is that it can do so only by restoring the Keynesian commitment to full employment that characterized the construction of the postwar welfare state and the solidaristic earnings structure in the first place.

The United States has been more sensitive than Europe to unemployment within its own frontiers. But it has been much less sensitive, indeed recklessly insensitive, to the catastrophic decline of the working and middle classes in our closest neighbors, Mexico and Canada, and still less to the threat of problems now emerging in Asia. Just as German policy anchors Europe, so U.S. policy anchors the Americas and the Pacific region. If the United States wants a free trading region, it cannot escape responsibility for anchoring the stability and growth of all the countries within it.

What would such a policy consist of? The minimum requirement is a financial mechanism that can effectively support the purchasing power of those countries that buy our capital goods and advanced intermediate exports, with special emphasis on our nearest neighbors. Currency stabilization, the resolution of leftover debt problems—still a hangover from the 1980s in much of Latin America and Africa—and the systematic discouragement of speculative hot money flows are also necessary. The American economic sphere requires, in other words, a new governing mechanism for its international finance, and one that is committed first and foremost to economic stabilization rather than to extracting the largest transfers from poor debtors to rich creditors. This is a daunting task, and perhaps the largest obstacle to the successful achievement of an income-equalizing strategy in the long run. But what alternative is there?

16

THE FATE OF THE MARKET

The toad beneath the harrow knows
Exactly where each tooth-point goes
The butterfly upon the road
Preaches contentment to that toad.

—Rudyard Kipling, "Pagett, M.P."

The discipline and profession of economics has a long tradition of acquiescence in the existing social order, punctuated only rarely by rebellion. We need a rebellion now. For, as John Maynard Keynes wrote in the different but equally perplexing context of 1930, "the world has been slow to realize that we are living . . . in the shadow of one of the greatest economic catastrophes of modern history."

As the Great Depression unfolded from 1929 to 1932, it became inescapable, visibly calamitous to millions. Our catastrophe, on the other hand, has been slow and insidious, stretched over a period of almost thirty years, difficult to measure and with far-reaching implications that are nevertheless subtle and easily left undetected. It has been a slow-motion event, to which many have adjusted themselves, some in insular satisfaction, more in sullen frustration. But the great rise in inequality from 1970 onward has been not less catastrophic for these reasons.

The orthodox economists awoke to the rise in inequality some years ago. But they were roused not by alarm over the rise of inequality *as such,* any more than Keynes's contemporaries were roused by the brute facts of mass unemployment. Instead, the economists took up the subject mainly because they rightly saw in rising inequality a threat to the legitimacy and acceptability of the free market that supposedly produced it.

What the economists did, in effect, was to reason backward, from the troublesome effect to a cause that would rationalize and justify it. After denying that rising inequality could stem from increases in trade, the orthodox agreed that it must be mainly an artifact of the demands that technology places on skill. They have therefore come to portray rising inequality as a bump on the road from the computer to the information age, unfortunate perhaps, but necessary to the efficient development of our economy and something to be accepted in the larger spirit of the times. In any case, it is the work of the efficient market, and the fundamental legitimacy of the outcome is not supposed to be questioned.

This *apologia* is a dreadful thing. It has distorted our understanding, twisted our perspective, and crabbed our politics. On the right, as one might expect, the winners on the expanding scale of wealth and incomes are given a reason for self-satisfaction and an excuse for gloating. Their gains are due to personal merit, the application of high intelligence, and the smiles of fortune. Those on the losing side are guilty of sloth, self-indulgence, and whining. Perhaps they have bad culture. Or perhaps they have bad genes. While no serious economist would take that last leap into racist fantasy, the underlying structure of the economists' argument has undoubtedly helped to legitimize, before a larger public, those who promote such ideas.

Yet the real tragedy of the mainstream response is not that it abets the complacent or even the vicious right. It is, rather, that the economists have deprived the *left* of an authentic response to the right-wing view. Having gone down on the field of battle in opposition to expanding trade, an error of judgment for which the left must ultimately answer, progressives now look homeward. Yet—apart from the spirited cry of the trade unions that "America needs a raise!" a scorned message that happens to be exactly on point—in looking homeward they find themselves sidetracked into an incoherent advocacy of personal skill development as a cure for the social malady of rising inequality. This is the meaning of the mantra of "investment in education," the dominant liberal interventionist response to the inequality crisis once the protectionist agitation has been put down.

Progressive voices have been attracted to this mantra and have placed their political energies behind it, in well-meant efforts to be useful. But while these efforts *are* useful, insofar as education is useful, they sum to nothing in the larger context of the inequality crisis. In an unequal meritocracy, education becomes, in effect, the purchase of tickets to a lottery, with high stakes and, as the investment in education grows, a larger and larger proportion of losing tickets. Meritocracy and egalitarianism are distinct values, both with their proper place. In the discussion of the inequality crisis and the role of education, they have become tragically confused, and in the rush of concern over access to lottery tickets, the structure of the prizes has slipped from view.

The focus on technology, productivity, the reward for skill, and the market mechanism thus serves a social function that goes far beyond the defense of free trade. Stripped bare, it is the modern version of the Horatio Alger myth. From the standpoint of the winners in the race for wealth, it immobilizes the losers, delegitimates them, deprives them of a political voice, sidetracks their champions into irrelevant policy stands, and permits the process of polarization to continue. Horatio Alger never looked back, to consider that his success was possible only because so many others were left behind.

As polarization of wages, incomes, and wealth develops, the common interests and common social programs of a society fall into decline. We have seen this too, in this country over thirty years, beginning with the erosion of public services and public investments, particularly in cities, with the assault on the poor and on immigrants and the disabled that led to the welfare bill of 1996, and continuing now with the manufactured crises of Medicare and the social security system. The haves are on the march. With growing inequality, so grows their power. And so also diminish the voices of solidarity and mutual reinforcement, the voices of civil society, the voices of a democratic and egalitarian middle class.

Professional economists remain important to this argument, because economics provides our leading interpreters of social cause and effect. The idea of a "labor market" has enormous power. It conjures spirits from the vasty deep, and they come. Labor supply, labor demand, the natural rate equilibrium, "market wages": each one of these ideas flows from a simple supply-and-demand diagram. Taken together, they describe conditions in a market that does not exist and never has existed, a market that is only an image, a market for a commodity that itself is only a vague abstraction, a figment of long-dead economics professors' imaginations. The notion that wages depend on personal skill, as expressed in the value of output, makes no sense in any organization where production is interdependent and joint—which is to say it makes no sense in virtually any organization.[1] The image holds together only because of the power of that supply-and-demand model.

What professional economics now needs is a rebellion against supply and demand. We need a rebellion against the idea that people are actually paid in proportion to the value of what they produce. We need a rebellion against the metaphor of the labor market—an entity that no one has ever seen, where no one has ever been, an entity that lacks the mechanisms of price adjustment that would be required for the marginal productivity theory to work. Economics needs a rebellion that is almost less against the system under which we live, as against the sources of our complacency about that system. We need a rebellion, not so much against existing market institutions, *as against the analytical tyranny of the idea of the market,* as it applies to pay.[2]

If we do not have an efficiently functioning labor market to set and justify our wages and salaries, what exactly do we have? The answer is: institutions, customs, privilege, social relations, history, law, and above all power, with an admixture of ingenuity and luck. But of course power, and particularly market or monopoly power, changes with the general level of demand, the rate of growth, and the rate of unemployment. In periods of high employment, the weak gain ground on the strong; in periods of high unemployment, the strong gain ground on the weak. One can trace variations on this theme, involving the growth rate, the exchange rate, inflation, and the minimum wage, and no doubt other factors under other historical conditions. All are best reconciled to a theory of differential power, rather than to a theory of differential skill.

I am not the first economist, even recently, to make an argument against the marginal productivity distribution theory. The pure theory of economic rent goes back to Adam Smith, with the full classical development given in the early nineteenth century by David Ricardo. The theory of monopoly and economic power has powerful development in this century in the works of Thorstein Veblen, Joseph Schumpeter—and I should be remiss not to mention John Kenneth Galbraith. In very recent years, we have the pathbreaking 1978 work on pay of Adrian Wood, a 1989 paper on economic rent and wages by Lawrence Katz and Lawrence Summers, a recent book on wages by David Blanchflower and Andrew Oswald, joined in a later paper by Peter Sanfey. We have the insightful work of David Card and Alan Krueger on the minimum wage, and that of Robert Frank and Philip Cook on winner-take-all phenomena.[3] All of these works challenge the orthodox theory of income distribution and the notion of the labor market in fundamental ways.

From the idea that pay is a struggle over economic rent, it follows that the major weapons in a struggle to reduce inequality are political. Some employ politics directly; others involve political decisions over economic policy. The direct variety include minimum wage laws, union legislation, social security programs, and national and international labor standards, including child labor laws and prohibitions against slavery and the use of prison labor. The indirect variety are the economic policy instruments that govern the general level of employment, the rate of economic growth, and the relative structure of prices in world trade. These determine the environment within which power relations are determined, and therefore whether direct measures will succeed or fail. And among economic policy instruments, by far and away the most important is the power to control the rate of interest, and with it to influence the rate of growth and the overall level of unemployment.

If it were true that the main determinants of rising inequality were skill-biased technological change or globalization, then the patterns we observe would not emerge. But in fact macroeconomic forces strongly influenced by public policy—the investment cycle and the general squeeze on middle-class consumption standards over the past thirty years—are the dominant patterns. This fact alone tells that we are not observing a random process generated in purely competitive and private markets. It tells that we are observing the enormous and catastrophic power of unstable policies to disrupt social relations, to create a war of all against all in which the strong prosper and the weak perish.

Mainstream economics these days is divided on the relationship between policy action and macroeconomic result. Many economists, including those most committed to a free-market explanation of inequality, also deny that government policy can effectively lower the rate of unemployment and tame the business cycle. I have not felt it necessary to argue this point at too great a length here, for two reasons. First, there is a substantial group of economists who do agree that sustained full employment is possible. And second, there is the power of an appeal to history, to the fact that for twenty-five years, from 1945 to 1970, we did enjoy near full employment, strong economic and productivity growth, and on the whole reasonably stable prices. There is no compelling argument that this achievement was anomalous or irreproducible. I believe, on the contrary, that it resulted from a sustained period of sensible policy, later abandoned.

The first task of citizens who are concerned about the splitting apart of America into a rich and an impoverished nation since 1970 must be to focus the mind on the essentials. The essential things, before anything else, are to keep reducing the rate of unemployment, to drive down the rate of interest. For these purposes, the control of monetary policy is the critical task. Although other matters are important, they are all secondary to this task, for the simple reason that those with the power to disrupt the macroeconomy control the supply of the unemployed and the direction of movement of in-equality. Until that power is again harnessed to the effective pursuit of full employment, as it was during the 1940s and in the 1960s, we are unlikely to see a return of anything resembling a middle-class wage structure. With ef-fective pursuit of full employment, other useful measures become possible, economically and politically, including a higher minimum wage, stronger so-cial security protections, universal health care, and programs of investment in shared public amenities. All of these steps would reinforce a trend toward greater equality in the private wage structure.

I call on those who read these pages, whether they are economists or not, in positions of influence or not, to consider the possibility of a politics of full employment, low and stable interest rates, stronger economic growth, higher minimum wages, and declining inequality. The way to restore the prosperity of the middle class is the way that prosperity was created in the first place. We need not an unfettered and enfeebled private economy, but a concerted part-nership between a strong and determined government and an energetic pri-vate sector, better regulated but also more vigorous than we have had. It has been done before. It can be done again. Success is not precluded by laws of economics.

This is no paradox, no contradiction. The failures after 1970 and again after 1980 came because government divested, deregulated, destabilized, and left private institutions to fend for themselves. The successes in the 1940s and the 1960s came because government took a firm leading hand at the highest levels of macroeconomic policy. No dreadful loss of efficiency will follow a concerted political program of inequality reduction. Quite to the contrary. We will discover that efficiency improves when a larger number of people feel they have a fair shot at being middle class, and when "middle-class values" come again to define our broader culture. We will find that people work harder under those conditions, that they are happier, that families are more stable, and that patterns of investment, consumption, and even techno-logical change will accommodate themselves to more equality in the nation at large. They do this, already, before the plain eyes of any visitor, in North-ern Europe and Japan.

The task is nevertheless very large. Economists can contribute, in a small way, by abandoning and renouncing cherished and convenient myths, by ac-cepting that the comfortable rationalizations so far offered to explain the rise of wage inequality fail in their scientific task of explaining what must be ex-plained. Short of full employment, the initiative of private markets plays little role in the evolution of the wage structure. Policy plays a large role, and inevitably therefore it is on policy, and not on markets, that an economic understanding of wage inequality must focus.

The market comes back into its own only *after* full employment is achieved. At that time, with inequality reduced and once again stable at low levels, economists can safely return to their traditional pursuits. Inequality may then revert to its status as a backwater subject, attracting little interest because nothing much changes, so long as full employment prevails. It is surely true that the classical economics applies, if at all, only at the special case of full employment. In all other conditions, in the general case, the controlling forces are assuredly policy, politics, the investment cycle, and effective aggregate demand.

Reducing wage inequality will not by itself solve the larger rise in inequality that stems from changing employment patterns, family structures, and the distribution of profits, interest, and wealth. But the measures leading to more equal wages will certainly help. Sustained full employment will stabilize the incomes of marginal and contingent workers. Low interest rates will reduce the vast net transfers from debtors in the middle class to creditors among the rich. Stronger economic growth will increase tax revenues, making possible new investments in shared public amenities and stronger social protections. Over time, more equal people are likely, in my view, to form more equal and more stable families, so that the patterns of the wage structure will again be reflected in the patterns of family income.

These would be vast benefits, but they will not be easily won. It requires first that political voices be found and that a political organization be developed. Neither party, and no large organized force in America today, yet exists with a determination to bring this about and a program focused accurately on measures that would be effective if put into practice. But with the beginning of understanding of what is required and what is at stake, perhaps that too can be changed. For surely the splitting apart of America remains, despite all the confusion and propaganda that surrounds it, the most important political, social, and economic issue that Americans face.

I end on a word of caution. Those who favor embarking on the large task of reducing inequality will need to accept, and acknowledge, a measure of discipline. By its nature, solidarity means self-restraint. If we wish to move to a new and more balanced equilibrium in the distribution of income and wealth, if we wish to restore the predominance of the middle class, we have to accept, as a nation and as individuals, that certain prizes will be unavailable, certain opportunities forgone. We will have to accept a certain social discipline on our individual chances, to increase the prospects of rising as a group. We shall also have to recognize the irreversible interdependence of nations within our trading region and act to stabilize growth and equality not only inside the United States, but across international frontiers. In other words, we shall have to sober up and act responsibly. This, and not the alleged trade-off between equality and efficiency, is the true sacrifice that a more equal society requires.

TECHNICAL APPENDIXES
TO CHAPTERS
2, 6, 7, AND 8

Appendix to Chapter 2

The Debate over Technology and Trade
(and a Note on Immigration)

The principal dissent from the skill-biased technology explanation of rising wage and salary inequality has come from a small group of economists who do not reject the general nexus between "skill" and pay, but who instead have an alternative explanation for increasing returns to skill. They suggest that the blame should be laid on increasing international trade, and in particular increasing trade between rich and poor countries. The leading advocates of this viewpoint are Adrian Wood, of the University of Sussex in the United Kingdom, and Edward E. Leamer, of UCLA.[1]

The core of the Wood-Leamer argument is that some countries—the "North"—hold a favored position in global competition for advanced goods produced by skilled labor. But other countries—the "South"—have unlimited reserves of semiskilled workers willing to work for low wages by northern standards. As a result, the expansion of trade between North and South acts like an increase in the supply of low-skilled workers in the northern labor market; it places downward pressures on the wages of the semiskilled and unskilled workers of the North.

Stripped to these essentials, both this trade and the technology explanations for rising inequality are about supply and demand in the market for labor. In one case, a technological development creates a scarcity in a new and particularly productive type of skill. This relative scarcity drives the wage rates paid to possessors of that skill—"the return to education"—upward. In the other case, the reduction of a barrier to trade in effect integrates the low-skilled part of the labor market across international frontiers. This expansion in the effective supply of less-skilled workers has the effect of driving their wages down— and once again raising the relative return to those activities in which the advanced country retains an advantage.

The issue between these stories is therefore not principally a matter of theories. Both Wood and Leamer rest their cases on orthodox, efficient market reasoning. Rather, the question they raise is an empirical one (though with plangent political reverberations).[2] Given the demand-side effect of skill differentials within countries, is the supply-side effect of skill differentials across countries also a substantial factor in rising inequality?

273

Wood's argument can be summarized by contrasting it with one of the most influential articles from the technology school, the 1992 lead article in the *American Economic Review* by John Bound and George Johnson. Bound and Johnson had estimated the causes of the decline in demand for unskilled labor in the United States—a decline that most observers agree has been on the order of 20 percent over twenty or twenty-five years. By calculating the replacement of unskilled American workers by manufactured imports (that is, by the products of unskilled foreign labor) Bound and Johnson were able to estimate the proportion of declining demand for the less skilled that is owing to the expansion of trade.

The number they came up with was very low. About one-half of 1 percent of estimated decline in demand for less skilled labor, they said, could be attributed to displacement by imports. This is just one-fortieth of the total decline in unskilled labor demand. Bound and Johnson therefore concluded that trade plays a negligible role in rising wage inequality. Indeed, it was this finding of a negligible role for the effects of rising trade that drove many scholars to the conclusion that technology had to be the principal cause of rising inequality.

Wood's criticism begins with the observation that Bound and Johnson make an error of applied technique. When calculating the displacement of American workers by imports, these authors used an estimate of the ratio of labor to output that was drawn by observation of the ratio of labor to output in surviving U.S. import-competing trades. The trouble with this is that foreign industries selling imports to the United States and U.S. industries in the same broad areas do not use the same technologies: low-wage countries use more labor. Partly this is because the activities are often not the same thing: the good are "noncompeting," even though they may be classified in the same industrial categories. For example, golf clubs and baseballs are both "sporting goods." But baseballs, which are entirely imported to the United States, require far more labor per dollar of product value than do golf clubs, a technology product. Thus, to use the labor-to-output ratio for golf clubs, say, as a proxy for labor displaced when the baseball industry moved to Haiti and similar venues leads to a large underestimate of the effect. Wood calculates that the error from this and similar problems is on the order of a factor of ten. On this account alone, rising imports account for 5 percent of declining demand for less skilled U.S. labor, or one-quarter of the total decline instead of just one-fortieth of it.[3]

Wood made considerable inroads with this argument, and he goes on to add two others that, if correct, would expand the estimated effect of trade on wages. First, many firms, when threatened by imports or the prospect of imports, engage in "defensive innovation" intended to cut their costs and reduce their demand for labor. This defensive innovation, though it produces technological progress and technological unemployment, should in fact be attributed to the causal pressures of trade. Wood estimates that this effect is at least as large as the first one, raising the total effect of trade on demand displacement to half.

Finally, there is the service sector. In terms of total employment, the service sector is four or five times larger than manufacturing. Yet very few data exist on international trade in services, and none of the estimates of the effects of expanded trade account for the export of service jobs, in data processing, communications, insurance, and related fields. Wood here makes another estimate: that overall these effects on the demand for less skilled labor are comparable to those in manufacturing. If so, then by Wood's accounting, the total effect of trade on the decline in demand for unskilled labor comes to 5 percent times two times two—or 20 percent in all, which is to say that virtually all of the decline in demand for unskilled labor in the United States can be attributed to trade, directly or indirectly.

Finally, Wood presents one additional argument, having to do with conditions in the developing countries—something that other researchers in the field have rarely examined. Wood finds that although the gap between the most and least skilled workers has been rising in the industrial nations of the North, it has been narrowing in some rapidly advancing industrializing nations of the South. Such a development would be flatly inconsistent with the notion of skill bias in technology change, since technology such as computers diffuses across the globe and should be presumed to have similar effects everywhere. But such a development would be consistent with the idea that northern firms are unloading relatively unattractive northern jobs to southern locales where, nevertheless, they are relatively attractive when compared to previously existing employments.

With these arguments, Wood and Leamer have made inroads on a consensus that had categorically denied the influence of trade on wage inequality. Yet their explanation has not prevailed. In part, this is due to some other empirical puzzles—inconsistencies between the findings and theoretical prediction. In particular, there is the troubling finding, emphasized by Robert Lawrence and Matthew Slaughter,[4] that Third World imports do not come into the northern economies on the cheap. Rather, they are sold on northern markets at the same prices as comparable goods produced domestically. That being so, it is somewhat difficult to specify a purely market mechanism according to which expanded trade would produce falling northern wages, in the absence of very high unemployment. How do the northern workers know that they are under threat?

There is a reasonable answer to the Lawrence-Slaughter objection: workers know they are under threat because their employers tell them. Import-competing manufacturers are well aware of their international competition. And they tell their workers. The media reinforce the message. So do the unions, if perversely, by seeking support for a protectionist policy. There is always the threat that the company will fail, or that its factory will move, and even if in practice workers could find other jobs, the costs of doing so are high. Thus, the pressures on import-competing domestic workers may be strong, even if there are few actual job losses or cut-rate imports on the domestic markets.[5]

But arguments like these run into the difficulty that they require a departure from textbook thinking about the working of competitive markets, in which market prices are the only sources of information. They cannot fit within the general framework of supply and demand for skill. You cannot use them to plug a gap in a theory based on competition and marginal productivity pricing, and still claim the theory itself as the coherent underpinning of your larger argument. (They fit quite well into a framework based on monopoly power, but in that framework trade tends to lose its distinctive character as a source of threats to workers. See Chapter 3.)

A more general problem lies in the difference between the scale of trade and the scale of the increase in inequality. In the United States, measured trade remains only about 15 percent of total economic activity, and most of that is trade between and among the richest countries. It is hard to see how North-North trade, which is most of the trade that we do, can raise inequality in the North. And once one subtracts the internorthern component from total trade, it is again hard to see how North-South trade, which remains comparatively minor, can have such pervasive effects on the wage structure. And yet the rise in inequality *is* pervasive, both in sectors heavily exposed to trade (such as manufactured consumers' goods) and in others for which trade is barely to be noticed (such as retailing).

On the whole, fair-minded reviewers have been comparatively receptive to the finding that North-South trade has had a significant, if not necessarily dominant, effect on manufacturing wages. But they have remained comparatively skeptical of the extended conjectures relating to induced technology and services. Thus, the claim that North-South trade can account for the remaining 15 percentage points of decline in demand for unskilled labor seems destined to stay controversial.[6]

The argument that North-South trade represents a de facto extension of the supply of low-skilled labor in the manufacturing sector raises the question of whether immigration of low-skilled southern workers, both legal and illegal, can have a similar effect directly in the labor markets of the northern countries. Immigration is a substantial phenomenon: about a million persons per year, most of them legal, of whom perhaps two-thirds are from Latin America and Asia, and many lacking high school diplomas. What is the effect of this influx on the wage structure?

A 1997 study by a panel of the National Research Council of the National Academy of Sciences examines this issue in depth for the United States.[7] The panel found large gaps between the average pay of new immigrants and those of native workers. Consistent with the overall rise in inequality, this gap has risen from 17 to 32 percent for male workers since 1970. New immigrants, particularly from Mexico, tend to be lacking formal education, and they compete for low-wage employment. The panel concludes that they may be responsible for as much as a 5 percent reduction over fifteen years in the average wage of native workers who also lack high school diplomas.

But the number of native-born American workers who lack a high school diploma is small and diminishing over time. Therefore, the wage effects associated with immigration are restricted mainly to the job segments for which immigrants compete, notably in hotel and restaurant trades and domestic service, as well as agriculture and, in the manufacturing sector, garments. Outside these sectors, the effects of immigration as such on the wage structure appear minor. Immigration, while possibly more significant than trade in its effects on the wage structure of the services sector, seems irrelevant to the differential between college- and high school–educated workers, and to most of the rising differentials within manufacturing.[8]

Do we then have an emerging consensus, under which "skill bias" gets credit for a quarter of the rise in inequality, trade for another quarter, immigration for a small amount, and the rest reserved to further research? Appealing though such a resolution might appear, it will not work, for the trade and technology schools are in fact arguing over the same part of the rise in inequality—the part that can be attributed to a change in the rate of return to skill, mostly in the manufacturing sector, and to a substantial extent the part that occurs after 1980. If there is to be a more comprehensive and thorough approach to the conundrum, it needs to come from a different direction.

My belief is that a macroeconomic approach, in which trade and technological change are presented as integrated aspects of increasing instability in the business cycle, provides the best way to resolve the essentially false opposition between the trade and technology schools.

Appendix to Chapter 6

Cluster Analysis and Industrial Grouping

A simple example may illustrate the need for a coherent analysis of industrial categories and the dangers of arbitrary taxonomy.[1] Suppose an economy has four workers: Ann, Bill, Chuck, and Diane. Ann makes computers. Bill sells computers. Chuck builds houses, and Diane paints houses. Ann and Bill earn $200 per week; Chuck and Diane earn $100 per week.

Now, let us ask, what is the influence of "industry" on wages? This will depend on how we define an industry, which we have not yet done. Here we have two obvious choices. One option is to divide the economy into two industries called "manufacturing" and "services." We might call this *horizontal stratification*. In this case, Ann and Chuck are in manufacturing; Bill and Diane are in services. The average wage in manufacturing is $150; that in services is also $150. Industry clearly does not matter to wages. An "industrial policy" that fostered manufacturing per se would have no effect on average wage levels.

But suppose we define our industries as "housing" and "computers": *vertical* (or perhaps *functional*) *stratification*. In this case, Ann and Bill are in computers; Chuck and Diane are in housing. Average wage in computers is $200; that in housing is $100. Now industry clearly *does* matter to wages. An industrial policy that fostered the computer industry might eventually reduce (because of diminishing returns) the relative wage advantage of computer workers, but in the meantime it would raise the average level of wages.

The above classifications are arbitrary; hence so is the answer to the question, Does industry matter to wages? This is the problem with the uncritical use of governmental industrial classifications. Some of the classification criteria are horizontal, some are vertical, some are merely vestiges of an outdated system. It is useful to have a standard industrial classification; otherwise no one could make valid year-to-year comparisons. But it is a mistake to accept these categories as though they were analytically valid as groups.

One way to approach this problem systematically, to reduce the arbitrary element in a classification scheme, is to examine the behavior and performance of subcategories through time. In the example, we have four subcategories: house building, house painting, computer assembly, and computer sales. Each has a history of good years and bad, of ebbs and flows in the business cycle. Since the technologies, the processes, and the mar-

278

kets are not the same, the histories will differ. We can measure those differences and compare them. If, say, the performances of the two housing subsectors, building and painting, are very similar, we should class "housing" as the industrial category. If house building and computer making resemble each other, while house painting and computer selling go their separate ways, then "manufacture" would be the activity that should attract our analytical interest. In contrast to the earlier example, this classification would *not* be arbitrary; it would be based systematically on the historical record.

Cluster analysis is merely a way to apply such a procedure to a large number of industrial subcategories over a fairly long span of time, and to do so quickly and efficiently on a computer. The output of a cluster analysis is a tree diagram, which shows the similarity and differences in the path of movement through time of a criterion variable, between all pairs of industries under observation. By looking at such a tree, we can develop an idea of the best way to reduce a large and cumbersome list of industrial groups, some nearly identical to each other and others wildly different, into a small number of groups whose members behave similarly to each other but exhibit the strongest differences from the behavior of members of other groups.

Cluster analysis works by measuring "distances" between "objects." In our case, we have measures not of objects themselves—the size, shape, or activities of particular industries—but rather the tracks of their performance through time. We have thirty-four measurements, one for each year, on the change of industrial performance for each of 139 manufacturing subcategories. By looking at rates of change in our measure of performance, year to year, we can achieve a particularly uniform, and highly comparable, set of measures, one for each industry or other subclassification we may be interested in observing. By treating these measures as if they were physical characteristics, we can effectively measure how similar, or how different, they are. Ordinary measures of distance can be adapted very easily to this task, even though the "space" through which distance is being measured contains many more than the standard three dimensions.

Our characteristic variable is the P-measure: the annual percentage rate of change of total employee earnings divided by production hours, from 1959 through 1992—essentially a measure of value-added per hour. We thus rest our analysis on a triangular matrix of 139 rows and columns, each of whose elements is a Euclidean distance in thirty-three dimensions, one for each year, computed by pairwise comparison of annual rates of change of wages *(w)*. The general formula for measuring the similarity of (distance between) two patterns of wage change over T years in industries X and Y is:

$$D = \sqrt{\sum_{t=1}^{T} (w_t^x - w_t^y)^2}$$

We used Ward's minimum variance method, a standard technique in cluster analysis programs. This method proceeds stage by stage, adding to clusters at each step so as to minimize the variance within (width of) newly formed clusters, relative to the variance remaining between clusters. Ward's method is well suited to producing compact and distinct groupings, whose members' behavior through time resembles each other fairly closely, while differing distinctly from that of members of other groups. This property means that the groups that result from our cluster analysis have as much between-group variation as possible, which will prove to be a very useful feature for the analysis in Chapter 7.

Clustering is hierarchical. It starts with 139 entities (in this instance) and ends up with just one single grouping with everything in it. Obviously neither extreme is very useful. The proper object of the exercise is to find some reasonable number of distinct groups, such that any natural patterns of association and difference in the data set are illustrated clearly.

Deciding where to stop is partly a matter of judgment: one wants enough different groups so that the main sources of difference are clearly represented, but not so many that the analysis becomes unwieldy or incoherent. A criterion of information lost by grouping, called the semipartial R^2, is useful to help choose a point at which to stop. In our case, this criterion suggests stopping with around thirty-six groups, of which nineteen turn out to be special cases with only one industry in them; in most cases, these outliers are very small in their employment. Thus, we work with seventeen major groups, and a half dozen of the larger outliers. Table 6.1 lists the classification scheme; only a few apparent misclassifications are omitted to simplify the exposition; these are listed at the bottom of the page.

A sample cluster analysis with a familiar data set, the national income and product accounts (NIPA), may help clarify the procedure as well as illustrate its power. The NIPA divides the great flows of expenditure in the economy into large and familiar categories of consumption, investment, government purchases, exports, and imports. Each of these is in turn broken into smaller subcategories. Consumption may be of durable or nondurable goods or of services; investment may be in producers' durables, business structures, or housing; government may be federal or state and local, defense or nondefense; and so on. The broad classifications depend on who is doing the spending (households, firms, units of government), while the subclassifications tend to reflect the type of expenditure undertaken (durables, nondurables, services, residential structures, and so on).

But is this classification scheme, which has been in use for more than fifty years, correct from an analytical point of view? Economic forecasters who are interested in predicting the stream of consumption or investment behavior should have a deep interest in this question. If the target of prediction—let's say overall consumption spending—is relatively homogeneous and reflective of just a few common causal factors, then a small number of predictors will do. But if total personal consumption expenditure is in fact an amalgam of types of expenditure that behave in very different ways, then careful disaggregation and multiple forecasting equations become essential. Otherwise, adding economically dissimilar time series to each other, and trying to estimate the behavior of personal consumption expenditure as a whole, will cause confusion and reduce the accuracy of the model. Similarly, the components of government spending and investment need to be shown to be homogeneous, or else treated as distinct objects.

Figure 6A.1 presents a tree diagram that is the output of a cluster analysis on the rates of change of the major components of nominal GDP, using quarterly data for the years from 1946 through 1995. (Like the other cluster trees in this book, it was produced by the very well-designed computational program Statistica.™) The horizontal axis of the diagram measures the similarity of paths through time of the eighteen time series. A small linkage distance indicates a high degree of comovement; large linkage distances show dis-

FIGURE 6A.1

A TREE DIAGRAM FOR THE NATIONAL INCOME AND PRODUCT ACCOUNTS CLUSTER ANALYSIS OF THE MOVEMENT OF NOMINAL TIME-SERIES, QUARTERLY DATA 1946–1995

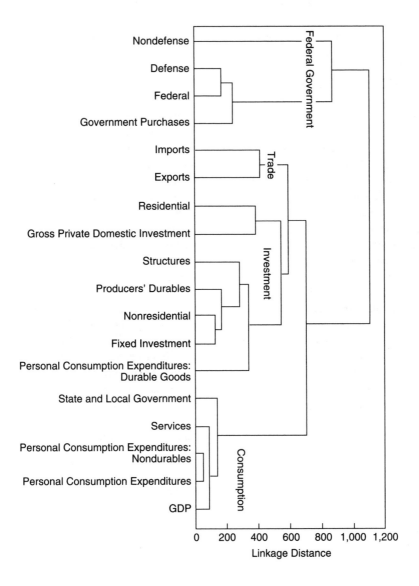

similarity. Thus, the trees of the diagram position each of the components of the national income and product accounts in relationship to all of the others.

The figure clearly divides into three great groups: the federal government on the left, trade and investment in the middle, and consumption expenditures on the right. But in fine detail the classification derived from clustering is quite different from the stock classification of the official accounts. For example, we see that state and local government purchases closely resemble personal consumption expenditures in their aggregate behavior; they do not at all resemble federal government purchases. Thus, to mix state and local government purchases in with those of the federal government in a model of "government expenditure policy" is clearly a mistake: the state and local series follow wholly different rules of behavior. The tree also shows that within the federal sector, defense and nondefense purchases follow very different rules.

We also find that the consumption of durable goods, a major component of personal consumption expenditures, quite closely tracks the behavior through time of business fixed investment, excluding residences. From this, we can see that an investment function will generally do a better job of predicting this component of consumption expenditure than would a consumption function. For this reason, in the analysis I group purchases of consumer durables with business investment rather than with consumption expenditure, and call the result a measure of "comprehensive investment." To do otherwise is to blur the distinction between forces in the economy that respond to credit conditions and expected profit rates on one side, and those that respond to fluctuations in current income on the other. This distinction is much more important analytically than the fact that some of these expenditures are done by households and others by business firms—the analytical basis of the official NIPA scheme.

Finally, although many standard textbook models treat exports as an exogenous variable and imports as a spin-off of the decision to consume, the cluster analysis illustrates that the behavior of exports and imports resemble each other more than they resemble anything else. Also, they both resemble the ebb and flow of investment more than they resemble the patterns of consumption spending. It is hard to know without further analysis what interpretation to place on this finding, but one possibility is that the movements of foreign trade in the aggregate are more influenced than we perhaps normally realize by transnational investment flows. The observed pattern is certainly consistent with exports of capital goods and intermediates generating flows of imports of consumer goods, a property of outsourcing and globalization.

Appendix to Chapter 7

Cluster Analysis and Discriminant Analysis with Time-Series Data

The following brief description of technique may be useful to some readers. It is not intended to give a complete account of the computations underlying Chapter 7 and the previous chapter, but rather to give some idea of the justification for my approach and to convey the flavor of the mathematical argument.

The essence of this analysis, like that of many others in social science, is a search for meaningful patterns in a mass of numbers. When the original data set is a sample survey or a single time series of economic data whose behavior one is attempting to explain, familiar statistical techniques like multiple regression analysis are often the most appropriate tools. But in this case, the original data are presented in partially aggregated, structured form, according to a hierarchical classification scheme—the SIC. There is information in data organized along these lines, but in raw form it is poorly suited to use in regression, whether as a dependent or independent variable. "Industries" as given by governmental accountants are not random observations, which makes explaining differences across industries problematic. Neither are they analytically distinct group structures, which also makes the use of "industry" as an explanatory variable in regression analysis questionable. This study attempts to circumvent some of these problems by deploying a set of organizing and analytical techniques that are appropriate to the nature of the data under study.

My main methods are an application of linear discriminant functions to a group structure derived from cluster analysis. Cluster analysis is a way of answering the question, How are objects best organized into groups? Discriminant analysis is a way of answering the question, How do groups differ? In this case especially, can we identify the main sources of difference between groups and the historical forces behind them?

I have based my cluster analysis on differences and similarities of behavior through time. (I class my birds not by their feathers but according to their flocks.) Behavior is based on time-series observation of a single criterion value—in this case, the rate of change of the performance measure (P-measure) for each original industrial category. This approach solves a number of technical problems in cluster analysis, but also leaves the resulting groups with a very intriguing property. They differ from each other in patterns that have been measured through time, that are, essentially, historical time-series variables. Moreover, I have constructed the groups so that as much as possible of the total variation inside the data set is expressed in between-group terms; as little as possible has been concealed within the groups. It follows that if we can sort through the time patterns of between-group variation in a systematic way, we may be able to isolate the principal historical forces that cause time paths in the original data set to differ from one another.

The full importance of this exercise may not be immediately apparent. But consider that we are dealing with time patterns in the change of hourly wages or, more precisely, an industrial performance measure that we know to be closely related to hourly wages. Wages, standard microeconomic theory tells, are determined by the marginal productivities of individual workers, and these are said to depend on the state of technology, the conditions of labor supply, and the underlying preferences of consumers for different types of product. It follows that changes in wages should reflect the evolution of these factors through time, and given the autonomy usually attributed to consumer and worker choice, one might expect a pattern of change that is essentially either inchoate—a kind of Brownian motion—or else driven by historical movements in technology and effective labor supply (e.g., the supply of skills or the expansion of trade).

But suppose we find instead that a very high fraction of the variations observed in the data are not random or clearly associated with education or trading patterns. Suppose, in fact, the major variations organize themselves into a small set of patterns that closely track macroeconomic variables like investment and growth or policy-driven parameters like the exchange rate or the military budget? It seems to me that this provides decisive evidence against the view that the major changes in the wage structure originate in the evolution of technological and social forces in the private sector. It seems to me rather to provide strong evidence in favor of a radical, contrary proposition: that the distribution of industrial performance and hence of wages is driven mainly by policy actions; it is coordinated not by the market but by the government. The government may be acting under private pressure or in the service of special interest, but that is beside the point for now.

My radical proposition is that *macro* drives *micro*. We do not need the "microfoundations for macroeconomics" that so many economists have made a project of seeking, largely in vain, over the past twenty-five years. We need instead to understand the *macrofoundations of microeconomic change*. Fundamentally, the empirical search for macrofoundations in quasi-microeconomic data is the task to which this study is addressed.

Given a group structure based on clustering of behavior through time, discriminant analysis has a very interesting application here. The point of discriminant analysis is the identification of clearly separated "dimensions"—weighted combinations of measured characteristics—along which previously defined groups of objects differ. A typical use in botany, for instance, might determine that three species of flower differ mainly in the length of their stamens, and secondarily in some characteristic of their petals. But here we have an original clustering based on the tracks of data through time. It follows that the weighting functions (eigenvectors) separating our different groups will be, by construction, a set of year-to-year coefficients—a constructed time series. If it turns out that these carefully separated constructions correspond to known or discoverable forces in economic history, that is precisely the sort of evidence for macrofoundations of divergent industrial performance and income distribution that we seek.

From this point, I offer a compact statement of the mathematical steps involved in moving from cluster to discriminant analysis with blocks of time-series data. The remainder of this appendix will be accessible to only a small number of readers. Everyone else may safely skip it.

1. We begin with an $N \times T$ matrix $\mathbf{R}$ of the P-measure for N officially defined industries for years $t = 1$ to T. We use information from industries aggregated to three-digit SIC codes, for which we have 139 industrial entities for the years 1958 to 1992. The P-measure is the ratio of total payroll to the number of production worker hours.

2. The next step is to convert $\mathbf{R}$ to an $N \times (T - 1)$ matrix $\mathbf{G}$ whose elements g_{it} are the rates of change of the P-measure for $i = 1$ to N industries for years $t = 2$ to T. Each row $\mathbf{g}$ is therefore a time series of rates of change.

3. We cluster the rows of $\mathbf{G}$ according to the Euclidean distance criterion (see the appendix to Chapter 6) using Ward's method, a hierarchical agglomerative procedure that minimizes within-group variance relative to between-group variance at each step. This yields a structure of association of patterns of wage change across industries.

4. Choose an appropriate level of grouping based on the agglomeration schedule and marginal loss of information as clustering progresses. That is, stop clustering at M groups when the algorithm starts forcing dissimilar objects into awkward and unwieldy clusters. This step, the choice of M, is essentially a matter of judgment, though the semipartial R^2 criterion often provides a guideline.

5. Consider the $(T - 1)$-dimensional square matrices $\mathbf{B}$ and $\mathbf{W}$, where the diagonal element of $\mathbf{B}$ is the sum of squared differences in rates of change between groups for each year $t = 2$ to T, and the diagonal element of $\mathbf{W}$ is the within-group sum of squared differences; off-diagonals are intertemporal cross-products. The problem is to find the $(T - 1)$-column vector $\mathbf{a}$ such that $\mathbf{a}'\mathbf{Ba}/\mathbf{a}'\mathbf{Wa} = \lambda$ is maximized. λ is the discriminant criterion.

6. The solutions to the problem stated in step 5 are found by maximizing the discriminant criterion, by finding the roots of $(\mathbf{W}^{-1}\mathbf{B} - \lambda\mathbf{I})\mathbf{a} = 0$. Each eigenvector $\mathbf{a}_i$ is a root ("canonical root") of the discriminant function, associated with an eigenvalue λ_i, and so forth. The eigenvalues may be ranked by size; they measure the relative proportion of the variation explained by each eigenvector.

7. The original element in this analysis consists in noting that the eigenvectors, though usually considered strictly as weighting functions or factor loadings, *are in this case themselves time series, whose elements are a_{12} through a_{1T}, and so forth.* The eigenvectors thus measure the set of forces through time that discriminate between the performance (wage) behavior of groups of industries. There are $M - 1$ eigenvectors, since $\mathbf{W}^{-1}\mathbf{B}$ has rank $M - 1$.

8. Are these "forces" themselves economic variables? To approach this problem, we first compute the canonical scores for each group of industries. If we have an $M \times (T - 1)$ matrix of the rates of change of mean wages by group, with time-

series rows g_j, then compute: $a'_i g_j$, and so on, for all eigenvectors and groups. Then rank the groups by canonical scores on each eigenvector, and examine for clues as to the economic force responsible for discrimination between groups.

9. Search for a historical rate-of-change time series corresponding to the force f hypothesized in step 8. Plot and compare to the movement of the eigenvector. Occasionally converting to index values can be helpful; often scaling is necessary so that the patterns can be compared visually. The decision that an eigenvector corresponds to a particular historical force is again essentially a matter of judgment, based on the distribution of scores and the resemblance of time series. Statistical techniques, such as analysis of correlation, may be employed to assess these judgments; however, they are often not definitive since any particular historical data series (such as GNP, unemployment, or the exchange rate) is at best an approximation of the force on wages. Since one can never exhaust all sources of information about the past, it is often possible that new historical data can improve on a previous identification.

Measuring the Evolution of Inequality
from Grouped Data

Originally drawn from information theory, Theil's T has the following formula:[1]

$$T = (1/n)\Sigma(Y_i/\mu)\log(Y_i/\mu).$$

Here, n is the number of individuals, Y_i is each person's income, and μ is average income for the whole population. "Log" is the natural logarithm.

Notice that whenever a group population consists of equal individuals, the final terms in T all reduce to $\log(Y_i/\mu) = \log(1)$, which is equal to zero. Thus *T* overall is zero for the case of perfect equality. And T increases as deviations away from the average value increase. Since deviations of Y_i below the mean have values between zero and one, whereas deviations above the mean are unbounded, T increases as more of the observations move away from the average. Thus, T is a reasonable way to measure the degree of dispersion about the average value for any group of observations, and that is, after all, what inequality is.

The formula for computing T from grouped data is this:

$$T = \Sigma(p_i\mu_i/\mu)\log(\mu_i/\mu) + \Sigma(p_i\mu_i/\mu)T_i,$$

where now p_i is the proportion of workers employed in the ith group, μ_i represents the average income for the ith group, μ represents average overall income, and T_i is the Theil T as measured strictly within the ith group. Thus, the grouped Theil statistic is the weighted sum of that part of inequality that occurs between groups (on the left of the above expression) and a part that occurs within groups (on the right).

The formula for T′, the between-group Theil statistic, is just the first element in the formula for computing the Theil T from grouped data:

$$T' = \Sigma(p_i\mu_i/\mu)\log(\mu_i/\mu).$$

Since the within-group element in variation is omitted, this is obviously a lower-bound estimate of dispersion.

My argument rests on the observation that the movement of T' will, in most cases, strongly resemble the movement of T itself; in that case, we can use the change in T' to approximate the unobserved, and unobservable, change in T. In principle, this is obvious enough: by finer and finer disaggregation of groups, T' will necessarily converge to T. I have checked this in practice by looking at fine and coarse disaggregations of the data on industrial structure and am satisfied that practice does follow principle in this respect.

The point is important because many people, on learning that a study examines data grouped by industry, tend to assume that only "interindustry" differences are being captured by the study. They therefore fear that a great many important sources of variation will be missed. But this is not actually the case. The very arbitrariness of industrial classification schemes comes to the rescue here. Because of the arbitrary character of the classification scheme to which it is applied—precisely because official dividing lines between "industries" are arbitrary, capricious, and often without well-defined economic meaning—the cross-boundary movements in dispersion that the between-group Theil statistic captures are *not* "interindustrial." They are, rather, a robust approximation of the general movement of the inequality of wages in the covered sector. Our measure of the movement of inequality is therefore very general, and it is not surprising that it correlates well with more broadly based inequality measures when these can be found.

The principle is essentially that of a fishnet. Imagine a fishnet that is highly elastic and unconfining, so as not itself to confine the movement of the fish. So long as the net is reasonably fine, few fish will escape. (Those that do must be uniformly smaller in size than the holes in the net, and are therefore less important.) And those that are caught will poke the net this way and that in their efforts to swim free. If there is a pattern to their individual efforts, it will show up in bulges in the surface of the net, here and there. If you watch the bulges, you can get a good idea of the movements of the fish. The finer the net, the better the image projected on it. (Alternatively, suppose you are standing in a dark cave with a sleeping bear. You throw a neon net over the bear. Though you can see only the net, and not the bear, it is nevertheless true that when the bear moves, so will the net.)

Our "net," in this case, is based on the government's long-standing group-wise disaggregation of the industrial structure, the SIC. Since at the three-digit level this net is in fact relatively fine, there is little reason to think that there exist major influences on relative wages that do not show up somewhere, as differences at the between-group level between some industrial unit and some other.

To take an example, consider the distinction in most manufacturing sectors between production workers, who are paid an hourly wage, and the salaried employees away from the production line. It may be—indeed, we shall see that it is the case—that average wages among salaried employees rise across all industries by fairly similar amounts, relative to production workers in the same industrial line. This is an effect, then, that is not industry specific. Will our interindustrial T' overlook it? No; it will not. This common shift within industries will raise average wages more in industries that use a higher proportion of nonproduction workers (such as aircraft, communications, and computers) and will therefore show up as an influence on between-group inequality, weighted by the relative importance of these groups. The finer the group structure, the more accurately the degree of movement in T' will track the movement of inequality overall.

In principle, therefore, we should be able to capture virtually all of the major causes of

TABLE 8A.1

REGRESSION ANALYSIS OF ALTERNATIVE MEASURES OF INEQUALITY

Variable	T'	Census CPS Gini	Grubb/Wilson CPS Theil
Unemployment	.55	.19	.36
	(.08)***	(.08)**	(.13)**
Economic growth	.29		
	(.09)***		
Inflation	.53		
	(.09)***		
Real exchange rate	.21	.29	
	(.10)*	(0.11)**	
Minimum wage	−.38	−.60	−.65
	(.11)***	(.11)***	(.13)***
Intercept term	.004	.42	.39
	(.003)	(.02)***	(.04)***
R^2	.87	.72	.72
N	33	33	22
Dates	1959–1992	1959–1992	1967–1988

* Significant at the 0.1 level.

** Significant at the .05 level.

*** Significant at the .01 level.

Note: Coefficients are standardized regression (beta) coefficients; standard errors are in parentheses.

T' is computed from *Census Reports'* average annual wage data for three-digit SIC industries by the author.

Census Gini is from Daniel Weinberg, "Income Inequality," U.S. Census Bureau P60-191 (June 1996), and is based on family income data.

Grubb and Wilson's Theil is from W. Norton Grubb and Robert H. Wilson, "Trends in Wage and Salary Inequality, 1967–1988," *Monthly Labor Review* (June 1992), 23–39.

Unemployment is the average monthly civilian unemployment rate.

Economic growth is the annual rate of change of real GDP.

Inflation is the annual change of the CPI.

RX101 is an index number of the 101-country trade-weighted real exchange rate, prepared by the Dallas Federal Reserve Bank, set equal to 1 for years before 1980 and earlier years; three-year moving average of the index taken for 1981–1992.

Minimum wage in 1995 dollars is as reported by the Center for Budget and Policy Priorities, "Assessing a $5.15 Minimum Wage" (Washington, D.C., March 27, 1996).

TABLE 8A.2

CORRELATION OF INEQUALITY MEASURES

	Census Gini	*Grubb and Wilson Theil*
T′	.77	.59
Census Gini		.72
	$N = 35$	$N = 22$

rising inequality within manufacturing, though not necessarily their precise absolute or relative importance, by looking at the movement of intergroup inequality across a sufficiently fine disaggregation of the group structure. So long as our groups are constructed in a way that breaks the underlying workforce into fairly small and fairly disparate groupings, which is in fact the case, then all of the major forces working at the level of individuals should have some effect on the comparative behavior of groups. Correspondingly, a statistical model that explains the comparative movements of average wages across a large number of disparate groups should do a reasonable job of capturing the significant forces operating through time at the unobserved, individual level (although one needs to be somewhat cautious about relying too much on precise estimates of coefficient values). Table 8.A1 presents such a statistical model, while 8.A2 shows the close relationship between T′ and two measures of inequality computed from Census data.

Measurement of Inequality for the Period 1920–1957

During the years 1920 to 1947, the National Industrial Conference Board, a business group based in New York City and forerunner of the present-day Conference Board, conducted regular surveys of wage rates in twenty-five major manufacturing industries. Over the same period, differing sources reported wage rates on an annual basis for farming, public road building, coal, gas and electric utilities, and the railroads. All in all, my coauthor Thomas Ferguson was able to locate some eighty-four industrial, regional, and occupational wage time series covering most of the American economy of that time.[2]

With a little bit of interpolation (to fill in some missing data points) and the help of the *Historical Statistics of the United States,* which provides employment estimates for different industries once a decade,[3] we were able to compute an estimate of T′ for the years 1920 to 1947. This estimate, reproduced in Figure 8.3, is comparable in every way to T′ computed from manufacturing data for the years 1958–1992—except for one thing. Since the series are computed from different group structures, the measured *level* of T′ in the earlier period cannot be compared to the level of T′ in the postwar years.

What to do? My solution takes advantage of the very high correlation between T′ for 1958–1992 and the Gini coefficient computed from CPS data and reported by the Census Bureau for those same years. We have the census Gini for years going back to 1947. Since T′ tracks the Gini in the years that follow 1958, it is reasonable to assume that T′ would also track the Gini for those earlier years. We can therefore make a fairly confident

TABLE 8A.3

A SINGLE VARIABLE REGRESSION MODEL OF INEQUALITY FOR 1920–1992

Dependent *Variable* : T'	*Coefficient* *(Standard error)*
Unemployment	.538 (.03)***
Constant	4.90 (1.42)***
R^2	.79
N, Degrees of Freedom	73, 71

*** Significant at the .01 level.

estimate of what our T' would look like if we had it, going back to 1947. (This is particularly true insofar as the Gini measures are fairly stable from 1947 to 1958; there is no reason to think T' is otherwise.)

But once we have two estimates of T' for 1947—one computed from the earlier data set and one extrapolated from the later data set—the problem is solved. We can simply adjust the estimate of T' for all years before 1947 to a level proportionate to the 1947 level estimate from the postwar data. In this way, we can construct a single continuous and consistent time-series measure of inequality in the wage structure in the United States, going all the way from 1920 to 1992, with confidence that it is both a fairly accurate measure of changing wage inequality and reasonable estimate of changes in overall income inequality through this entire time. Table 8.A3 shows the statistical relationship between this measure and the unemployment rate.

NOTES

Chapter 1

1. John Rawls, *A Theory of Justice.*

2. This is the view, I think, of Andrew Hacker in his wide-ranging new survey, *Money.*

3. No less a leading light among academic economists than Harvard's N. Gregory Mankiw remarks that technology is "what you say when you don't understand something." John Cassidy, "The Decline of Economics," p. 52.

4. Robert Topel of the University of Chicago has made this explicit: "Wage inequality has risen in modern economies because rising demands for skills have made talented people more scarce. As in other market situations, this 'problem' of a demand-driven rise in price contains the seeds of its own solution. Supply is more elastic in the long run than in the short run. Rising returns to skill encourage people to invest in human capital, which in the long run will increase the proportion of skilled workers in the labor force." Robert H. Topel, "Factor Proportions and Relative Wages," p. 69. Robert Z. Lawrence makes a similar statement in *Single World, Divided Nations?* p. 129.

5. There is also no evidence that any similar adjustment ever happened in the past. In a recent paper addressed to this question, Thomas Ferguson and I show (in "The American Wage Structure: 1920–1947") that there was no systematic change in skill premiums within industries during the period 1920 to 1947, despite a large increase in the supply of educated labor during this time. After having held a somewhat contrary view, focused on apparently declining skill premiums for some groups in the 1930s, the Harvard economists Claudia Goldin and Lawrence Katz now appear to agree. See Goldin and Katz, "The Decline of Non-Competing Groups" and "The Origins of Technology-Skill Complementarity."

6. Martin Carnoy, *Faded Dreams.*

7. The short-lived credit crunch of 1966–1967 was a kind of dress rehearsal.

8. Prominent nationalists include William Greider, *One World, Ready or Not,* and Michael Lind, *The Next American Nation.*

9. See Edward R. Tufte, *Political Control of the Economy.*

10. "Household Income Climbs After Long Stagnation," *New York Times,* September 27, 1996, p. A3.

11. Citizens for Tax Justice, *Inequality and the Federal Budget Deficit*, p. 6. Obviously the 1992 figure in this study is a projection.

12. Edward N. Wolff, *Top Heavy*, provides a judicious summary of the evidence on the increasing inequality of wealth, which, like the inequality of income, began to deteriorate around 1970. This study was sponsored by the Twentieth Century Fund.

13. The increase in interest payments tailed off in the late 1980s, as debt burdens and interest rates declined. Net capital gains and partnership profits soared between 1982 and 1988, indicating that the top 1 percent did well on its rentier income in the recovery, relative to the top 10 percent who presumably include the receivers of a large part of interest income.

14. According to Wolff, op. cit., p. 64, over half of financial assets are owned by the wealthiest 1 percent of American families and over 85 percent by the top 10 percent. Joel Slemrod, "On the High Income Laffer Curve," p. 197, Table 13, gives figures that range from 20 to just above 50 percent ownership by the top percentile for major classes of financial assets in 1989. According to the *1997 Economic Report of the President,* total personal interest income was about $750 billion in 1996; federal net interest payments less than one-third of that figure; while state and local governments are net interest earners. Interest flows to persons are therefore an amalgam of private and public payments, but mainly represent interest on private debts.

15. The government also pays interest on its own debts, and when interest rates rise, the increase in this burden works through the budget process to crowd expenditures on social programs.

16. And especially of a small group of dedicated public interest advocates whose influence is vastly out of proportion to their budgets—naming names: Robert Greenstein, Center for Budget and Policy Priorities, and Robert McIntyre, Citizens for Tax Justice. Interestingly, this has also been one of the few areas where liberal social policy has the partial blessing of orthodox economics, since neither taxes nor transfers interfere greatly with the freedom of markets to set pretax, pretransfer wage rates.

17. Charles Murray's *Losing Ground* exemplified the conservative campaign against the welfare system.

18. In the 1996 presidential campaign, candidate Patrick J. Buchanan had added immigrants, Mexicans in particular, to the list of villains. (A Maginot Line was duly proposed.) More willful ignorance lay behind these attacks, including overstatement of the number of Mexican illegals, due to a failure to count returns across the border to Mexico, and deliberate neglect of the large numbers of white Europeans who arrive at airports on tourist visas and disappear, attracting no political or enforcement attention.

19. For example, the much-discussed proposal to enact a balanced budget amendment to the Constitution includes a provision requiring a supermajority of the Congress—a 60 percent vote—in order to approve tax increases.

20. Notably, the relentless former commerce secretary Peter G. Peterson. See Peter G. Peterson, *Will America Grow Up Before It Grows Old?* and *Facing Up.*

21. That social security is the target became unmistakably clear in late 1996 and early 1997 when a pair of commissions, one from Congress and the other appointed by the president, recommended dual blows to the system: cuts in cost-of-living adjustments and partial privatization. The first commission, chaired by a former chairman of the Council

of Economic Advisers, Michael Boskin, called for a recalculation of cost-of-living indexation in the social security benefit formulas, in a way that would drastically reduce the future benefit flow. The second, chaired by Edward Gramlich of the University of Michigan, issued a split recommendation widely viewed as endorsing partial privatization of the trust funds. Social security survived the first round of these discussions, but the argument is far from over.

22. Various efforts from academic quarters to tar the rise of social security with the decline of national saving were long ago shown to be fallacious, so this line of argument, while still made, plays only a small supporting role in debates now. On the other hand, the role of rising inequality in fostering privatization plans receives explicit recognition in the *1997 Economic Report of the President,* which quotes the report of the Quadrennial Advisory Commission on social security to the effect that privatization contains the "seeds of dissolution": "there would be every reason for many average and above-average earners, particularly, to press for further reductions in contributions to Social Security in order to make more available in their individual accounts. Thus, the [Individual Account] plan is inherently unstable, and could lead to an unraveling of the redistributional provisions that are so integral to Social Security and so crucial to its effectiveness" (pp. 116–117).

23. The *1997 Economic Report of the President* provides a reliable survey of the controversy.

Chapter 2

1. *The 1982 Economic Report of the President,* hearings before the Joint Economic Committee, March 10, 1982.

2. Barry Bluestone and Bennett Harrison, *The Great U-Turn.* See also Robert Kuttner, "The Declining Middle."

3. In an early riposte, McKinley Blackburn and David Bloom challenged the Bluestone-Harrison findings. Blackburn and Bloom argued that over the period 1967 to 1985, family income inequality had increased but individual earnings inequality did not; hence they questioned whether labor demand factors can be responsible. The Blackburn-Bloom paper is a useful survey of pitfalls and caveats in inequality research up to the mid-1980s, but since then, there seems to have developed a consensus that inequality in both earnings and incomes did rise. McKinley Blackburn and David Bloom, "The Effects of Technological Change on Earnings and Income Inequality in the United States." See also Frank Levy's 1987 book, *Dollars and Dreams,* whose major theme was the seeming stability of the U.S. income distribution up to that time. Levy's book was largely based on 1980 census results; thus it could not capture what was happening in the years since that census was taken.

4. Sheldon Danziger and Peter Gottschalk, *America Unequal.* Robert Z. Lawrence, *Single World, Divided Nations.* Danziger and Gottschalk briefly mention unemployment as a cause of inequality; Lawrence does not.

5. Danziger and Gottschalk, op. cit, p. 128.

6. *Relative* demand shifts can be positive or negative, good news or bad. They can re-

flect forces that improve prospects for the skilled, or they can reflect forces that undercut prospects for the less skilled. In the former case, the demand shift is a positive one associated with technological modernization and increasing demand for skills required to manage new technologies and to make them work. In the latter, it may be a negative shift associated with downsizing and the rooting out of the comparatively obsolescent.

7. Juhn, Murphy, and Pierce, "Wage Inequality and the Rise in Returns to Skill," "attribute the increased inequality to an increased demand for high-skilled workers and accompanying 'wage changes' that put a premium on high skills" (quote taken from an accompanying press release).

8. The decline in skill premiums in the 1970s is perhaps first noted by Richard Freeman, in "Over Investment in College Training?" and is reconfirmed in tables presented by Kevin Murphy and Finis Welch, "The Structure of Wages," for both younger and experienced workers.

9. See Murphy and Welch, op. cit., and "The Role of International Trade in Wage Differentials." Murphy and Welch do not believe that any single cause can suffice: "Even if all changes in relative wages could be attributed to growth in skill premiums, still the source of growth would be an open question. But because the growth in skill premiums is not the only explanation for observed changes, the question is refocused. We do not believe that simple technological shifts with substitution counterparts provide adequate answers. Something else must be involved" (p. 52).

10. Influential papers in 1992 by John Bound and George Johnson and a 1994 study by Bound, Eli Berman, and Zvi Griliches have been widely cited to reject both of these hypotheses. These studies found little evidence of shifts in employment across industrial lines, such as one might have found a century ago from agrarian horse raising toward mechanical automotive manufacture and maintenance. They also found that while trade in manufactures has undoubtedly expanded, the growth of demand for labor in the export trades approximately offsets the decline for labor in the trades that compete with imports, so that the net effect of trade on the relative demand for skilled and unskilled labor has been very small. The first judgment is widely accepted; the second remains controversial. John Bound and George Johnson, "Changes in the Structure of Wages in the 1980s"; Eli Berman, John Bound, and Zvi Griliches, "Changes in the Demand for Skilled Labor Within U.S. Manufacturing."

11. Danziger and Gottschalk, op. cit., p. 141.

12. George E. Johnson, "Changes in Earnings Inequality." An early dissent appears in a 1987 report of the Panel on Technology and Employment of the National Academy of Sciences, who complain that "the methodologies and data used in studies of technological changes and skills are weak and imprecise." The panel goes on to note that "case studies of the impacts of specific technologies or of technological change within a specific industry rarely consider a lengthy period of time; thus they are unable to trace changes in skill requirements as a technology, industry or production process passes through different stages of its development or diffusion." The NAS panel goes on to downplay any role of any kind for technological change in the increasing inequality of incomes, writing that "demographic trends and slow economic growth, rather than technological change, appear to be the primary causes of any tendency toward earnings polarization." This interesting perspective has been substantially neglected by later researchers. Richard Cyert and David Mowery, eds., *Technology and Employment,* pp. 100, 110.

13. Johnson, op. cit., is again explicit about the indirect and inferential nature of this research: "The *lack of evidence in favor of trade* as an explanation of shifts in the relative demand function during the 1980s led many of the early researchers to the conclusion that *something else* must have shifted the aggregate production function in favor of skilled workers. Within a conventional supply-demand model, the *only plausible candidate* that could have done this is skill-biased technological change." (Emphases added.)

14. To elaborate on a previous note, whether these hypothetical effects were "between" or "within" industries depends on how you define "industry." If all "transportation supplies" were grouped together as industry, then the literature on the effect of automobiles might conclude that they did not change the structure of industrial employment very much. If, on the other hand, the classifications were "machinery" and "leather goods," the answers might be very different.

15. Johnson acknowledges this point by subtitling his discussion "The Indirect Argument for a Shift in Demand." Op. cit., p. 41. It is interesting that the same argument—lack of direct evidence—used to discount the role of trade is not acknowledged as telling against the role of "technology." The reason is that technology is a catch-all category and trade is not.

16. The Bound, Berman, and Griliches paper, op. cit., is an especially notable example, given the econometric credentials of its authors.

17. An early example is Adam Smith's immortal pin factory; the division of labor is nothing more than a form of technological change. In 1888 Henry George began *Progress and Poverty* by noting that "the present century has been marked by a prodigious increase in wealth-producing power. The utilization of steam and electricity, the introduction of improved processes and labor-saving machinery, the greater subdivision and grander scale of production, the wonderful facilitation of exchanges, have multiplied enormously the effectiveness of labor."

18. Lawrence points to an accelerated decline in the ratio of production to nonproduction workers in the 1980s as a sign of more intensive use of "skilled" labor during this decade. But this decline could as easily be due to outsourcing or other factors as to technological change, and Lawrence himself agrees that at a minimum, "organizational change" needs to be considered alongside technology in the usual sense as a source of these changes. Op. cit., pp. 63–64. The problem here is that counting "organizational change" as a type of "technological change" distorts the meaning of the word, suggesting a scientific or engineering basis for events that might easily be political or sociological instead, or for that matter symptoms of globalization.

19. Indeed, if one looks back a few years, one highly reputable suggestion was that it should be attributed to the effect of commodity price shocks in the early and mid-1970s, and those shocks are described as a form of *technological regress*. See Michael Bruno and Jeffrey Sachs, *The Economics of Worldwide Stagflation*, p. 20.

20. There is a discussion in my 1989 book, *Balancing Acts*. Chapter 5 in this book contains further details on the latest contributions to this argument, which is not without interest. But surely there comes a point where one is entitled to lose interest in a chase that leads only from one rabbit hole to the next.

21. Alan Krueger, "How Computers Have Changed the Wage Structure." With careful statistical controls for occupation and schooling, Krueger finds a 10 to 15 percent wage pre-

mium associated with computer use. It is the interpretation of this finding, not its accuracy, that is open to question.

22. David Howell, *Institutional Failure and the American Worker.* See also his "The Collapse of Low-Skill Male Earnings in the 1980s" and David Howell and Edward Wolff, "Trends in the Growth and Distribution of Skills in the U.S. Workplace, 1960–1985" and their "Skills, Bargaining Power and Rising Interindustry Wage Inequality Since 1970."

23. Juhn, Murphy, and Pierce, op. cit., trace the rise in skill premiums to the early 1980s. Robert Lerman also finds that hourly wage inequality topped out in 1984. Lerman distinguishes between inequality in hourly wages and inequality in earnings or incomes; the latter continued to rise while the former stabilized. But it is inequality in hourly wages that technological change can account for; rising inequality in the broader measures of income after wage inequality stabilizes must have to do with changes in relative hours or in family structure. Robert I. Lerman, "Is Earnings Inequality Really Increasing?"

24. For example, see Lawrence Katz and Kevin Murphy, "Changes in Relative Wages, 1963–1987," esp. Figure 1. Juhn, Murphy, and Pierce, op. cit., report similar time patterns.

25. Ken Polsson, "Chronology of Events in the History of Microcomputers."

26. Larry Hirschhorn, "Computers and Jobs," p. 405.

27. *1996 Electronic Market Data Book,* Electronic Industries Association, Table 2-19.

28. Modern business software, including WordStar, Lotus 1-2-3, Microsoft Word, and WordPerfect, were all introduced after 1980. "Personal Computers: History and Development," *Jones Telecommunications and Multimedia Encyclopedia: Update,* June 12, 1997.

29. Lawrence, op. cit., reaches the conclusion that technological change must be defined broadly to include organizational change if it is effectively to explain rising inequality. George Johnson has also distanced himself from the computer-centered view, declaring that it is "probably too early to determine just how much of the post-1980 technological change is due to computers as opposed to the long-run trend of increased complexity of work environments in general" (op. cit., p. 49). The difficulty with this is that there is no evidence that the "long-run complexity of work environments"—whatever that phrase means—increased after 1980.

30. The full quotation, a masterpiece of satire, is in the essay, "Why Is Economics Not an Evolutionary Science?" *Quarterly Journal of Economics* (1898).

Chapter 3

1. Robert Kuttner's *Everything for Sale* is a wonderful corrective to the cultural fixation on this topic. This work was sponsored by the Twentieth Century Fund. A classic critique of marginal productivity distribution theory is Lester Thurow, *Generating Inequality,* esp. Appendix A.

2. Robert Heilbroner, ed., *The Essential Adam Smith,* pp. 211, 217–219. Citations are from *Wealth of Nations,* bk. I, chap. X, pt. II, "Inequalities Occasioned by the Policy of Europe."

3. David Card and Alan Krueger, *Myth and Measurement;* Philip Cook and Robert Frank, *The Winner-Take-All Society.*

4. When a janitor in a factory earns more than a janitor in a school, the difference is, in some deep sense, a pass-through of monopolistic profit rather than return to the value of work done. It reflects the market position of the firm or industry, rather than the value or irreplaceability of the employee; it is a part of pay not tied to "marginal product." See especially Lawrence F. Katz and Lawrence H. Summers, "Industry Rents," pp. 209–290. David Blanchflower, Andrew Oswald, and Peter Sanfey, "Wages, Profits and Rent-sharing," pp. 227–251, suggest that a very large part of wage differentials across industries are attributable to the phenomenon of differential rents.

5. Early leads provided in Richard R. Nelson and Sidney G. Winter, *An Evolutionary Theory of Economic Change*, remain substantially unexplored since that time. Nicole Fortin and Thomas Lemieux, "Institutional Changes and Rising Wage Inequality," is a significant exception, as is David Howell, *Institutional Failure and the American Worker*. Fortin and Lemieux argue that institutional changes can account for about one-third of the rising wage inequality in the United States in the 1980s, with deunionization being particularly important for men and the minimum wage for women (p. 75). Fortin and Lemieux point out that few studies have even considered the role of the minimum wage, partly because most work has been restricted to the study of inequality among full-time male workers, while the minimum wage is particularly important for women. Results in Chapter 8 strongly support Fortin and Lemieux on the importance of the minimum wage to the overall wage distribution. See also Fortin, Lemieux, and John DiNardo, "Labor Market Institutions and the Distribution of Wages."

6. A move to deregulate doctoring, say by granting more liberal recognition to foreign medical degrees, would have exactly the same sort of depressing effect on doctors' wages as deregulation in trucking had on truckers, except in that case the overall effect would tend to compress, rather than stretch, the education premium. But in fact the deregulation of trucking did occur in 1980, while deregulation of doctoring and lawyering did not; this could well account for part of the increasing education premium observed immediately thereafter. Nicole Fortin and Thomas Lemieux report quantitative estimates of the effects of deregulation on wage inequality, though they conclude that the "direct impact of economic deregulation on rising wage inequality [is] comparatively small." Op. cit. (1997), p. 76.

7. Michael Keane and Eswar Prasad, "The Employment and Wage Effects of Oil Price Changes."

8. In a beautiful paper, DiNardo and Pischke report similar findings for pencils, as well as calculators and other tools, in the German wage structure, and reach the same conclusion I do, namely, that toys trickle down. John DiNardo and Jorn-Steffen Pischke, "The Returns to Computer Use Revisited."

Chapter 4

1. The "degree of monopoly," a concept devised a half-century ago by the pioneering Polish economist Michał Kalecki, is a useful way of characterizing just how much monopoly power any particular business enjoys. Technically, the degree of monopoly power is the inverse of the elasticity of the firm-specific demand curve. The more inelastic the

firm's demand curve, the greater the markup between price and marginal cost, and the greater the degree of monopoly. Perfect competition implies infinite elasticity—a horizontal demand curve in which the firm has no influence whatever over price.

2. This process is known as rent seeking in the economic literature. Most scholarly work in that area focuses on how people extract rents from the government, the biggest monopolist of them all, but the same principles apply to all the smaller forms of monopoly in the private sector.

3. In an experiment with ultra-free-market practices, the city of Prague, Czech Republic, completely deregulated taxi pricing. The results were supposed to lead to competitive pricing, but in fact they generated extreme forms of monopolism, as every taxi driver sought to negotiate for the maximum each customer might be willing to pay. In the end, astute residents developed long-term relationships with particular cabbies, whom they summon by cell phone; in this way they gain some protection from extortion at the price of inordinately long waits. For the casual visitor to the city, an unchaperoned taxi ride remains a very risky business.

4. The classic work remains John Kenneth Galbraith, *The New Industrial State.*

5. A trip to the Balkans or to Northern Ireland reminds one that religion, not ethnicity, is the conventional marker of intergroup conflict in these unhappy parts of Europe. For a fine discussion of ethnic and religious identity in Bosnia, see Tone Bringa's *Being Muslim the Bosnian Way.*

6. Richard Herrnstein and Charles Murray, *The Bell Curve.* This dreadful book has inspired several good collections in rebuttal, including Russell Jacoby and Naomi Glauberman, *The Bell Curve Debates,* and Claude S. Fischer et al., *Inequality by Design.*

7. In the 1970s, when skill premiums declined sharply, two independent forces were at work. One was an increasing level of credentials in the workforce, which will slowly erode a skill premium even if the composition of jobs and distribution of pay does not change. The other was a sharp rise in economic instability, and a consequent inability of well-educated labor force entrants to find decent employment. This second force, unlike the first, did affect the wage structure. The rise in education levels did not change the structure of jobs on offer, but a rise in unemployment did increase the gap between the top and the bottom. The fact that a large proportion of new labor force entrants were also well qualified exacerbated the decline in the average premium for holders of college degrees that occurred during these years.

8. The equal pay for equal work movement affecting wages in "women's professions" such as nursing, teaching, and office work is, on the other hand, about the shape of the wage structure. But perhaps for this reason it almost entirely lacks official standing and has never enjoyed the respectability accorded to affirmative action.

9. The point is not quite so clear-cut for gender as for race. Gender issues are to some extent structural in our economy, insofar as whole categories of economic life are categorized as "women's professions" and paid accordingly. In contrast, professions strictly identified with blacks, such as sharecropping, domestic service, and sleeping car porters, substantially declined decades ago. Yet even allowing for the existence of women's professions and some sex-segregated manufacturing sectors, notably apparel, the larger movements in inequality are not movements between male and female occupations or industries, but rather within and among industries and occupations whose workforces are predominantly male.

These larger movements probably account for another false paradox: the decline of the average gap between men's and women's wages even as overall inequality was rising. Women's median wages rose from 62 to 79 percent of men's median wages from 1979 to 1993. But rather than reflecting gains for women, this mainly resulted from the collapse of high-wage male-dominated manufacturing employments (the same force that *reduced* the average wage of black workers relative to white). The average gap between men and women workers therefore narrowed, even as overall inequality increased. In the mid-1990s, economic recovery put the paradox in motion in reverse: overall inequality declined while male-female differentials widened, provoking certain neoclassically inclined economists to express puzzlement. See *New York Times*, "Wage Difference Between Women and Men Widens," September 16, 1997, p. A1. Contrary to speculation, there is no evidence that increasing female labor supply—for instance, due to welfare reform—had anything to do with this.

10. John Maynard Keynes, *Essays in Persuasion*, p. 176. In the *General Theory*, Keynes extends this argument to the interest rate: "It might be more accurate, perhaps, to say that the rate of interest is a highly conventional, rather than a highly psychological, phenomenon. For its actual value is largely governed by what its value is expected to be" (p. 203).

11. This idea of a group defined by common patterns of behavior is very close to the idea of a wage contour, which was developed in institutional labor economics. In 1957 the Harvard labor economist (and later, secretary of labor) John T. Dunlop offered this definition of a wage contour: "A stable group of wage-determining units . . . which are so linked together by (1) similarity of product markets, (2) resort to similar sources for a labor force, or (3) common labor-market organization (custom) that they have common wage-making characteristics. . . . The level of wage rates by occupations within the contour need not be equal, *but changes in compensation are highly interrelated*." J. T. Dunlop, "Wage Contours."

12. In much of the academic work involving analysis of industries, analysis therefore proceeds as though, for example, "transportation equipment" or "special industrial machinery" were collections of actually similar items, produced by corporations with common interests, or in establishments that resembled each other in some economically meaningful way. This, of course, is not the case. Boeing and Ford, though both producers of transportation equipment, are very different industrial operations, with differing markets, different technologies, and differing political interests. It is a mistake to group them together and to expect that the characteristics of the artificial grouped entity, "producers of transportation equipment," will be other than a formless amalgam of its divergent underlying components.

Chapter 5

1. Sheldon Danziger and Peter Gottschalk, *America Unequal*, present a characteristic view on this question: "It is the post-1983 period that is the anomaly. During this period mean income increased, but so did inequality. . . . First, there was a long economic recovery, but total gains in income were modest. . . . Second, the economic growth had uneven distributional effects" (p. 66).

2. The starting year of the Korean War was 1950. Apart from this, military spending

probably boosted first-year performances in 1961 (the Berlin crisis) and 1983 (Reagan's military buildup). Taking all of these into account would not materially change my view. There are not enough consistent cases to back up the "bounce-back" theory; one can much more readily argue that strong recoveries occurred when strongly expansionary policies were put into effect, as in 1961, 1976, and 1983.

3. The correlation coefficient between these two series is .78 over five business cycle expansions, whereas the correlation ratio between the depth of the previous recession and the strength of the recovery over four years is only .07.

4. There are economists who argue that a slower expansion, building steadily on past accomplishments, will last longer and prove less inflationary than a rapid one—a view that is indeed held at the Federal Reserve. But the historical record provides little basis for this view. Although there are not many cases to examine, since the early 1960s the more rapid expansions have generally lasted a longer time: the correlation between cumulative growth over five years and length of the recovery is a robust .84. It also appears that there is no close or definite relationship between the strength of an economic expansion and the progress of rising inflation over its lifetime. The inflationary expansions of the 1970s were neither very strong nor very long lived, and the overall correlation between cumulative growth and the increase of inflation is not significantly different from zero.

5. This final combination might be tolerable if it lasts a great deal longer than the eight- and ten-year expansions that were the norm over the preceding three decades. But the evidence on the durability of past expansions suggests that weak ones have early mortality, and this does not lend confidence that the present period of modest growth will last so long.

6. William Greider, *Secrets of the Temple,* provides an account of monetary policy at this time. Edward Denison, *Accounting for Slower Economic Growth,* provides a more comprehensive listing of competing explanations.

7. Philadelphia Federal Reserve Bank economist Leonard Nakamura argues that 2 to 3 percent should be added to the growth of real personal consumption expenditure after 1974, virtually wiping out the decline in measured productivity growth. Nakamura's case rests partly on an alleged unmeasured contribution of computers to multifactor productivity growth, and partly on an argument about structures of consumption (Engel curves), which are changing "as though" income growth were faster than the data show. Leonard Nakamura, "Is U.S. Economic Performance Really That Bad?"

8. Richard Nixon instituted three important policy changes immediately. The first was the abolition of the wage-price guideposts, a decision that led to rising inflation almost immediately. Second was a signal to the Federal Reserve Board that it could raise interest rates and fight inflation with some increase in unemployment if it so chose, a decision that led to the 1970 recession. And third was the enactment of the investment tax credit, later repealed, which raised the after-tax rate of return for business investment. See Charles David Shreve, *A Precarious and Uncertain Liberalism,* for an excellent treatment of this critical transition.

9. Robert Z. Lawrence and Matthew J. Slaughter, "International Trade and American Wages in the 1980's."

10. As we shall explore in later chapters, this does not mean that American workers who produce capital goods have done badly relative to workers who produce consumption

goods. In fact, the reverse is true: the burden of a stagnant consumption wage has fallen more heavily on consumption goods workers. The redistribution of wages within manufacturing toward the technology-producing sectors accounts for this apparent paradox.

11. The 1996 report of a commission chaired by Professor Michael Boskin, "Toward a More Accurate Measure of the Cost of Living," placed the overstatement of inflation in the CPI at 1.1 percent per year. Economist Dean Baker reports that this implies that half the population would have been in poverty by modern standards thirty years ago. The Boskin estimate, which is almost certainly too high, also implies a doubling of estimates of productivity growth over the past thirty years.

12. An early attempt to come to grips with the effects of diversification is David Warsh, *The Idea of Economic Complexity.*

13. Nakamura's intriguing evidence about consumption is relevant here. It is that American consumers have continued to diversify their purchases away from basic commodities at rates consistent with much higher rates of real income growth than official measurements display. Nakamura argues that there has been "unmeasured consumer surplus" from the increasing diversity of products, which accounts for a widely shared perception of improved well-being not picked up in the official statistics. However, a counterargument might be made: that the increased dispersion of incomes is actually responsible for the increased diversity of consumption goods, which are appealing to ever more finely stratified market segments. In that case, efforts to raise the estimate of the average gain in social welfare from product diversification may not be meaningful, in the absence of explicit consideration of distributive values.

14. Land rents have collapsed even more, from some 3 percent of total incomes in the 1940s and 1950s to next to nothing, though this reflects, among other things, the rise of home ownership in society, perhaps not particularly disturbing.

15. In the most recent data, there was a sharp increase in inequality in 1993–1994, which was followed by a small decline in 1995. Part of this latest increase is, however, the result of changes in the data set rather than in the population, and probably should not be taken very seriously. It is due to an increase in the "top-code" bracket from $300,000 to $1 million. This increase means that we now have a more accurate measure of actual income inequality, since the incomes of the highest reporting group are now more accurately reported. But by the same token, the measured increase between 1993 and 1994 is partly artificial.

Chapter 6

1. Robert B. Reich, *The Work of Nations,* chap. 14.

2. I discuss the K-sector/C-sector relationship in detail in an earlier book, *Balancing Acts.*

3. Joseph A. Schumpeter, *Capitalism, Socialism and Democracy,* p. 74. This is essentially the winner-take-all phenomenon to which Robert Frank and Philip Cook call attention in *The Winner-Take-All Society.*

4. An industry-sponsored study of software manufacture, done by Nathan Associates and reported by the *New York Times* on June 3, 1997, p. C2, finds that 619,400 Ameri-

cans are currently employed in software-related trades at an average earnings of $57,300, twice the national average earnings of $27,900. This is a quintessential K-sector business, though unfortunately not yet classified as a manufacturing category in the SIC.

5. In an important footnote, Schumpeter described the behavior of certain C-sector firms—he had in mind autos in the 1930s and rayon in the 1920s—toward each other as "*corespective* rather than competitive: they refrain from certain aggressive devices (which, by the way, would also be absent in perfect competition); they keep up with each other and in doing so play for points at the frontiers." *Capitalism, Socialism and Democracy,* p. 90.

6. James Galbraith and Paulo Du Pin Calmon, "Industries, Trade and Wages."

7. Lawrence F. Katz and Lawrence H. Summers, "Industry Rents," provide evidence on the existence of industry-specific wage differentials at one moment in time. Our argument extends the Katz-Summers case by arguing that changing industry-specific rents should lead to changing wage differentials.

8. The moment came when I asked my research assistant, Lu Jiaqing, to compute first a series on average annual earnings of all employees in each industry and then to compute a second series for the hourly wages of production workers. Lu shifted the denominator of the fraction he was computing but neglected to shift the numerator. It proved to be a brilliant mistake.

9. Indeed, because total payroll is very highly correlated with industrial value-added through time in most SIC categories, with correlation coefficients approaching .99 in most cases, this variable gives essentially the same results as would the use of value-added per production hour. By the same token, however, once we had the P-measure, there was no particular reason to rerun the analysis with a value-added measure.

10. See Robert Bakker, *The Dinosaur Heresies,* for a great read on this subject. The movie *Jurassic Park* introduced the dinosaur-bird hypothesis to millions.

11. These are essentially all manufacturing industries for which complete data are available at the three-digit level of disaggregation.

12. In this case, there are 9,591 distinct relationships, and each involves computing a single number from the thirty-three original pairs of yearly change rates in the P-measure.

13. The prime virtue of the technique is that it produces groupings only by merging entities that are truly similar; we stop grouping up when the underlying groups differ by too much. Thus, the total amount of differences that existed in the original data set is largely preserved in the later one. And we can analyze the differences between the resulting small number of groups, with great confidence that we are looking at the principal differences that actually exist in the economy as a whole.

14. In earlier work, using data through 1988, Paulo Calmon and I were struck by the internal homogeneity of the garment-apparel sector. This is evidently no longer the case; the P-measure distributes the clothing sector over three separate clusters: food and clothing, printing, and other women's apparel.

15. Clearly this is at least as plausible as grouping aircraft with automobiles under "Transportation Equipment," which is the official approach.

16. The performance of the greeting cards industry was a mystery I did not probe.

17. These are nominal figures, not corrected for inflation; an inflation correction would change the scale of the axes but not the positions of each group on the chart.

18. One can compare the change in total production worker hours as a fraction of total

employment by drawing rays from the origin to each point in the diagram. The more shallow the slope of the ray, the greater the change. Thus, only apparel and the tobacco-hats group, at the bottom of C-sector, showed the kind of transformation that characterizes the K-sector. And, of course, apparel workers could not protect their relative wages.

19. Thus, low-wage sectors have large average differentials even though their average salaries are low by comparative standards. These comparisons are based on a standard estimate of 2,000 production worker hours per year.

20. These are the differences that some other studies have failed to find. I believe the reason is that they did not perform the taxonomic sorting of their industrial data that is required before such differences become visible.

21. Not surprisingly, this pattern of bifurcation emerges only as industrial performance patterns diverge after 1970. A graph drawn during the first half of the period would not have shown it. Computers and electronics are significant outliers combining a high share of nonproduction employment with a larger premium—about twofold, comparable to garment workers—between hourly and salaried pay on average. These calculations, of course, conceal all the variation that exists within the salaried sector.

22. We shall return to the S-sector, which requires a larger though in many other ways inferior data set, in Chapter 9.

Chapter 7

1. That is, once industrial groups are properly differentiated, it appears that between-industry sources of variation account for a large part of the difference in wage performance across groups of workers, a finding obscured when industrial classification schemes mix winning and losing groups. We also observe that among consumption goods industries, interindustrial earnings divergences appear to be larger, on the whole, than does the also-growing split in earnings between production and nonproduction workers.

2. Details in the appendix for this chapter (at the back of the book). Here I deploy a statistical technique known as taking the canonical roots of a discriminant function, which reduces the differences between our groups to a small number of underlying forces, or patterns of change through time. Technically, each root is a weighting function; in matrix terms they are eigenvectors of a normalized between-group variance-covariance matrix. The trick in the analysis is to treat this sequence of annual weights "as if" it were an economic time series, and then to look to economic history to try to determine what each force actually represents.

3. As a technical matter, the calculation of how much variation is explained by each root or eigenvector is made from the associated discriminant criterion or eigenvalue; we choose to analyze those eigenvectors with the largest associated eigenvalues. However, it is important to realize that this measure of the amount of variation across groups is not weighted by the size of those groups. For this reason, even if the underlying performance variable were wage change rather than the P-measure, a finding that four roots explain 60 percent of the between-group variation would not imply that these forces account for 60 percent of a between-group Theil index calculated from the same information, since the

Theil index is employment weighted. In principle, it could happen that a high degree of variability contributed by a few small sectors would generate a large proportion of the total between-group variation, even though the number of workers involved is insignificant. However, in this data set, it appears that the main forces or roots do each represent sources of variation affecting large groups of workers; a possible exception is the third root, which appears to capture the effects of trade protection and seems to have large effects on only a small set of industries.

4. My particular measure includes both business investment and household investment as measured by purchases of consumer durables, grouped together to form what may be called "comprehensive investment." This reflects another reality revealed by a different cluster analysis, on the rates of change of components of the national income and product accounts—namely, that the movement in time of consumers' durable purchases, normally listed as a consumption item, in fact corresponds more closely to the movement in time of business fixed investment than it does to the other elements of the consumption package. This analysis is presented briefly in the appendix to Chapter 6 (at the back of the book.)

5. Given the large size of the food and clothing and chemicals sectors, one could make an argument that this pattern is more important, relatively, than its eigenvalue-discriminant criterion suggests. There is, unfortunately, no way to weight these patterns by the size of the groups that form them. However, Chapter 8 will present an analysis of the movement of wage inequality across industrial groups that is weighted by the size of the groups. Both analyses form part of our picture of industrial change and wage inequality.

6. Interestingly, the missiles industry scores low on the "war force." But this is no anomaly. Strategic nuclear missiles are not used in actual military conflict, and expenditure on their procurement fell as the claims of the Vietnam War grew in the mid-1960s, to rise again as the war wound down in the early 1970s. More problematic is the difference between the high quality of the fit for the periods before the start and after the end of the Vietnam War and the poor fit during the years 1965–1975. The explanation is probably that during an actual war, industries supplying war materiel add production hours very rapidly. This cuts into their financial and industrial performance. The ideal time for war industries is when spending is high but no war is actually being fought.

7. If r_t is the coefficient value in period t, then over T periods the cumulative value is $R = 100*(1 + r_1)(1 + r_2) \ldots (1 + r_{(T-1)})(1 + r_T)$.

8. The absence of steel and automobiles from the sectors strongly benefited by protection is possibly explained by the type of protection these sectors received in the 1980s. This took the form of voluntary export restraints by the major Japanese competitors, who then moved up-market in the product mix of their industries, particularly automobiles. Thus, the mechanism tended to distribute the "protection rents" to the foreign rather than to the domestic companies, a process that explains, in part, why it was possible to negotiate such programs in the first place.

9. In the next chapter I will add in that part of the officially defined services sector that might reasonably be described as behaving like the K-sector; this will raise the number toward 12 million, still only a tenth of the workforce at the very most.

10. Correspondingly, in industries with the lowest uptake of new technology—hous-

ing, motorbikes, and cars and metals—the competitive pressure of technology on wages diminishes to the point where the effect is no longer clearly perceptible.

Chapter 8

1. Two important papers have recently reached conclusions similar to mine: Nathan S. Balke and Daniel J. Slottje, "A Macroeconometric Model of Income Inequality in the United States," and George J. Borjas and Valerie A. Ramey, "The Relationship Between Wage Inequality and International Trade."

2. Anne E. Polivka and Jennifer M. Rothgeb, "Redesigning the CPS Questionnaire," provides a good survey of problems with the employment-related questions in the CPS.

3. Chinhui Juhn, Kevin Murphy, and Brooks Pierce, "Wage Inequality and the Rise in Returns to Skill," p. 419.

4. Juhn et al. (ibid.) summarize for their entire period: "The percentage increase in wages is roughly a linear function of the percentile, with wage increases being 1.4 percent higher for each 10 percentile points up in the wage distribution."

5. Lynn Karoly, "The Trend in Inequality Among Families, Individuals and Workers in the United States."

6. In other words, T' and the unobservable T will be highly correlated over time. To be confident of this in any given case, the grouping rules need to satisfy two further conditions. First, they must be consistent over time, so that individuals are not arbitrarily reclassified from one period to the next. Second, the groups should not overlap. Fortunately, the SIC scheme meets both of these conditions fairly well. It remains possible that wage inequality within SIC classes behaves somewhat differently through time than wage inequality across these classes, but the likelihood that the differences are large or important is quite small.

7. Recently, these data have become available in electronic format on CD-ROM, through the *Census Reports* published by the Bureau of the Census.

8. The details of this reduction have been presented in Chapter 6.

9. A regression of T' on the Gini also reveals that over the full time period, the two series move proportionately: a 10 percent change in T' predicts a 10 percent change in the Gini.

10. Robert Lerman reaches his similar conclusion—that hourly wage inequality peaked in 1984—from a broadly based data source on wages: the Survey of Income and Program Participation (SIPP). Lerman, "Is Earnings Inequality Really Increasing?" Also, the Juhn, Murphy, and Pierce finding (op. cit.) that skill premiums rise most sharply in the early 1980s is inconsistent with an effect of computers in the late 1980s and 1990s.

11. The construction of a suitable exchange rate series posed puzzles of its own. I started with the comprehensive trade-weighted series (RX101) computed by the Dallas Federal Reserve Bank, which takes into account the currencies of 101 countries with which the United States trades and adjusts each one for the difference in inflation rates between the United States and that country. To allow for so-called J-curve (time-lag) effects, I used a three-year, lagged moving average of the raw Dallas series. And finally, because trade in manufactures became vastly more important with the huge surge of

imports that followed the recessions of 1980 and 1981, I effectively neutralize pre-1981 values of this series by artificially setting the value to one. Thus, the hypothesis being tested is that a trade-weighted exchange rate started to have an important effect on inequality for the years 1981 and after. My argument is that my particular form of this time series is well adapted to capture the structural change that actually occurred at this time.

12. I use the minimum wage in 1995 dollars, as computed by the Center for Budget and Policy Priorities, "Assessing a $5.15-an-Hour Minimum Wage."

13. Nicole Fortin, Thomas Lemieux and John DiNardo, "Labor Market Institutions and the Distribution of Wages." Thomas Ferguson and I find similar effects on women's wages from the introduction of the minimum wage in the early 1930s. Ferguson and Galbraith, "The American Wage Structure, 1920–1947.

14. The second is the census Gini measure of household income inequality, reported by Daniel H. Weinberg, "A Brief Look at Postwar U.S. Income Inequality." The third is a shorter but population-based Theil statistic reported by W. Norton Grubb and Robert H. Wilson, "Trends in Wage and Salary Inequality, 1967–1988." Insignificant variables were dropped from the equations for these two series.

15. The equation shows no strong evidence of serial correlation in the residuals (DW coefficient of 1.48), time trends in the dependent variables, or other statistical problems.

16. It is also obvious that trade and the exchange rate are closely related. From a statistical perspective, the effects of trade, which others have documented, appear here to be artifacts of U.S. exchange rate movements, when one takes into consideration the patterns of American trade with both advanced and developing countries. On the other hand, the weight of less-developed countries in the basket of currencies whose values go into the exchange rate index is itself an outcome of globalization. As trade with low-wage countries has grown, so has the importance of their currencies in the measurement of a properly trade-weighted exchange rate. In this way, the trade hypothesis is supported by this analysis, but also subordinated at the same time, for if North-South trade could have expanded without the structural overvaluation of the dollar in relation to the currencies of low-wage countries, particularly as occurred beginning in the early 1980s, then the effect of trade on wage inequality would have been much less severe.

17. Steven G. Allen, "Updated Notes on the Interindustry Wage Structure," Figure 1, presents strikingly similar series drawing on a variety of sources, including the Conference Board. Allen also presents a useful survey of previous work on interindustry wage structures, noting that "very few studies in recent years have examined *changes* in compensation by industry."

Chapter 9

1. The vertical distance separating any two industries or services measures the degree of similarity or difference in their wage evolutions through time.

2. But not life insurance, a pure service, interestingly enough.

3. As with Chapter 7's taxonomy of manufacturing proper, the overall quality of the grouping appears good. Only a handful of classifications—grocery stores with sensitive materials, beauty shops as a manufacturing satellite—appear suspect on prima facie

grounds. But then, compared to the P-measure, the rate of change of average hourly wages is not a superior clustering variable, and we are working with fifteen fewer years of data than were available in Chapter 7. On the whole it is remarkable that the group structures are as clean as they are.

4. The two fringe clusters have less than 2 million total employees apiece.

5. A failure to do so is not simply a question of accounting. It means that the sector that is labeled "services" will behave in ways that resemble manufacturing more than it should, because elements that are strongly influenced by the behavior of manufacturing industries have been added unwittingly to the mix.

6. The problem of computing a consistent between-groups Theil is complicated by rapidly changing classification schemes and the addition of large new sectors to the data in several recent years.

7. The dotted line is the first canonical root of the discriminant function that best separates the movements of earnings across four large groups: manufacturing and satellites, pure services, materials-sensitive sectors, and the outliers. Both investment series are averaged over the first four years after they occur, allowing for a surge in investment to have a delayed effect on wage differentials. For an explanation of discriminant analysis, see the appendix to Chapter 7 at the back of the book.

8. The pattern of gross private domestic investment by business firms is closely correlated with the pattern of durable goods purchases, or household investment. Thus, in a broad sense, wages in goods production track trends in goods consumption, with a lag of several years' time.

9. The presence of intercity and rural bus transportation on the list is a bit of a puzzle. Perhaps the fortunes of this sector went up when rising gasoline prices forced people to reconsider long-distance driving in the 1970s.

10. New and used car dealers, who work on commission, are also high on this list for obvious reasons. Less obvious high scorers include beauty shops, coal miners, parking services, and crushed and broken stone. But overall the pattern is clear. Low scorers on this force include various construction crafts, day care, logging, nonstore retail, and retail bakeries—all about as far from the cutting edge of technology as one can get.

11. Comparisons of earnings between industries officially classed as manufacturing and those not so classed can be tricky. Here we use a measure of average hourly wages for production workers alone in the manufacturing sector and of average hourly earnings for all employees in the services industries.

12. A simple regression of the average difference between manufacturing and services wages and the within-manufacturing Theil statistic yields the finding that the former explains about 75 percent of the variation in the latter.

13. And this *despite* historically high real interest rates that might on some theoretical accounts have been expected to reduce expenditure on investment goods. The resolution of this apparent paradox lies in the fact that increasing volatility of the business cycle raises the rate of scrapping of old equipment in slumps and therefore the rate of capital renewal in the expansion.

14. Even the economic theory that relates individual wages to marginal productivity does not predict that average sectoral wages will rise with average sectoral productivity. Many people appear to think that it does, confusing the notions of marginal and average

productivity. The result is a hopeless muddle, which, of course, can be taken advantage of by the winners in the distribution game to assert the justice of their position.

15. This is more or less the position of Jeremy Rifkin and his followers. See, for example, Rifkin's *The End of Work*.

Chapter 10

1. To be precise, the calculation of the natural rate of unemployment then incorporates a divide-by-zero.

2. Robert Lucas, "Tobin and Monetarism."

3. Paul A. Samuelson and Robert M. Solow provided the canonical treatment: "Analytical Aspects of Anti-Inflation Policy."

4. Only a few voices, including Robert Eisner in the United States and Nicholas Kaldor in the United Kingdom, never accepted the short-run Phillips curve as a theory of inflation, and so were in a position to resist. But their voices were not widely heeded in the economics profession, and only three decades later have Robert Eisner's continuing and cutting critiques of the natural rate hypothesis found the hearing that they deserve. See Robert Eisner, "A New View of the Nairu." This working paper has appeared in several versions with increasing effect, for those seriously interested in econometric evidence. It is published in Paul Davidson and Jan Kregel, eds., *Improving the Global Economy.*

5. I have published this illuminating figure on numerous previous occasions and apologize to readers who may have seen it before.

6. Eisner, op. cit., explores this issue in persuasive detail.

7. Robert J. Gordon, "The Time-Varying NAIRU and Its Implications for Economic Policy," Table 1. Robert J. Gordon's textbook, *Macroeconomics,* was an important source of NAIRU estimates for the economics profession, as Gordon himself acknowledges.

8. Charles Adams and David Coe, "A Systems Approach to Estimating the Natural Rate of Unemployment and Potential Output for the United States."

9. Mercifully, Akerlof, Dickens, and Perry have produced estimates of the NAIRU ranging from 4.6 to 5.3 percent, in good time for the September 1996 reduction of the actual unemployment rate to 5.1 percent and its continued decline to 4.8 percent as of May 1997. See George Akerlof, William T. Dickens, and George Perry, "The Macroeconomics of Low Inflation," Table 5.

10. In general, the estimated NAIRU in a variety of studies has tracked the actual unemployment rate, sluggishly. When unemployment rises, analysts tend to discover that the demographic characteristics of workers are deteriorating or that the job-wage and wage-price dynamics have become unstable. See David M. Gordon, "The Un-Natural Rate of Unemployment." And as the unemployment rate drifts down again, those flaws mysteriously began to disappear, and a lower NAIRU is estimated. Recent empirical studies like Eisner (op. cit.) and Ray Fair's "Testing the Standard View of the Long-Run Unemployment-Inflation Relationship" have confirmed this instability, both across time and in transnational comparisons.

11. The recent innovation of a "time-varying NAIRU," in which the estimated natural rate varies according to the predictions of a model, is the latest rabbit to be pulled from the hat of the natural raters. Such models are attractive in the face of the record of

stationary models. But they seem unlikely to resolve the practical problem, for to move to a general consensus on time variation, we need agreement not only on a value but on the process generating the value. How likely is this, given, for instance, the disagreement over so basic an issue as whether wages belong in a price equation? Or consider what time variation adds to policy discussion. If the implication of time-varying natural rate models is that unemployment can be pushed down slowly, well past previously imagined limits, with the NAIRU in tow, well and good. But you can reach that conclusion without any such model; nobody argues for a crash program to achieve 3 percent unemployment next year. If, on the other hand, the implication is that one must base interest rate policy on the ever-changing output of a computer model, policymakers will wisely assign varying natural rate estimates a low weight. And if the implication is that next year's NAIRU is a random walk from this year's, the practical consequence is not different from that of abandoning NAIRU models altogether. See Gordon, op. cit.

12. There is a second cost to this style of thinking, one that falls on the economists rather than on the economy. This is a loss of influence. It is one thing to position oneself in the center of gravity of a national political debate, where one can condition theory with circumstance, address important problems, and recommend now one thing, now another, as conditions change. It is something else again to be always singing the same note, always revisiting the same issue, always revising past estimates, coming up with the "new NAIRU" and the "new new NAIRU" as though it were a matter of a political makeover. People stop paying attention, and rightly so.

Chapter 11

1. George Gilder's *Wealth and Poverty* and Jude Wanniski's *The Way the World Works* were the pop tracts of the moment.

2. For example, Robert Blecker reports that 57 cents of every dollar received on corporate mergers and acquisitions in the 1980s was consumed rather than reinvested. Robert Blecker, *Are Americans on a Consumption Binge?*

3. Edward N. Wolff, *Top Heavy*, Figure 3-3.

4. Blecker, op. cit., provides a comprehensive critique of the savings shortage arguments. See also his book, *Beyond the Twin Deficits*.

5. There is, to be sure, a political dynamic. If the voters have been propagandized into thinking that the budget should be balanced, then each party can be penalized by the other for deviations from the faith. The safe stand, under such circumstances, is in favor of balance. But this fact of American political life tells us nothing about the economics.

6. Congressional Budget Office, *Reducing the Deficit: Spending and Revenue Options*, pp. 1–2.

7. Here, we may usefully recall another passage from Keynes: "The absurd, though almost universal, idea that an act of individual saving is just as good for effective demand as an act of individual consumption, has been fostered by the fallacy . . . that an increased desire to hold wealth . . . must, by increasing the demand for investments, provide a stimulus to their production; so that current investment is promoted by individual saving to the same extent as present consumption is diminished. It is of this fallacy that it is most difficult to disabuse men's minds." *The General Theory of Employment, Interest and Money*, pp. 211–212.

8. Congressional Budget Office, *The Economic and Budget Outlook: An Update.*

9. A further passage from Keynes: "The reader will readily appreciate that the problem here under discussion is a matter of the most fundamental theoretical significance and of overwhelming practical importance. For the economic principle, on which the practical advice of economists has been almost invariably based, has assumed, in effect, that, *cet.par.,* a decrease in spending will tend to lower the rate of interest and an increase in investment to raise it. But if what these two quantities determine is, not the rate of interest, but the aggregate volume of employment, then our outlook on the mechanism of the economic system will be profoundly changed." *The General Theory,* pp. 134–135. There is nothing new in economics!

10. This estimate takes the average rise in interest rates across the yield spectrum at about 1 percent. See Congressional Budget Office, *Economic and Budget Outlook* (January 1994): 76.

11. I have so far not discussed the specific proposal of a balanced budget amendment to the U.S. Constitution. Suffice it to say that this dangerous proposition has no serious economic rationale, because the goal of balancing the budget itself makes no economic sense. By the same token, those who argue for a "gradual approach" or a legislated as opposed to a constitutional move toward a balanced budget should not be seen as "moderates" in this discussion. Rather, the burden should be on them to show why their radical goal should be preferred to a policy of stable debt in relation to GDP, taking into account the large tax increases and expenditure cuts they would impose to achieve it.

12. The late Nobel Prize–winning economist William Vickrey especially has argued that a steady expansion of the federal debt is necessary to meet the demand for safe financial assets as economic growth proceeds. Absent a rising federal debt, households increasingly bid up the prices of common stocks, a process that cannot continue indefinitely without subjecting the system to the risk of a financial collapse. See Vickrey's last article, "A Trans-Keynesian Manifesto."

13. At the same time, a realization that there is no economic rationale for balancing outlays and revenues at the federal level drives home another progressive point. It would make sense to split investment from consumption expenditures in the federal budget, and so to legitimate bond financing of public investment spending. The purpose of this would not be, as many imagine, to create a favored environment for capital spending or to impose a "workable" requirement that consumption support be funded from current tax revenues. Federal expenditures to support mass consumption are just as needful, in our time and situation, as federal capital expenditures, and occasions arise when they are just as legitimately financed by deficit spending. The point, rather, is to emphasize the actually conservative character of public fiscal policy and to encourage instead a policy whose design and objective is actually to raise social well-being and living standards—not in the sweet hereafter, but today, tomorrow, and the day after that.

Chapter 12

1. See Robert Reich, *The Work of Nations;* Robert Kuttner, *Managed Trade and Economic Sovereignty;* Clyde Prestowitz, *Trading Places;* Steven Cohen and John Zysman, *Manufacturing Matters.*

2. Some of these ideas were first expressed in a review of Paul Krugman's *Pop Internationalism,* published in *Dissent* (winter 1997).

3. Both of these are explicitly defended in, for example, the *1997 Economic Report of the President,* a concise and authoritative statement of supply-side liberal views.

4. See, for example, Paul Krugman, "Is Free Trade Passé?"

5. Schumpeter summarized as follows: "I have stated that, broadly speaking, relative shares in national income have remained substantially constant over the last hundred years. This, however, is true only if we measure them in money. Measured in real terms, relative shares have changed substantially in favor of the lower income groups. This follows from the fact that the capitalist engine is first and last an engine of mass production which unavoidably means also production for the masses, whereas, climbing upward in the scale of individual incomes, we find that an increasing proportion is being spent on personal services and on handmade commodities, the prices of which are largely a function of wage rates." *Capitalism, Socialism and Democracy,* p. 67.

6. The leading advocate of this position is David Alan Aschauer, whose views are summarized in "Genuine Economic Returns to Infrastructure Investment." Edward Gramlich, "Infrastructure Investment, A Review," provides a critical survey.

7. Launched, as my colleague Michael Oden has reminded me, in response to an unusually successful early 1960s tour of the Bolshoi Ballet.

Chapter 13

1. Before the Accord of 1953, an agreement between the Federal Reserve and the Treasury that launched the modern period of independent central banking, the Federal Reserve was charged with maintaining the value of the long government bond at par, which meant maintaining the long-term interest rate equal to the coupon on that bond, which was 2 percent.

2. It is a matter, as Keynes wrote in the *General Theory,* of liquidity preference, which governs the demand for money as compared with interest-bearing assets of different maturities. The Federal Reserve's role is to supply liquidity as it is demanded and to set the terms on which it is supplied—that is, the rate of interest that induces financial market speculators to choose interest-bearing instruments rather than cash.

3. Rudiger Dornbusch and Mario Henrique Simonsen, *Inflation Stabilization with Incomes Policy Support,* was an early entry in a now-extensive literature on this issue. See also Rudiger Dornbusch, Federico Sturzenegger, and Holger Wolf, "Extreme Inflation"; Rudiger Dornbusch, "From Stabilization to Growth"; Lourdes Sola, "Heterodox Shock in Brazil"; Stanley Fischer, "The Israeli Stabilization Program"; Daniel Heymann, "The Austral Plan."

4. Hugh Rockoff, *Drastic Measures.*

5. The Germans, a famous case, famously pretend to believe that their price stability is due to the effective monetary control of the independent Bundesbank. But in fact intricate relationships between the authorities and the trade unions are also critically involved. The literature on the German case documents this quite effectively. A further discussion of the German case follows in Chapter 14.

6. Dimitri Papadimitriou and Randall Wray, "Targeting Inflation."

7. An interesting implication of the Papadimitriou-Wray thesis is the following: Sup-

pose the government were to flood the market with low-income public housing. Actually housing rents would decline, and so would the much larger imputed rents to home owners in the CPI. Inflation would decline! It may be that under CPI targeting, the Department of Housing and Urban Development would be a better inflation fighter than the Federal Reserve!

8. It follows that for Congress to adopt legislation making this the de jure statutory responsibility of the Federal Reserve, as Senator Connie Mack has proposed, would be a disaster. You cannot legislate the goals of monetary policy without also, in effect, legislating the theory under which monetary policy has to be conducted. This is a point that Senator Mack understands perfectly well.

9. Press reports on the "credit crunch" began in 1991 and ended in 1994. During this time, Federal Reserve officials repeatedly promised that the crunch would soon end; business journalists called for it to be alleviated by lower interest rates, and certain conservative economists, associated with the Shadow Open Market Committee, repeatedly asserted that no such thing was happening. In fact, the crunch was real, and was ended only when the Federal Reserve raised interest rates to restore the relative profitability of business loans to banks.

Chapter 14

1. This chapter omits consideration of a class of anti-inflation policy suggestions associated with American economists over the years: the tax-based inflation policy (TIP) proposal of Henry Wallich and Sidney Weintraub, the market anti-inflation plan (MAP) of David Colander and Abba Lerner, and numerous variations. Readers interested in these suggestions, which I do not believe to be practical, should consult Colander's *Incentive-Based Incomes Policies*.

2. The general statement of the theoretical argument is in Wendy Carlin and David Soskice, *Macroeconomics and the Wage Bargain*, pp. 408–414. See also L. Calmfors and J. Driffill, "Bargaining Structure, Corporatism, and Macroeconomic Performance."

3. Paulo Du Pin Calmon, Pedro Conceicao, James K. Galbraith, Vidal Garza Cantu, and Abel Hibert, "The Evolution of Inequality in Brazil, Mexico and the United States."

4. James K. Galbraith, *Balancing Acts*.

5. There would very likely be an election cycle in the adjustment. With elections every two years, this is not all that much of a problem from an economic standpoint, though political objections can, of course, be raised.

Chapter 15

1. A very useful compilation of previous work is Lars Osberg, ed., *Economic Inequality and Poverty*. John Hills, ed., *New Inequalities*, is a very wide-ranging collection of papers on inequality in Britain. See also Stephen Nickell and Brian Bell, "Changes in the Distribution of Wages and Unemployment in OECD Countries," and David Card, Francis Kramarz, and Thomas Lemieux, "Changes in the Relative Structure of Wages and Employment."

2. A 1996 paper by Christopher Niggle, "New Evidence from the Luxembourg Income Surveys," summarized the extent of these measures at that time. Interested readers can contact the LIS for regularly updated information.

3. Most notably, the sharp drop shown in wage inequality in Belgium in the early 1970s does not appear plausible and does not show up when the same analysis is run at a higher level of industrial aggregation (e.g., a two-digit decomposition). A less visible defect apparently produces discontinuity in the data for France in 1977. This defect emerged from a comparison of and apparent inconsistency between fixed and variable-weighted Theil measures, discussed below.

4. "During the 1970s, Italy experienced an extreme compression of wage differentials, similar to the better-known situation in Sweden. Most evidence suggests that this compression came to a stop around 1982–83, coincident with a major institutional change (in the form of the escalator clause in Italian union contracts), a major economic change (the slowdown in inflation), a major technological change (industrial restructuring and the computer revolution), and a major political change (the loss of support for unions and their egalitarian pay policies)." Christopher L. Erickson and Andrea Ichino, "Wage Differentials in Italy."

5. Noncomparabilities may be due to cross-country differences in the composition of industrial employment, cross-country differences in the proportion of total employment in covered manufacturing, or cross-country differences in the allocation of nonwage incomes.

6. Where more than one Gini coefficient was available, the most recent was used as a benchmark. The resulting coefficient, which is a kind of reverse-engineered Gini time series, is not strictly a guess at the Gini. For years other than the benchmark, what it estimates technically is the contribution of changing inequality in the dispersion of earnings to changes in the income distribution. The concept appears useful, but I am not arguing that it should be given more weight than it can bear.

7. The shift from a variable to a fixed-weighted measure doubles the estimated increase in wage in equality in the United Kingdom after 1979, from about 8 to over 16 percent, making the rise of inequality in the United Kingdom measured in this way much more closely comparable to that in the United States than the variable-weighted measures indicate. Moreover, the rise in non-wage sources of inequality in the United Kingdom, due to cuts in public assistance programs and rising interest rates, has been greater than in the United States, so that overall inequality has actually risen more in the United Kingdom.

8. As we did for measurements of industrial performance in the United States, we compute a matrix of Euclidean distances between the vectors of rates of change—one for each country. We then construct a hierarchical table of association between countries according to the distance between them in this $(t-1)$-dimensional "phase-space," where t is the number of years for which one has observations. Our standard clustering method that minimizes, at each step, the ratio of variance within groups to variance between groups (Ward's method) produces a tree diagram illustrating the covariation of each variable across the countries under analysis.

9. This difference is measured by the "linkage distance" between movements of inequality and movements of unemployment, across countries.

10. And also the Canadians, whose relative equality was also shattered in the 1980s by developments to their south.

11. One might also mention the decision to place a Harvard graduate, Carlos Salinas de Gortari, in the Mexican presidency in 1988.

Chapter 16

1. Equally, the idea that relative pay across organizations might depend on organizational skill makes sense only if all other considerations (such as monopoly power) are deliberately excluded—which is to say it makes no sense in the real world. Anyway, the competitive story is necessarily based on individuals rather than groups.

2. Such a rebellion almost got going in the 1960s, when a dispute known as the "Cambridge controversies" challenged the concept of capital as a factor of production and hence the coherence of the notion of marginal productivity. But the marginal productivity theory of the labor market survived that challenge, and its success in so doing is the root of the difficulty today.

3. Adrian J. B. Wood, *A Theory of Pay;* Lawrence Katz and Lawrence Summers, "Industry Rents"; David G. Blanchflower and Andrew J. Oswald, *The Wage Curve;* Blanchflower, Oswald, and Sanfey, "Wages, Profits and Rent-sharing"; David Card and Alan Krueger, *Myth and Measurement;* Robert Frank and Philip Cook, *The Winner-Take-All Society.*

Appendix to Chapter 2

1. Adrian J. B. Wood, *North-South Trade, Employment and Inequality;* Edward E. Leamer, "In Search of Stolper-Samuelson Effects on U.S. Wages."

2. The political cross-currents are occasionally convoluted. Those who dismiss the evidence for a role of trade in inequality tend to be fervent advocates of free trade. However, neither Wood nor Leamer deploys the contrary evidence to support a protectionist position.

3. Further, Wood's argument transforms the underlying "facts of the case" as we understand them from the standard emphasis on rising relative demand for skilled labor in the North (consistent with the skill-biased-technology explanation) to rising relative employment of unskilled labor when North and South are taken together—which would be consistent with his emphasis on increased supply of unskilled labor.

4. Robert Z. Lawrence and Matthew J. Slaughter, "International Trade and American Wages in the 1980's." Another critique of Lawrence and Slaughter can be found in Jeffrey Sachs and Howard Shatz, "Trade and Jobs in U.S. Manufacturing." Sachs and Shatz argue that the relative price of unskilled-labor-intensive goods did fall, something that, if true, undercuts the Lawrence-Slaughter argument completely.

5. A 1996 paper by Paulo Calmon and myself finds a relationship between trade competitiveness and wages that must rest essentially on some such outside-of-market-channels flow of information. James K. Galbraith and Paulo Du Pin Calmon, "Wage Change and Trade Performance in U.S. Manufacturing Industries."

6. After a long period in which mainstream economists simply ignored Wood's argument, Lawrence presents a reasoned counterargument.

7. National Research Council, *The New Americans*.

8. Moreover, as elsewhere in these studies, there is an important question about directions of causality. With a more equal wage structure, native-born Americans would want jobs that now only immigrants will take, and the demand for migrant labor would decline.

Appendix to Chapter 6

1. This section is adapted from James K. Galbraith and Paulo Du Pin Calmon, "Industries, Trade and Wages."

Appendix to Chapter 8

1. Henri Theil, *Statistical Decomposition Analysis*.

2. Thomas Ferguson and James K. Galbraith, "The American Wage Structure: 1920–1947. This long and technical paper will be published separately.

3. To achieve a match between the time series for wages and the industrial groups of the *Historical Statistics* for 1940 on which I rely for employment weightings, it was necessary to combine the eighty-four time series of the former into the twenty-six grouped categories of the latter.

BIBLIOGRAPHY

Articles and Reports

Abell, John D. "Military Spending and Income Inequality." *Journal of Peace Research* 31, no. 1 (1994): 35–43.

Adams, Charles, and David Coe. "A Systems Approach to Estimating the Natural Rate of Unemployment and Potential Output for the United States." *IMF Staff Papers* 37 (June 1990) 232–293.

Akerlof, George, William T. Dickens, and George Perry. "The Macroeconomics of Low Inflation." *Brookings Papers on Economic Activity* 1 (1996).

Allen, Steven G. "Updated Notes on the Interindustry Wage Structure." NBER Working Paper No. 4664, February 1994.

———. "Relative Wage Variability in the United States, 1860–1983." *Review of Economics and Statistics* 69 (1987): 617–626.

———. "Technology and the Wage Structure." Mimeo. North Carolina State University, 1993.

Alogoskoufis, George. "Test of Alternative Wage Employment Bargaining Models with an Application to the UK Aggregate Labor Market." *European Economic Review* 35, no. 1 (1991): 23–38.

Alpert, William T. "Employment, Unemployment and the Minimum Wage: A Causality Model." *Applied Economics* 20 (1988): 1453–1465.

Altonji, Joseph G. "Variation in Employment Growth in Canada: The Role of External, National, Regional, and Industrial Factors." *Journal of Labor Economics* 8 (1990): 198–237.

Armah, Bartholomew. "Trade Sensitive Manufacturing Employment: Some New Insights." *Review of Black Political Economy* 2 (1992): 37–55.

Aschauer, David Alan. "Genuine Economic Returns to Infrastructure Investment." *Policy Studies Journal* 21 (summer 1993): 380–391.

Balandi, Gianguido. "Introduction to Social Europe." *European Letter* (January 1996).

Balassa, Bela. "The Employment Effects of Trade in Manufactured Products Between Developed and Developing Countries." *Journal of Policy Modeling* 8 (1986): 371–391.

Baldwin, Marjorie. "Estimating the Employment Effects of Wage Discrimination." *Review of Economics and Statistics* 74 (1992): 446.

Balke, Nathan S., and Daniel J. Slottje. "A Macroeconometric Model of Income Inequality in the United States." In J. H. Bergstrand et al., eds., *The Changing Distribution of Income in an Open U.S. Economy,* pp. 244–278. Amsterdam: Elsevier Science, 1994.

Bell, Linda A. "Union Wage Concessions in the 1980s: The Importance of Firm-Specific Factors." *Industrial and Labor Relations Review* 48 (1995): 258–275.

Belman, Dale, and Thea Lee. "International Trade and the Performance of U.S. Labor Markets." Mimeo. Economic Policy Institute, 1994.

Belous, Richard S. "Trade Has Job Winners, Too: The Very Strong Job-Generating Effect of Exports Is Often Overlooked." *Across the Board* 24 (1987): 53–58.

Berman, Eli, John Bound, and Zvi Griliches. "Changes in the Demand for Skilled Labor Within U.S. Manufacturing: Evidence from the Annual Survey of Manufactures." *Quarterly Journal of Economics* 109 (May 1994): 367–397.

Bernstein, Jared, and Lawrence Mishel. "Good Jobs at Good Wages: The Characteristics of Jobs Created by Lifting Line-of-Business Restrictions in Telecommunications for Baby Bells." Washington, D.C.: Economic Policy Institute, 1993.

Birdsall, Nancy, David Ross, and Richard Sabot. "Inequality and Growth Reconsidered." Paper presented at the meeting of the American Economic Association, 1994.

Blackburn, McKinley L. "Interpreting the Magnitude of Changes in Measures of Income Inequality." *Journal of Economics* 42 (1989): 21–25.

Blackburn, McKinley L., and David Bloom. "The Effects of Technological Change on Earnings and Income Inequality in the United States." In Richard Cyert and David Mowery, eds., *The Impact of Technological Change on Employment and Economic Growth.* Cambridge, Mass.: Ballinger, 1988.

Blanchflower, David, Andrew Oswald, and Peter Sanfey. "Wages, Profits and Rent-sharing." *Quarterly Journal of Economics,* no. 1 (February 1996): 227–251.

Blau, Francine D. "Real Wage and Employment Uncertainty and the Labor Force Participation Decisions of Married Women." *Economic Inquiry* 29 (1991): 678–696.

Blau, Francine D., and Lawrence M. Kahn. "The Impact of Wage Structure on Trends in U.S. Gender Wage Differentials: 1975–87." NBER Working Paper No. 4748, 1994.

———. "Rising Wage Inequality and the U.S. Gender Gap." *American Economic Review* 84 (May 1994): 23–28.

Bluestone, Barry. "The Growth of Low-Wage Employment: 1963–1986." *American Economic Review* 78 (1988): 124.

———. "The Impact of Schooling and Industrial Restructuring on Recent Trends in Wage Inequality in the United States." *American Economic Review* 80 (1990): 303–307.

Bluestone, Barry, and Stephen Rose. "Overworked or Underemployed? Changing Working Time in an Era of Job Insecurity." Prepared for presentation at the Southern Economics Association meetings in Washington, D.C., 1996.

———. "Overworked or Underemployed? Unravelling an Economic Enigma." *American Prospect* 31 (March–April 1997): 58–94.

Boal, William M. "The Effect of Labor Unions on Employment, Wages and Days of Operation Coal Mining in West Virginia." *Quarterly Journal of Economics* 109 (1994): 267.

Borjas, George J., Richard B. Freeman, and Lawrence F. Katz. "On the Labor Market Effects of Immigration and Trade." NBER Working Paper No. 3761, 1991.

Borjas, George J., and Valerie A. Ramey. "The Relationship Between Wage Inequality and International Trade." In J. H. Bergstrand et al., eds., *The Changing Distribution of Income in an Open U.S. Economy,* pp. 215–241. Amsterdam: Elsevier Science, 1994.

———. "Time-Series Evidence on the Sources of Trends in Wage Inequality." *American Economic Review* 84 (May 1994): 10–16.

Boskin, Michael J. "Toward a More Accurate Measure of the Cost of Living: Final Report to the Senate Finance Committee of the Advisory Commission to Study the Consumer Price Index." Washington: Senate Finance Committee, December 4, 1994.

Bound, John, and George Johnson. "Changes in the Structure of Wages in the 1980s: An Evaluation of Alternative Explanations." *American Economic Review* 82 (June 1992): 371–392.

Brauer, David A. "The Effect of Imports on U.S. Manufacturing Wages." *Quarterly Review* 16 (1991): 14–26.

Brown, Charles, and James Medoff. "The Employer Size-Wage Effect." *Journal of Political Economy* 97 (1989): 1027–1057.

Buchele, Robert. "Economic Dualism and Employment Stability." *Industrial Relations* 22 (1983): 410–418.

Buchinsky, Moshe. "Changes in the U.S. Wage Structure, 1963–1987: Application of Quantile Regression." *Econometrica* 62 (March 1994): 405–458.

Bureau of Labor Statistics. "Employment in Industries: Bureau of Labor Statistics Report—The American Work Force: 1992–2005." *Occupational Outlook Quarterly* 37 (1993): 20–34.

Burgess, Simon. "Labor Markets Under Trade Unionism: Employment, Wages and Hours." *Economic Journal* 102 (1992): 1293–1296.

———. "Labor Demand Quantity Constraints or Matching the Determination of Employment in the Absence of Market-Clearing." *European Economic Review* 37 (1993): 1295–1315.

Callaghan, Polly, and Heidi Hartmann. "Contingent Work: A Chart Book on Part-time and Temporary Employment." *Economic Policy Institute* (1991).

Calmfors, L., and J. Driffill. "Bargaining Structure, Corporatism, and Macroeconomic Performance." *Economic Policy* 6 (1988): 13–61.

Calmon, Paulo Du Pin, Pedro Conceicao, James K. Galbraith, Vidal Garza Cantu, and Abel Hibert. "The Evolution of Inequality in Brazil, Mexico and the United States." Mimeo. University of Texas at Austin, 1997.

Campbell, Duncan. "Foreign Investment, Labor Immobility and the Quality of Employment." *International Labor Review* 133 (1994): 185.

Cappelli, Peter. "Rethinking Employment." *British Journal of Industrial Relations* (January 1996).

Card, David. "Do Minimum Wages Reduce Employment? A Case Study of California, 1987–89." *Industrial and Labor Relations Review* 46 (1992): 38–54.

———. "Measuring the Effect of Subsidized Training Programs on Movements In and Out of Employment." *Econometrica* 56 (1988): 497–531.

Card, David, Francis Kramarz, and Thomas Lemieux. "Changes in the Relative Structure of Wages and Employment: A Comparison of the United States, Canada and France." Mimeo. Princeton University, 1994.

Card, David, and Thomas Lemieux. "Changing Wage Structure and Black-White Wage Differentials." *American Income Review* 84 (May 1994): 29–33.

Carnoy, Martin, Manuel Castells, and Chris Benner. "What Is Happening to the U.S. Labor Market? Part I: A Review of the Evidence." Mimeo. Stanford University, 1996.

Cassidy, John. "The Decline of Economics." *New Yorker,* December 2, 1996.

Center on Budget and Policy Priorities. *Assessing a $5.15-an-Hour Minimum Wage.* Washington D.C., March 27, 1996.

Chen, Paul, and Jeffrey L. Coles. "Compensating Wage Differentials and the Welfare Cost of Unemployment: 1929–1967." *Quarterly Review of Economics and Finance* 32 (1992): 3–25.

Citizens for Tax Justice. *Inequality and the Federal Budget Deficit.* Washington, D.C., September 1991.

Clark, Andrew. "Trade Union Utility Functions: A Survey of Union Leaders' Views (Employment versus Salary in Labor Negotiations)." *Industrial Relations* 32 (1993): 391–411.

Cohen, Yinon. "Temporary Help Service Workers: Employment Characteristics and Wage Determination." *Industrial Relations* 32 (1993): 272–287.

Congressional Budget Office. *The Economic and Budget Outlook: An Update.* Washington, D.C.: CBO, September 1993.

———. *The Economic and Budget Outlook.* Washington, D.C: CBO, January 1994.

Conway, Delores A. "Analysis of Employment Discrimination Through Homogeneous Job Groups." *Journal of Econometrics* 61 (1994): 103.

Costrell, Robert M. "The Effects of Industry Employment Shifts on Wage Growth: 1948–1987." Mimeo. Prepared for the Joint Economic Committee, Congress of the United States, 1988.

Couch, Kenneth A. "New Evidence on the Long-Term Effects of Employment Training Programs." *Journal of Labor Economics* 10 (1992): 380–389.

Council of Economic Advisers. Office of the Chief Economist. "Job Creation and Employment Opportunities: The United States Labor Market, 1993–1996." Report by the Council of Economic Advisers with the U.S. Department of Labor. Mimeo. April 23, 1996.

Crenshaw, Edward. "Cross-National Determinants of Income Inequality: A Replication and Extension Using Ecological-Evolutionary Theory." *Social Forces* 71 (December 1992): 339–363.

Currie, Janet. "Employment Determination in a Unionized Public-Sector Labor Market: The Case of Ontario's School Teachers." *Journal of Labor Economics* 9 (1991): 45–67.

———. "Labor Markets Under Trade Unionism: Employment, Wages, and Hours." *Journal of Economic Literature* 30 (1992): 1525–1527.

Cutler, David M., and Lawrence F. Katz. "Rising Inequality? Changes in the Distribution of Income and Consumption in the 1980s." NBER Working Paper No. 3964, 1992.

Daly, Michael. "The Impact of Regional Investment Incentives on Employment and Productivity: Some Canada Evidence." *Regional Science and Urban Economics* 23 (1993): 559–576.

Danthine, Jean-Pierre. "Wage Bargaining Structure, Employment and Economic Integration." *Economic Journal* 104 (1994): 528–542.

Davis, J. B., and A. F. Shorrocks. "Optimal Grouping of Income and Wealth Data." *Journal of Econometrics* 42 (1989): 97–108.

Davison, Carlos, and Michael Reich. "Income Inequality: An Inter-Industry Analysis." *Industrial Relations* 27 (1988): 263–284.

Dean, Jayne. "Sex-Segregated Employment, Wage Inequality and Labor-Intensive Production: A Case Study of 33 U.S. Manufacturing Industries." *Review of Radical Political Economics* 23 (1991): 244–268.

De Melo, Jaime, and David Tarr. "Industrial Policy in the Presence of Wage Distortions: The Case of the US Auto and Steel Industries." *International Economic Review* 34 (November 1993): 833–851.

DiNardo, John, and Thomas Lemieux. "Diverging Male Wage Inequality in the United States and Canada, 1981–1988: Do Unions Explain the Difference?" Mimeo. University of California-Irvine, undated.

DiNardo, John, and Jorn-Steffen Pischke. "The Returns to Computer Use Revisited: Have Pencils Changed the Wage Structure Too?" NBER Working Paper No. 5606, June 1996.

Doiron, Denise J. "Bargaining Power and Wage-Employment Contracts in a Unionized Industry." *International Economic Review* 33 (1992): 583–605.

Dornbusch, Rudiger. "From Stabilization to Growth." NBER Working Paper No. 3302. Cambridge: NBER, 1990.

Dornbusch, Rudiger, Federico Sturzenegger, and Holger Wolf. "Extreme Inflation: Dynamics and Stabilization." BPEA No. 2, 1991, 1–64.

Dornbusch, Rudiger, and Mario Henrique Simonsen. *Inflation Stabilization with Incomes Policy Support: A Review of the Experience in Argentina, Brazil and Israel.* New York: Group of 30, 1986.

Dunlop, John T. "Wage Contours." In M. J. Piore, ed., *Unemployment and Inflation: Institutionalist and Structuralist Views,* pp. 61–74. Armonk, N.Y.: M. E. Sharpe.

Dunne, Timothy, and James A. Shumitz, Jr. "Wages, Employment, Size-Wage Premia: Their Relations to Advanced-Technology Usage at US Manufacturing Establishments." *Economica* 62 (1995): 89–107.

Durlauf, Steven N. "Theory of Persistent Income Inequality." NBER Working Paper No. 4056, 1992.

Dutt, Amitava Krishna. "North-South Models: A Critical Survey." Mimeo. Florida International University, 1988.

———. "Uneven Development in Alternative Models of North-South Trade." Mimeo. Florida International University, 1987.

Eckstein, Otto, and Thomas Wilson. "The Determination of Money Wages in American Industry." *Quarterly Journal of Economics* (1962): 379–414.

Eisner, Robert. "A New View of the Nairu." In Paul Davidson and Jan Kregel, eds., *Improving the Global Economy: Keynesianism and the Growth in Output and Employment.* Cheltenham: Edward Elgar, 1997.

Elliott, R. F., and M. J. White. "Recent Developments in the Industrial Wage Structure of the UK." *Cambridge Journal of Economics* 17: (1993): 109–129.

Erickson, Christopher L. "Wage Rule Formation in the Aerospace Industry." *Industrial and Labor Relations Review* 45 (April 1992): 507–522.

Erickson, Christopher L., and Andrea Ichino. "Wage Differentials in Italy: Market Forces, Institutions and Inflation." NBER Working Paper No. 4922, November 1994.

Fair, Ray. "Testing the Standard View of the Long-Run Unemployment-Inflation Relationship." Mimeo. Yale University, April 1996.

———. "Testing the NAIRU Model for the United States." Mimeo. Yale University, April 1997.

Feenstra, Robert C., and Gordon Hanson. "Foreign Investment, Outsourcing and Relative Wages Proceeding of Political Economy of Trade Policy." Mimeo. University of Texas at Austin, 1994.

Ferguson, Thomas, and James K. Galbraith. "The American Wage Structure, 1920–1947." Manuscript, 1997.

Fischer, Stanley. "The Israeli Stabilization Program." *American Economic Review* (May 1987): 275–278.

FitzGerald, Valpy. "International Markets and Open Economy Macroeconomics: A Keynesian View." Mimeo, University of Oxford, paper presented at the International Conference, The Relevance of Keynesian Economic Policies Today, University of East London, 1995.

Flamm, Kenneth. "Semiconductor Dependency and Strategic Trade Policy." *Brookings Papers on Microeconomics* 1 (1993): 249–333.

Fortin, Nicole, and Thomas Lemieux. "Institutional Changes and Rising Wage Inequality: Is There a Linkage?" *Journal of Economic Perspectives* 11, no. 2 (spring 1997).

Fortin, Nicole, Thomas Lemieux, and John DiNardo. "Labor Market Institutions and the Distribution of Wages: A Semi-Parametric Approach." *Econometrica* 65 (September 1996): 1001–1044.

Freeman, Richard. "Over Investment in College Training?" *Journal of Human Resources* 10 (summer 1975): 287–311.

Freeman, Richard B., and Karen Needles. "Skill Differential in Canada in an Era of Rising Labor Market Inequality." NBER Working Paper No. 3827, 1991.

Friedman, Milton. "The Role of Monetary Policy." *American Economic Review Papers and Proceedings* (May 1968): 1–17.

Galbraith, James K. "Inequality and Unemployment: An Analysis Across Time and Countries." *Review of Economic Inequality* (forthcoming).

———. "Time to Ditch the NAIRU." *Journal of Economic Perspectives* 11 (winter 1997): 93–108.

———. "Dangerous Metaphor: The Fiction of the Labor Market." Rhinebeck, N.Y.: Jerome Levy Economics Institute Policy Brief, 1997.

———. "Unemployment, Inflation and the Job Structure." Rhinebeck, N.Y.: Jerome Levy Economics Institute, Working Paper No. 154, 1996.

———. "Uneven Development and the Destabilization of the North." *International Review of Applied Economics* 10 (1996): 107–120.

———. "Global Keynesianism in the Wings." *World Policy Journal* 12 (fall 1995): 65–69.

———. "A Global Living Wage." *Political Quarterly* (special issue) (1995): 54–60.

———. "John Maynard Nosferatu." *Journal of Post Keynesian Economics* 17 (winter 1994): 249–260.

———. "Keynes, Einstein and Scientific Revolution." *American Prospect,* no. 16 (winter 1994): 62–67.

———. "Labor and the NAFTA: A Short Report." *Economic Development Quarterly* 7 (1993): 323–326.

———. "A New Picture of the American Economy." *American Prospect* (fall 1991): 24–36.

———. "Trade and the Planning System." In Samuel Bowles, Richard Edwards, and William G. Shepherd, eds., *Unconventional Wisdom: Essays in Honor of John Kenneth Galbraith,* pp. 231–256. Boston: Houghton Mifflin, 1989.

Galbraith, James K., and Paulo Du Pin Calmon. "Wage Change and Trade Performance in U.S. Manufacturing Industries." *Cambridge Journal of Economics* 20 (July 1996): 433–450.

———. "Industries, Trade and Wages." In Michael Bernstein and David Adler, *Understanding American Economic Decline,* pp. 161–168. New York: Cambridge University Press, 1994.

Gang, Ira N. "Allocating Jobs Under a Minimum Wage: Queues vs. Lotteries." *Economic Record* 66 (1990): 186.

Garber, Steven. "The Reserve-Labor Hypothesis, Short-Run Pricing Theories, and the Employment-Output Relationship." *Journal of Econometrics* 42 (1989): 219–246.

Gibbons, Robert, and Lawrence Katz. "Does Unmeasured Ability Explain Inter-Industry Wage Differences?" Mimeo. Harvard University, 1989.

Gill, Andrew, and Stewart Long. "Is There an Immigration Status Wage Differential Between Legal and Undocumented Workers? Evidence from the Los Angeles Garment Industry." *Social Science Quarterly* 70 (March 1989): 164–173.

Gittleman, Maury B., and David R. Howell. "Changes in the Structure and Quality of Jobs in the United States: Effects by Race and Gender," *Industrial Labor Relations Review* 48, no. 13. (1995): 420–440.

Gleicher, David. "Net Employment Reserves and Occupational Wage Rate Determination." *Journal of Post Keynesian Economics* 15 (1992): 125–147.

Godley, Wynne. "U.S. Foreign Trade, the Budget Deficit and Strategic Policy Problems: A Background Brief." Jerome Levy Economics Institute Working Papers No. 138, April 1995.

Goldin, Claudia Dale, and Lawrence F. Katz. "Decline of Non Competing Groups Changes in the Premium to Education 1890 to 1940." NBER Working Paper No. 5202, 1995.

———. "The Origins of Technology-Skill Complementarity." Mimeo, Harvard University, 1997.

Goldin, Claudia Dale, and Robert A. Margo, "Great Compression: The Wage Structure in the United States at Mid-Century." NBER Working Paper No. 3817, 1991.

Gordon, David M. "The Un-Natural Rate of Unemployment: An Econometric Critique of the NAIRU Hypothesis." *American Economic Review Papers and Proceedings* (May 1988): 117–123.

Gordon, Robert J. "The Time-Varying NAIRU and Its Implications for Economic Policy." *Journal of Economic Perspectives* 11, no. 1 (1997): 11–32.

Gramlich, Edward. "Infrastructure Investment, a Review." *Journal of Economic Literature* 32, no. 3 (September 1994): 1176–1197.

Greenberg, David. "Multistate Employment and Training Program Evaluations: A Tale of Three Studies." *Industrial and Labor Relations Review* 47 (1994): 679–691.

Gritz, R. Mark. "The Impact of Training on the Frequency and Duration of Employment." *Journal of Econometrics* 57 (1993): 21–52.

Groshen, Erica L. "The Structure of the Female/Male Wage Differential: Is It Who You Are, What You Do, or Where You Work?" *Journal of Human Resources* 26 (1991): 454–472.

Grubb, W. Norton, and Robert H. Wilson. "The Effects of Demographic and Labor Market Trends on Wage and Salary Inequality, 1967–1988." LBJ School Working Paper Series, 1991.

———. "Trends in Wage and Salary Inequality, 1967–1988." *Monthly Labor Review* (June 1992): 23–39.

Guerrieri, Paolo. "Technology and International Trade Performance in the Most Advanced Countries." *Berkeley Roundtable on the International Economy* (1991).

Haber, Sheldon, and Roberts S. Goldfarb. "Does Salaried Status Affect Human Capital Accumulation?" *Industrial and Labor Relations Review* 48 (January 1995): 322–337.

Hall, Robert E. "Why Is the Unemployment Rate So High at Full Employment?" *Brookings Papers on Economic Activity* 3 (1970): 369–402.

Hamermesh, Daniel. "Inflation and Labor Market Adjustment." *Economic* 53 (1986): 63–73.

Hansen, Niles. "Regional Employment Implications of a Free Trade Agreement." *Labor Law Journal* 43 (1992): 518–522.

Hanson, Gordon H. "Industry Agglomeration, Regional Trade, and the Pioneer Firm: Theory and Evidence from Mexico." Mimeo, The University of Texas at Austin, 1992.

Hanson, Gordon H., and Ann Harrison. "Trade, Technology, and Wage Inequality." Mimeo. University of Texas at Austin, 1995.

Hercowitz, Zvi. "Output Growth, the Real Wage, and Employment Fluctuation." *American Economic Review* 81 (1991): 1215.

Heymann, Daniel. "Inflation and Stabilization Policies." *Cepal Review* 28 (1986): 67–97.

———. "The Austral Plan." *American Economic Review* (May 1987).

Hirschhorn, Larry. "Computers and Jobs: Services and the New Mode of Production." In Richard M. Cyert and David C. Mowery, eds., *The Impact of Technological Change on Employment and Economic Growth*. Cambridge, Mass.: Ballinger, 1988.

Holzer, Harry J. "Employment, Unemployment and Demand Shifts in Local Labor Markets." *Review of Economics and Statistics* 73 (1991): 25–33.

Holzer, Harry J., Lawrence F. Katz, and Alan B. Krueger. "Job Queues and Wages: New Evidence on the Minimum Wage and Inter-Industry Wage Structure." NBER Working Paper No. 2561, 1988.

Howell, David R. "The Collapse of Low-Skill Male Earnings in the 1980's: Skill Mismatch or Shifting Wage Norms?" Jerome Levy Economics Institute Policy Brief, 1995.

———. "Institutional Failure and the American Worker". Rhinebeck, N.Y.: Jerome Levy Economics Institute of Bard College Policy Brief, 1997.

———. "The New Competitive Labor Market: Higher Skills and Lower Wages?" Unpublished manuscript, New School for Social Research, 1993.

———. "Production Technology and the Interindustry Wage Structure." *Industry Relations* (1989): 32–50.

———. "Technological Change and Demand for Skills in the 1980's: Does Skill Mismatch Explain the Growth of Low Earnings?" Mimeo. New School for Social Research, 1993.

Howell, David R., and Maury B. Gittleman. "Job, Labor Market Segmentation and Earnings Inequality: Effects of Economic Restructuring in the 1980's by Race and Gender." Mimeo. New School for Social Research, 1992.

———. "Job, Labor Market Segmentation in the 1980's: A New Perspective on the Effects of Employment Restructuring by Race and Gender." Mimeo. New School for Social Research, 1993.

Howell, David R., and Edward N. Wolff. "Changes in the Information-Intensity of U.S. Employment Since 1950: Has Information Technology Made a Difference?" C. V. Starr Economic Research Report 93–08, New York University, March 1993.

———. "Technical Change and the Demand for Skills by U.S. Industries." *Cambridge Journal of Economics* (1992): 127–146.

———. "Skills, Bargaining Power and Rising Inderindustry Wage Inequality Since 1970." *Review of Radical Political Economics* 22 (1990): 30–37.

Hulten, Charles R. "Growth Accounting When Technical Change Is Embodied in Capital." *American Economic Review* 82 (1992): 964–980.

Jensen, J. Bradford, and Nathan Musick. "Trade, Technology, and Plant Performance." Working Papers on Industrial and Economic Performance, U.S. Department of Commerce, Economics and Statistics Administration, Office of Policy Development, April 1996.

Jocoby, Sanford M. "Sticky Stories: Economic Explanation of Employment and Wage Rigidity." *American Economic Review* 80 (1990): 33–38.

Johnson, George E. "Changes in Earnings Inequality: The Role of Demand Shifts." *Journal of Economic Perspectives* 11, no. 2 (spring 1997).

Johnson, Nancy Brown. "Airline Workers' Earnings and Union Expenditures Under Deregulation." *Industrial and Labor Relations Review* 45 (1991): 154–165.

Juhn, Chinhui, Kevin Murphy, and Brooks Pierce. "Wage Inequality and the Rise in Returns to Skill." *Journal of Political Economy* 101, no. 3 (1993).

Juhn, Chinhui, Kevin M. Murphy, and Robert H. Topel. "Why Has the Natural Rate of Unemployment Increased over Time?" *Brookings Papers on Economic Activity* 2 (1991): 75–142.

Kahn, Charles M. "Introducing Work Rules into Models of Wage-Employment Contracts." *Quarterly Review of Economics and Finance* 33 (1993): 217–232.

Karier, Thomas. "A Note on Wage Rates in Defense Industries." *Industrial Relations* 26 (1987): 195–200.

Karoly, Lynn. "The Trend in Inequality Among Families, Individuals and Workers in the United States: A Twenty-five Year Perspective." Santa Monica, Calif.: Rand Corporation, 1992.

Karoly, Lynn A., and Jacob Alex Klerman. "Using Regional Data to Reexamine the Contribution of Demographic and Sectorial Changes to Increasing U.S. Wage Inequality." In J. H. Bergstrand et al., eds., *The Changing Distribution of Income in an Open U.S. Economy*, pp. 183–215. Amsterdam: North-Holland, 1994.

Katz, Lawrence F. "Some Recent Developments in Labor Economics and Their Implications for Macroeconomics." *Journal of Money, Credit, and Banking* 20 (1988): 508–530.

———. "Recent Developments in Labor Economics." Mimeo. Harvard University, 1992.

Katz, Lawrence F., and Kevin Murphy. "Changes in Relative Wages, 1963–1987: Supply and Demand Factors." *Quarterly Journal of Economics* (February 1992): 35–78.

Katz, Lawrence F., and Ana L. Revenga. "Changes in the Structure of Wages: The U.S. vs. Japan." *Journal of the Japanese and International Economies* (December 1989).

Katz, Lawrence F., and Lawrence H. Summers. "Can Inter-industry Wage Differentials Justify Strategic Trade Policy?" NBER Working Paper No. 2739, 1988.

———. "Industry Rents: Evidence and Implications." *Brookings Papers on Economic Activity: Microeconomics 1989*. Washington, D.C.: Brookings Institution, 1989.

Kaufman, Bruce E., and Paula E. Stephan. "Determinants of Interindustry Wage Growth in the Seventies." *Industrial Relations* 26 (1987): 186–194.

Keane, Michael. "Skill Levels and the Cyclical Variability of Employment, Hours, and Wages." *International Monetary Fund Staff Papers* 40 (1993): 711–744.

Keane, Michael, and Eswar Prasad. "The Employment and Wage Effects of Oil Price Changes: A Sectoral Analysis." *Review of Economics and Statistics* 78, no. 3, 389–400.

Kim, Benjamin J. C. "A Time-Series Study of the Employment–Real Wage Relationship: An International Comparison." *Journal of Economic and Business* 40 (1988): 67–79.

Kletzer, Lori. "Industry Wage Differentials and Wait Unemployment." *Industrial Relations* 31 (1992): 250–269.

Kosters, Marvin H. "Schooling, Work Experience, and Wage Trends." *American Economic Review* 80 (1990): 308–312.

Krueger, Alan. "How Computers Have Changed the Wage Structure: Evidence from Microdata, 1984–1989." *Quarterly Journal of Economics* 108 (February 1993): 33–60.

Krueger, Alan B., and Lawrence H. Summers. "Efficiency Wages and the Inter-Industry Wage Structure." *Econometrica* 56 (1988): 259–293.

Krugman, Paul R. "Globalization and the Inequality of Nations." *Quarterly Journal of Economics* 110 (November 1995): 857ff.

———. "Technology's Revenge." *Wilson Quarterly* 18 (autumn 1994): 56–65.

———. "Trade, Jobs and Wages." *Scientific American* 270 (April 1994): 44–49.

———. "Technology and International Competition: Overview." Mimeo. National Academy of Science, presented at the National Academy of Engineering Symposium, Linking Trade and Technology Policies: An International Comparison, 1991.

———. "Is Free Trade Passé?" *Journal of Economic Perspectives* 1 (1987): 131–144.

Kruse, Douglas L. "International Trade and the Labor Market Experience of Displaced Workers." *Industrial and Labor Relations Review* 41 (1988): 402–417.

Kuehn, John A. "Technology and Foreign Trade Impacts on U.S. Manufacturing Employment, 1975–80." *Growth and Change* 17 (1986): 46–61.

Kuttner, Robert. "The Declining Middle." *Atlantic* 252 (1983): 60–72.

Lambert, Peter. "Inequality Reduction Through the Income Tax." *Economica* 60 (1993): 357–365.

Lane, Timothy. "Wage Controls and Employment in Economies in Transition." *Journal of Comparative Economics* 19 (1994): 171–188.

Lawrence, Colin, and Robert Z. Lawrence. "Manufacturing Wage Dispersion: An End Game Interpretation." *Economic Activity* 1 (1985): 47–116.

Lawrence, Robert Z., and Matthew J. Slaughter. "International Trade and American Wages in the 1980's: Giant Sucking Sound or Small Hiccup?" *Brookings Papers on Economic Activity,* no. 2 (fall 1993).

Leamer, Edward E. "In Search of Stolper-Samuelson Effects on U.S. Wages." NBER Working Paper No. 5427, January 1996.

———. "Optimal Aggregation of Linear Net Export Systems." In Terry Barker and M. Hashem Pesaran, eds., *Disaggregation in Econometric Modelling.* London Routledge, 1990.

———. "A Trade Economist's View of U.S. Wages and "Globalization." Mimeo. UCLA, 1995.

———. "Trade, Wages and Revolving Door Ideas." NBER Working Paper No. 4716, 1994.

Lebow, David E., John M. Roberts, and David J. Stockton. "Economic Performance Under Price Stability." Division of Research and Statistics, Board of Governors of the Federal Reserve System, Working Paper Series No. 125, 1992.

Lee, Hiro. "Shifting Comparative Advantage and the Employment Effects of US-Japan Trade." *World Economy* 17 (1994): 323–346.

Leonard, Jonathan S. "Unions and Employment Growth." *Industrial Relations* 31 (1992): 80–94.

———. "Wage Structure and Dynamics in the Electronics Industry." *Industrial Relations* 28 (1989): 251–275.

Leonard, Jonathan S., and Louis Jacobson. "Wage Trends and the Job Creation Debate: Earnings Inequality and Job Turnover." *American Economic Review* 80 (1988): 298–302.

Lerman, Robert I. "Is Earnings Inequality Really Increasing?" *Urban Institute: Economic Restructuring and the Job Market,* no. 1 (March 1997).

Lerman, Robert L., and Shlomo Yitzhaki. "Improving the Accuracy of Estimates of Gini Coefficients." *Journal of Econometrics* 42 (1989): 43–47.

Levy, Frank S., and Richard C. Michel. "Work for Welfare: How Much Good Will It Do?" *AEA Papers and Proceedings* 72 (1986): 399–404.

Lockwood, Ben. "Dynamic Wage–Employment Bargaining with Employment Adjustment Costs." *Economic Journal* 99 (1989): 1143–1158.

Loh, Eug Seng. "Technological Changes, Training, and the Interindustry Wage Structure." *Quarterly Review of Economics* 32 (1992): 25–44.

Lucas, Robert. "Tobin and Monetarism: A Review Article." *Journal of Economic Literature,* 29, no. 2 (June 1981): 558–567.

Maasoumi, Esfandiar. "Continuously Distributed Attributes and Measures of Multivariate Inequality." *Journal of Econometrics* 42 (1989): 131–144.

Madsen, Jacob B. "Wage Gap and Technology." *Kyklos* 47 (1994): 95–108.

Mandler, Michael. "Policy Responses to Deindustrialization and Wage Inequality: Competitiveness Strategies and Labor Market Policy." Mimeo. Harvard University, 1992.

Mangum, Garth L. "Twenty Years of Manpower Training and Economic Development." *Labor Law Journal* 32 (1981): 508–514.

Maynard, Rebecca. "Evaluating Employment and Training Programmes: Lessons from the USA." *International Journal of Manpower* 14 (1993): 94–105.

Miller, Bernard F. "The Airline Industry: Labor Relations in the Era of Deregulation, Mergers, Bankruptcies, and Layoffs." *Labor Law Journal* 43 (1992): 388–394.

Miller, Paul W. "Low-Wage Youth Employment: A Permanent or Transitory State?" *Economic Record* 65 (1989): 126–136.

Mincer, Jacob. "Human Capital, Technology, and the Wage Structure: What Do Time Series Show?" NBER Working Paper No. 3581, 1991.

Mishel, Lawrence, and Jared Bernstein. "Is the Technology Black Box Empty? An Empirical Examination of the Impact of Technology on Wage Inequality and the Employment Structure." Paper presented to the Labor Economics Workshop at Harvard University, April 1994.

———. "Technology and the Wage Structure: Has Technology's Impact Accelerated Since the 1970s?" Paper presented to the NBER Labor Studies Workshop, July 1996.

Mitchell, Daniel J. B. "Keynesian, Old Keynesian, and New Keynesian Wage Normalism." *Industrial Relations* 32 (1993): 1–29.

Montgomery, Edward, and William Wascher. "Race and Gender Wage Inequality in Services and Manufacturing." *Industrial Relations* 26 (1987): 284–290.

Moore, Basil. "Why Wage and Price Flexibility Is Destabilizing: A Critique of Walras." Mimeo. Wesleyan University and University of Stellenbosch, 1996.

Murphy, Kevin, and Finis Welch. "The Role of International Trade in Wage Differentials." In Marvin Kosters, ed., *Workers and Their Wages: Changing Patterns in the United States.* pp. 39–69. Washington, D.C.: American Enterprise Institute, 1990.

———. "The Structure of Wages." *Quarterly Journal of Economics,* 107 (1992): 285–327.

———. "Wage Differentials in the 1980s: The Role of International Trade." Mimeo. 1989.

Nakamura, Leonard. "Is U.S. Economic Performance Really That Bad?" Philadelphia Federal Reserve Bank Working Paper No. 95–21, 1995.

Nantz, Kathryn. "The Labor-Managed Firm Under Imperfect Monitoring: Employment and Work Effort Responses." *Journal of Comparative Economics* 14 (1990): 33–51.

Neumark, David. "Employment Effects of Minimum and Subminimum Wages: Panel Data on States." *Industrial and Labor Relations Review* 46 (1992): 55–81.

Nickell, Stephen, and Brian Bell. "Changes in the Distribution of Wages and Unemployment in OECD Countries." *American Economic Review Papers and Proceedings* (May 1996): 302-308.

Nickell, Stephen, and James Symons. "The Real Wage-Employment Relationship in the United States." *Journal of Labor Economics* 8 (1990): 1–15.

Nielsen, François. "Income Inequality and Industrial Development: Dualism Revisited." *American Sociological Review* 59 (1994): 654–677.

Niggle, Christopher. "New Evidence from the Luxembourg Income Surveys." Mimeo. Redlands University, 1996.

Nissan, Edward, and George Carter. "Income Inequality Across Regions over Time." *Growth and Change* 24 (1993): 303–319.

Nord, Stephen. "The Relationship Among Labor-Force Participation, Service-Sector Employment, and Underemployment." *Journal of Regional Science* 29 (1989): 407–422.

Nunn, Sam. "Training for the Future." *Labor Law Journal* 34 (1983): 611–617.

Obey, David R., and the staff of the Joint Economic Committee. "Potential Economic Impact of NAFTA: An Assessment of the Debate." United States Congress, 1993.

O'Neill, June. "Can Work and Training Programs Reform Welfare?" *Journal of Labor Research* 4 (1993): 265–282.

Papadimitriou, Dimitri B., and L. Randall Wray. "Targeting Inflation: The Effects of Monetary Policy on the CPI and Its Housing Component." *Public Policy Brief,* no. 27 (1996).

Parguez, Alain. "Full Employment and Inflation." Mimeo. University of Besançon and ISMEA, Paris, 1994.

Pemberton, James. "Wage and Employment Determination When Employment Adjustment Is Costly." *Bulletin of Economic Research* 41 (1989): 77–81.

Pencavel, John. "The Determination of Wages, Employment, and Work Hours in an Economy with Centralized Wage-Setting: Sweden, 1950–1983." *Economic Journal* 98 (1988): 1105–1127.

Perry, George. "Changing Labor Markets and Inflation." *Brookings Papers on Economic Activity* 3 (1970).

Petersen, Carol Dawn. "Can Jobs Help the Underclass Break the Cycle of Poverty?" *Journal of Economic Issues* 26 (1992): 243–255.

Phelps, Edmund S. "Low-Wage Employment Subsidies versus the Welfare State." *American Economic Review* 84 (1994): 54–59.

Phillips, Keith. "Regional Wage Divergence and National Wage Inequality." *Economic Review* (fourth quarter 1992): 31–44.

Pissarides, Christopher A. "Loss of Skill During Unemployment and the Persistence of Employment Shocks." *Quarterly Journal of Economics* 107 (1992): 1371–1392.

Podgursky, Michael. "Labor Market Policy and Structural Adjustment." *Reprint Series of LRRC Publications* 74 (1984): 74–96.

Polivka, Anne E., and Jennifer M. Rothgeb. "Redesigning the CPS Questionnaire." *Monthly Labor Review* (September 1993).

Raffer, Kunibert. "Disadvantaging Comparative Advantages: The Problems of Decreasing Returns." In Renee Prendergast and Frances Stewart, eds., *Market Forces and World Development,* pp. 75–89. New York: St. Martin's Press, 1994.

———. "International Financial Institutions and Accountability: The Need for Drastic Change." In S. Mansoob Murshed and Kunibert Raffer, eds., *Trade, Transfers and De-*

velopment: Problems and Prospects for the Twenty-First Century, pp. 151–165. Brook-field: E. Elgar, 1993.

Reagan, Patricia B. "On-the-Job Training, Layoff by Inverse Seniority, and the Incidence of Unemployment." *Journal of Economics and Business* 44 (1992): 317.

Rebitzer, James B., and Renee M. Landers. "Human Resources Practices and the Demographic Transformation of Professional Labor Markets." Mimeo. MIT, 1994.

Rebitzer, James B., and Lowell J. Taylor. "The Consequences of Minimum Wage Laws: Some New Theoretical Ideas." *Journal of Public Economics* 56 (1995): 245–255.

Rebitzer, James B., Renee M. Landers, and Lowell J. Taylor. "Rat Race Redux: Adverse Selection in the Determination of Work Hours." Mimeo. MIT, 1994.

Rector, Robert. "Welfare Reform, Dependency Reduction, and Labor Market Entry." *Journal of Labor Research* 14 (1993): 283.

Revenga, Ana L. "Exporting Jobs? The Impact of Competition on Employment and Wages in US Manufacturing." *Quarterly Journal of Economics* 107 (1992): 255–285.

———. "Wage Determination in an Open Economy: International Trade and U.S. Manufacturing Wages." Mimeo. Harvard University, 1989.

Rhoades, Stephen A. "Wages, Concentration, and Import Penetration: An Analysis of the Interrelationships." *Atlantic Economic Journal* 12 (1984): 23–31.

Rizvi, S. Abu Turab. "The Microfoundations Project in General Equilibrium Theory." *Cambridge Journal of Economics* 18 (1994): 357–377.

Robinson, James C. "Market Structure, Employment, and Skill Mix in the Hospital Industry." *Southern Economic Journal* 55 (1988): 315–326.

Rones, Philip L. "Moving to the Sun: Regional Job Growth, 1968–1978." *Monthly Labor Review* 103 (1980): 12–20.

Rostow, W. W. "Policy for a Viable American Economy." Submission for the Senate Committee on Banking, Housing and Urban Affairs. Mimeo. University of Texas, Austin, 1992.

Rowthorn, R. E. "Centralisation, Employment and Wage Dispersion." *Economical Journal* 102 (1992): 642.

Rudebusch, Glenn D., and David W. Wilcox. "Productivity and Inflation: Evidence and Interpretations." Mimeo. Federal Reserve Board, Washington, D.C., 1994.

Sachs, Jeffrey, and Howard Shatz. "Trade and Jobs in U.S. Manufacturing." *BPEA* 1, no. 1 (spring 1994): 1–84.

Samuelson, Paul A., and Robert M. Solow. "Analytical Aspects of Anti-Inflation Policy." *American Economic Review* 50 (May 1960): 177–194.

Saunders, Norman. "BLS Employment Projections for 1990: An Evaluation." *Monthly Labor Review* 115 (1992): 15–32.

Scott, Robert E. "Flat Earth Economics: Is There a New International Trade Paradigm?" *Challenge* (September-October 1993): 32–39.

———. "Sectorial Strategies and Participant Commitments: The Keys to Effective Trade and Industrial Policies." *Stanford Law and Policy Review* (Fall 1993): 127–142.

Scott, Robert E., and Randy Barber. "Jobs on the Wing: Trading Away the Future of the U.S. Aerospace Industry." Economic Policy Institute, Washington D.C., 1995.

Scott, Robert E., and Thea M. Lee. "The Costs of Trade Protection Reconsidered: U.S. Steel, Textiles, and Apparel." In Robert A. Blecker, ed., *U.S. Trade Policy and Global Growth,* pp. 108–135. Armonk, N.Y.: M. E. Sharpe, 1996.

Shapiro, Robert J. "Cut-and-Invest to Compete and Win: A Budget Strategy for American Growth." Progressive Policy Institute, Policy Report No. 18, 1994.

Slemrod, Joel. "On the High Income Laffer Curve." In Joel Slemrod, ed., *Tax Progressivity and Income Inequality.* New York: Cambridge University Press, 1994.

Slottje, D. J., R. L. Basmann, and M. Nieswiadomy. "On the Empirical Relationship Between Several Well-Known Inequality Measures." *Journal of Econometrics* 42 (1989): 49–66.

Slottje, D. J., Joseph G. Hirschberg, Kathy J. Hayes, and Gerald W. Scully. "A New Method for Detecting Individual and Group Labor Market Discrimination." *Journal of Econometrics* 61 (1994): 43–64.

Slottje, D. J., and Joseph G. Hirschberg. "An Empirical Bayes Approach to Analyzing Earnings Functions for Various Occupations and Industries." *Journal of Econometrics* 61 (1994): 65–79.

Slottje, D. J., Joseph G. Hirschberg, and Esfandiar Maasoumi. "Cluster Analysis for Measuring Welfare and Quality of Life Across Countries." *Journal of Econometrics* 50 (1991): 131–150.

Sola, Lourdes. "Heterodox Shock in Brazil: *Tecnicos,* Politicians and Democracy." *Journal of Latin American Studies* (February 1991).

Solon, Gary. "Intergenerational Income Mobility in the United States." *American Economic Review* 82 (1992): 393–408.

Spinnewyn, Frans. "Optimal Membership, Employment, and Income Distribution in Unionized and Labor-Managed Firms." *Journal of Labor Economics* 8 (1990): 317–341.

Spriggs, William E., and Robert E. Scott. "Economists' Views of Workers' Rights and U.S. Trade Policy." College of Business and Management, University of Marland at College Park, Occasional Paper No. 60, 1995.

Stanley, Fischer. "Stopping High Inflation: The Israeli Stabilization Program, 1985–86." *American Economic Review* 77 (1987): 275–292.

Stergio, Anthony. "Clinton's Effect on Labor and Employment Law." *Labor Law Journal* 44 (1993): 239–245.

Stowsky, Jay. "America's Technical Fix: The Pentagon's Dual Use Strategy, TRP, and the Political Economy of U.S. Technology Policy." Mimeo. University of California, 1996.

Svhettkat, Ronald. "Compensation Differentials? Wage Differentials and Employment Stability in the US and German Economies." *Journal of Economic Issues* 27 (1993): 153–171.

Symons, James. "The Real Wage-Employment Relationship in the United States." *Journal of Labor Economics* 8 (1990): 1–16.

Topel, Robert H. "Factor Proportions and Relative Wages: The Supply-Side Determinants of Wage Inequality." *Journal of Economic Perspectives* 11, no. 2 (spring 1997).

Van Ark, Bart, and Erik Monnokhof. "Size Distribution of Output and Employment: A Data Set for Manufacturing Industries in Five OECD Countries, 1960s–1990." OECD Economics Department Working Papers No. 166, 1996.

Van Wijnberger, Sweder. "Tariffs and Employment and the Current Account: Real Wage Resistance and the Macroeconomics of Protectionism." *International Economic Review* 28 (1987): 691–707.

Vickrey, William. "A Trans-Keynesian Manifesto (Thoughts About an Asset-Based Macroeconomics)." *Journal of Post Keynesian Economics* 19, no. 4 (summer 1997): 495–510.

Wedde, Erich. "Democracy and Income Inequality Reconsidered." *American Sociological Review* 54 (1989): 865–868.

Weinberg, Daniel H. "A Brief Look at Postwar U.S. Income Inequality." Department of the Census, *Current Population Reports: Household Economic Studies.* Washington, D.C., June 1996.

Weitzman, Martin L. "A Theory of Wage Dispersion and Job Market Segmentation." *Quarterly Journal of Economics* (1989): 121–137.

Wellington, Alison J. "Effects of the Minimum Wage on the Employment Status of Youths: An Update." *Journal of Human Resources* 26 (1991): 27–47.

Wessels, Walter John. "The Minimum Wage and Tipped Employees." *Journal of Labor Research* 14 (1993): 213–227.

Williams, Nicolas. "Regional Effects of Minimum Wage on Teenage Employment." *Applied Economics* 25 (1993): 1517–1529.

Wood, Adrian. "The Factor Content of North-South Trade in Manufactures Reconsidered." *Review of World Economics* 4 (1991): 719–743.

———. "How Much Does Trade with the South Affect Workers in the North?" Mimeo. Institute for Development Studies, 1990.

———. "A New-Old Theoretical View of North-South Trade, Employment and Wages." Mimeo. Institute for Development Studies, 1991.

———. "North-South Trade and Female Labor in Manufacturing: An Asymmetry." *Journal of Development Studies* 27 (1991): 168–190.

Zappala, Gianni. "The 'Structure-Unionism-Wage' Paradigm in Labor Economics: Resolving the Stalemate." *Journal of Economic Issues* 28 (1994): 819–841.

Zimmerman, Don A. "The National Labor Relations Act and Employment-at-Will: The Federal Preemption Doctrine Revisited." *Labor Law Journal* 37 (1986): 223–234.

Zweimüller, Josef, and Erling Barth. "Bargaining Structure, Wage Determination, and Wage Dispersion in 6 OECD Countries." *KYKLOS* 47 (1994): 81–93.

Books

Backman, Jules. *Wage Determination: An Analysis of Wage Criteria.* Princeton: D. Van Nostrand, 1959.

Bakker, Robert. *The Dinosaur Heresies: New Theories Unlocking the Mystery of the Dinosaurs and Their Extinction.* New York: Morrow, 1986.

Berryman, Sue E. *The Adjustments of Youth and Educational Institutions to Technologically Generated Changes in Skill Requirements.* Washington, D.C.: National Commission for Employment Policy, 1985.

Bhagwati, Jagdish, and Marvin H. Kosters, eds. *Trade and Wages: Leveling Wages Down.* Washington, D.C.: AEI Press, 1994.

Blanchflower, David, and Andrew Oswald. *The Wage Curve.* Cambridge: MIT Press, 1994.

Blecker, Robert. *Are Americans on a Consumption Binge? The Evidence Reconsidered.* Washington, D.C.: Economic Policy Institute, 1990.

———.*Beyond the Twin Deficits.* Washington, D.C.: Economic Policy Institute, 1992.

Bluestone, Barry, and Bennett Harrison. *The Great U-Turn.* New York: Basic Books, 1988.

Bowers, John. *Trade Union Reform and Employment Rights Act 1993: A Practical Guide.* London: Longman, 1993.

Bringa, Tone. *Being Muslim the Bosnian Way.* Princeton: Princeton University Press, 1995.

Bruno, Michael, and Jeffrey Sachs. *The Economics of Worldwide Stagflation.* Cambridge: Harvard University Press, 1985.

Bureau of Labor Statistics. *Employment Data Under the New Standard Industrial Classification: First Quarter 1988.* Washington, D.C.: U.S. Department of Labor, Bureau of Labor Statistics, 1989.

Bureau of the Census and Bureau of Labor Statistics. *Trade and Employment.* Washington, D.C.: U.S. Department of Commerce, Bureau of the Census and U.S. Department of Labor, Bureau of Labor Statistics, 1984.

Burns, E. M. *Wages and the State: A Comparative Study of the Problems of State Wage Regulation.* London: P. S. King & Son, 1926.

Card, David, and Alan Krueger. *Myth and Measurement: The New Economics of the Minimum Wage,* Princeton: Priceton University Press, 1995.

Carlin, Wendy, and David Soskice. *Macroeconomics and the Wage Bargain.* Oxford: Oxford University Press, 1990.

Carnoy, Martin. *Faded Dreams: The Politics and Economics of Race in America.* Cambridge: Cambridge University Press, 1995.

Citizens for Tax Justice. *Inequality and the Federal Budget Deficit.* Washington, D.C., September 1991.

———. *A Far Cry from Fair.* Washington, D.C., April 1991.

Clark, Jerry, and Michael Martin. *The Impact of International Trade on U.S. Employment Levels and Composition.* Corvallis: Agricultural Experiment Station, Oregon State University, in cooperation with Oregon Wheat Commission, 1985.

Cohen, Steven, and John Zysman. *Manufacturing Matters: The Myth of the Post–Industrial Economy.* New York: Basic Books, 1987.

Colander, David, ed. *Incentive-Based Incomes Policies: Advances in TIP and MAP.* Cambridge, Mass.: Ballinger, 1985.

Congressional Budget Office. *Reducing the Deficit: Spending and Revenue Options.* Washington, D.C.: CBO, March 1994.

Cook, Philip, and Robert Frank. *The Winner-Take-All Society.* New York: Free Press, 1995.

Council of Economic Advisers. *The 1997 Economic Report of the President.* Washington, D.C.: Government Printing Office, 1997.

Cox, Jacob D., Jr. *The Economic Basis of Fair Wages.* New York: Ronald Press, 1926.

Creedy, John. *Income, Inequality and the Life Cycle.* Brookfield: Edward Elgar, 1992.

Cyert, Richard M., and David Mowery, eds. *Technology and Employment: Innovation and Growth in the U.S. Economy.* Washington, D.C.: National Academy Press, 1987.

————. *The Impact of Technological Change on Employment and Economic Growth.* Cambridge, Mass.: Ballinger, 1988.

Danziger, Sheldon, and Peter Gottschalk. *America Unequal.* Cambridge: Harvard University Press, 1995.

Davidson, Paul, and Jan Kregel, eds. *Improving the Global Economy: Keynesianism and the Growth in Output and Employment.* Cheltenham: Edward Elgar, 1997.

Denison, Edward. *Accounting for Slower Economic Growth: The United States in the 1970s.* Washington, D.C.: Brookings Institution, 1979.

Denzau, Arthur. *How Import Restraints Reduce Employment.* St. Louis: Center for the Study of American Business, 1987.

Dovring, Folke. *Inequality: The Political Economy of Income Distribution.* New York: Praeger, 1991.

Duchin, Faye. *Trading Away Jobs: The Effects of the US Merchandise Trade Deficit on Employment.* Washington, D.C.: Economic Policy Institute, 1988.

Eberts, Randall W., and Joe A. Stone. *Wage and Employment Adjustment in Local Labor Markets.* Kalamazoo: W. E. Upjohn Institute for Employment Research, 1992.

Economic Policy Institute. *Strategy for Public Investment-Led Growth.* Washington, D.C., 1992.

————. *Free Trade with Mexico: The Potential Economic Impact.* Washington, D.C., 1991.

Economics and Statistics Administration. *Technology, Economic Growth and Employment: New Research from the Department of Commerce.* Washington, D.C.: U.S. Department of Commerce, Economics and Statistics Administration, 1994.

Eisner, Robert. *How Real Is the Federal Deficit?* New York: Free Press, 1986.

————. *The Misunderstood Economy: What Counts and How to Count It.* Boston: Harvard Business School Press, 1994.

Employment and Training Administration. *If Imports Cost You Your Job . . . Apply for Trade Adjustment Assistance.* Washington, D.C.: U.S. Department of Labor, Employment and Training Administration, 1990.

Ferguson, Thomas. *Golden Rule.* Chicago: University of Chicago Press, 1996.

Fischer, Claude S., et al. *Inequality by Design: Cracking the Bell Curve Myth.* Princeton: Princeton University Press, 1996.

Galbraith, James K. *Balancing Acts: Technology, Finance and the American Future.* New York: Basic Books, 1989.

Galbraith, James K., and William Darity, Jr. *Macroeconomics.* Boston: Houghton Mifflin, 1994.

Galbraith, John Kenneth. *The New Industrial State.* Boston: Houghton Mifflin, 1967.

George, Henry. *Progress and Poverty.* New York: Robert Schalkenbach Foundation, 1938.

Gilder, George. *Wealth and Poverty.* New York: Basic Books, 1981.

Gould, Jay M., and Bentley H. Paykin. *The Structure of U.S. Business: A Guide to the Analysis of Concentration, Employment Trends and Wage and Salary Levels in 900 U.S. Industries.* New York: Economic Information Systems, 1981.

Greider, William. *One World, Ready or Not: The Manic Logic of Global Capitalism.* New York: Simon & Schuster, 1997.

———. *Secrets of the Temple.* New York: Simon & Schuster, 1987.

Guille, Bruce R., and James Brian Quinn, eds. *Technology in Services: Policies for Growth, Trade, and Employment.* Washington, D.C.: National Academy Press, 1988.

Hacker, Andrew. *Money: Who Has How Much and Why?* New York: Scribner, 1997.

Haslag, Joseph H., William R. Russell, and Daniel Slottje. *Macroeconomic Activity and Income Inequality in the United States.* London: JAI Press, 1989.

Heilbroner, Robert, ed. *The Essential Adam Smith.* New York: Norton, 1986.

Herrnstein, Richard, and Charles Murray. *The Bell Curve: Intelligence and Class Structure in American Life.* New York: Free Press, 1994.

Hills, John, ed. *New Inequalities: The Changing Distribution of Income and Wealth in the United Kingdom.* Cambridge: Cambridge University Press, 1996.

Hugh-Jones, E. M., ed. *Wage-Structure in Theory and Practice.* Amsterdam: North-Holland, 1966.

International Labour Office. *The Employment Effects in the Clothing Industry of Changes in International Trade.* Geneva: International Labour Office, 1980.

———. *Rural Employment Promotion: Seventh Item on the Agenda.* Geneva: International Labour Office, 1988.

Jacoby, Russell, and Naomi Glauberman. *The Bell Curve Debates.* New York: Times Books, 1995.

Jencks, Christopher. *Rethinking Social Policy: Race, Poverty and the Underclass.* Cambridge: Harvard University Press, 1992.

Kalecki, Michal. *Capitalism, Business Cycles and Full Employment.* Oxford: Clarendon Press, 1990.

Keynes, John Maynard. *Essays in Persuasion.* New York: W. W. Norton, 1963.

———. *The General Theory of Employment Interest and Money.* London: Macmillan, 1936.

———. *The Economic Consequences of the Peace.* London: Macmillan, 1920.

Krueger, Anne O. *Trade and Employment in Developing Countries.* Chicago: University of Chicago Press, 1981.

Krugman, Paul R. *Pop Internationalism.* Cambridge: MIT Press, 1996.

Kuttner, Robert. *Managed Trade and Economic Sovereignty.* Washington, D.C.: Economic Policy Institute, 1989.

———. *Everything for Sale: The Virtues and Limits of Markets.* New York: Knopf, 1997.

Labor and Employment Law Institute. *Labor and Employment Relations in the Age of the Robot, Computer, and Foreign Competition.* 3rd Annual Labor and Employment Law Institute, University of Louisville, April 24–25, 1986. Littleton, Colo.: F. B. Rothman, 1987.

———. *Significant Problems in Labor and Employment Law in the Late Eighties.* 5th Annual Labor and Employment Law Institute, University of Louisville, May 19–20, 1988, Littleton, Colo.: F. B. Rothman, 1990.

Lawrence, Robert Z. *Single World, Divided Nations? OECD Labour Markets and International Trade.* Washington, D.C.: Brookings and OECD Development Centre, 1996.

Levy, Frank. *Dollars and Dreams: The Changing American Income Distribution.* New York: Russell Sage Foundation, 1988.

Lind, Michael. *The Next American Nation: The New Nationalism and the Fourth American Revolution.* New York: Free Press, 1995.

Lipsey, Robert E. *Price and Quantity Trends in the Foreign Trade of the United States.* Princeton: Princeton University Press, 1963.

Madrick, Jeffrey, *The End of Affluence: The Causes and Consequences of America's Economic Dilemma.* New York: Random House, 1995.

Marx, Karl. *Capital.* New York: International Publishers, 1967.

Maxwell, Nan L. *Income Inequality in the United States, 1947–1985.* Westport, Conn.: Greenwood Press, 1990.

Mehl, Georg. *US Manufactured Exports and Export-Related Employment: Profiles of the 50 States and 33 Selected Metropolitan Areas for 1983.* Washington, D.C.: U.S. Department of Commerce, International Trade Administrations, 1987.

———. *US Manufactured Exports and Export-Related Employment: Profiles of the 50 States and 49 Selected Metroprofiles Areas for 1986.* Washington, D.C.: U.S. Department of Commerce, International Trade Administrations, 1990.

Mintz, Alex, ed. *The Political Economy of Military Spending in the United States.* London: Routledge, 1992.

Mishel, Lawrence, Jared Bernstein, and John Schmitt. *The State of Working America 1996–97.* New York: Economic Policy Institute, M. E. Sharpe, 1996.

Murray, Charles. *Losing Ground: American Social Policy, 1950–1980.* New York: Basic Books, 1984.

National Center on Education and the Economy. *America's Choice: High Skills or Low Wages!* New York: National Center on Education and the Economy, 1990.

National Industrial Conference Board. *The Economic Almanac, 1948.* New York: Conference Board, 1947.

———. *The Economic Almanac, 1949.* New York: Conference Board, 1948.

———. *The Economic Almanac, 1950.* New York: Conference Board, 1950.

———. *The Economic Almanac, 1951–52.* New York: Conference Board, 1951.

———. *The Economic Almanac 1953–54.* New York: Conference Board, 1953.

———. *The Economic Almanac, 1956.* New York: Conference Board, 1956.

———. *The Economic Almanac, 1958.* New York: Conference Board, 1958.

National Research Council. *The New Americans: Economic, Demographic, and Fiscal Effects of Immigration.* Washington, D.C.: National Academy Press, 1997.

Nelson, Richard R, and Sidney G. Winter. *An Evolutionary Theory of Economic Change.* Cambridge: Harvard University Press, 1982.

Nicholson, Stephen R. *Chief Executive Officers: Contracts and Compensation: A Study of Employment Contracts of Chief Executive Officers of Two-Year Colleges Effective in 1986, Including General Provisions, Benefits and Compensation Data.* Washington, D.C.: The National Academy Press, 1988.

Osberg, Lars, ed. *Economic Inequality and Poverty: International Perspectives.* Armonk, N.Y.: M. E. Sharpe, 1991.

Peterson, Peter G. *Facing Up: How to Rescue the Economy from Crushing Debt and Restore the American Dream.* New York: Simon & Schuster, 1993.

———*Will America Grow Up Before It Grows Old?* New York: Random House, 1996.

Pettengill, John S. *Labor Unions and the Inequality of Earned Income*. Amsterdam: North-Holland, 1980.

Prestowitz, Clyde, *Trading Places: How We Allowed Japan to Take the Lead*. New York: Basic Books, 1982.

Rawls, John. *A Theory of Justice*. Cambridge: Belknap Press of Harvard University Press, 1971.

Reich, Robert B. *The Work of Nations: Preparing Ourselves for 21st Century Capitalism*. New York: Alfred A. Knopf, 1991.

Rifkin, Jeremy. *The End of Work: The Decline of the Global Labor Force and the Dawn of the Post-Market Era*. New York: Putnam, 1995.

Rockoff, Hugh. *Drastic Measures: A History of Wage-Price Controls in America*. Cambridge: Cambridge University Press, 1985.

Salkever, Louis R. *Toward a Wage Structure Theory*. New York: Humanities Press, 1964.

Saunders, Christopher, and David Marsden. *Pay Inequalities in the European Community*. London: Butterworths, 1981.

Schafer, Todd, and Jeff Faux, eds. *Reclaiming Prosperity: A Blueprint for Progressive Economic Reform*. Armont, N.Y.: M. E. Sharpe, 1996.

Schumpeter, Joseph A. *Capitalism, Socialism and Democracy*. New York: Harper & Row, 1943.

Sen, Amartya. *Inequality Reexamined*. Cambridge: Harvard University Press, 1992.

Sen, Amartya, and Jean Dreze, eds. *The Political Economy of Hunger*. London: Clarendon Press of Oxford University Press, 1990.

Sharma, Soumitra. *John Maynard Keynes: Keynesianism into the Twenty-first Century*. Cheltenham, UK: Edward Elgar, 1998.

Shreve, Charles David. *A Precarious and Uncertain Liberalism: Lyndon Johnson and the New Economics*. Baton Rouge: Louisiana State University Ph.D. dissertation, 1996.

Slottje, D. J. *The Structure of Earnings and the Measurement of Income Inequality in the U.S.* Amsterdam: North-Holland, 1989.

Smith, Adam. *An Inquiry into the Nature and Causes of the Wealth of Nations*. New York: Dutton, 1970.

Technology Administration. *Correlations of Productivity, Compensation, and Corporate Profits*. Washington, D.C.: U.S. Department of Commerce, Technology Administration, 1995.

Theil, Henri. *Statistical Decomposition Analysis: With Applications in the Social and Administrative Sciences*. Amsterdam: North-Holland Publishing Company, 1972.

Thurow, Lester C. *Generating Inequality: Mechanism of Distribution in the U.S. Economy*. New York: Basic Books, 1975.

———. *Head to Head: The Coming Economic Battle Among Japan, Europe and America*. New York: Morrow, 1992.

Tufte, Edward R. *Political Control of the Economy*. Princeton, N.J.: Princeton University Press, 1978.

Tyson, Laura D'Andrea, William T. Dickens, and John Zysman, eds. *The Dynamics of Trade and Employment*. Cambridge, Mass.: Ballinger, 1988.

U.S. Congress. *Goals 2000: Educate America Act.* Message from the president. Washington, D.C.: U.S. GPO, 1993.

U.S. Congress. Committee on Banking, Housing, and Urban Affairs. *Challenges and Opportunities for the Conduct of Monetary Policy.* Hearing before the Committee on Banking, Housing, and Urban Affairs, 1993.

———. *Conduct of Monetary Policy.* Hearing before the Committee on Banking, Housing, and Urban Affairs, 1986.

U.S. Congress. Committee on the Budget. *Interest Rates, Wages, Employment, and Inflation.* Hearing before the Committee on the Budget, 1994.

U.S. Congress. Committee on Education and Labor. *Achieving Full Employment: Legislative and Policy Consideration.* Hearing before the Subcommittee on Employment Opportunities of the Committee on Education and Labor, 1988.

———. *Economic Dislocation and Worker Adjustment Assistance Act, H.R. 1122.* Hearing before the Subcommittee on Labor-Management Relations and Employment Opportunities of the Committee on Education and Labor, 1988.

———. *Hearing on Employment and Training Needs in the Current Recession.* Hearing before the Subcommittee on Employment Opportunities of the Committee on Education and Labor, 1992.

U.S. Congress. Committee on Finance. *Social Security Domestic Employment Reform Act of 1994.* Washington, D.C.: U.S. GPO, 1994.

———. *Trade Adjustment Assistance: A Failure for Displaced Workers.* Hearing before the Committee on Finance, 1993.

U.S. Congress. Committee on Governmental Affairs. *Job Training and Employment Services.* Hearing before the Subcommittee on Government Efficiency, Federalism, and the District of Columbia of the Committee on Governmental Affairs, 1988.

U.S. Congress. Committee on Government Operations. *NAFTA: A Negative Impact on Blue Collar, Minority, and Female Employment?* Hearing before the Employment, Housing, and Aviation Subcommittee of the Committee on Government Operations, 1994.

———. *North American Free Trade Agreement: Are There Jobs for American Workers?* Hearing before the Employment, Housing, and Aviation Subcommittee of the Committee on Government Operations, 1993.

———. *Steps Toward a Comprehensive Employment and Training System.* Hearing before the Employment, Housing, and Aviation Subcommittee of the Committee on Government Operations, 1994.

U.S. Congress. Committee on Labor and Human Resources. *Creating a National Employment Training System.* Hearing before the Subcommittee on Labor and Human Resources, 1994.

U.S. Congress. Committee on Veterans' Affairs. *The Transition Assistance Program.* Hearing before the Subcommittee on Education, Training, and Employment, 1994.

U.S. Congress. Committee on Ways and Means. *The Impact of International Trade on US Employment: A Survey of Literature.* Hearing before the Subcommittee on Trade of Committee on Ways and Means, 1977.

U.S. Congress. Joint Economic Committee. *The 1982 Economic Report of the President.* Hearings before the Joint Economic Committee, March 10, 1982.

———. *Employment-Unemployment.* Hearing before the Joint Economic Committee, 1990.

———. *Manufacturing Job Losses and the Future of Manufacturing Employment in the United States.* Hearing before the Joint Economic Committee, 1994.

———. *The Swedish Experience: Assuring Industrial Competitiveness in a High-Wage, Full-Employment Economy.* Symposium before the Joint Economic Committee, 1988.

U.S. Department of Commerce. *Building the American Dream: Jobs, Innovation, and Growth in America's Next Century.* Washington, D.C.: Department of Commerce, 1996.

U.S. General Accounting Office. *U.S.-Mexico Trade: The Maquiladora Industry and U.S. Employment.* Washington, D.C.: General Accounting Office, 1993.

U.S. International Trade Commission. *U.S. Trade-Related Employment, 1978–84: Report on Investigation.* Washington, D.C.: U.S. International Trade Commission, 1986.

Veblen, Thorstein. *The Theory of the Business Enterprise.* Clifton, N.J.: A. M. Kelley, 1973.

Wanniski, Jude. *The Way the World Works.* New York: Simon & Schuster, 1983.

Warsh, David. *The Idea of Economic Complexity.* New York: Viking Press, 1984.

Weicher, John C. *The Distribution of Wealth: Increasing Inequality?* Washington, D.C.: American Enterprise Institute Press, 1996.

Weintraub, Sidney. *Some Aspects of Wage Theory and Policy.* Philadelphia: Chilton Books, 1963.

Wilson, William Julius. *When Work Disappears: The World of the New Urban Poor.* New York: Knopf, 1996.

Wolff, Edward N. *Top Heavy: The Increasing Inequality of Wealth in America and What Can Be Done About It.* New York: New Press, 1996.

Wood, Adrian J. B. *North-South Trade, Employment and Inequality.* Oxford: Clarendon Press of Oxford University Press, 1994.

———. *A Theory of Pay.* Cambridge: Cambridge University Press 1978.

News Articles, Internet Citations, and Electronic Data Sets

Bureau of Economic Analysis of the U.S. Department of Commerce. *Census Reports.*

"Household Income Climbs After Long Stagnation." *New York Times,* September 27, 1996.

"Personal Computers: History and Development." *Jones Telecommunications and Multimedia Encyclopedia: Update,* June 12, 1997.

Polsson, Ken, "Chronology of Events in the History of Microcomputers." http://www.islandnet.com/~kpolsson/comphist.htm.

1996 Electronic Market Data Book. Electronic Industries Association.

INDEX